Happiness Studies Book Series

For further volumes:
http://www.springer.com/series/10117

Happiness Studies Book Series

Aims and Scope

Exploring features and implications for personal and social empowerment from a substantially interdisciplinary point of view.
Like the Journal of Happiness Studies, the series explores happiness through both objective and subjective indicators. Subjective aspects comprise cognitive evaluations (like life satisfaction), positive affect and emotions, development of meanings, competences, and goals.
Key issues include appraisal of life, work conditions, mental and physical health, developmental trajectories throughout the life span, socio-economic conditions, cultural aspects, and their impact on individual and social wellbeing.

Antonella Delle Fave
Editor

The Exploration of Happiness

Present and Future Perspectives

Springer

Editor
Antonella Delle Fave
Department of Pathophysiology
and Transplantation
University of Milano
Milan
Italy

ISSN 2213-7513 ISSN 2213-7521 (electronic)
ISBN 978-94-007-5701-1 ISBN 978-94-007-5702-8 (eBook)
DOI 10.1007/978-94-007-5702-8
Springer Dordrecht Heidelberg New York London

Library of Congress Control Number: 2012952292

Printed on acid-free paper

Springer is part of Springer Science+Business Media (www.springer.com)

Contents

Contributors

Robert A. Cummins Deakin University, Melbourne, VIC, Australia, e-mail: cummins@deakin.edu.au

Edward L. Deci University of Ottawa, Ottawa, ON, Canada

Antonella Delle Fave Department of Pathophysiology and Transplantation, University of Milano, Settore Didattico Ospedale Sacco, Via G.B. Grassi 74, 20157 Milan, Italy, e-mail: antonella.dellefave@unimi.it

Ed Diener University of Illinois and Gallop Organization, 901 West Illinois Street, Urbana, IL 61801, USA

Marissa Diener University of Utah, 1901 East South Campus Drive, Salt Lake City, UT 84112, USA

Grant Duncan School of People, Environment and Planning, Massey University Albany, Private Bag 102-904, North Shore MSC, Auckland, New Zealand, e-mail: L.G.Duncan@massey.ac.nz

Richard Eckersley 23 Garland Rd, Bundanoon, NSW 2578, Australia, e-mail: richard@richardeckersley.com.au

Tak Fung Information Technologies, University of Calgary, Alberta, Canada

Linda Fung Statcomp Consulting Services Ltd, Calgary, AB, Canada

Tan H. Hoon Psychological Sciences, University of Missouri-Columbia, McAlester Hall, Columbia, MO 65211, USA

Veronika Huta University of Ottawa, Ottawa, ON, Canada

M. Joseph Sirgy Department of Marketing, Virginia Polytechnic Institute and State University, Blacksburg, VA 24061-0236, USA, e-mail: sirgy@vt.edu

Cheryl Kier Psychology Centre, Athabasca University, Athabasca, AB, Canada

Chu Kim-Prieto Department of Psychology, The College of New Jersey, 2000 Pennington Road, Ewing, NJ 08628, USA, e-mail: kim@tcnj.edu

Shinobu Kitayama University of Michigan, Ann Arbor, MI, USA

Ambrose Leung Department of Policy Studies, Mount Royal University, Calgary, AB, Canada, e-mail: acleung@mtroyal.ca

Mike W. Martin Department of Philosophy, Chapman University, One University Drive, Orange, CA 92866, USA, e-mail: mwmartin@chapman.edu

Vinai Norasakkunkit Minnesota State University, Mankato, MN, USA; Gonzaga University, Spokane, WA, USA

Jan Ott Erasmus University Rotterdam, Rotterdam, The Netherlands, e-mail: jan.ott@planet.nl

Nansook Park Department of Psychology, University of Michigan, 525 East University, Ann Arbor, MI 48109-1109, USA

Christopher Peterson† Department of Psychology, University of Michigan, 525 East University, Ann Arbor, MI 48109-1109, USA

Richard M. Ryan University of Rochester, Rochester, NY 14627, USA, e-mail: ryan@psych.rochester.edu

Carol D. Ryff Institute on Aging and Department of Psychology, University of Wisconsin-Madison, Madison, MI, USA, e-mail: cryff@wisc.edu

Jörg Schimmel United Nations Development Programme, PO Box 101, UN House, Deloitte Tower, Level 14, Douglas Street, Port Moresby, Papua New Guinea , e-mail: jorg.schimmel@undp.org

Christie Scollon Texas Christian University, 2800 West Bowie Street, Fort Worth, TX 76109, USA

Martin E. P. Seligman Department of Psychology, University of Pennsylvania, Philadelphia, PA 19104, USA

Kennon M. Sheldon Psychological Sciences, University of Missouri-Columbia, McAlester Hall, Columbia, MO 65211, USA, e-mail: sheldonk@missouri.edu

Burton H. Singer Office of Population Research/Institute on Aging, Princeton University/University of Wisconsin-Madison, Madison, USA

Robert Sproule Department of Economics, Bishop's University, Sherbrooke, QC, Canada

Maya Tamir Stanford University, 450 Serra Mall, Stanford, CA 94305, USA

Yukiko Uchida Graduate School of Human and Environmental Studies, Kokoro Research Center, Kyoto University, Sakyo-ku, Kyoto 606-8501, Japan, e-mail: yuchida@umich.edu; yukikou@educ.kyoto-u.ac.jp

Jukka Varelius Department of Behavioural Sciences and Philosophy, University of Turku, 20014 Turku, Finland, e-mail: varelius@hotmail.com

Ruut Veenhoven Erasmus University Rotterdam, P. O. Box 1738, 3000 Rotterdam, The Netherlands; North-West University, Mmabatho 2745, South Africa, e-mail: veenhoven@fsw.eur.nl

Jiyun Wu Management and Marketing Department, School of Management, Rhode Island College, Providence RI 02908, USA, e-mail: JWU@ric.edu

During the preparation of this book Christopher Peterson—the first author of Chap. 9—suddenly and untimely passed away. With this publication we would like to pay homage to a colleague whose commitment and dedication to the study and teaching of well-being has been recognized by the whole academic and professional community of positive psychology.

Part I
Individual Well-Being: Theory and Research

Chapter 1
The Exploration of Happiness: Present and Future Perspectives

Antonella Delle Fave

Happiness is gaining increasing momentum as a core topic in research and intervention programs. The Journal of Happiness Studies was launched in 2000 as the first international scientific forum open to scientists and researchers belonging to the most diverse disciplines, who aimed at proposing and discussing conceptualizations, empirical findings, intervention programs, and social policy strategies related to this multifold and controversial construct.

In the last few years the number of submissions to the Journal of Happiness Studies steadily increased, and in June 2011 the Journal received its first Impact Factor. This success represents both an indicator of the high scientific quality of the contributions, and an uncontroversial sign of the ceaselessly growing interest in the investigation of happiness, well-being and related topics from a variety of epistemological perspectives, ranging from economics to sociology, from psychology to philosophy, from education to medicine.

This book represents the first volume of a series that aims at complementing the Journal of Happiness Studies. Each book will provide readers with an articulated overview of a specific topic, investigating it from various points of view. The distinctive feature of gathering multidisciplinary contributions around a unifying theme will be unique for this series in the current domain of well-being publications. It will help strengthen cross-disciplinary synergies among authors investigating the same topic, and it will raise the interest in happiness research among professionals and experts belonging to a broad range of domains.

This first volume includes a selection of contributions published in the Journal of Happiness Studies during its first decade of life, with the aim to provide readers with a general overview of the prominent issues, problems and challenges that well-being research has been facing since its appearance on the scientific stage.

The chapters address issues that lie at the core of the lively debate going on around happiness, ranging from theoretical frameworks and models to social and

A. Delle Fave (✉)
Department of Pathophysiology and Transplantation, University of Milano,
Settore Didattico Ospedale Sacco, Via G.B. Grassi 74, 20157 Milano, Italy
e-mail: antonella.dellefave@unimi.it

A. Delle Fave (ed.), *The Exploration of Happiness*, Happiness Studies Book Series,
DOI: 10.1007/978-94-007-5702-8_1, © Springer Science+Business Media Dordrecht 2013

political action. They tackle still controversial issues, such as the contextualization of happiness within the subjective or the objective realm, the adequacy of the instruments used to assess it, its relevance for individuals and societies as a goal *per se*, or rather as a means or a by-product of a life well-lived.

1.1 Book Overview

1.1.1 Part 1: Individual Well-Being—Theory and Research

The first two chapters of this volume address the nature of happiness and its function in human life. Varelius (2004) contrasts objective and subjective theories of happiness; the former are grounded into the assumption that well-being can be described through behaviors and activities that contribute to shape the good life in accordance with shared values, moral principles, and universal features of the "human nature"; the latter identify happiness with the fulfillment of subjectively perceived desires and aspirations. Varelius offers a solution to this conceptual opposition, suggesting that while subjective well-being (SWB) can be empirically evaluated, no scientifically sound techniques are currently available to measure the objective components of happiness. Therefore, considering that subjective evaluations of well-being are necessarily contextualized within an external system of social values and moral principles, and that they arise from the individual interaction with this system, further developments in the empirical investigation of SWB can fruitfully help shed light on its relationship with objective dimensions.

Martin (2008) offers an overview of some paradoxes that the conceptualization of happiness conveys. Moving from the well-known assumption "to get happiness, forget about it", he discusses a set of paradoxical statements that characterize the history of happiness investigation, categorizing them as paradoxes of aim, success, freedom, and attitude. His final summary focuses on the need for an integrated perspective, interpreting these paradoxes as one-sided truths that are in tension with each other, rather than conflicting and mutually exclusive perspectives. Martin calls for a broader framework in which the subjective experience of happiness is interwoven with socially constructed values, standards, and ideals, rather than being identified with them. He also stresses the dynamic nature of happiness, whose subjective evaluation changes with time in relation with the individual development process and life experiences.

The subsequent chapters are grounded in well-defined psychological theories developed in the last three decades. Their authors conceptualize individual wellbeing from two different but complementary perspectives: hedonism and eudaimonism, both rooted in ancient Greek philosophical systems. The origins of the hedonic view of happiness can be traced back to Aristippus of Cyrene (IV century B.C), who equated happiness with pleasure, stating that only what is pleasant or has pleasant consequences is intrinsically good. Today, the hedonic approach to happiness is centered on the concept of SWB that includes positive affect and global life satisfaction judgements (SWB; Kahneman et al. 1999). The eudaimonic view stems from Aristotle's concept of eudaimonia, described as the fulfillment of one's true nature, that includes both self-actualization and commitment to socially shared goals. Today this approach to the study of well-being comprises a wide range of constructs, such as self-actualization and self-acceptance, perception of purpose and meaning, self-determination, cultivation of competences, trust in relationships, and cooperation. One of the basic differences between these two perspectives is that the eudaimonic approach focuses on the process of living well, investigating the factors that contribute to it; the hedonic approach is instead prominently focused on the outcomes of this process.

Two chapters endorse the hedonic perspective. Kim-Prieto et al. (2005) propose a integrated and time-sequential framework for the investigation of SWB. In particular, they highlight the dynamic structure of SWB, grounded in the sequential addition and integration of new information that takes place throughout the individual life, thus contributing to changes in SWB ratings. This sequential framework is articulated into four stages: the first one refers to objective aspects, such as life circumstances and events occurring in the individual life; the second stage is represented by the subjective emotional reactions to these circumstances and events; the third stage is constituted by the retrospective recall and reconstruction of the emotional reactions previously experienced; the fourth stage refers to global life satisfaction judgements. Kim-Prieto et al. discuss objective and subjective factors that can influence each of these stages, and emphasize their interrelationship rather than their developmental progression. More than one sequence can take place at the same time; reciprocal influences can be hypothesized between sequences and stages; each stage can exert an influence on other stages in the same sequence, in parallel sequences or in future ones. This integrated framework can allow researchers to better disentangle the specific contribution of the different components considered in each stage to the global construct of SWB.

The dynamic structure of SWB is also taken into account by Cummins (2010), but from a different point of view. He hypothesizes the evolution of a homeostatic mechanism aimed at safeguarding the widely observed stability of SWB values within a narrow range, situated toward the positive pole of the satisfaction rating scale. This hypothesis can help clarify the psychological processes underlying individuals' adaptation and successful coping with life challenges, as well as the negative consequences of the disruption of homeostasis generated by an excessively demanding situation. Within this framework, depression can be interpreted as the long-term outcome of a chronic impairment in the homeostatic mechanism that allows for the stability of functional levels of SWB.

Two other chapters refer instead to the eudaimonic perspective. Ryff and Singer (2008) offer a synthetic overview of the historical and conceptual roots of the multidimensional construct of psychological well-being (PWB; Ryff 1989). They contextualize PWB within the eudaimonic framework, identifying a set of theoretical precursors for each of its components—purpose in life, self-acceptance, mastery, autonomy, positive relations, and personal growth. They finally provide updated findings showing the relations between PWB and biological correlates, and suggesting the positive impact of PWB on health.

Ryan et al. (2008) include in their conceptualization of eudaimonia subjectively pursued aims, as well as individual characteristics that are judged as exemplary and excellent in relation to objective and shared values. They propose a model of good life based on self-determination theory, suggesting that the pursuit of intrinsic aspirations and goals is connected at the motivational level with the three basic needs for competence, autonomy and relatedness, and at the cognitive level with reflectivity and mindfulness, defined as the ability to clearly and appropriately evaluate events and situations, and to consequently act and make choices in a meaningful and integrated way.

The authors of the last three chapters in this part propose unified frameworks, in which both hedonic and eudaimonic aspects of well being can be combined.

Peterson et al. (2005) propose an operalization of well-being grounded in the identification of three orientations to happiness: pleasure, engagement, and meaning. They provide empirical evidence of the relative impact of each orientation on the overall ratings of life satisfaction. In particular, their findings show that a life filled with all three orientations leads to the greatest life satisfaction in comparison to a life with low levels of all three orientations. However, engagement and meaning contribute to happiness more significantly than pleasure.

A multidimensional approach is also adopted by Sheldon and Hoon (2007), who provide empirical evidence of the independent contribution to SWB of a set of psychological and environmental determinants, the former including personality traits, need satisfaction, progress toward personal goals, and self-esteem, the latter comprising social support and a favorable cultural context. Thanks to its unique and specific contribution to SWB, each of these six determinants represents a distinct level within a unified hierarchical model.

Sirgy and Wu (2009) finally propose to expand the orientations to happiness model by adding to it the contribution of balance, defined as a state "reflecting satisfaction or fulfilment in several important domains with little or no negative affect in other domains" (Sirgy and Wu 2009, p. 185). Sirgy and Wu move from two basic assumptions: each life domain is structured around a limited set of needs, that can be related to survival, to growth, or to both; each life domain—according to the kind of needs it satisfies, and to the extent it allows for their fulfilment—is characterized by a specific salience, that makes it more or less effective in contributing to the overall well-being. Therefore, because of the satisfaction limit that can be derived from a single domain, people have to invest their resources in multiple life domains in order to satisfy the full spectrum of survival and growth needs. These considerations lead the authors to consider balance as the potentially prominent source of SWB.

1.2 Part 2: Socio-Economic and Cultural Issues

This second part of the book includes contributions specifically addressing social and cultural aspects of happiness, prominently derived from studies conducted within the sociological and economic perspectives.

The first three chapters focus on theoretical models and constructs that substantially contribute to contextualize well-being research within a broad sociocultural perspective. Veenhoven (2000) proposes a 4-fold model to describe quality of life, identifying two major dimensions—chances and outcomes—and distinguishing in each of them outer (objective) and inner (subjective) qualities. The model is thus constituted of four quadrants. Outer chances refer to the livability of the environment and social context; inner chances refer to the personal abilities to cope with the environmental demands. Outer outcomes can be summarized in the concept of "utility of life", assuming that a good life is based on higher values transcending the individual; inner outcomes are represented by appreciation of life that can be operationalized as the assessment of subjective well-being. After providing examples of how this 4-fold classification can be used in different disciplines, for example to evaluate the quality of health conditions or the qualities of a social system, Veenhoven warns against the tendency to sum up factors belonging to each of the four quadrants of the model in the attempt to get an aggregated quality of life score, since they assess qualitatively different dimensions, many of them not being directly and reliably measurable (such as utility of life). He also emphasizes the importance of implementing the assessment of subjective aspects, that can be measured and compared more effectively than some of the outer indicators of quality of life.

Leung et al. (2011) focus on social capital, a construct that is gaining increasing attention in well-being research. Relying on empirical evidence obtained from a large national survey, they discuss the relationship between subjective well-being ratings and four dimensions of social capital: trust and obligations; information channels; norms and sanctions; and belongingness. Their results suggest that these dimensions can be fruitfully used as predictors of subjective well-being, and can thus represent an implementation target for social policies aimed at promoting citizens' well-being.

The need for contextualizing happiness studies within cultures is effectively highlighted by Uchida et al. (2004). They bring empirical evidence of the different evaluation of well-being among European American and East Asian participants: while among Westerners happiness is best predicted by self-esteem, and positive and negative emotions are perceived as opposite poles negatively correlated with each other, among Asians happiness is best predicted by embeddedness, and as balance between positive and negative effect. These differences can be related to the specific patterns of independent and interdependent self-construal (Markus and Kitayama 1991), promoted in individualistic and collectivistic cultures respectively. Individualistic cultures encourage people to use subjective cues and dimensions to define themselves, their goals, and their achievements; on the contrary, individuals raised in collectivistic contexts build their selfdefinition according to interpersonal and group dimensions: goals are settled within the community; and other people's needs are crucially important in goal setting and achievement.

The last four chapters tackle the problematic issue of the relationship between happiness and indicators of national development. This issue is problematic in that it calls into play theoretical assumptions about two crucial points: the selection of the socioeconomic indicators that can best represent development; the identification of subjective well-being with the *summum bonum* to be pursued by individuals and governments. Far from being neutral and objective, these assumptions stem from values that are historically and culturally grounded.

From this problematic stance, Eckersley (2000) addresses the relationship between progress and happiness. On the basis of empirical evidence showing that growth in national wealth is not correlated with increasing values of well-being, especially in developed nations where basic needs are satisfied, he critically discusses the assumption that maximizing subjective well-being should be the ultimate goal of progress. As an alternative approach, he suggests the pursuit of a balance between individual and social dimensions of happiness, grounded in collective agency, prudence, and responsibility.

On the same vein, Duncan (2010) criticizes the view according to which governments should aim at maximizing their citizens' happiness. He emphasizes the risks entailed in the promotion of a consumerist perspective that reduces policies to products, generating in citizens a spiral of progressively rising expectations that would be impossible to fulfill. Considering that there is no clear empirical evidence of a positive relationship between governments' policy performance and citizens' political trust and participation, Duncan recommends to clearly distinguish between government actions and citizens' levels of happiness and life satisfaction. The two phenomena do not necessarily overlap, and thus cannot be jointly used to assess governments' overall performance.

The problematic consequences of equating well-being with wealth and material abundance is a concern for Schimmel (2009), who discusses the conceptualization of development endorsed by the United Nations Development Program (UNPD), and operationalized through the Human Development Index (HDI). HDI focuses of three major indicators of well-being: standard of living (GDP), health, and education. Schimmel argues that this approach evaluates poverty exclusively in terms of lack and deficiency, adopting as norm of reference the life conditions of an ideal young, affluent, healthy, and educated citizen. From this perspective, well-being is synonymous with abundance of resources. Several studies however contradict this assumption, showing very uncertain relationships between the position of a country in the HDI ranking and the level of subjective well-being reported by its citizens. This contradictory finding holds true also considering each of the three indicators separately. Schimmel concludes that objective and subjective dimensions have to be combined in any evaluation of development, outlining the problems that can derive from confounding the potential to be happy with the actual state of being happy.

On the contrary, Jan Ott (2010) suggests that governments should more systematically rely on citizens' evaluations of happiness in order to develop adequate policy interventions. He summarizes empirical evidence on the influence of governments' technical quality and of social equality on citizens' levels of subjective well-being. On the basis of this evidence, Ott suggests that collecting information on the life conditions of citizens reporting different levels of happiness can shed light on the sources of these differences, and can thus offer governments useful hints about specific social needs and problematic issues, providing direction for the promotion of more equal levels of happiness among citizens, through a more equal distribution of resources.

1.3 Future Directions

1.3.1 Beyond Reduction, Towards Integration

While each of the chapters in this book is grounded into well-defined theories and perspectives, and focuses on specific constructs and dimensions of well-being, it is possible to identify a fil-rouge, a shared concern that crosses most of them. This concern consists in the tension toward a unified framework that encompasses the variety of well-being dimensions as exhaustively as possible. This goal is surely ambitious, and cannot be successfully pursued without ignoring some crucial aspects.

In particular, there is the necessity to gain deeper insight into the multiple psychological dimensions of well-being, avoiding simplified and reductionist perspectives. For example, empirical evidence clearly highlighted that eudaimonic and hedonic happiness are two correlated but separate constructs (Delle Fave et al. 2011a, b; Gallagher et al. 2009; Huta and Ryan 2010; Linley et al. 2009; Keyes and Annas 2009). The models proposed in this book by Peterson and his colleagues, Sheldon and Hoon, and Sirgy and Wu represent laudable and heuristically relevant attempts to address this issue.

A second aspect to be carefully considered when studying well-being is its contextualization within cultural and situational constraints. Uchida et al. effectively raise the issue of the cultural rootedness of well-being concepts. Veenhoven distinguishes between chances and results, thus pointing to the interplay between environmental opportunities and constraints, on the one hand, and individual evaluations of well-being. Eckersley, Duncan, and Schimmel unveil the cultural biases underlying widespread assumptions on well-being at the social and individual levels. Ott points to the fact that when people evaluate their level of happiness by averaging positive and negative aspects of their life, thus making the relationship between happiness and objective conditions ambiguous. Several other studies have delved into the role of well-being dimensions in dealing with unfavorable circumstances. In periods of uncertainty or change and in the adjustment to stressful events people report high levels of meaning making, even though associated with low levels of SWB (Folkman and Greer 2000; Park 2005; Shmotkin et al. 2006). In the case of traumatic events, a post-traumatic growth process can arise from the elaboration and contextualization of the event in the individual's life and representation of reality (Tedeschi and Calhoun 2004). People with chronic diseases or disabilities, who face disadvantages related to both their biological impairments and to the social attitudes toward them, often perceive themselves as ordinary persons coping with extraordinary circumstances (Saravanan et al. 2001) and report good levels of well-being, prominently from the eudaimonic point of view (Arnold et al. 2004; Delle Fave and Massimini 2005; Cortinovis et al. 2011).

1.3.2 Harmonizing Perspectives

Peterson et al. (2005) remark that the different approaches developed in order to study well-being have proceeded autonomously and without seeking for connections with other perspectives, thus leading to a variety of definitions of happiness, each one grounded into a well-defined framework, but no one capturing the complexity and multidimensionality of the concept. Similarly, Ryff and Singer (2008) note that clinging to highly specific and defined approaches entails the risk to overlook other important dimensions.

The clear delimitation of the field of analysis is however a necessity in science, and it is related to the need for maximizing precision and specificity in the assessment and measurement of phenomena. This need is especially compelling when the objects under examination consist in exquisitely psychological dimensions—thus requiring the use of assessment tools based on subjective self-reports—but also when researchers deal with collective phenomena, that call into play a great variety of variables and components that can be only partially taken into account in a single study.

The "constructive tensions" (Ryff and Singer 2008, p. 33) presently running across the broad and multifaceted field of well-being studies have to be interpreted as opportunities for progressively expand and deepen our knowledge and understanding, rather than as threats and sources of disorder and fragmentation. From this perspective, to unilaterally contrast universalism and relativism, objective data and self-reports, quality and quantity, hedonia and eudaimonia cannot take researchers very far in their attempts to provide an exhaustive description of happiness.

The complexity of human behavior can hardly be captured through simplified paradigms, and the current state of the art in well-being studies does not allow for a unified perspective yet. Individuals and societies, like any other living system, show dynamic features clearly taken into account in the models proposed by Cummins and by Kim-Prieto et al.

Biological, psychological, and social systems tend toward progressively higher levels of complexity through the exchange of information with the environment (Khalil and Boulding 1996; Maturana and Varela 1986; Prigogine and Stengers 1984) leading to the system's transformation (Pribram 1996). In particular, the acquisition of new information is transformed into stable neural connections at the biological level; into personal skills, beliefs, meanings and purposes at the psychological level; and into codified rules, norms, and values at the social level. However, at none of these level the system configuration is stable, by virtue of the progressive and ceaseless integration of new information.

On the basis of these premises, any scientist interested in the study of wellbeing has to take into account both the specific configuration of the system under examination and its relationships with higher order and lower order systems, as well as its modifiability according to progressive increases in complexity (Delle Fave 2007). By the way, ceaseless change represents a core concept endorsed by a variety of worldviews across history and cultures. Just to mention few examples, Heraclitus conceptualized reality as an uninterrupted flux of change. The Hindu and Buddhist traditions focused on the concept of Maya as illusoriness of the phenomenal reality. In much more recent times, the studies conducted by Heisenberg, Einstein, and De Broglie in the domain of physics determined that our observations dynamically contribute to shape reality, in that have an effect on the behavior of elementary physical entities. Evidence emerging from different disciplines supports the dynamic and ever-changing nature of reality, that too often we tend to ignore, due our preoccupation to achieve fixed and definitive descriptions of individuals and societies.

From this perspective, a peculiar relevance assumes the concept of balance, repeatedly echoed by the contributors to this volume. Sirgy and Wu directly include it in their model of well-being. Ryff and Singer call for higher attention to the concept of balance in the conceptualization of well-being by referring to Aristotle's invitation to seek "the intermediate", avoiding any excess or deficiency in behaviors, attitudes, beliefs, and expectations, even as concerns the "positive" or "good" ones. Ryan et al. refer to the feelings of inner peace, inner harmony, and connectedness with the environment and a "greater whole" transcending the self as one of the outcomes of the eudaimonic life. Eckersley claims for a definition of well-being grounded into the "balance between personal happiness and social bonds, obligations, and responsibility" (p. 286).Veenhoven refers to the definition of quality of life as "harmony between self-interest and transcendent utility" (p. 32). Uchida et al. provide evidence of the non-contradictory coexistence of positive and negative emotions in evaluations of well-being among East Asian participants, suggesting the relevance of emotional balance rather than of maximization of positive affect. These findings are consistent with the focus on another kind of balance, namely social harmony, as a prominent goal of collectivistic societies, that influence self construals, daily behaviors, and social policies.

Other studies suggest the relevance of balance in well-being research, be it evaluated across life domains (Cummins and Nistico 2002; WHOQOL Group 2004; Wu 2009), as a psychological state (Delle Fave et al. 2011a; Lu 2001; Jason et al. 2001; Muñoz Sastre 1998), as a social dimension (Ho and Chan 2009; Leung et al. 2002; Ferriss 2002).

A historical and interdisciplinary overview of harmony as a concept related to quality of life (Delle Fave 2013) has recently highlighted that, beyond philosophical and conceptual differences, in all cultural traditions harmony has been directly or indirectly related to well-being, and it represents an indicator of a good quality of life, at both the individual and social levels.

An harmonization effort should be also made by researchers involved in the definition and operationalization of well-being components, due to its multiplicity of dimensions and levels of analysis. The patterns of interaction between these multiple levels can be widely different according to cultural features, values, worldviews, and meanings. The impact of policies and social provisions can differentially affect individuals and groups according to the structure and access to resources, as well as to basic social values. In the broad and still unexplored planet of well-being there is a wide range of issues, topics, and dimensions still waiting to be investigated, and maybe even to be discovered.

References

Arnold R, Ranchor A, Sanderman R, Kempen GIJM, Ormel J, Suurmeijer TPBM (2004) The relative contribution of domains of quality of life to overall quality of life for different chronic diseases. Qual Life Res 13:883–896

Cortinovis I, Luraschi E, Intini S, Sessa M, Delle Fave A (2011) The daily experience of people with achondroplasia. Appl Psychol: Health and Well-Being 3:207–227

Cummins RA (2010) Subjective well-being, homeostatically protected mood and depression: a synthesis. J Happiness Stud 11:1–17

Cummins RA, Nistico H (2002) Maintaining life satisfaction: The role of positive cognitive bias. J Happiness Stud 3:37–69

Delle Fave A (2007) Theoretical foundations of the ESM. In: Hektner J, Schmidt J, Csikszentmihalyi M (eds) Experience Sampling Method. Measuring the quality of everyday life, Sage, New York, pp 15–28

Delle Fave A (2013) Harmony. In: Michalos A (ed) The Quality of Life Encyclopedia, Springer, Dordrecht

Delle Fave A, Massimini F (2005) The relevance of subjective well-being to social policies: optimal experience and tailored intervention. In: Huppert F, Keverne B, Baylis N (eds) The Science of Well-being, Oxford University Press, Oxford, p 379–404

Delle Fave A, Brdar I, Freire T, Vella-Brodrick D, Wissing MP (2011a) The Eudaimonic and hedonic components of happiness: qualitative and quantitative findings. Soc Indic Res 100:185–207

Delle Fave A, Massimini F, Bassi M (2011b) Psychological selection and optimal experience across cultures, Springer Science, Dordrecht

Duncan G (2010) Should happiness-maximization be the goal of government? J Happiness Stud, 11:163–178

Eckersley R (2000) The mixed blessing of material progress: diminishing returns in the pursuit of happiness. J Happiness Stud 1:267–292

Ferriss AL (2002) Does material well-being affect non-material well-being? Soc Indic Res 60:275–280

Folkman S, Greer S (2000) Promoting psychological well-being in the face of serious illness: when theory, research and practice inform each other. Psycho-Oncol 9:11–19

Gallagher MW, Lopez SJ, Preacher KJ (2009) The hierarchical structure of well-being. J Pers 77:1025–1049

Ho SSM, Chan RSY (2009) Social harmony in Hong Kong: level, determinants and policy implications. Soc Indic Res 91:37–58

Huta V, Ryan RM (2010) Pursuing pleasure or virtue: the differential and overlapping well-being benefits of hedonic and eudaimonic motives. J Happiness Stud 11:735–762

Jason LA, Reichler A, King C, Madsen D, Camacho J, Marchese W (2001) The measurement of wisdom: a preliminary effort. J Community Psychol 29:585–598

Kahneman D, Diener E, Schwarz N (eds) (1999) Well-being: the foundations of hedonic psychology. Russell Sage Foundation, New York

Keyes CLM, Annas J (2009) Feeling good and functioning well: distinctive concepts in ancient philosophy and contemporary science. J Posit Psychol 4(3):197–201
Khalil EL, Boulding KE (eds) (1996) Evolution, Order and Complexity, Routledge, New York
Kim-Prieto C, Diener E, Tamir M, Scollon C, Diener M (2005) Integrating the diverse definitions of happiness: a time-sequential framework of subjective well-being. J Happiness Stud 6:261–300
Leung K, Tremain Koch P, Lu L (2002) A dualistic model of harmony and its implications for conflict management in Asia. Asia Pac J Manag 19:201–220
Leung A, Cheryl K, Fung T, Fung L, Sproule R (2011) Searching for happiness: The importance of social capital. J Happiness Stud 12:443–462
Linley PA, Maltby J, Wood AM, Osborne G, Hurling R (2009) Measuring happiness: the higher order factor structure of subjective and psychological well-being measures. Pers Individ Differ 47:878–884
Lu L (2001) Understanding happiness: a look into the Chinese folk psychology. J Happiness Stud 2:407–432
Markus HR, Kitayama S (1991) Culture and the self: implications for cognition, emotion and motivation. Psychol Rev 98:224–253
Martin MW (2008) Paradoxes of happiness. J Happiness Stud 9:171–184
Maturana H, Varela F (1986) The tree of knowledge: a new look at the biological roots of human understanding. New Science Library, Boston
Muñoz Sastre MT (1998) Lay conceptions of well-being and rules used in well-being judgements among young, middle-aged, and elderly adults. Soc Indic Res 47:203–231
Ott J (2010) Greater happiness for a greater number: some non-controversial options for government. J Happiness Stud 11:631–647
Park C (2005) Religion as a meaning-making framework in coping with life stress. J Soc Issues 61:707–729
Peterson C, Park N, Seligman MEP (2005) Orientations to happiness and life satisfaction: the full life versus the empty life. J Happiness Stud 6:25–41
Pribram KH (1996) Interfacing complexity at the boundary between the natural and social sciences. In: Khalil EL, Boulding KE (eds) Evolution, Order and Complexity, Routledge, New York, p 40–60
Prigogine I, Stengers I (1984) Order Out of Chaos, Bantam, New York
Ryan RM, Huta V, Deci EL (2008) Living well: a self-determination theory perspective on eudaimonia. J Happiness Stud 9:139–170
Ryff CD (1989) Happiness is everything, or is it? Exploration on the meaning of psychological well-being. J Pers Soc Psychol 57:1069–1081
Ryff CD, Singer BH (2008) Know thyself and become what you are: a eudaimonic approach to psychological well-being. J Happiness Stud 9:13–39
Saravanan B, Manigandam C, Macaden A, Tharion G, Bhattacharji S (2001) Re-examining the psychology of spinal cord injury: a meaning centered approach fom a cultural perspective. Spinal Cord 39:323–326
Schimmel J (2009) Development as happiness: the subjective perception of happiness and UNDP's analysis of poverty, wealth and development. J Happiness Stud 10:93–111
Sheldon KM, Hoon TH (2007) The multiple determination of well-being: independent effects of positive traits, needs, goals, selves, social support and cultural context. J Happiness Stud 8:565–592
Shmotkin D, Berkovich M, Cohen K (2006) Combining happiness and suffering in a retrospective view of anchor periods in life: a differential approach to subjective well-being. Soc Indic Res 77:139–169
Sirgy MJ, Wu J (2009) The Pleasant life, the Engaged life, and the Meaningful life: what about the balanced life? J Happiness Stud 10:183–196
Tedeschi RG, Calhoun LG (2004) Post-traumatic growth: conceptual foundations and empirical evidence. Psychol Inq 15:1–18
Uchida Y, Norasakkunkit V, Kitayama S (2004) Cultural constructions of happiness: theory and empirical evidence. J Happiness Stud 5:223–239

Varelius J (2004) Objective explanations of individual well-being. J Happiness Stud 5:73–91
Veenhoven R (2000) The four qualities of life. J Happiness Stud 1:1–39
WHOQOL Group (2004) Can we identify the poorest quality of life? Assessing the importance of quality of life using the WHOQOL-100. Qual Life Res 13:23–34
Wu C (2009) Enhancing quality of life by shifting importance perception among life domains. J Happiness Stud 10:37–47

Chapter 2
Objective Explanations of Individual Well-Being

Jukka Varelius

Abstract Empirical research on questions pertaining to individual well-being is informed by the researchers' philosophical conception of the nature of well-being and, consequently, the adequacy of such research is partly determined by the plausibility of this conception. Philosophical theories of human well-being divide into subjective and objective. Subjective theories make our well-being dependent on our attitudes of favour and disfavour. Objective theories deny this dependency. This article discusses objective theories of individual well-being from the point of view of their explanatory power and argues that these theories are unable to provide an acceptable account of the prudential goodness of what they consider to be good for human beings. The article concludes by discussing some implications of its main argument to empirical research on questions pertaining to individual well-being.

Keywords Subjectivism • Objectivism • Happiness • Well-being • Prudential value • Explanation

Empirical research on questions pertaining to individual well-being is informed by the researchers' conception of the nature of well-being and, consequently, the adequacy of such research is partly determined by the plausibility of this conception. Questions pertaining to the nature of well-being are philosophical in character. In philosophy, these questions concerning individual well-being are seen as questions pertaining to the value that a life has for the person who is living it, to prudential value that is. However valuable a person's life may be in other terms, it has prudential value only if it is also good for the person who is living it.

In philosophical literature, theories of prudential value, or human well-being, are usually divided into subjective and objective (see, e.g., Arneson 1999; Bernstein 1998; Parfit 1984; Scanlon 1993; Sumner 1996; Thomson 1987). Subjective theories see our well-being as determined by our attitudes of favour and disfavour. Objective theories deny this kind of determination. On a subjective theory of well-being, it is easy

J. Varelius (✉)
Department of Behavioural Sciences and Philosophy, University of Turku, 20014 Turku, Finland
e-mail: varelius@hotmail.com

A. Delle Fave (ed.), *The Exploration of Happiness*, Happiness Studies Book Series, DOI: 10.1007/978-94-007-5702-8_2,

to understand why attaining some purported prudential good makes a person better off: either that thing gives the agent pleasure or satisfies a desire she has (or both). Accepting the common subjectivist point of departure that the attitudes that should be taken to be relevant in determining what is prudentially good for a person should be sufficiently informed, the subjectivist can be taken to have a plausible sounding explanation for the prudential goodness of her prudential goods. But dissociating prudential goodness from the attitudes of the agent whose well-being is being assessed gives rise to the question: why would some purported prudential good be good for an (informed) agent? In this article I will argue that the objective theories of well-being cannot provide an acceptable explanation of the prudential goodness of what they claim to be good for human beings. I conclude by discussing some implications of my argument to empirical research on questions pertaining to individual well-being.

2.1 Subjective and Objective Theories of Well-Being and Happiness

As was said above, subjective theories of prudential value see our well-being as determined by our attitudes of favour and disfavour. Thus, when our task is to determine whether some particular thing or activity is good for an agent or not, the subjective theories of well-being advise us to consult the agent whose well-being is being assessed, to pay attention to her own preferences and attitudes of favour and disfavour. Objective theories, in their turn, maintain that an agent's well-being is not determined by her own desires and attitudes of favour and disfavour. Instead of concentrating on these kinds of subjective states, objective theories usually make well-being dependent on such objective issues as whether a thing or an activity satisfies human needs, realises the human nature, etc. Often objective theories provide a list of things and activities that they consider to be good for a person and, accordingly, these theories are called objective list theories of well-being. Usually the lists of objective prudential goods include such entries as moral goodness, rational activity, the development of one's abilities, having children and being a good parent, knowledge, and the awareness of true beauty (see, e.g., Parfit 1984, p. 493 ff.), and these objective theories maintain that a life is good for the person who is living it only when it contains these particular elements. Importantly, an objective theory of well-being denies that there is a necessary connection between what an agent desires or has a pro-attitude towards and what is good for her, and maintains that something can be directly and immediately good for a person although that person does not regard it favourably. In addition to this desire or pro-attitude independence requirement, a theory of well-being must satisfy at least one of two further kinds of requirements in order to qualify as an objective theory of well-being.[1] On an objective theory of well-being, what is considered as prudentially good must either

[1] Otherwise we could determine the objective good of a particular agent on the basis of the irrational opinions of any other individual. It is thus clear that there must be something more to an objective theory of well-being than mere independence of the desires of the agent whose well-being is being assessed.

(1) be regarded as good intersubjectively or (2) be good in a (stronger) realist sense.[2] Thus, if in addition to fulfilling the desire independence condition, a theory of well-being satisfies either the requirement of intersubjectivity or the requirement of realism (or both), then the theory qualifies as an objective theory of well-being.[3]

In addition to prudential value and well-being, in everyday common language as well as in philosophical literature there are several notions available for evaluating how well a life is going for the person who is living it, including happiness, welfare, contentment, satisfaction, flourishing, etc. None of these concepts have commonly accepted precise meanings and, partly as a consequence of this, the exact relationships between them remain unclear. However, since the notion of happiness is of central importance for the readers of this journal, I will now briefly discuss the relationship between the notions of prudential value and happiness. Most importantly, the notion of happiness concerns a person's own subjective experience and assessment of how well or badly she is faring.[4] The nature of the relationship between prudential value or well-being and happiness depends on whether or not we accept that only things that enter an agent's experience can have an effect on her well-being. If we accept this experience requirement, then it is reasonable to accept that happiness is quite the same as prudential value, for then only things that enter an agent's experience can have an effect on her well-being. And it seems to me plausible that things that have an effect on how well a life is going for the person who is living it, i.e., on that person's well-being, will influence the person's happiness as understood in the present sense.[5] I do think that the experience requirement should be accepted and thus that well-being is quite the same as happiness in the present sense, but I am not able to explicate my arguments to this effect here.[6] So, those who accept the experience requirement may

---

[2] Here I thus understand 'realism' in the traditional way which maintains that something has real existence only if it exists independently of peoples' mental states. It may be that there is no stronger sense of objectivity than intersubjectivity in the evaluative sphere. Whether this is the case is a question I will not now go into.

[3] It has been pointed out that not all objective theories are list theories, nor are all list theories necessarily objective theories. I will not now go into such questions as whether a list with only one entry is really a list or whether desire theories can sometimes properly be called list theories.

[4] Although the precise meanings given to this concept differ from each other significantly, they seem to have this reference to the agent's subjective experiences and evaluations in common.

[5] It is perhaps useful to point out that the reference to the subject's own experience and evaluation in the above definition of happiness does not imply that what enhances a person's happiness is necessarily determined by her attitudes and desires in the sense that subjective theories of well-being see prudential value as being determined. If objectivism about happiness is accepted, then what promotes a person's happiness is not determined by her desires and attitudes of favour and disfavour, but her own experience of how well she is faring would, of course, be subjective in the sense used in this definition of happiness. For an objective conception of happiness see, e.g., Kraut (1979).

[6] I think that it would be counter-intuitive to maintain that things that do not enter an agent's experience could have an effect on that agent's well-being. However, it has been suggested to me that, e.g., a person's losing a substantial amount of money may have an effect on her well-being even if she is unaware of this loss and that a posthumous dishonour may have an effect on how well the dishonoured person's life went in prudential terms. I leave discussion on these points for another occasion.

assume that what I say below is directly relevant from the point of view of happiness, whereas those who reject the experience requirement must assume that I will be talking about well-being only.[7]

2.2 Explaining Prudential Goodness

When talking about prudential value, some philosophers simply put forward a list of things and activities they consider to be good for a person, irrespective of whether that person has any pro-attitude towards these things or not (see, e.g., Finnis 1980, 1983). This kind of account of individual well-being does fulfil the condition of desire independence, but it does not satisfy the requirement of intersubjectivity nor the requirement of realism, at least when the latter kind of requirements are interpreted as demanding that a theory must make the prudential goodness of its prudential goods objectively intelligible. According to this kind of interpretation of the requirements of intersubjectivity and realism—which I find plausible—an objective theory of well-being must provide an objective—in the sense understandable by all normal agents—explanation of what it is that makes its prudential goods prudentially good and how this something produces individual well-being.[8] Since the kind of accounts of well-being that simply put forward a list of what their proponents consider to be prudentially good things and activities do not satisfy this kind of requirement of intersubjectivity or realism, they do not qualify as full-blown objective theories of prudential value.

2.2.1 Are Prudential Goods Self-Evident?

What the proponents of these kind of list accounts of human well-being would present as a reply to this criticism is, I think, that what they consider to be prudentially good things and activities are self-evidently good for individual

---

[7] In the history of philosophy such prominent figures as Aristotle and J.S. Mill have equated, or at least have usually been interpreted as equating, happiness and well-being with each other. A modern equation of happiness with well-being is found, e.g., in Den Uyl and Machan (1983).

[8] Usually objective list theories of well-being provide a list of things which they consider to be prudentially good for all persons. There could however be objective theories which provided different lists for different individuals. The latter kind of theories qualify as objective theories of well-being if what they claim to be good for a particular individual is objectively recognisable as such. I thus presuppose that there are no objective or real values that are recognisable for one person only. An objective list theorist committed to the existence of these kind of prudential values could only come up with one objective list theory of well-being that is applicable to one person only.

human beings and thus no explanations of the sort I here require are needed. Finnis (1980, Chap. 3, see also 1983, Chap. 2), e.g., maintains that knowledge is good for one irrespective of desires and whether it is pleasurable to have it or not. Finnis (1980, p. 72) writes:

> It is obvious that a man who is well-informed, etc., simply *is* better off (other things being equal) than a man who is muddled, deluded, and ignorant, that the state of the one is better than the state of the other, not simply in this particular case or that, but in all cases, as such, universally and *whether I like it or not.* Knowledge is better than ignorance.[9] (emphasis in original)

The problem with this kind of conception is that it is not at all obvious that knowledge is good prudentially. There is a plausible criticism of the view that knowledge has intrinsic prudential value. Would I, the proponents of this criticism ask, be better off if I knew exactly how many grains of sand lie on my local beach (other things being equal) (see, e.g., Nozick 1989, p. 116; Goldsworthy 1992, p. 12)? That is, there is much knowledge that seems clearly to be worthless. Finnis (1980, p. 62) accepts that not all knowledge is of equal value. But why not? If knowledge is prudentially valuable, period, why should one item of knowledge be of more value than another (in this sense)? If the value of knowledge were instrumental or had something to do with the desire for it or the pleasures it could give, it would be understandable that some items of knowledge could be held to be more valuable than others. But with an intrinsic value[10] of knowledge, this none-quality claim is hard to accept. Thus, someone who holds that knowledge has intrinsic prudential value is committed to the view that all knowledge is of equal value. And this view is implausible. It therefore seems that there is no sufficient

---

[9] However, at the end of his discussion on knowledge and its prudential value he presents an argument, according to which it would be self-refuting to deny that knowledge is in itself necessarily good for us. If it is self-evident that some proposition is true, then it is not necessary to provide an argument to show it to be true. Thus, the fact that Finnis provides an argument for his claim that knowledge is a prudential good suggests that he does not after all believe this claim to be self-evidently true. I do not consider this to be a problem, for I think it is not self-evident that knowledge has intrinsic prudential value. But for a view which holds there to be self-evidently prudentially valuable things, this kind of lack of self-evidence is a problem. Finnis' argument proceeds as follows: "… one who makes such an assertion (that knowledge is not a prudential good), intending it as a serious contribution to rational discussion, is implicitly committed to the proposition that he believes his assertion is worth making, and worth making *qua* true; he thus is committed to the proposition that he believes that truth is a good worth pursuing or knowing. But the sense of his original assertion was precisely that truth is not a good worth pursuing or knowing. Thus he is implicitly committed to formally contradictory beliefs." (Finnis 1980, pp. 74–75) The argument Finnis presents here is implausible. One who makes the kind of assertion Finnis talks about does not logically commit herself to the proposition that all knowledge is intrinsically good, but only to the instrumental goodness of this particular assertion. See also Goldsworthy (1992, pp. 13–14).

[10] By the intrinsic value of an entity I understand the value that that entity has independently of its value as an instrument in attaining some other value or its consequences.

reason to hold that to have knowledge is, as such, of prudential value. Knowledge is of course not the only thing that could be said to be obviously prudentially valuable irrespective of whether it satisfies desires or brings pleasure. In addition to knowledge, Finnis' list of the 'basic forms of human good'—which seems representative of its kind—contains the following entries: life, play, aesthetic experience, sociability (friendship), practical reasonableness, and 'religion' (Finnis 1980, Chap. 4). Rather than examining all these things, I will merely state that it is equally implausible to hold that any, or all, of them are self-evidently intrinsically prudentially valuable as such as it is to hold that knowledge as such is intrinsically prudentially valuable.

2.2.2 Backgrounding Self-Evidence

Those objectivists who are not content with simply stating that some things are (self-evidently) prudentially valuable usually have a background story the purpose of which is to make the reader sufficiently perceptive—or what is considered as such—for the issues discussed, and the claims to self-evidence are then expressed against a background story of this kind.[11] Instead of going into the different kinds of background stories found in discussions on different kinds of value,[12] I will consider simply one, that of Foot (1995). I have chosen to discuss Foot's view here because it appears to be a novel kind of defence of the objective account. However, I will argue that ultimately it succumbs to a problem that, to my knowledge at least, haunts all present accounts of this kind. For this reason, it is also representative of many other objective views.

Foot accepts that moral judgements are practical and action-guiding, but argues that subjectivists are mistaken when they infer from this claim the corollary that moral judgements cannot be purely factual and objective. Foot's argument proceeds, roughly, as follows. Acting morally is part of practical rationality. This can be shown by considering the nature of moral virtues. It is in the concept of a moral virtue that in so far as someone possesses it his actions are good, i.e., he acts well. What distinguishes the morally virtuous persons from others is that for the virtuous, certain considerations count as reasons

[11] It could be maintained that to hold that we are able to see the self-evidence of something only after we have been given reasons and arguments for it is nonsensical. For if seeing or understanding something is impossible without these reasons and arguments, then this something is not self-evident. I will now ignore this problem.

[12] Some of them are found in discussions on moral value without explicit claims concerning whether they are purported to apply to other kinds of value as well or not. However, it seems that many of these background stories could *mutatis mutandis* be used in discussions on prudential value, if they are not purported to apply to the case of prudential value to begin with.

for action and as reasons with a certain weight. These considerations have to do with human excellences and human defects. Human defects and excellences are determined by what human beings are and by what they do. What determines our nature and doings are the facts of human life—e.g., that we are social animals that depend on each other—which are such that it is rational for us to be moral (Foot 1995, p. 3 ff.).

However, as Foot herself acknowledges, accepting a view like hers does not necessarily persuade one to reject the subjectivist points of departure, for it is possible to require that the fact that an agent has a reason for action is itself dependent on his desires and attitudes. Foot considers the following example. A person throws away his supply of cigarettes. He does so because he wants to give up smoking, and he wants to give up smoking because he wants a healthy old age. The series goes on—A for the sake of B—but, it is assumed, it cannot go on forever. And must it not, Foot imagines her critic asking, end with something that the agent 'simply wants', i.e., with some conative element in his psychological state (Foot 1995, pp. 12–13)?

Obviously, Foot's answer to this question is 'No'. In her view, we must ask what gives the agent this goal. Does he find himself trembling at the thought of cancer at 50? Is he in a state of anxiety at the thought of how much he smokes? Perhaps, Foot replies, but nothing of this kind has to be part of the story. She continues by posing the following questions: Why could it not simply be that the agent recognises that there is a reason for him, as for anyone else, to look after his future so far as the circumstances allow? Why should not this be where the series of questions 'why?' comes to an end? Why should we not take the recognition of a reason for acting as bringing the series to a close? Recognition of a reason, Foot says, gives the rational person a goal, and this recognition is based on facts and concepts, not on some prior attitude, feeling, or goal. The only fact about the individual's state of mind that is required for the explanatory force of the proposition about the requirement of rationality is, Foot concludes, that he does not 'for some bizarre reason' deny its truth (Foot 1995, pp. 12–13).

2.2.3 Problems with Backgrounding

The problem with this kind of argument for objectivism is that it simply begs the central question. Instead of providing good reasons to believe that evaluative judgements could be purely factual, it simply states that they are. All arguments of the form in which the objectivist or realist describes some evaluatively salient situation in purely factual or descriptive terms and then asks—rhetorically—whether that description determines some particular kind of evaluative judgement concerning that situation or not are, I think, doomed to failure for the following reason. Either the description does not determine the evaluative judgement the objectivist or realist is after, or the description is not after all purely descriptive or factual as it is claimed to be.[13, 14]

It could be objected that the most important part of the realist or objectivist argument consists of the background story—which in Foot's case is that concerning the relationship between morality and practical rationality—and putting forward the evaluatively salient cases with the intentions of establishing realism are simply ways of demonstrating the point of that story. But the problem is that these evaluatively salient cases do not necessarily determine a particular evaluative judgement even if the background story is given the attention it deserves. Assuming that the objectivist's examples are well chosen, the fact that they do not succeed in what they are purported to do simply throws doubt on the background story, or more doubt, if it is found problematic to begin with. To my knowledge at least, there is no plausible background story which would force one to accept that a description of some evaluatively salient situation as such determines some particular evaluative judgement concerning that situation.

It might be claimed that the subjectivist stance is equally question-begging when it does not accept that an evaluative judgement can be determined by a description in the way the realists maintain. Why, the realist could ask, does not the subjectivist accept the obvious? The subjectivist's answer to this kind of criticism is of course that what the realist claims to be obvious is not really obvious.

---

[13] I have here assumed that the realist does not hold values to be recognisable from some epistemically privileged value-laden point of view only. However, what I will say below applies to these views as well.

[14] It could be objected that there are straightforward cases of deriving value judgements from facts or purely descriptive statements. For example, from the fact that a shopkeeper has provided me with some goods (which cost money and which I have asked for, etc.), it follows that I owe the shopkeeper some money. And from the fact that I owe the shopkeeper money, follows the value judgement that I ought to give the shopkeeper money. Cases like this, it has been claimed, demonstrate that we can derive judgements of value from purely factual statements. Hare has provided a plausible criticism of this kind of arguments that make use of what have been called 'institutional facts'. Without now going more deeply in this issue, I will just quote a passage of Hare's criticism. Hare writes: "Talking about 'institutional facts', though it can be illuminating, can also be a peculiarly insidious way of committing the 'naturalistic fallacy'.... There are moral and other principles, accepted by most of us, such that, if they were not generally accepted, certain institutions like property and promising could not exist. And if the institutions do exist, we are in a position to affirm certain 'institutional facts' (for example, that a certain piece of land is my property), on the ground that certain 'brute facts' are the case (for example, that my ancestors have occupied it form the time immemorial). But from the 'institutional facts', certain obviously prescriptive conclusions can be drawn (for example, that nobody ought to deprive me of the land). Thus it looks as if there could be a straight deduction, in two steps, from brute facts to prescriptive conclusions via institutional facts. But the deduction is a fraud. For the brute fact is a ground for the prescriptive conclusion only if the prescriptive principle which is the constitutive rule of the institution be accepted; and this prescriptive principle is not a tautology. For someone (a communist for example) who does not accept this non-tautologous prescriptive principle, the deduction collapses like a house of cards—though this does not prevent him from continuing to use the word 'property' (with his tongue in his cheek)." Hare (1964).

I find this answer convincing. I accept that the conclusion of a logically valid argument cannot say anything that is not either explicitly or implicitly included in its premises.[15] And if a description of a state of affairs logically implies an evaluative judgement, then that description cannot be evaluatively neutral in the way the realist claims it to be. Thus, I take it that a realist should not see the relation between the description of the evaluatively salient case, and the evaluative judgement she sees that case as determining, as one of logical entailment. For this reason, the realist needs something to fill in the gap between the description and the evaluative judgement. And this filler is usually something like Griffin's (1996) sensitivity to something in the world,[16] a sensitivity that is 'complex in its workings and fairly rich in its connections'. In other words, what the realists put forward to fill in the gap between description and evaluation is usually something quite obscure and mysterious,[17] if indeed they offer anything to fill this gap at all. Consequently, I take it that the subjectivist does not beg the question when she refuses to accept an evaluative judgement which the objectivist or realist claims to be determined by a description. The burden of proof in showing that some particular evaluative judgement follows from a description of an evaluatively salient state of affairs is thus on the realist's side.[18]

---

[15] For a discussion on this principle in connection with questions pertaining to values see, e.g., Brink (1989).

[16] For a good discussion on the kind of sensitivity realists usually talk about, see Norman (1997).

[17] A possible way for a realist to answer this kind of criticism is to claim that her filler is not that mysterious after all since similar fillers are presupposed by our knowledge about many other things, such as inertia, identity, necessity and possibility in general, causation, etc. (see Mackie 1977). In order to evaluate this reply, we would have to examine the presuppositions of knowledge about inertia, identity, etc. and find out whether they are in this respect relevantly similar to the case of evaluative knowledge. This cannot be done here. And further, even if it were the case—which need not be—that similar fillers were presupposed in other areas as well as in the evaluative sphere, we do not have to conclude from this that we have evaluative knowledge. Perhaps the more reasonable conclusion to draw is that, contrary to what we may have believed, we do not have knowledge in these other areas.

[18] These kinds of arguments for objective views and against subjective ones are of course not the only ways in which the objectivist can argue for her stance (and against the subjectivist). In a recent article, Ronald Dworkin attacks in an original way views that deny the possibility of objectivity and truth for evaluative judgements. Since subjective theories of well-being hold judgements of prudential value to be subjective and—at least in the sense I have defined them—not capable of being true in the sense in which factual judgements are, I take it that Dworkin is also attacking subjective theories of well-being. Dworkin sees the subjectivists as purporting to establish the view that first-order substantial moral judgements such as 'Abortion is wrong', 'It is not right to torture babies for fun', etc., are neither objective nor capable of being true from points of departure that are neutral and austere. According to Dworkin, subjectivists claim neutrality about the substance of ordinary positive moral convictions, since they take no sides in questions such as whether terrorism is immoral or not. By subjectivist austerity Dworkin means that she purports to rely on nonmoral—and presumably also nonprudential in the realm of prudential value—arguments to defeat the objectivist stance. The main point of Dworkin's lengthy argument can be, I think, recapitulated as follows. Consider the following sentences:

2.3 Possible Objections Considered

Before concluding this article, I will consider some possible objections to the kind of position I have adopted above.

2.3.1 Does Being Independent of an Individual's Desires and Belonging to a List Make a Thing Good?

In discussing the claim that the kind of objective accounts which simply provide a list of what their proponents consider to be prudentially good things do not qualify as objective theories of well-being, Arneson draws attention to the fact that what the subjectivists consider as prudentially good may change with changes in the subjective attitudes considered as relevant from the point of view of determining prudential value whereas the objective goods remain what they are even if people's attitudes change. He then writes as follows (Arneson 1999, p. 119):

> … the objective-list theory is not merely the provision of a list of putative goods. It is also a claim that what it is to be intrinsically valuable for a person, to make that person's life go better for herself, is to be an item that belongs on such a list.

Arneson presupposes that all versions of the objective list theory of well-being are such as not to provide reasons for their objective goods being prudentially

Footnote 18 (continued)

1. Abortion is wrong.
2. What 1. says is true.
3. What 1. and 2. say is really and objectively so.

According to Dworkin, there is no plausible interpretation of either 2. or 3. that would not make them restatements or clarifications of 1. And thus neutrality and austerity is not compatible with denying such statements as 2. and 3. (see Dworkin 1996, pp. 87–139). As a criticism of subjectivism as I have defined it, Dworkin's argument is clearly a nonstarter. A subjectivist need not purport to be either austere or neutral, at least in Dworkin's sense of these terms. Subjectivists hold that the grounds for evaluative judgements are different from what objectivists think them to be. But a subjectivist need not accept that everything goes in prudential and moral life and that no rational answer can be given to prudential or moral questions. According to subjectivists, what is good for a person is determined—in one way or another—by this person's attitudes, and when the requirements of a subjective theory are obeyed in this determination, it is rational according to that theory. As the case of Hare's theory shows, an anti-realist—or prescriptivist to use Hare's own term—need not accept that rationality has no place in morality (see, e.g., Hare 1981).

Even if Hare did not succeed in showing moral rationality to have a morally neutral basis in moral language this would not of course mean that anti-realists could not show morality to be rational. Thus, although Dworkin is directing his criticism against all views that deny the possibility of truth and objectivity in evaluative contexts, it does not succeed in refuting subjective theories of well-being, for subjectivists need not accept the points of departure Dworkin claims they accept. And it is of course not clear that Dworkin's argument succeeds even if subjectivists did accept neutrality and/or austerity.

good. And he also maintains that, in order to qualify as an objective theory of well-being, it is sufficient that an account keeps its goods independent of possibly changing subjective attitudes and such that they belong to a list of putative prudential goods. This is confusing.

First, there are objective list theories of well-being that give grounds for holding their goods to be prudentially good. Perfectionism, e.g., maintains that exemplifying the human virtues is good because it realises the human essence. Second, it is clearly question-begging to maintain that a view qualifies as a theory of objective prudential value simply by keeping its goods independent of individual desires and gathering them into a list. Being independent of subjective attitudes and belonging to a list does nothing to explain why a particular alleged objective prudential good would really be prudentially good. Thus, what Arneson writes presents no real threat to what I have argued above.

2.3.2 Can a Coherentist Theory of Evaluative Justification Save Prudential Objectivism?

Kitcher acknowledges that explaining the prudential goodness of their goods is a problem for objective theories of well-being. In order to avoid this problem, he maintains, objectivism must pick out some property whose ascription can be made in a value-free fashion, seeing this as the criterion of human well-being. Kitcher (1999, pp. 59–60) calls this the Reductivist Challenge. He proposes that objectivists can avoid answering this challenge by adopting a coherence theory of justification. Kitcher (1999, p. 82) writes:

> The Reductivist Challenge can be generated from a very simple foundationalist theory of moral justification; it can be avoided by adopting a very simple coherentist theory of moral justification.

Since Kitcher's Reductivist Challenge is, at least, very similar to the problem that I claimed to undermine the present forms of objectivism, I will briefly consider Kitcher's proposition concerning how objectivists could avoid this problem.

Kitcher thus poses his answer to the Reductivist Challenge in terms of foundationalism, the view that evaluative judgements are justified when they are self-evident or follow logically from self-evident evaluative judgements, and coherentism which considers an evaluative judgement to be justified when it coheres with other evaluative judgements and plausible factual knowledge. He then argues as if an objectivist committed to a foundationalist theory of evaluative justification could, when she realises that she is threatened by the Reductivist Challenge, simply switch into a different kind of theory of evaluative justification, i.e., coherentism, avoid this problem, and then go on as if nothing had happened. This is implausible. Objectivists may indeed commit themselves to a coherentist theory of prudential justification when, e.g., they accept the claim that some objectively existing value is graspable only from a privileged epistemic point of view that necessarily involves some prudentially evaluative components as parts of it.[19] But switching from foundationalism to coherentism is not an answer to the Reductivist Challenge. The Reductivist Challenge cannot be answered by ignoring it. And those who accept the kind of coherentist stance described above commit themselves to the existence of some mysterious kind of sensitivity needed in order to recognise objective values, which is itself problematic in a way similar to that in which the Reductivist Challenge is problematic for foundationalist objectivism. Thus, to offer adopting coherentism as an objectivist answer to the Reductive Challenge is not plausible.

2.3.3 Are Metaprudential Arguments Irrelevant to Theories of Well-Being?

It could be claimed that what I have said above is not problematic for the objective theories of well-being, because theories of well-being are normative theories whereas the questions I have raised belong to the metaprudential sphere.[20] Since, this objection would proceed, the metaprudential sphere deals with questions pertaining to the nature of judgements about what benefits or harms individuals and the nature of the property of being beneficial and the property of being harmful, etc., the issues it addresses are independent of the questions with which theories of well-being are concerned. And, consequently, we need not worry about the problems confronted by realism when we are discussing the objective theories of well-being.

[19] Roughly, in the moral and prudential spheres, such theories as foundationalism and coherentism purport to provide answers to problems of moral and prudential epistemology: most importantly, perhaps, to the question concerning the epistemic status of moral and prudential judgements. But the epistemic status of moral and prudential judgements is clearly dependent on the mode of existence of the referents of these judgements. We cannot decide that we know some evaluative judgement to be true or justified in some particular way without adopting a view concerning the existence of what that judgement is about (see also Hare 1985, p. 95). It might be claimed that subjectivists can adopt coherentism as readily as objectivists, and that for this reason the move proposed by Kitcher is a legitimate one for an objectivist to make. However, if subjectivists can be coherentists or foundationalists, they cannot be this in the same sense as objectivists, for the former deny the possibility of evaluative knowledge and justification in the sense the latter try to establish it. When anti-realists or subjectivists present theories of evaluative knowledge these theories and their aims look quite dissimilar compared to those put forward by objectivists (see, e.g., Hare 1996).

[20] I here assume the common distinction between such normative and practical questions as what things and activities are good and what should be done to attain these goods, etc. and the metaquestions pertaining to the nature of the property of good, the logical character of normative discourse, etc. The branch of moral philosophy that deals with these kind of metaquestions as they arise in connection with moral values is called metaethics. In connection with prudential value, I will call these metaquestions metaprudential problems.

The question of whether normative theories are in this way independent of the issues arising in the metaprudential and metaethical spheres divides philosophers quite sharply. On the one hand, there are those who consider these kind of meta-level questions to be of crucial importance from the point of view of normative issues (see, e.g., Hare 1952, 1963, 1981) and, on the other hand, there are those who take these two domains to be, at least largely, independent of each other (see, e.g., Blackburn 1993; Hooker 1991; Hurka 1993). I find the latter view implausible. It seems to me obvious that the evaluative question about what has, or is conducive to, individual welfare is not independent form metaprudential questions pertaining to the nature of judgements about what benefits or harms individuals or to the nature of the property of being beneficial and harmful. However, since what I find obvious is not obvious to everybody, I will try to come up with some reasons to back up my position on this issue.

Consider first the case in which people disagree over the prudential goodness of some particular thing or activity. When we want to know what to make of a disagreement of this kind, we run into the question of whether it is possible for two mutually incompatible evaluative judgements to apply to the same thing or activity at the same time. And this clearly raises questions belonging to the metaprudential sphere. Second, some of the most important problems relating to the objectivity of theories of well-being and to the questions arising in connection with realism have to do with desires and their role in constituting well-being and value. I take it that the notion of desire used in the metaprudential sphere is similar to that from which the objective theorists see well-being as independent. Further, I assume that the notion of desire used in both of these domains is at least very reminiscent of, if not the same as, what we mean by desire in everyday language. If theories of well-being were not metaprudentially neutral, then the different theories of well-being could use, at least, two notions of desire that were different from each other in a metaprudentially relevant respect. First, there could be the kind of desires from which preference hedonism and the desire theories would talk about. The objects of these desires would be determined by the agents having them, and these desires would then determine what is prudentially valuable. I will call this kind of desires 'value-determining' desires. Second, there could be the kind of desires the objects of which were determined by realistically existing values. I will call this kind of desires 'value-determined' desires.

Consider now the common definition of an objective theory of well-being. According to this definition, something can be prudentially good for an agent whether that agent desires it or not. The desires talked about in this connection cannot be of the value-determining kind, for prudential value cannot be independent of this kind of desires. Thus, the desires the objective theorist talks about must be of the value-determined kind, which means that at least the objective theories of well-being are not metaprudentially neutral. It could be objected to this that if what is prudentially valuable necessarily gives rise to desires, then it does not make sense to define an objective theory of well-being to say that something can be prudentially good for an agent whether that agent desires it or not, for an agent necessarily desires what is prudentially valuable. Thus, the common definition of an objective theory of well-being would be nonsensical if it were put in terms of value-determined desires.

However, even though prudential value would necessarily give rise to desires, the common definition of an objective theory of well-being would be reasonable because of the possibility of confusions and irrationality. Indeed, it seems that the main motivation behind the acceptance of objective theories of well-being has to do with fears that the agents themselves could be illogical, confused, etc. in their own assessments of what is good for them. So, even though prudential value necessarily gave rise to desires, it would still be reasonable to define an objective theory of well-being in the usual way.

The above argument concerning value-determined and value-determining desires presupposes that values are necessarily connected to motivation, i.e., the view that philosophers call motivational internalism is true. However, since motivational internalism has not been shown to be true or acceptable, the view that there is no necessary connection between prudential values and motivational desires, motivational externalism that is, remains a viable option. But assuming that motivational externalism instead of motivational internalism is true, or acceptable, is of no help for those who hold the metaprudential sphere to be independent from normative questions. For even externalist objectivism takes a stand concerning the acceptability of notions of desire which are different from each other in a metaprudentially relevant respect. That externalist objectivism in fact rejects both value-determining and value-determined desires could perhaps be taken to speak for its metaprudential neutrality. However, that a view is incompatible with either value-determined or value-determining desires is sufficient to make it metaprudentially substantive. That it is incompatible with both of these kind of desires does not change this fact. I take it that metaprudential issues are not independent of normative questions and thus that my criticisms of objectivism and realism are not irrelevant from the point of view of objective theories of well-being.

2.4 Conclusion

Objective theories of individual well-being separate what is good for a person from that person's attitudes of favour. In this article, I argued that this separation makes it difficult for an objectivist to explain the prudential goodness of her prudential goods. In explaining why what they take to be good for a person would actually be good for that person the objectivists resort to unacceptable claims of self-evidence and/or to some mysterious faculty that they take to be necessary for grasping prudential goodness. This problem makes current objective theories of individual well-being unappealing.

This result is theoretical in character but, as it concerns the nature of prudential value, it is also relevant from the point of view of empirical research concentrating on issues pertaining to individual well-being. In recent social indicators research approaches making use of subjective appraisals of well-being have come under attack for two general reasons. First, it has been maintained that subjective appraisals of well-being can be objectively wrong, and that trained experts are more able to determine what makes a life good for the person who is living it than the person herself. Second, it has been argued that since subjective appraisals of well-being are imprecise, unstable, and incomparable with each other, studies making use of them do not produce the kind of exact data that would be of use to policy makers.

In the light of the above argument, the first kind of criticism of the subjective approach to empirical questions pertaining to well-being is without sufficient grounds. It is, of course, true that when individuals evaluate whether or not something is good for them they must have as much of the relevant information concerning that thing or activity at hand as possible and be 'cool, calm, and collected'. But since the objective theories, in their current incarnations at least, do not qualify as plausible theories of individual well-being, subjective theories provide a better basis for empirical research on well-being than they do.

The second criticism of the subjective approach to empirical research on well-being does not concern studies adopting a subjective theory of well-being exclusively, since subjective satisfaction with objectively defined constituents of well-being can be, and has been, examined also. However, in the light of the above argument, to the extent that this criticism is justified, it provides reason for further development of the methods used to study subjective well-being rather than for adopting an objectivist approach to empirical research on well-being. Importantly, this involves clarifying the meanings of the concepts and terms used in these studies so that they can produce as precise data as possible. The above argument may also be taken as a modest step towards reaching that goal. Further work on these issues must however be left for another occasion.

References

Arneson RJ (1999) Human flourishing versus desire satisfaction. Soc Philos Policy 16(1):113–142

Bernstein M (1998) Well-being. Am Philos Quarterly 35(1):39–55

Blackburn S (1993) Essays in quasi-realism. Oxford University Press, New York

Brink DO (1989) Moral realism and the foundations of ethics. Cambridge University Press, Cambridge

Den Uyl D, Machan TR (1983) Recent work on the concept of happiness. Am Philos Quarterly 20(2):115–134

Dworkin R (1996) Objectivity and truth: you'd better believe it. Philos Public Aff 25(2):87–139

Finnis J (1980) Natural law and natural rights. Clarendon Press, Oxford

Finnis J (1983) Fundamentals of ethics. Clarendon Press, Oxford

Foot P (1995) Does moral subjectivism rest on a mistake? Oxford J Legal Stud 15(1):1–14

Goldsworthy J (1992) Well-being and value. Utilitas 4(1):1–26

Griffin J (1996) Value judgement: improving our ethical beliefs. Clarendon Press, Oxford

Hare RM (1952) The language of morals. Clarendon Press, Oxford

Hare RM (1963) Freedom and reason. Clarendon Press, Oxford

Hare RM (1964) The Promising Game, Revue Internationale de Philosophie 70. Reprinted in Hare RM (1989) Essays in ethical theory. Clarendon Press, Oxford

Hare RM (1981) Moral thinking: it's levels, method, and point. Oxford University Press, Oxford
Hare RM (1985) Ontology in ethics. In: Honderich T (ed) Morality and objectivity: essays in memory of John Mackie. Routledge & Kegan Paul, London
Hare RM (1996) Foundationalism and coherentism in ethics. In: Sinnott-Armstrong W, Timmons M (eds) Moral knowledge?: new readings in moral epistemology. Oxford University Press, New York
Hooker B (1991) Theories of welfare, theories of good reasons for action, and ontological naturalism. Philos Papers 20(1):25–36
Hurka T (1993) Perfectionism. Oxford University Press, New York
Kitcher P (1999) Essence and perfection. Ethics 110:59–83
Kraut R (1979) Two conceptions of happiness. Philos Rev 88(2):167–197
Mackie JL (1977) Ethics: inventing right and wrong. Penquin, Harmondsworth
Norman R (1997) Making sense of moral realism. Philos Inv 20(2):117–135
Nozick R (1989) The examined life. Simon and Schuster, New York
Parfit D (1984) Reasons and persons. Clarendon Press, Oxford
Scanlon T (1993) Value, desire, and quality of life. In: Nussbaum MC, Sen A (eds) The quality of life. Clarendon Press, Oxford
Sumner LW (1996) Welfare, happiness, and ethics. Clarendon Press, Oxford
Thomson G (1987) Needs. Routldege and Kegan Paul, London

Chapter 3
Paradoxes of Happiness

Mike W. Martin

Abstract To get happiness forget about it; then, with any luck, happiness will come as a by-product in pursuing meaningful activities and relationships. This adage is known as *the* paradox of happiness, but actually it contains a number of different paradoxes concerning aims, success, freedom, and attitudes. These paradoxes enhance our understanding of the complexity of happiness and its interaction with other values in good lives, that is, lives which are happy as well as morally decent, meaningful, and fulfilling. Yet, each paradox conveys a one-sided truth that needs to be balanced with others. Happiness, understood as subjective well-being, involves positively evaluating our lives and living with a sense of well-being. As such, it should not be confused with either pleasure or normative conceptions of "true" happiness.

Keywords Happiness • Paradox of happiness • Values • Good lives • Self-fulfillment • Hedonism • Success • Freedom • Attitudes

To get happiness forget about it; then, with any luck, it will come as a by-product in pursuing meaningful activities and relationships. This adage is known as *the* paradox of happiness, but in fact it contains a number of different paradoxes. Without claiming completeness, I distinguish a dozen of them, grouped under the headings of aim, success, freedom, and attitude. With one exception, they are not paradoxes in the sense of logical contradictions, and most of them are not even seeming contradictions; instead, they express psychological incongruities and empirical ironies that contradict widely-held beliefs about how to obtain happiness. Each of them expresses a one-sided and sometimes dangerous truth. Nevertheless, together they reveal some of the complexity in pursuing good lives, that is, lives which are happy as well as morally decent, meaningful, and fulfilling. For this reason the paradoxes have attracted the attention of philosophers (whom

M. W. Martin (✉)
Department of Philosophy, Chapman University, One University Drive,
Orange, CA 92866, USA
e-mail: mwmartin@chapman.edu

A. Delle Fave (ed.), *The Exploration of Happiness*, Happiness Studies Book Series,
DOI: 10.1007/978-94-007-5702-8_3,

I emphasize), psychologists, and economists alike, and at least some of the paradoxes warrant further empirical investigation.

By happiness I mean subjective well-being. We are happy insofar as we are satisfied with our lives overall, taking into account all their major aspects. The scope of happiness might be specified further as the immediate present, some other time-slice of perhaps several years, or our entire lives—past, present, and future. In any case, overall satisfaction is shown by (1) evaluating our lives as meeting our major expectations, given our values and aspirations, and (2) experiencing them with a sense of well-being and a high level of enjoyment (Sumner 1996). Typically, both aspects involve satisfying at least many of what we belief to be our most valuable desires (without assuming those beliefs and values are objectively justified) (Kekes 1988). In this way, subjective well-being differs from normative conceptions of "true" or "genuine" happiness, such as "activity of soul in accordance with virtue" (Aristotle 1941, p. 943). I am interested in how the paradoxes link happiness to other values in good lives, but adopting a value-neutral definition avoids begging questions while staying close to the predominant use of the term "happiness."

3.1 Aim: Hedonism, Self-Interest, Guidance, and Constituents

Paradoxes of aim claim that pursuing happiness directly, deliberately, and devotedly is self-defeating or otherwise problematic. Instead, we should concentrate our energies on other goals, activities, and relationships that can yield satisfactions contributing to happiness. This need for indirectness seems paradoxical because usually we assume that attentive effort is needed in pursuing important goals, in particular happiness. Paradoxes of aim have different foci, the most famous of which is pleasure.

3.1.1 Paradox of Hedonism

According to the paradox of hedonism, it is self-defeating to pursue pleasures directly because most happiness-contributing pleasures come indirectly from pursuing meaningful endeavors for their own sake. John Stuart Mill discusses this paradox in connection with his recovery from a major psychological depression during his early twenties.

> I never, indeed, wavered in the conviction that happiness is the test of all rules of conduct, and the end of life. But I now thought that this end was only to be attained by not making it the direct end. Those only are happy (I thought) who have their minds fixed on some object other than their own happiness; on the happiness of others, on the improvement of

> mankind, even on some art or pursuit, followed not as a means, but as itself an ideal end. Aiming thus at something else, they find happiness by the way (Mill 1989, p. 117).

As the passage continues, Mill slides from happiness to pleasure. Indeed, throughout his writings he conflates happiness (long-term overall satisfaction) with pleasure (briefer episodic enjoyment). One moment he stipulates that "by happiness is intended pleasure" and another moment he defines happiness as a "manner of existence" that is "exempt as far as possible from pain, and as rich as possible in enjoyments, both in point of quantity and quality" (Mill 1979, pp. 7, 11). Either way, Mill construes the paradox of happiness as the paradox of hedonism. It is self-defeating, he contends, to fix attention on our happiness because doing so results in excessive critical scrutiny of our pleasures. This scrutiny erodes a given pleasure, either by making it appear less grand than we had hoped for, so that it is "felt to be insufficient," or by distancing ourselves from the full and immediate experience of it, whether by "putting it to flight by fatal questioning" or by "forestalling it in imagination" (Mill 1989, p. 118).

The paradox of hedonism contains an important truth. The most enriching enjoyments are tied to activities and relationships valued for their own sake, and not merely for the pleasures they produce. They yield pleasures because we first desire them, and find them desirable, on broader grounds than simply their pleasure-producing aspect (Feinberg 2002, p. 551). Psychologically, this truth is important for Mill in grappling with depression, a mental state that tends to collapse us inwardly. Philosophically, it plays a role in his development of utilitarianism, specifically in his conception of the good—the good which is to be maximized, considering everyone affected by our actions impartially. For Mill, intrinsic goods are reducible to pleasures, but some pleasures have greater value than others, in particular those found through pursuing love, friendship, and intellectual activities as "ideal ends," that is, for their own sake rather than simply for the pleasures or further consequences they produce. A happy life is rich in these "higher" pleasures.

Henry Sidgwick, another great nineteenth-century utilitarian, invokes the paradox of hedonism in arguing against egoistic hedonism, that is, the version of ethical egoism that says we ought always and only to maximize our own pleasures. Egoistic hedonism is self-defeating because it enjoins pleasure-seeking and yet results in diminished pleasure. Happiness, understood as "the greatest attainable surplus of pleasure over pain," cannot be pursued successfully by concentrating on our pleasures because the fullest and richest pleasures come from being fully stimulated by people, events, and things in the world which "must be temporarily predominant and absorbing" (Sidgwick 1907, p. 120). To his credit, Sidgwick states the paradox of hedonism more cautiously than Mill does, and he understands it as advising us to restrict rather than to abandon the direct pursuit of happiness: "Happiness is likely to be better attained if the extent to which we set ourselves consciously to aim at it be carefully restricted" (Sidgwick 1907, p. 405). In this way, Sidgwick provides an important corrective to Mill by affirming that it is appropriate to adopt happiness as one of our direct aims, as long as we avoid narrow preoccupation with it.

3.1.2 Paradox of Self-Interest

A second paradox widens the focus from pleasures to self-interest, that is, to our overall good. According to the paradox of self-interest, aiming directly and exclusively at self-interest is self-defeating. It fosters self-absorption and thereby constricts the range and depth of gratifications available in pursuing interests in other people, activities, and events. The paradox of self-interest is frequently voiced from the pulpit, and Bishop Joseph Butler examined it with psychological acuity in his remarkable eighteenth-century sermons: "how much soever a paradox it may appear, it is certainly true, that even from self-love we should endeavour to get over all inordinate regard to, and consideration of ourselves" (Butler 1964, p. 171). The iconoclast Bertrand Russell makes the theme equally salient in his writings. He presents it as a momentous discovery in moving away from his agonized self-preoccupation during youth into his richly satisfying adulthood. Self-absorption destroys meaningful and happy personal relationships. Equally bad, it causes boredom by blocking the development of deep interests and zestful pursuits. Accordingly, "the secret of happiness is this: let your interests be as wide as possible, and let your reactions to the things and persons that interest you be as far as possible friendly rather than hostile" (Russell 1996, p. 123).

For their part, classical economists and psychologists assumed psychological egoism, the view that humans are only motivated by self-interest, and hence they tended to be oblivious to the paradox of self-interest. Today, renegade economists are beginning to appreciate the importance of personal commitments to the well-being of others that restrict narrow self-interest and require some personal sacrifice. Indeed, Robert Frank argues that we evolved as animals with capacities for love and loyalty because of "a simple paradox, namely, that in many situations the conscious pursuit of self-interest is incompatible with its attainment" (Frank 1988, p. ix). Likewise, positive psychologists explore how other-directed virtues contribute to our enlightened self-interest and our happiness (Seligman 2002; Haidt 2006; Martin 2007).

Belliotti would have us go further in abandoning happiness as central to our self-interest. Happiness, he insists, is overrated. We should not and "do not pursue happiness directly. We pursue worthwhile, meaningful, valuable, exemplary lives. If we are reasonably successful in that quest, happiness may follow. If not, we can still take pride and derive satisfaction from living well" (Belliotti 2004, p. xi). Belliotti's suggestion seems off the mark, both as description and prescription. Most of us actively seek happiness in and through activities we find meaningful, and at least part of what makes them meaningful is their contribution to our happiness. Indeed, the notion of meaningful lives that bring no happiness whatsoever is problematic. Happiness and meaning are distinct but interwoven in ways that make it impossible to pry them apart as sources of motivation in good lives.

The paradox of self-interest, properly understood, concerns *excessive* self-seeking and self-preoccupation. Periodic self-reflection about whether we are sufficiently happy is entirely compatible with maintaining genuine interests in the world and zestful pursuits. Indeed, it seems likely to promote those interests and pursuits by ensuring they are meaningful and fulfilling. The paradox of self-interest, like the paradox of hedonism, is a corrective to one-sided self-seeking, not a basis for rejecting all direct regard for happiness in conjunction with other important values.

3.1.3 Paradox of Guidance

The next paradox shifts from motivation to guidance. According to the paradox of guidance, usually we lack a clear conception of what will make us happy, and hence in pursuing happiness directly we are pursuing a will-o'-the-wisp. Immanuel Kant formulates the paradox in terms of practical reason, that is, reasoning in moral and other practical matters rather than in matters of abstract theory: "the more a cultivated reason purposely occupies itself with the enjoyment of life and with happiness, so much the further does one get away from true satisfaction" (Kant 1996, p. 51). This is because the complexities of the world and the vagaries of individual psychology render us hapless victims who lack a reliable guide to happiness: "one can form no determinate and sure concept of the sum of satisfaction of all inclinations under the name of happiness" (Kant 1996, p. 54). Kant defines happiness in different ways, sometimes as uninterrupted pleasure, sometimes as satisfaction of all our desires (which is different, for not all satisfied desires yield pleasure–witness buyers' remorse), and sometimes as both (Wike 1994; Hill 2002). In any case, his point is that usually we do not have a clear concept of what will bring us happiness. Seeking riches can lead to troubles and anxiety; seeking knowledge can result in pained awareness of tragedy; seeking long life can lead to ill health in advanced age; and so forth (Kant 1996, pp. 70–71). Our aim in exercising practical reason should be to lead moral lives and then partial happiness will come along the way, postponing full happiness as a gift in a spiritual life after death.

Surely matters are not that bleak, at least not today. Indeed, studies show that most people are mostly happy (Biswas-Diener et al. 2004, p. 21). Admittedly, our practical reason is highly fallible (Gilbert 2006), but it serves us 'reasonably' well in pursuing happiness. Kant gives a one-sided analysis of reason's role in seeking happiness because he has a philosophical ax to grind. He seeks to establish that the primary role of practical reason is to discern universal and absolute (exceptionless) moral duties, but it is utterly unreliable as a guide to happiness. Yet, contrary to Kant, the limitations of reason do not render the pursuit of happiness futile, and whatever flaws reason has carry over to morality. Few ethicists share Kant's optimism that reason can discern absolute duties, and our practical reason is as flawed in discerning and integrating our various duties as it is in pursuing happiness. Whether in pursuing morality or happiness, we must make do with our flawed reasoning capacities.

Inspired by Kant, but deepening his skepticism, Nicholas White locates the paradox of guidance in the very concept of happiness, rather than the limitations of our practical reason. The concept of happiness, he says, is essentially the notion that there is a best or right way to harmonize our myriad desires, interests, aims, and values (White 2006, pp. vii, 162, 166). Each of us repeatedly faces conflicting aims, and the concept of happiness arises from the expectation of finding a guide about how best to harmonize our wants, akin to how the picture in a puzzle guides us in fitting together its pieces. This expectation is futile, and a unifying picture for an entire life is a chimera. Coordinating our desires, interests, and values is a matter of ongoing contextual decision-making rather than applying a general guide to our lives overall.

In some passages, White seems to recommend abandoning the concept of happiness altogether because it is based on the "unrealizable hope for some kind of coherence of aims" (White 2006, pp. vii–viii). That conclusion is unwarranted. Coherence is often possible through reasoned attempts to live good lives. Moreover, the fact that many of us lack clear and reliable *conceptions* of what will make us happy does not mean we lack a clear *concept* of happiness. That concept is subjective well-being, which is not exactly White's concept of an overall evaluation of our lives, for that could instead mean an evaluation of our lives as good in all major respects (not just happiness). I agree that coherence must emerge within practical situations rather than from grand schemas, but I do not share his postmodernist doubts about the contribution of sound conceptions of good lives to promoting coherence and happiness.

3.1.4 Paradox of Constituents

Although most paradoxes of happiness express empirical incongruities and ironies, one paradox highlights a logical truth. According to the paradox of constituents, it is a matter of logic that happiness cannot be pursued directly and exclusively as an end, for happy lives are comprised of other things that must be sought for their own sake. Elizabeth Telfer provides a charming statement of the paradox: "In the case of most ends, the means are logically separable from them: thus if I play the piano [solely] to earn money, it makes sense for a fairy godmother to say, 'Forget about the playing; here is the money.' But this does not apply to happiness. If I marry in order to be happy it would not make sense for her to say 'Forget about the marriage, here is the happiness', since the happiness I sought (the argument goes) was by definition happiness in marriage" (Telfer 1980, p. 30). Because the marriage is a constituent of this individual's happiness, her happiness cannot be pursued as an independent end.

By underscoring that happiness is a response to meaningful activities and relationships, the paradox of constituents conveys an insight bearing on all the paradoxes of happiness. Nevertheless, as Telfer points out, the paradox does not provide a basis for denying that happiness can itself be pursued as an end in itself. For, the activities and relationships that produce happiness are contingent matters for each of us, not matters of logic. It is intelligible for persons, young or old, to say they want to be happy even though they have yet to discover which activities and relationships will make that possible. And having discovered those activities and relationships, they can pursue them (in part) as means to (the sought-after end of) happiness.

To sum up, paradoxes of aim convey insights that are half-truths. Yes, we should avoid excessive self-preoccupation and instead focus outwardly on people and projects, but in doing so we should not disregard our happiness, for it remains one important dimension of fully desirable lives, interwoven with meaning, morality, and self-fulfillment. Indeed, we do well to periodically review our primary endeavors and relationships to appreciate their meaning and to assess whether they are making us happy (Telfer 1980, pp. 32–33). We do and should consider our happiness in making major life decisions, for example about whether to pursue a job offer or to marry a particular person. And even in situations where we must sacrifice our happiness for higher ideals, we do well to be clear that we are indeed sacrificing something of great value in order to achieve something of even greater value.

3.2 Success: Getting, Money, and Status

Shifting the focus from aims to results, *paradoxes of success* challenge widely-held beliefs that obtaining certain things will automatically make us happy. The paradoxes caution against equating happiness with specific results that we pursue single-mindedly, and they advise that happiness tends to come indirectly along the way in pursuing goals. In one colloquial sense, success refers to obtaining material goods such as money and consumer products, as well as social status and other external rewards, by contrast with intrinsic satisfactions from what we believe to be valuable endeavors and relationships (O'Neil 1993). In another sense, with which I begin, success simply means getting what we seek.

3.2.1 Paradox of Getting

The paradox of getting is that happiness has less to do with acquiring what we seek than with the journey in seeking it. By their very nature, desires promise pleasure (satisfaction) when they are fulfilled (satisfied), and we have a deep-seated tendency to think that happiness will come from reaching what we regard as our primary goals in life. Yet, there is no tight correlation between satisfying desires and being satisfied with what we get. Indeed, as the saying goes, we need to be careful what we wish for, lest we get it.

The paradox of getting conveys several insights. On the one hand, happiness has more to do with liking what we already have than with constantly getting more. On the other hand, happiness often comes more from making progress toward meaningful goals than from success in achieving them (Haidt 2006, p. 84). And sometimes "anticipation is better than realization" (Nozick 1989, p. 116). Moreover, experiencing progress can promote happiness even when it is accompanied by feelings of frustration due to temporary setbacks, periodic exhaustion, and temporary depression. The experiences that most directly promote happiness come from what Csikszentmihalyi (1997) famously calls "flow": engaging in valued activities that challenge and engage us, while providing immediate and positive feedback, whether or not episodic pleasures are involved. In addition to the enjoyments or gratifications obtained from flow activities, myriad everyday pleasures contribute to happiness, especially when we learn to savor them (by concentrating on them in ways at odds with the paradox of hedonism).

3.2.2 Paradox of Money

The paradox of money is that money does not bring or buy happiness, contrary to the widespread illusion that it does. Insofar as money is pursued in the belief it will make us happy, the paradox of money is a special instance of the paradox of getting. But it stands on its own in challenging our tendency to regard money as the solution to all our problems. Much money simply feeds the "hedonic treadmill": the more we buy and have, the more we want (Brickman and Campbell 1971). In macroeconomic terms, the paradox of money has been called the paradox of (economic) progress: Average incomes in western democracies have doubled over the last fifty years, but levels of happiness have remained virtually unchanged. Even after adjusting for rising costs, there is a genuinely surprising failure of increased wealth to increase happiness (Lane 2000; Argyle 2001; Easterbrook 2003).

The paradox of money expresses a partial truth. Money does contribute to happiness, although less than we usually believe. It increases happiness dramatically by moving individuals out of poverty, but thereafter it contributes little and haphazardly to happiness. Part of the explanation for this surprising result is that we tend to misuse money once we have it, becoming caught up in endless routines of getting and spending, rather than building wealth to increase freedom and peace of mind (Frank 1999, 2004). Also, we are made unhappy by envy and by feeling we are not making what we deserve compared to others, which brings us to the next paradox.

3.2.3 Paradox of Status

According to the paradox of status, our prestige-oriented comparisons with others do not promote happiness, even though we constantly act as if they do. It is not enough to have a comfortable life; we need to keep up with the Joneses and then surpass them. Insofar as having money is as much about status as survival, at least once beyond poverty, it is not surprising that the paradoxes of status and money overlap. When a group was asked whether they would prefer an income of $50,000 when others earned $25,000, or an income of $100,000 when others earned $200,000, they chose the $50,000–half of what they could have had, but preferable to half of what others have (Solnick and Hemenway 1998, pp. 373–383).

Envy and snobbery partly explain this preference for lower amounts of money over lower status, but the primary explanation seems to be our need for self-esteem and our tendency to attach self-esteem to social status. Money, luxury cars, large houses, expensive jewelry, and virtually any conspicuous consumption that favorably sets us apart from others are symbols of personal significance (Layard 2005, pp. 41–45). Yet, insofar as we remain preoccupied with assessing well-being in terms of these shifting standards, driven by status anxiety, we place our happiness and perhaps our other values at risk (Botton 2004).

3.3 Freedom: Submission, Choice, and Self-Conflict

Paradoxes of freedom assert that (happiness-promoting) freedom is won by surrendering or limiting it. Like paradoxes of aim, they suggest we should not pursue happiness directly, but this time the emphasis is on liberation and choice.

3.3.1 Paradox of Submission

The paradox of submission is that surrender can liberate us in ways contributing to happiness. We feel happily liberated not by maintaining complete control but instead through loyalty to ideals, standards, and meaningful causes and relationships (Martin 1994, pp. 156–160). Harry Frankfurt asks, "How are we to understand the paradox that a person may be enhanced and liberated through being seized, made captive, and overcome? Why is it that we find ourselves to be most fully realized, and consider that we are at our best, when—through reason or through love—we have lost or escaped from ourselves?" (Frankfurt 1989, p. 89). He answers that our very identity is shaped by deep caring, and that deep caring has a selfless element, by contrast with our usual self-preoccupation. This selflessness contributes to a sense of meaning and self-respect and thereby indirectly promotes happiness. We are liberated by choosing freely and decisively to close some options, as when spouses promise to love, honor, and cherish each other, forsaking (adultery with) all others. Deep caring reshapes our will and identity, establishing a "volitional necessity" that makes it difficult or even impossible to abandon who and what we love. Happiness, as well as self-realization, comes from caring relationships and submission to standards and ideals of excellence.

The paradox of submission is also a familiar theme in religious conceptions of happiness which enjoin submission to a deity. William James expresses it in nonsectarian terms: "Give up the feeling of responsibility, let go your hold, resign the care of your destiny to higher powers, be genuinely indifferent as to what becomes of it all, and you will find not only that you gain a perfect inward relief, but often also, in addition, the particular goods you sincerely thought you were renouncing" (James 1902, p. 108). The idea is also central in twelve-step recovery programs such as Alcoholics Anonymous which enjoin admitting powerlessness over our addictions and submitting to a "higher power" so as to become empowered to overcome the addictions.

Although the paradox of submission makes a psychological claim, then, it is generally tied to normative claims about which loyalties and submissions are desirable. The distinction is important and bears on all the paradoxes of happiness in thinking about fully good lives. A sense of happiness and meaning is one thing; a justified sense of meaning produced by valid ideals is something else. Terrorists provide a painful reminder of the difference. For this reason, the paradox of submission expresses a partial and dangerous truth—a truth easily misunderstood and abused. In general, the value of happiness increases insofar as it is interwoven with other justified values.

Frankfurt tends to slide over the distinction between desirable and undesirable loyalties, but Alan Gewirth (1998) highlights it. He distinguishes two conceptions of self-fulfillment: satisfaction of our most strongly motivating desires (aspiration-fulfillment), and effective pursuit of what is most worthwhile in us (capacity-fulfillment). Corresponding, there are two conceptions of happiness: satisfaction of our strongest desires (aspiration-happiness), and normative conceptions of developing what is best in us (capacity-happiness). The two go together ideally, but not always in practice. In some cases, "You may be made very unhappy if you develop your highest talents; for example, a person who by intense concentration and practice becomes a superb violinist may come to feel very discontented with his life" (Gewirth 1998, p. 50). Alluding to the paradoxes of aim, Gewirth points out that aspiration-fulfillment and happiness are often best pursued indirectly by focusing on valuable activities and relationships. Yet, in light of his violinist example—suppose the violinist turns to alcohol and abandons his talents altogether—Gewirth might have added that capacity-fulfillment sometimes requires the pursuit of aspiration-happiness. In any case, the two are interwoven and should be pursued together in good lives.

3.3.2 Paradox of Choice

The paradox of choice, as Barry Schwartz calls it, is that multiplying the number of options sometimes lessens happiness, contrary to the belief that it increases our autonomy and thereby our happiness. In one study, 65 % of people claim that if they had cancer they would want to make their own treatment choices, yet only

12 % of people who actually got cancer wanted to make their treatment decisions (Schwartz 2005, p. 32). As this example suggests, too many choices can be burdensome because they place responsibility (and potentially blame) on us, but also because evaluating options takes time and adds complexity and confusion. Thus, President Bush's 2005 Medicare drug benefit program gave senior citizens as many as sixty options, thereby causing confusion, anxiety, and "choice overload." In addition, the more desirable choices we have the greater the "opportunity costs," such as regrets in having to turn down attractive options in settling for others. Again, having the options to return purchased goods would seemingly increase our happiness in making choices. Yet, Schwartz marshals evidence that we are more satisfied when our decisions are not so easily reversible, probably because reversible decisions keep us anxiously alert to better options we have missed. Of greater consequence, the paradox of submission overlaps with the paradox of choice: When we commit ourselves in a spirit of permanence, as in getting married, we tend to be happier than if we feel free to walk away at any time.

In practice, the paradox of choice applies most to "maximizers" who habitually learn about and assess all options in order to make the very best choice. "Satisficers," in contrast, quickly locate a satisfactory choice and then act. Most of us do well to be maximizers in only the most important areas of our lives. In everyday choices such as buying food and clothes, we tend to be happier when we settle for what is good enough rather than worrying about the ideal choice (Schwartz 2005, pp. 77–116). The goal is to find the proverbial joys of a simple life while grappling with sufficient options to avoid boredom.

3.3.3 Paradox of Self-Conflict

Conflicting desires are so commonplace that most of them provide no basis for speaking of paradox, rather than simply dilemma, ambivalence, and indecision. Yet, some conflicts are so ubiquitous, intense, and complex that they deserve to be called paradoxes of self-conflict. For example, we desire to be thin and to exercise self-control but also to eat and drink whatever we want; we desire financial security but also to walk away from secure but frustrating jobs; we desire intimacy and also the freedom that places intimacy at risk.

The last example is explored by Marar as what he calls "the Happiness Paradox": we have elemental needs both to break free and to belong (Marar 2003, p. 32). More fully, "it is not simply that these needs contradict one another, they are literally paradoxical in that the successful expression of the one requires the assertion of its opposite" (Marar 2003, p. 187). Thus, we desire to be free from the constraining judgments of other individuals and groups and to choose our own values; simultaneously, as we exercise our freedom we seek justification in their eyes, which we know is attached to their values. The problem is inherent in human nature, but it intensifies in a postmodern world where belief in objectively-defensible values is at risk or has evaporated.

I do not share Marar's postmodernist vision of endless and tortured oscillation between seeking freedom from other's values and obeisance to the values of our selected audiences whose approval we desire, with no anchor in reasoned moral judgments that apply to ourselves and others. I retain belief in the possibility of objectively-justified values in terms of which we ground our identity, self-respect, and good lives. Marar powerfully illuminates, however, how our desires for individuality and intimacy are sometimes so sharply at odds that they reveal paradoxical aspects of our identity. He is also correct that at least some such conflicts can only partly be diminished through practical wisdom and reasonable compromise, not to mention therapy, so as to make happiness possible. Sometimes happiness requires accepting, rather than fully resolving, our conflicts. This acceptance brings us to the last set of paradoxes.

3.4 Attitude: Affirmation and Hope

Paradoxes of attitude assert that locating happiness in things we lack is futile; for the most part, we already have everything we need to be happy—if we change our attitudes. This idea, which generalizes the paradoxes of success, is paradoxical because we tend to assume that our happiness is derived from things we currently lack. In addition, we overlook how much of our experience of the world is filtered through attitudes that are substantially up to us and that give us more control over our happiness than we usually believe. Happiness itself is defined in terms of attitudes of positive evaluation of our lives, and it turns largely on other attitudes that we can cultivate: self-respect and self-esteem, hope and optimism for a brighter future, gratitude for what we have received, humility in our expectations, relinquishing painful regrets, forgiving offenses, and working through our grief until we can accept tragedy. Paradoxes of attitude take various forms, two of which emphasize affirmation of the present and hope for the future.

3.4.1 Paradox of Affirmation

According to the paradox of affirmation, happiness lies in affirming what we have already, who we are at present, and the world as it is now. The more we pursue happiness outside ourselves the unhappier we become (a claim at odds with paradoxes of aims). Instead, we need to change our attitudes from negation and self-denigration to affirmation and self-esteem (Pollan 2005).

In smell-the-roses moments, affirmation seems the simplest of things, for goodness and beauty are everywhere if only we are attuned to them. Far more challenging, however, is the task of developing habits of appreciation that enable us to affirm the ubiquitous good despite the equally ubiquitous bad. Such habits might be cultivated through spiritual disciplines centered on humility, gratitude, and love. In this connection, the religious thinker Camenisch celebrates how gratitude can become "an entire outlook on life" in which individuals "live with a joyful sense of the interrelatedness of things whereby life is enriched by the generosity of persons or powers outside themselves" (Camenisch 1981, p. 23). Solomon echoes the same theme in secular lines: "we are the beneficiaries of a (more or less) benign universe, or even the lucky beneficiaries of good fortune in a cruel universe. This should dictate gratitude, even if there is no one or nothing in particular to whom that gratitude is directed" (Solomon 2002, p. 104).

The Greek and Roman Stoics, for whom happiness meant serenity, proposed an even more demanding transformation of attitude. Epictetus advises, "Do not seek to have events happen as you want them to, but instead want them to happen as they do happen, and your life will go well" (Epictetus 1983, p. 13). Of greatest importance, we must accept the inevitability of death of ourselves and people we love: "What upsets people is not things themselves but their judgments about the things. For example, death is nothing dreadful... but instead the judgment about death that it is dreadful—*that* is what is dreadful" (Epictetus 1983, p. 13). According to Epictetus, happiness comes from what we can control and from what we must otherwise accept.

3.4.2 Paradox of Hope

Another paradox of attitude suggests that happiness comes from positive attitudes concerning the future, such as hope, faith, and optimism—not from getting what we hope for, but rather from the impact of these future-oriented attitudes in the present. In particular, hope generates positive thoughts about the promise of goods that will emerge from the present. This theme permeates the writings of Peale: "the happiness habit is developed by simply practicing happy thinking," and "we manufacture our unhappiness by thinking unhappy thoughts, by the attitudes which we habitually take, such as the negative feeling that everything is going to turn out badly, or that other people are getting what they do not deserve and we are failing to get what we deserve" (Peale 2003, pp. 60–61). Peale is not quite as Pollyannaish as first appears. He emphasizes that changing attitudes requires discipline in changing habits, and he acknowledges that tragedies cannot and should not be brushed aside with superficially upbeat thoughts. Still, Peale's excessive emphasis on positive-thinking is best supplanted by the more sober stance of Martin Seligman who tempers optimism with accuracy and honesty (Seligman 1991, p. 221, 2002, p. 96).

In general, paradoxes of attitude convey only partial truths, for our happiness depends on both our attitudes and actual events in the world—to which our attitudes are attuned when we are reasonable and truthful. Certainly Epictetus goes too far in advocating serenity-promoting attitudes by weakening our ties to people whom we love. This stance was appropriate amidst the horror and radical uncertainty of the Roman Empire, but it is unappealing in today's world where happiness lies in the kinds of deep love and caring that Frankfurt emphasizes, and that are incompatible with the stoics' emotional distancing.

Furthermore, despite the insights contained in paradoxes of attitude, we lack complete control over our attitudes and hence our happiness. Indeed, many psychologists suggest that each of us has a largely fixed point or range of happiness. Studies of identical twins reveal they have comparable ranges of happiness, whether raised together or apart from each other, suggesting that our happiness range is part of our genetic inheritance (Lykken 1999, p. 56). This should not be surprising, given that roughly half of our personalities are genetically given.

The twin studies also help explain why some people are by nature and temperament happier than others. They are also compatible with some puzzling, indeed paradoxical, facts about good and bad fortune. Common sense tells us that our happiness would soar permanently if we won a multimillion dollar lottery, and it would sink irreversibly if we became quadriplegics. These emotional highs and lows do occur, but only for a short time. In tune with our range of happiness, within a year of these events, levels of happiness usually return to about where they were before (Brickman et al. 1978). Although we are extremely sensitive to dramatic changes, we tend to adapt psychologically to the status quo, adjusting our expectations and desires to the situation before us (Haidt 2006, p. 86). To be sure, fixed-point and fixed-range approaches to happiness are themselves contested, and it seems that at least some major life events, for example marriage, divorce, and unemployment, do modify our happiness range (Biswas-Diener et al. 2004; Easterlin 2004).

Finally, shifts in our attitudes can alter our assessments of when and how much we are happy during other periods of our lives. It makes sense to say, for example, "I thought I was happy when I was married (or single), but now I know I wasn't." Again, "I thought I could never be happier than I was in my youth, but now I know that was an illusion." As we live longer and more deeply, we acquire a wider range of comparisons to use in assessing our lives and our attitudes can shift. In this way, our conceptions of happiness are dynamic rather than static (White 2006, pp. 109–115).

3.5 Conclusion

The pursuit of happiness might be a simple matter for individuals blessed with a happy temperament, but for most of us it can be precarious and perplexing. The paradoxes of happiness help illuminate why this is so. All the paradoxes suggest that happiness is pursued indirectly as the by-product of meaningful activities and relationships. The paradoxes have different emphases, however, and each conveys one-sided truths that are sometimes in tension with each other.

Paradoxes of aim tell us that we should not focus narrowly on our pleasures (hedonism) and our personal good (self-interest); nor should we assume that we can have a pellucid picture of what will make us happy (guidance); nor should we conceive of happiness as separable from meaningful activities and relationships (constituents). Paradoxes of success remind us that getting what we want does not always lead to wanting what we get (getting), and that happiness is easily lost amidst illusions about material goods (money) and comparisons with others (status). Paradoxes of freedom emphasize that submitting to causes, loyalties, and standards can bring happiness-promoting liberation (submission), that too many choices can threaten happiness (choice), and that we can undermine our happiness when we fail to reasonably resolve or accept our conflicting desires for belonging and breaking free (conflict). Paradoxes of attitude tell us that pursuing happiness in things we lack can be futile unless we learn to cherish what we already have (affirmation) and derive peace from hope and faith (hope).

Whereas the paradox of constituents conveys the logical truth that (subjectively) meaningful activities and relationships partly constitute happy lives, the other paradoxes highlight psychological incongruities and empirical ironies that might warrant further empirical study. At the same time, the paradoxes contribute to understanding the role of happiness in good lives, in particular how it is interwoven with meaning, morality, and self-fulfillment. Distinct from the paradoxes of happiness discussed here, classical Greek, Roman, and religious thinkers often affirm a moral paradox that happiness and morality are fused, rather than merely interwoven (White 2006, p. 120), a notion linked to normative conceptions of happiness. But that is a topic for another paper.

References

Argyle M (2001) The psychology of happiness, 2nd edn. Routledge, New York

Aristotle (1941) Nicomachean Ethics (trans: Ross WD) In: Richard McKeon (ed) The basic works of Aristotle, Random House, New York, pp 927–1112

Belliotti RA (2004) Happiness is overrated. Rowman and Littlefield Publishers, Lanham

Biswas-Diener R, Diener E, Tamir M (2004) The psychology of subjective well-being. Daedalus 133(2):18–25

Botton A (2004) Status anxiety. Pantheon, New York

Brickman P, Campbell DT (1971) Hedonic relativism and planning the good society. In: Apley MH (ed) Adaptation-level theory: a symposium. Academic, New York, pp 287–302

Brickman P, Coates D, Janoff Bulman R (1978) Lottery winners and accident victims: is happiness relative? J Pers Soc Psychol 36:917–927

Butler J (1964) Fifteen sermons. G. Bell and Sons, London

Camenisch PF (1981) Gift and gratitude in ethics. J Religious Ethics 9:1–34

Csikszentmihalyi M (1997) Finding flow. Basic Books, New York

Easterbrook G (2003) The progress paradox. Random House, New York

Easterlin RA (2004) The economics of happiness. Daedalus 133(2):26–33

Epictetus (1983) The handbook of Epictetus (trans: Nicholas PW). Hackett Publishing, Indianapolis

Feinberg J (2002) Psychological egoism. In: Feinberg J, Shafer-Landau R (eds) Reason and responsibility (Wadsworth, Belmont, pp 547–559

Frank RH (1988) Passions Within Reason. W.W. Norton and Company, New York

Frank RH (1999) Luxury fever. Free Press, New York

Frank RH (2004) How not to buy happiness. Daedalus 36:69–79

Frankfurt HG (1989) The importance of what we care about. Cambridge University Press, New York
Gewirth A (1998) Self-fulfillment. Princeton University Press, Princeton
Gilbert D (2006) Stumbling on happiness. Alfred A Knopf, New York
Haidt J (2006) The happiness hypothesis. Basic Books, New York
Hill TE (2002) Human welfare and moral worth: kantian perspectives. Clarendon Press, Oxford
James W (1902) The varieties of religious experience. Modern Library, New York
Kant I (1996) Practical philosophy (trans: Mary JG). Cambridge University Press, New York
Kekes J (1988) The examined life. Bucknell University Press, Lewisburg
Lane R (2000) The loss of happiness in market democracies. Yale University Press, New Haven
Layard R (2005) Happiness. Penguin Press, New York
Lykken D (1999) Happiness. St. Martin's Griffin, New York
Marar Z (2003) The Happiness paradox. Reaktion Books, London
Martin MW (1994) Virtuous giving: philanthropy, voluntary service, and caring. Indiana University Press, Bloomington
Martin MW (2007) Happiness and virtue in positive psychology. J Theory Soc Behav 37:1 (forthcoming)
Mill JS (1979) Utilitarianism. Hackett Publishing, Indianapolis
Mill JS (1989) Autobiography. Penguin, New York
Nozick R (1989) The examined life. Simon and Schuster, New York
O'Neil JR (1993) The paradox of success. G.P. Putnam's Sons, New York
Peale NV (2003) Power of positive thinking. Simon and Schuster, New York
Polland SM (2005) It's all in your head: thinking your way to happiness. HarperCollins, New York
Russell B (1996) The conquest of happiness. Liveright, New York
Schwartz B (2005) The paradox of choice. Harper Perennial, New York
Seligman MEP (1991) Learned optimism. Alfred A Knopf, New York
Seligman MEP (2002) Authentic happiness. Free Press, New York
Sidgwick H (1907) Methods of ethics, 7th edn. University of Chicago Press, Chicago
Solnick SJ, Hemenway D (1998) Is more always better?: a survey on positional concerns. J Econ Behav Organ 37:373–383
Solomon RC (2002) Spirituality for the skeptic. Oxford University Press, New York
Sumner LW (1996) Welfare, happiness, and ethics. Clarendon Press, Oxford
Telfer E (1980) Happiness. St. Martin's Press, New York
White N (2006) A brief history of happiness. Blackwell Publishing, New York
Wike VS (1994) Kant on happiness in ethics. State University of New York Press, Albany

Chapter 4
Integrating the Diverse Definitions of Happiness: A Time-Sequential Framework of Subjective Well-Being

Chu Kim-Prieto, Ed Diener, Maya Tamir, Christie Scollon and Marissa Diener

Abstract The field of subjective well-being (SWB) is primarily concerned with people's evaluation of their lives; however, it includes a wide range of concepts, from momentary moods to global life satisfaction judgments. We propose a framework that integrates these diverse constructs. Our sequential temporal framework of subjective well-being describes experiences of well-being from the events and circumstances that cause evaluative reactions, through the emotional reactions to these events, to recall of these reactions, and finally to global judgments of well-being based on the previous stages. The hypothesized processes that translate the various steps in the sequence into one another are described, and supporting evidence is reviewed. We outline the implications of our framework for understanding subjective well-being, and discuss the research that is needed to further explore the proposed framework.

Keywords Emotion • Subjective well-being • Mood • Happiness

C. Kim-Prieto (✉)
Department of Psychology, The College of New Jersey,
2000 Pennington Road, Ewing, NJ 08628, USA
e-mail: kim@tcnj.edu

E. Diener
University of Illinois and Gallop Organization,
901 West Illinois Street, Urbana, IL 61801, USA

M. Tamir
Stanford University, 450 Serra Mall, Stanford, CA 94305, USA

C. Scollon
Texas Christian University, 2800 West Bowie Street, Fort Worth, TX 76109, USA

M. Diener
University of Utah, 1901 East South Campus Drive, Salt Lake City, UT 84112, USA

A. Delle Fave (ed.), *The Exploration of Happiness*, Happiness Studies Book Series,
DOI: 10.1007/978-94-007-5702-8_4,

4.1 Integrating the Diverse Definitions of Happiness: A Time-Sequential Framework of Subjective Well-Being

Subjective well-being (SWB) encompasses a wide range of components, such as happiness, life satisfaction, hedonic balance, fulfillment, and stress, and holds at its core affective and cognitive evaluation of one's life. It also extends from the specific and concrete to the global and abstract: momentary experiences versus people's global judgments about their entire lives.

Research on SWB has grown in prominence in the scientific literature in recent years. Over 4,000 studies are listed in PsychInfo under "life satisfaction," and almost 4,000 studies are listed for "happiness." On the negative end of the subjective well-being dimension, PsychInfo lists over 30,000 studies about major depression and approximately 40,000 studies on stress. SWB has been extensively studied in relation to demographic factors such as marriage (Lucas et al. 2003; Reis and Gable 2003) and income (Diener and Biswas-Diener 2002 for a review), personality factors (Diener and Lucas 1999) coping (e.g., King et al. 2000) and goal pursuit (Emmons 1986). Research on its heritability (e.g., Tellegen et al. 1988) and cross-cultural generalizability (see Diener et al. 2003 for a review) has been growing, and scientists have examined the benefits of positive emotions (Fredrickson 1998) and SWB (e.g., Diener et al. 2002).

This boom in scientific inquiry is also reflected in the importance of happiness to the lay mind: In a recent survey of over 9,000 college students in 47 nations, happiness was rated at 8.1 on a nine-point scale of importance, making it the highest regarded of the 20 given values (e.g., love, wealth, health, and getting into heaven). Over half of the respondents rated the importance of happiness as a "9", while only 3 % indicated that they did not value happiness at all.

The interest in SWB by academics as well as the lay public is high, and the extent of research that is encompassed by SWB is far flung: The variables representing SWB are manifold, as are the measures. This booming popularity bodes well for the future of SWB research. But it has also resulted in confusion and contention regarding the measurement and meaning of SWB. We propose a framework for integrating the variables in the area of SWB, and review the factors that influence the relationship between the components. However, before we outline and explain our framework, we first review the current status of SWB research.

4.1.1 Current Approaches to SWB Research

People gauge their SWB in a number of different ways. For example, one can appraise large segments of one's life, such as work, social relationships, or marriage. Or, one can gauge happiness by recalling emotions felt during a specific event, such as Christmas dinner. Or, one can rely on current mood or spontaneous emotional reactions.

Given these multiple components that are involved in the estimation of SWB, three main approaches to SWB can be identified. Each approach offers a unique conceptualization of SWB, and relies on different kinds of measures. The first approach views SWB as a global assessment of life and its facets. According to this approach, knowledge of SWB requires access to personal global judgments of satisfaction and quality of life. Research based on this approach often involves large surveys, in which respondents are asked to self-report on their general happiness or satisfaction with large global domains, such as work or social relationships. An example of this approach is the Eurobarometer questions administered to a thousand respondents twice a year in each of the European Union nations.

A second approach views SWB as a recollection of past emotional experiences. Within this framework, researchers assess people's evaluations of their lives by asking participants about their emotions over the last week, last month, or other specific timeframes. Instead of inquiring about how happy or satisfied a person is in general, researchers in the second tradition ask respondents to recall whether they experienced a number of relevant feelings, such as "depressed," "joyful," or "on top of the world" during a certain period of time (Bradburn 1969). Rather than relying on a global judgment of satisfaction, this approach focuses on memories of past emotions.

A third approach views SWB as an aggregation of multiple emotional reactions across time (Kahneman 1999). Because this approach emphasizes on-line emotional experiences, it often relies on the experience sampling method (ESM). In ESM, people report on their current emotions several times a day, over a set period of time, usually varying from one week to several weeks. The researcher obtains an estimate of SWB by aggregating the participants' reports and examining average mood, emotional intensity, affect variability, and other temporal affective variables. In some cases, the researcher might also assess the respondent's feelings in different situations (e.g., Fleeson 2001).

In sum, because researchers have addressed SWB from multiple perspectives, measures of SWB have also varied. Research on SWB can include huge international samples (e.g., Suh et al. 1998), small samples of undergraduate students (Emmons 1986), adolescents (McKnight et al. 2002), groups of elderly respondents (Baltes and Mayer 1999; Smith et al. 1999) or clinical populations (e.g., Frisch et al. 1992); it may use general surveys, specific questionnaires, or experience sampling methods. Such variety inevitably raises questions about what these different measures are assessing.

4.1.2 Explaining the Variety of SWB Measures

To what degree do the different facets of SWB converge? If the measures used by the different approaches fully converge, this would justify the use of SWB as an overarching construct, but at the same time call for a reconceptualization of its different components. On the other hand, if the measures are unrelated, researchers would need to reconsider the usefulness of SWB as a general construct, and focus on the unique and more specific concepts emphasized by each approach.

Much research exists on the convergent validity of SWB assessments. For example, do people's global judgments of their happiness correlate with their recall of events or their average reported happiness when they are signaled at random moments? The correlations between different measures tend to be positive, but modest. For example, Balatsky and Diener (1993) found that Russian students' recall of good versus bad events in their lives correlated 0.22 with a global measure of life satisfaction. Pavot et al. (1991) also found a correlation of 0.42 among these measures in a U.S. sample. Thomas and Diener (1990) estimated correlations in the range of 0.50 to 0.58 between on-line reports of the frequency of positive versus negative affect and recalled affect, and estimated correlations ranging from 0.02 to 0.62 for the intensity of affect. Wirtz et al. (2004) reported correlations between recall after one month and on-line affect in the 0.53–0.75 range. Lucas et al. (1996) examined across a series of studies the correlation between global life satisfaction and recalled affect, and found correlations ranging from 0.42 to 0.52 between life satisfaction and recalled positive affect, and between −0.30 and −0.51 between life satisfaction and recalled negative affect. Thus, the various SWB measures appear related, but only at moderate levels.

When assessing the correlation between different measures of SWB, researchers often assume that the assessments tap with a varying degrees of measurement error an underlying latent construct of SWB. For instance, Sandvik et al. (1993) found a single factor underlying self-report and non self-report measures of SWB. Following this view, using different measurement methods are desirable because each measurement approach contains different measurement error (Diener and Fujita 1995).

Some researchers have questioned the inherent validity of specific SWB measures. Veenhoven (1993), for example, argues that the concept that comes closest to reflecting SWB is global life satisfaction. Although momentary moods might be assessed accurately, they might not reflect true long-term subjective well-being. For example, a person might experience enjoyable moments, but end up concluding that his or her life was meaningless (e.g., see Seligman 2002). Kahneman (1999) however, argues the opposite. He suggests that on-line moods are the most accurate and least biased measurement of SWB, and therefore should have a privileged place among the measures.

However, the moderate correlations between various measures of SWB do not seem to be due to unreliability or invalidity of the scales. In his review, Diener (1984) points to substantial temporal reliabilities of the SWB scales, often in the 0.55–0.70 range. He further reviews studies showing that correlation of peer reports and self-reports are in the 0.40 range (see also Lucas et al. 1996), and self-report of SWB converges with expert, researcher, and staff ratings on average of 0.52 when measures are corrected for unreliability (e.g., Sandvik et al. 1993). Sandvik et al. (1993) found significant correlations between SWB scales and troubles (e.g., parental divorce), health symptoms, and personality inventories such as Optimism and Extraversion scales. Thus, the SWB measures show substantial validity and reliability, in spite of the less than satisfactory correlations between the measurements of SWB.

Another explanation for the moderate correlations between the measures is that they tap different constructs. This explanation argues that moods, emotions, and long-term cognitive judgments of one's life each capture something different about respondents' reactions to their lives. According to this approach, different measures are seen as addressing different constructs, all grouped under the capacious canopy of SWB.

In sum, several explanations exist for the modest correlations among the measures. One explanation views the different measures as tapping a single construct with varying degrees of error, suggesting the existence of a single underlying SWB latent trait. Another approach suggests that some of the measured constructs are of superior validity in assessing SWB than other methods of measurement. A third approach views each measure as tapping a distinct construct, suggesting that a single underlying latent trait does not exist, although the different constructs might be correlated with each other.

The approach that we propose moves beyond the idea that SWB is merely a vague term encompassing many independent constructs, or that it is an underlying unitary construct for which we are searching out the best measure. We propose that while SWB is a unitary construct, it changes through the passage of time. As such, the different components that make-up the time-sequential framework of SWB are related to each other in systematic ways.

Our framework is built on the idea that reactions to events unfold over time, and that different measures of SWB reflect different temporal stages in this developing process. It incorporates what is known about how current moods, as well as the recall of emotions, influence global satisfaction judgments. Our framework also includes findings on the memory for emotions, and the factors besides on-line hedonic experiences that can influence reports of recalled affect. Finally, it incorporates what is known about how global SWB judgments are constructed. Thus, we bring conceptual coherence to the diverse definitions of SWB and to the manifold measures of this construct.

4.2 Key Points and Implications of the Framework

Our framework makes several major points about SWB, and has implications for interventions, measurement, and life choices in the pursuit of well-being.

1. We frame SWB as a sequence of stages that unfold over time, from instigating events and circumstances to global evaluations of life.
2. The four major stages of SWB are related to one another and follow a temporal sequence: (A) life circumstances and events; (B) affective reactions to those events; (C) recall of one's reactions; and (D) global evaluative judgment about one's life.

3. In addition to the temporal unfolding, new factors also influence SWB at each stage. Thus, although each stage correlates with the stages before it and after it, the correlations are less than unity, even when controlling for measurement error.
4. Understanding SWB requires comprehending the entire sequence of stages; no single stage is adequate by itself. Thus, measurement of any single stage provides an incomplete picture of SWB, and assessing all four stages is necessary for a complete understanding of subjective ill-being and well-being.
5. The four stages, and the transition processes between them, indicate why people's circumstances are only modestly related to the global judgments they make about their lives.
6. The reason that personality has such a pervasive influence on subjective well-being is that it influences all four of the stages.
7. The framework points to tradeoffs people might make in trying to maximize their SWB. For example, people might sacrifice positive hedonic experience at the second stage in order to maximize positive global judgments of well-being at the fourth stage.
8. We hypothesize return loops in the model such that later stages in the framework may influence a new set of events and reactions to them in the future by influencing people's behavior and reactions.

In the following sections, we present the steps of our sequential framework in greater detail and discuss the relations between the stages in the model. We also review how various measures map onto specific stages, and discuss some of the variables that influence each stage, as well as the relation between the stages. Finally, we conclude with suggestions for future research that is needed in order to further test our framework. Our overarching aim is to demonstrate that different concepts and measures of SWB can be understood within a comprehensive temporal framework.

4.3 The Sequential Framework of Subjective Well-Being

The framework presented in Fig. 4.1 follows an event as it is gradually modified and integrated into the complex network that includes the various measurements of SWB. The sequences are not necessarily causal in nature, but rather reflect major components of life evaluations as they evolve in time. The model begins with objective events and circumstances that elicit emotional reactions from the individual. Quality of life can be measured by assessing objective life circumstances, and economists and sociologists have often assessed well-being at this level. It should be noted, however, that this first stage is not strictly *subjective* well-being because this stage does not include people's reactions to their world. Nevertheless, because objective events are often the initial targets of subjective evaluations, they appear as the first step of our conceptual temporal sequence.

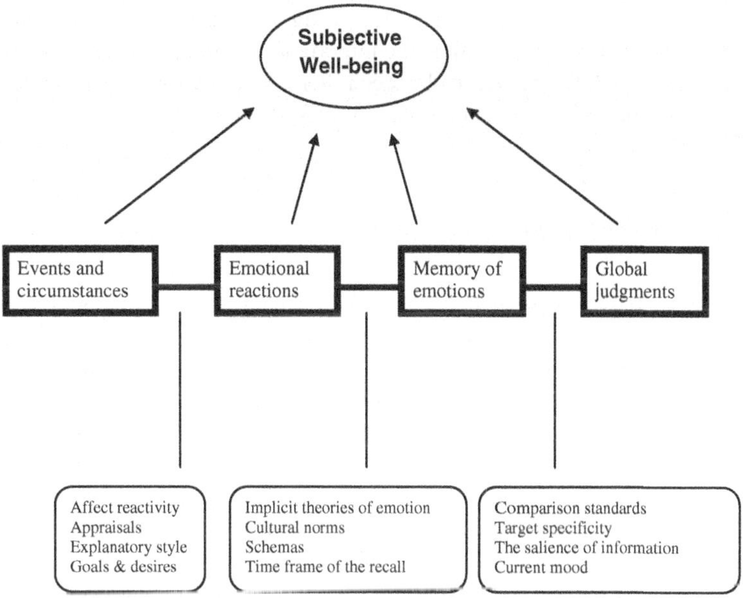

Fig. 4.1 A sequential framework for the study of subjective well-being

The next stage involves the emotional responses to the events. Emotional reactions involve multiple components, such as cognitive appraisal, physiological reactions, and behavioral tendencies. On-line recording of reactions, both in the laboratory and in the natural world, have been used to assess SWB at this stage. The experience sampling method invented by Csikszentmihalyi and Larsen (1978) has been particularly popular for obtaining self-reports of on-line emotional reactions (see Reis and Gable 2000; Scollon et al. 2004, for reviews of this method ology). Figure 4.1 lists several of the processes that influence the ways in which events and circumstances can lead to emotional reactions, and these will be reviewed later.

After the immediate emotional reactions diminish, they can later be recalled. But as Fig. 4.1 indicates, multiple factors beyond emotional reactions are reflected when emotions are recalled. Additional factors, such as the person's self-concept or current goals and concerns, can influence the recall of the emotion.

In the last stage, people can think back about events and the circumstances of their lives, and their reactions to them, and address global evaluative questions, such as whether they are satisfied with their marriage, are fulfilled at work, or feel happy. This last stage can include information from any of the previous stages, including the immediately preceding stage of emotion recall. Figure 4.1 shows some of the factors that are now understood to influence global evaluations.

The following sections describe each stage of the framework in more detail, and also provide information about some of the factors that can influence the associations among the stages. The following discussion is not meant to be exhaustive, but serves to highlight some important factors that influence each stage in the sequence and the transitions between them, to allow for a better understanding of the multiple components that play into SWB.

4.3.1 Life Events and Circumstances

People's lives vary enormously in ways that would seem to potentially have a huge impact on their well-being. Sociologists, economists, and policy scholars often examine the differences in life circumstances as direct measures of quality of life, without recourse to subjective indicators. Economists often focus on variables such as the per capita gross domestic product of nations, in the belief that indices of income indicate individuals' quality of life. Indeed, earnings correlate with variables such as health, longevity, victimization, and mental health (Diener and Biswas-Diener 2002; Diener and Diener 1995). Sociologists and policy scholars often analyze additional objective indicators besides those traditionally studied by economists. For example, they assess variables such as infant mortality, educational equality, longevity, and levels of violent crime to indicate the quality of life of societies (for review, see Diener Suh 1997).

4.3.1.1 The Relation of Circumstances to the Later Stages

What is the relation between life events and circumstances and SWB? Brickman and Campbell (1971) contended that we adapt to life circumstances, and therefore live on a "hedonic treadmill," where neither good nor bad circumstances make a difference due to habituation. Despite the importance of this insight, research has shown that adaptation is often not complete, and that life circumstances do matter for various measures of SWB. Even the data collected by Brickman et al. (1978) revealed that differences between people's SWB correlated with differences in life circumstances. For example, Brickman et al. found that people with spinal cord injuries had significantly lower SWB than others, although the authors suggested that these differences were not as large as we might expect. The lottery winners they studied had higher SWB than their control group, but the difference was not significant, perhaps because of the small sample size and consequent lack of statistical power. Moreover, other researchers have found that lottery winners do report higher levels of SWB than various comparison groups (Smith and Razzell 1975).

Other studies also point to the power of people's circumstances in influencing their SWB. For example, the correlation between the average income of nations and the average SWB of these societies is often around 0.70 (Diener and Biswas-Diener 2002). Most people in America report positive levels of SWB (Diener Diener 1995), whereas people living in the slums of Calcutta more often have low SWB (Biswas-Diener and Diener 2001). Similarly, we find that homeless individuals in California, Oregon, and Calcutta all show low levels of SWB (Biswas-Diener and Diener 2003).

Longitudinal studies also suggest that life events and circumstances can influence SWB. In a large and representative sample of Germans, we analyzed the longitudinal associations between life satisfaction and life events. For example, women who started out with high life satisfaction showed a large drop when their husbands died, and then slowly recovered over a period of many years (Lucas et al. 2003). People who lost their jobs showed a decline in life satisfaction and never fully recovered to their former levels (Lucas et al. 2004).

As noted earlier, our framework indicates a temporally evolving sequence, but one that does not imply a causal connection. On the contrary, as we describe later on, each stage in the sequence is influenced by different factors, including earlier as well as later steps in the sequence. Thus, the direction of influence from events to reactions is not always unidirectional. For example, happy people tend to make more money (Diener et al. 2002), get married (Harker and Keltner 2001), and have better health (e.g., Danner et al. 2001; see Lyubomirsky et al. 2002, for a review). Furthermore, extraverts tend to experience a greater number of positive events, while neurotics experience a greater number of negative events (Headey and Wearing 1989; Magnus et al. 1993). Clearly, objective events do not occur in a vacuum, but reflect multiple forces (both external as well as internal) that operate in concert. We will refer to this issue again when we discuss multiple sequence scenarios later in the chapter.

Overall, life events and circumstances do appear to influence later stages of SWB. However, such relations are often surprisingly small. For example, Emmons and Diener (1985) found correlations ranging from −0.06 to 0.10 for objective standing in a domain and satisfaction with that domain. Suh et al. (1996) found that young people largely adapt to many common life events, such as promotions at work. Even in the case of extremely negative events, such as mass shootings or plane crashes, more than half of victims are able to find benefits in the tragedy (Tennen and Affleck 2002). In addition, demographic factors such as education, marriage, income, and ethnicity together usually account for a small percentage of the variance in measures of SWB (e.g., Campbell et al. 1976). Taken together, these findings suggest that while life circumstances can influence reports of well-being, reactions to most life circumstances vary so substantially that there is on average only a modest relation between these circumstances and SWB. Several factors can account for this modest relation, two of which are described below.

4.3.1.2 Habituation and Adaptation

Compared to facets of the environment that remain stable, changing events can have special significance for a person's SWB; however, people tend to habituate to their environments such that life circumstances often do not have an intense influence on the person's affect (Brickman et al. 1978; Suh et al. 1996). Adaptation also occurs to the aspects of the environment that have remained stable for a long time. Because recent events and changes in circumstances can have a large impact on SWB, and long-standing circumstances often have a very small influence, the correlation of circumstances and measures of SWB is often modest across people. Long-term stable life circumstances can have some influence on SWB (e.g., Biswas-Diener and Diener 2001), but recent events are more likely to produce strong reactions that include substantial changes in SWB (e.g., Lucas et al. 2004; Suh et al. 1996). There is now clear evidence that although important life events such as losing one's job or spouse have a strong immediate impact on measures of SWB, the impact diminishes over time, although the individual may never completely return to his or her original level of SWB (Lucas et al. 2003, 2004). Over time, events and circumstances that are stable come to have a diminishing impact, thereby reducing the correlation between life circumstances and SWB in studies that do not also examine how long the circumstances have remained in place.

4.3.1.3 The Context of Situational Circumstances

Researchers studying the effects of events and demographic variables on SWB have often concluded that the effects tend to be relatively small. For example, Campbell et al. (1976) concluded that all of the demographic variables they studied, taken together, accounted for less than 20 % of the variance in SWB. However, the effects of variables such as marriage and age probably depend heavily on the situational specifics of those variables. Good health enjoyed by a 70 year old may contribute more to SWB than good health enjoyed by a 20 year old. Or, the effects of widowhood on SWB may be different for a person surrounded by friends and family versus another woman who only recently moved to a new location where she has little social support. Thus, one reason that demographic and other "objective" social indicators correlate only modestly with the subjective stages is that they are relatively imperfect indicators of quality of life, and do not take into account important contextual factors which moderate people's subjective reactions to life.

4.3.2 Emotional Reactions to Events and Circumstances

The next stage in our framework moves from the events and life circumstances to the person's reaction to these events. When a life event occurs, a person appraises the event—how desirable it is, whether she or he has the resources to cope with it, why the event occurred, and so forth. The evaluation of events might occur consciously as well as unconsciously (e.g., Robinson 2000), and these appraisals lead to varying emotions (e.g., Ortony et al. 1988). Central to feelings of SWB is that reactions to events are evaluative (feeling whether the events are good or bad), and include feelings of pleasantness and unpleasantness.

We cannot give a thorough description of all the processes that comprise emotional reactions, but simply emphasize that such reactions are complex phenomena that involve parallel processes at multiple levels. For example, in addition to immediate evaluations and later cognitive appraisals, an emotional reaction often involves outward motor expression, such as facial expressions, posture, vocalizations, and verbal expressions. Emotional reactions also involve changes in physiological systems, such as neurochemical processes and activation of specific brain regions. In addition, emotional responses to events also include people's verbal labels for their emotions, which contain information about the explanation for the emotional feeling. Because emotional reactions involve many systems, measurement of such reactions have been based not only on self-reports, but also on biological (Cacioppo et al. 2000) and nonverbal measures (Keltner et al. 1999; Oettingen and Seligman 1990). Because an emotional reaction is a complex set of responses to events, no single measure can fully capture it.

On-line verbal reports of emotional reactions can be complemented by nonverbal, physiological, and behavioral measures (e.g., Larsen and Fredrickson 1999) to yield a richer understanding of emotional reactions. These measures of various components of emotional reactions are usually moderately correlated with one another. Thus, whereas well-being researchers have focused mainly on self-report scales to assess on-line emotion, additional measurements can offer an invaluable contribution to the understanding and assessment of well-being judgments.

4.3.2.1 The Transition from Objective Events to Emotional Reactions

Emotional reactions are responses to either internal or external events. Although some events affect virtually all people because they are almost universally appraised as good or bad, most events produce varying reactions across people. Thus, the transition from life events and circumstances to people's emotional reactions to these events and circumstances has been a central task in understanding SWB. Of course, importance of individual interpretation in understanding the emotional response to external events has been undeniable from early days of emotion theory (e.g., James James 1884), and one that has been much researched by emotion scholars (e.g., Lyubomirsky and Tucker 1998). Providing an exhaustive mapping of all the variables that have been linked to emotional response would require an extensive review onto itself, and beyond the scope and aim of our current task. Thus, we merely provide some key examples from the emotion literature of the ways that different variables affect the transition from objective events to emotional reactions.

Personality appears to be one such key element. Personality traits, such as extraversion and neuroticism, have been related to reactivity to emotional stimuli (Canli et al. 2001; Larsen and Ketelaar 1991; Rusting and Larsen 1997; Tamir et al. 2002; Zelenski and Larsen 1999). People differ in how intensely they respond to emotional events (Larsen and Diener 1987; Larsen et al. 1986, 1987), and in the duration of their emotional reactions (Schimmack et al. 2000).

Another important element is appraisal and explanatory style (Buchanan and Seligman 1995). Several theories explain how appraisals are made, and how habitual appraisal tendencies can influence SWB (e.g., Ortony et al. 1988; Seligman 1995). At the most basic level, appraisal processes lead to a valenced evaluation of events in terms of their personal significance. In addition to appraising whether an event is positive or negative, people also assess causal factors, personal control, and their ability to cope. Some appraisals are learned and habitual. For example, fear can be conditioned without conscious mediation (e.g., Robinson 2000). Appraisal also occurs at the level of interpretation; people differ in the way they interpret and explain situations (Lyubomirsky and Ross 1999; Lyubomirksy and Tucker 1998). For example, people who are aggressive tend to appraise situations in more aggressive terms (e.g., Cohen et al. 1998). Indeed, learned helplessness (Peterson and Seligman 1984; Peterson et al. 1993), which is a pessimistic explanatory style coupled with stable and global self attributions of negative outcomes, predict strong and persistent negative emotions (see also Jackson et al. 2002).

4.3.2.2 Emotional Reactions and Well-Being

Thus far, we have discussed the nature of emotional reactions and few select variables that mediate events and evaluative responses to them. However, even the approach that places the greatest emphasis on specific emotional experiences does not view single experiences as a reflection of long-term feelings of well-being. Rather, multiple emotional reactions are aggregated in order to reflect people's feelings of well-being over time. Considering the fact that researchers often aggregate multiple emotional reactions across time, it is important to identify the key factors that influence the selection of the emotional reactions that have long-term effects. One important factor that influences long-term effects of emotional reactions is goals and personal desires. This is because although people can respond emotionally to events at any given moment, only the reactions that are relevant to general goals and concerns are likely to influence SWB. For example, a person might encounter a snake in the woods and experience intense fear, but such a reaction does not necessarily have implications for that person's sense of happiness and satisfaction with life because they hardly ever go for a walk in the woods. Thus, life circumstances and events most influence SWB when they either hinder or benefit major goal progress, or signify whether an important goal has been obtained or lost (Cantor and Sanderson 1999; Emmons 1986).

Factors that are closely linked to personal goals appear to have most impact on people's reports of SWB. For example, Andrews and Withey (1976) found that people's evaluations of things that are generally distant from their own lives, such as the government and other institutions, have little relation to measures of SWB. On the other hand, people's evaluations of factors closer to their lives, such as their social relationships and jobs, correlate more closely with their reports of SWB. Events such as recent widowhood strongly influence the reports of SWB of most people (Lucas et al. 2003). While the reason is not clear, we theorize that the death of a spouse has a pervasive effect on most people's ability to meet many of their desires and goals simply due to the fact that their spouse is no longer present.

Goals and motivational concerns also mediate the relation between external events and reactions to them, to the extent that resources influence people's ability to reach their goals. Diener and Fujita (1995) found that resources, such as income, were most relevant to measures of SWB if they were related to the person's goals (see also Crawford-Solberg et al. 2002). Furthermore, personal resources, such as social support and self-confidence, were more important for reports of SWB than were material goods. Objective social indicators of quality of life are only modestly related to later stages in the SWB sequence because people have different goals and values, and have different amounts of resources for obtaining their particular goals.

In sum, the model described thus far indicates that external events and circumstances are related to people's affective and cognitive reactions, but that this relation is mediated by processes that vary considerably across individuals. Further, while no one-to-one correspondence between events and circumstances and evaluative reactions to them exist, the two are related in a systematic manner and depend on a variety of factors, such as explanatory style, adaptation, and the availability of resources for meeting one's goals.

4.3.3 The Recall Stage

The next stage involves later recollections of an emotional reaction to an event. Substantial research has been conducted on the relation between memory and emotion, focusing on how emotion is encoded, how it is recalled, and how emotion and memory affect one another (e.g., Christianson 1992). As suggested by our framework, research findings show that although on-line reports and recalled reports of the same emotional event are related, they are not identical (e.g., Thomas and Diener 1990). One cause of the discrepancy between on-line and retrospective reports of emotion is that memories of emotion are not encoded in memory in a permanent form. Instead, emotional memories are constantly being reconstructed based on present emotional experiences, current values, beliefs, and motivations (e.g., Ross and Wilson 2000). Figure 4.1 indicates several factors that influence the reconstruction of emotional memories, including implicit theories of emotion, cultural norms regarding emotions, and information conveyed in surveys, such as the recall time frame.

Indeed, one factor that influences the reconstruction of memory is people's implicit theories about emotion. In this regard, McFarland et al. (1987) demonstrated that when women were asked to recall their mood during menses, they recalled more negative emotions than they previously reported on-line: Implicit theories about the relation between menstruation and mood moderated the amount of negative emotion that was remembered. Implicit theories about gender also operate in a similar manner in that gender differences that are apparent in retrospective reports of emotion can disappear when researchers measure on-line emotion (Robinson and Clore 2002; Robinson et al. 1998).

Cultural beliefs also influence the transition from on-line to remembered emotion. For example, Oishi (2002) found that Asian Americans and European

Americans differed in their retrospective ratings of emotion but not in their on-line reports of emotion. When asked to recall their on-line moods, European Americans remembered their week as very good and Asian Americans remembered their week as mildly good, although the two groups reported their mood as being equally mildly good on their on-line reports. It is possible that people are more likely to recall feeling emotions that are normative for their culture, or recall feeling the emotions that fit culturally with the events they have been experiencing (see Markus and Kitayama 1994, for why this might occur).

Other factors underlying the relation of on-line emotion labeling and recalled affect include current appraisals of the object or event causing the reaction. The recall of emotional events can depend on the current state of the individual. Levine and her colleagues (Levine 1997; Levine et al. 2001) demonstrated that people reconstruct their memories for emotion in the direction of their current appraisals. In their study, changing evaluations of the presidential candidate Ross Perot led to reconstructing one's memory of how one felt earlier about Perot's actions. Thus, changes in appraisal of circumstances or events can result in changes in memory for one's previous reactions to them.

Why are emotional memories susceptible to reconstruction? Robinson and Clore (2002) suggest that when recalling emotions over a wide time frame, individuals do not retrieve specific instances and aggregate them to compute mean levels of affect. The recall task is difficult, and respondents prefer to provide quick answers to researchers' questions. Consequently, people rely on heuristic information such as their general self-concept, implicit beliefs about emotion, or current mood, to inform their estimates of past emotional experience. In support of this, Feldman Barrett (1997) showed that individuals who score high on self-report measures of neuroticism overestimated in their recalled reports the amount of negative emotion they experienced on-line. On the other hand, individuals who scored high on self-reports of extraversion recalled more pleasant affect then they actually experienced on-line. Diener et al. (1984) showed a similar effect with happy versus unhappy people: Happy people overestimated the amount of pleasant affect in recall, whereas unhappy people overestimated the amount of negative affect in recall.

One final influence on recall is that the survey questions presented by the researcher can stimulate respondents to search for different information. Winkielman et al. (1998) asked respondents about how much anger they had experienced, but over time frames of either one week or one year. People reported large amounts of anger for the week compared to what would be expected for a year if extrapolated from the weekly reports to a full year. Respondents appeared to set a threshold for reporting that depended on the questions asked by the researcher. When the interviewer asked about anger in a short period, such as a day, the participant assumed that she/he must be interested in any experience, even mild irritation, because intense anger would be unlikely in such a brief period, and the short time frame implied that the experience is frequent. When the interviewer asked about anger over the course of a year, however, the respondents assumed that she/he was inquiring about intense anger episodes that could be recalled over a long period, and provided an estimate of only intense anger experiences. The two estimates are incommensurable in terms of the translation of the frequency of anger from one time period to the other because the subjects in the two conditions provide information about different emotional experiences. Thus, reports of recall are not only influenced by memory factors, but also by survey design variables that influence how participants interpret the questions.

The above review indicates that recall does not provide a precise duplicate of on-line experience, and that other influences such as personality and culture can influence what is remembered. Thus, measures of SWB that depend on recall are likely to be influenced by these other factors in addition to on-line past experiences. When people recall that they are more joyful than other individuals, it might be because of on-line emotional reactions, or it might be because of norms, interpretations of survey items, or implicit beliefs about emotions.

Thus, memories of emotions are dynamic reflections of the way emotions are being shaped and modified through time. Emotion memories cannot be simply dismissed as biased reflections of the "real" on-line emotions because research indicates that remembered emotions are sometimes better predictors of behaviors than the actual on-line emotions themselves. For example, Wirtz et al. (2004) found that participants' memory of their spring break vacation was a better predictor of whether they wanted to go on a similar vacation in the future than their on-line emotions assessed during the vacation. Oishi (2004) also found that people's on-line feelings with their romantic partner were not as important as the recall of these feelings in predicting whether the partners would still be in the romantic relationship six months later. Within our framework, on-line affect and recalled affect no longer need to vie for the position of "true emotional well-being." Instead, both on-line affect and recalled affect are two different ways of understanding subjective well-being.

4.3.4 Constructed Satisfaction Judgments

Global evaluations of one's life occur at the final phase of the emotion sequence. For example, respondents can think about and report whether their lives are meaningful, whether their work is fulfilling, and whether their marriage is satisfactory. Such global evaluations are distinctly different from both online affective experiences and the recall of such experiences. Indeed, one of the approaches to SWB mentioned earlier focuses on global evaluations as the best indicator of SWB. In this section, we describe this stage in further detail, emphasizing how it relates to earlier stages in the framework.

Schwarz, Strack, and their colleagues (see Schwarz and Strack 1999, for a review) examined how people construct life satisfaction judgments. Figure 4.1 lists several of the processes these researchers have examined, including the accessibility of specific standards of comparison, the salience of specific information, the specificity of the evaluated target, and the influence of current mood. Schwartz et al. shed considerable light on the processes that influence the construction of global satisfaction judgments, and we describe some of these factors below.

4.3.4.1 Comparison Standards

One process that affects people's constructions of satisfaction judgments is the standards that people use, whether consciously or unconsciously, in making SWB judgments (Campbell et al. 1976). Schwarz and Strack (1999) showed that the comparison standards against which one judges one's life could be altered by priming. They asked participants to respond to satisfaction questions when a person in a wheelchair was in the respondent's view. In this case, life satisfaction was higher because respondents compared themselves to the person with a disability. A similar finding was presented by Dermer et al. (1979), who showed that people's life satisfaction was higher if life in the past was presented in an unfavorable light. In another study, Schwarz and Scheuring (1988) varied the response scales on items prior to the satisfaction judgment: Some subjects had response scales with low options (suggesting that most people are not that well off in the domain), whereas other participants received items with response scales that were high (indicating that most subjects are well off in this domain). The response scales set standards against which subjects could gauge their own level of success, and this influenced their later satisfaction (for a review of this line of research, see Schwarz 1996).

4.3.4.2 Target Specificity

People can evaluate their satisfaction with their life as a whole, but they can also rate their satisfaction with specific life domains, including romantic relationships, career, physical appearance, and many more. Because different targets could be related to different experiences and goals, the target specificity of satisfaction judgments might also influence the resulting evaluations. Some research suggests that people may rely on different sources of information when evaluating their satisfaction with specific versus general life domains. For example, Schwarz et al. (1987) suggested that people access domain-specific information when evaluating specific life-domains, but rely on heuristic cues (e.g., their current mood) when evaluating their satisfaction with life as a whole. Although further research is needed to compare general to specific life satisfaction judgments, the available research indicates that different sources of information might be salient to different degrees when evaluating life satisfaction.

4.3.4.3 Salience

The information that is salient, and therefore highly accessible, at the time of satisfaction judgment can strongly influence the judgment (Schwarz and Strack 1999). For example, in one study (Strack et al. 1988) college student respondents were asked about both their dating satisfaction and their life satisfaction, but the question order was counterbalanced, with half of the subjects receiving the dating question first. When the dating question came before the life satisfaction question, the two correlated substantially, but when the dating question came second, the correlation was low. Presumably the concrete dating question could influence the life satisfaction response by making certain information salient, but the life satisfaction question would be unlikely to influence the respondents' satisfaction with their romantic lives because this judgment is more bounded by the reality of the situation. Schimmack et al. (2002) extended these findings to the individual difference domain by showing that for some individuals, information about romantic life is more chronically salient than for other individuals, and therefore is more likely to influence their life satisfaction judgment. Thus, both situationally primed information and material that is chronically salient for individuals are likely to be used in the construction of life satisfaction judgments.

Later investigators built on the impressive work of Schwarz and Strack. Schimmack et al. (2002) explored why, if momentary situational factors influence reports of life satisfaction, these reports tend to be very stable across time and situations (Diener and Larsen 1984; Eid and Diener in press). They found that the information people use in their judgments also tends to be stable. People tend to use the same sources of information repeatedly over time, and the information itself tends to be somewhat stable. For example, Schimmack et al. found that whether individuals used their family relationships in judging their life satisfaction was moderately stable over time. In addition, the ratings of family relationships were themselves somewhat stable over time. It appears that some information is chronically accessible to individuals, and tends to be used repeatedly when they report their satisfaction, unless other information is made more salient by the situational context. Thus, global satisfaction judgments are likely to be based on some chronically salient information, as well as information that has recently been primed by situational factors.

In addition to individual differences in the domains of information people use when making life satisfaction judgments, individual differences also exist in the way people use information.

Diener et al. (2002) found that some individuals most heavily weight the domains in which they have the biggest problems in judging their life satisfaction, whereas other individuals most heavily weight their best domains.[1] At the societal level, some cultures focus people more on positive or on negative information (e.g., Elliot et al. 2001; Lee et al. 2000), and this can change the emotional information they recall when making global life judgments. In a similar vein, Diener et al. (2000) found that a general positivity disposition predicts average life satisfaction judgments across nations. Thus, it is clear that both stable individual differences and situational factors influence global judgments of life satisfaction.

A strength of a life satisfaction measure is its flexibility: People can consider or ignore information that they personally consider relevant or irrelevant when

[1] It might be, however, that there is a universal tendency to weight negative events more heavily than positive ones, based on the idea that negative information in general is more salient than positive information (Ito and Cacioppo 1999; Rozin and Royzman 2001). Future research is needed to better understand this tendency and its relevance to SWB.

making judgments about life satisfaction. However, this flexibility leaves open the possibility that situational factors can influence the judgment by making certain information more salient to the respondent. This also explains why objective predictors are often only modestly related to global satisfaction judgments; some respondents might view the predictor as relevant to his or her global evaluation, whereas others may not. Schimmack et al. (2002) found, for example, that almost all student respondents considered progress toward their academic goals when making life satisfaction judgments, but only about half of them considered their current mood or housing arrangement to be relevant. Individual differences in goals, as well as culture (Oishi and Diener 2001), are likely to influence what people consider important when evaluating their lives.

4.3.4.4 Relation of Global Judgments to Previous Stages in the Model

In order to compute a judgment of life satisfaction or fulfillment, people can use affective information, such as their recall of positive emotions. Suh et al. (1998) found that recall of affect correlated with life satisfaction judgments, and Schimmack et al. (2002) found evidence suggesting that individuals retrieve emotional information when forming life satisfaction judgments. However, both studies suggest that individual differences exist in the relative degree to which people rely on past emotional experiences when making global judgments of life satisfaction.

Alternatively, although life satisfaction and on-line emotion are related, they are not the same thing. Lucas et al. (1996) used a multitrait-multimethod approach to examine the relation between emotional experience and life satisfaction. Although significantly correlated, global reports of positive affect and negative affect showed separability from reports of life satisfaction. Similarly, Eid and Diener (in press) found a correlation of 0.74 between the variables at the latent trait level. Thus, long-term affect accounted for about half of the variability in life satisfaction when the effects of current mood and situational variability were removed from each measure. When constructing global SWB judgments, people take more than their pleasant and unpleasant emotions into account. For example, Schimmack et al. (2002) found that objective circumstances, such as college grades, housing, and romantic relationships, held some importance in life satisfaction judgments.

4.3.5 Conclusion

Figure 4.1 presents a sequence that includes the major temporal components of SWB. These stages incorporate objective events and circumstances that people experience in their lives, the subjective emotional reactions to such events, the memories of specific emotional reactions, and the global judgments of life satisfaction. While these stages unfold over time, we do not imply progressive development such that one stage turns into another. Instead, these stages in the SWB sequence are related, but not identical. Most current research on well-being is related to one of three approaches outlined earlier in this chapter. Whereas each of these approaches emphasizes one stage in the sequence, our framework suggests that each stage is one of several different forms of evaluation that people make about their SWB. No stage in the framework can single-handedly provide a full account of subjective well-being; rather, the interrelationship of the stages is crucial to a full understanding of how people evaluate their lives. The framework therefore incorporates several important factors that influence both specific stages and the transitions between them.

4.3.6 Multiple Sequence Scenarios

Our framework shows a simplified version of emotional experiences in real life. In everyday life, people are exposed to multiple events, which lead to multiple emotions that can later be recalled separately or in combination. Thus, a sequential path as the one depicted in Fig. 4.1 does not occur in a vacuum; rather, it constantly influences and is influenced by other sequences along the temporal continuum. Thus, an event that occurs at stage, whether it be the occurrence of an emotional event, a memory of an emotional event, or global evaluation, influences what happens at other stages of other events. As shown in Fig. 4.2, one can examine the relation between two adjacent sequences, where sequence 1 occurs on a temporal continuum before sequence 2. Because a thorough overview of all possible relations is beyond the scope of this chapter, we will briefly discuss two

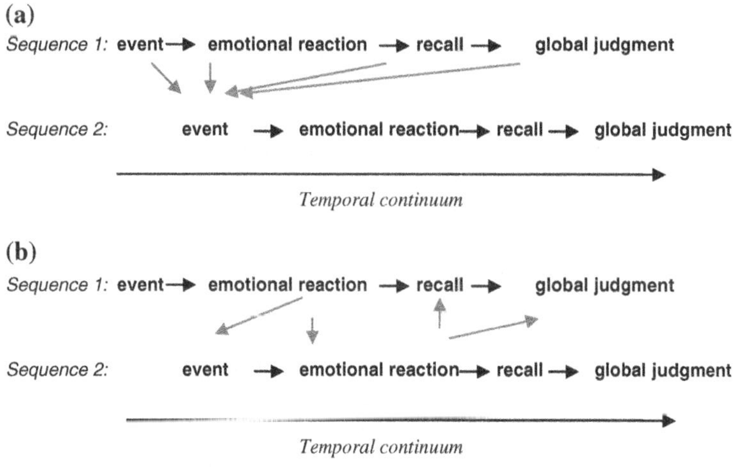

Fig. 4.2 Examples for relations between multiple sequences

examples: Effects of previous stages on future events and circumstances, and the effects of concurrent events on emotional experience.

4.3.6.1 Effects on Future Objective Outcomes

Our daily experiences are constantly shaped and modified by experiences from our past. This is especially true in the field of emotion and SWB, because valenced evaluations of life can influence patterns of choice and behavior, reactivity, and evocation.

By using our framework, one can examine how different components of SWB influence objective life outcomes. As shown in Fig. 4.2a, each stage in an earlier sequence can contribute to the prediction of future life events and circumstances.

In this respect, positive emotional states are likely to elicit positive reactions from others (Lyubomirsky et al. 2002). Positive emotions can also alter performance by increasing creativity, income, work performance, health, and other variables that are valued in many cultures. Thus, emotional reactions can influence later events and life circumstances. For example, research shows that recalled emotions can be a better predictor of future events than the actual on-line experiences (Wirtz et al. 2004; Oishi 2004). Furthermore, global judgments of job satisfaction can mediate the relation between work environment and turnover (Lambert et al. 2001), as well as predict outcome variables such as productivity and company profit (Harter et al. 2002). Thus, each of the three subjective stages can influence later objective events and circumstances.

4.3.6.2 Multiple Effects of On-line Emotions

In addition to noting possible relations between past stages and future outcomes, our framework also points to the multiple effects each stage can have on stages in future or parallel sequences. For example, Fig. 4.2b indicates the potential effects of current emotions on each of the four stages in a subsequent SWB sequence.

We have already mentioned the possible effects of emotional reaction on the prediction of future outcomes. However, on-going emotional reactions can also influence the way people respond emotionally to other events in the environment. For example, positive affect increases selective attention to positive information (Tamir and Robinson 2004), which might serve to maintain positive feelings. Indeed, many studies have documented the effects of emotion on concurrent cognition and evaluation. In addition, reactions to one event can influence the recall of other events. For example, people in a positive mood might be more likely to recall positive events from their past, whereas people in a negative mood might be more likely to recall negative events.

Finally, people's current mood can influence their global judgments of life satisfaction, but they can also discount this information if they believe that it is due to irrelevant sources (Schwarz and Clore 1983; see also Robinson 2000). Schimmack et al. (2002) found that about one-half of respondents report that they use their current mood in evaluating their lives. Those individuals who say that they use their current mood show a much larger correlation between their moods and life satisfaction reports than do individuals who say that they do not use their current mood information. Although individuals differ in whether they use this information, they tended to do so with some stability across time. However, when a particular piece of information becomes particularly salient, such as one's mood on a beautiful spring day after a long spate of bad weather, or when one's nation has just won a soccer championship, this material might become salient even for individuals for whom it is not chronically salient.

4.3.6.3 Summary

The above examples demonstrate that stages in sequences that involve different eliciting events can influence one another. Revealing such intricate interrelationships is an important task for future research. Despite the fact that our framework must be made more complex to accommodate all paths of influence between variables, it nevertheless points to major steps in the SWB sequence, and alerts us to the importance of searching for the interconnections among those stages. Thus, the current framework should have heuristic, conceptual, and empirical value in terms of stimulating theory and empirical work on the ways that the major stages in the sequence are related to one another.

4.3.7 On the Primacy of the Various Stages

As mentioned earlier, scholars have argued for the primacy of one stage over the other stages in terms of reflecting SWB. For example, in terms of eliciting events, many sociologists and economists favor economic and social indicators, which reflect life circumstances in a society. In terms of emotional experience, Kahneman (1999) argued that on-line emotional reactions to events have priority in terms of assessing hedonic outcomes because this measure is not as biased as recall and global judgments. Others have focused on retrospective memories, preferring a broader perspective on a person's life than how the respondent feels at the moment of the survey. Finally, Veenhoven (1993) argued that global judgments, such as life satisfaction, are primary in assessing SWB because it best reflects the philosophical notion of the good life. The preference for one perspective over another can be based on philosophical reasons, or because one method might be considered less biased than another.

However, an important point of this chapter is that a scientific understanding of people's evaluations of their lives requires knowledge of each of the stages because they are connected to one another in an integral fashion. Each stage indicates new information about the quality of a person's life, and a comprehensive theoretical understanding is not possible without understanding the complete sequence. There is evidence that each of the various stages predict important behaviors. For example, laboratory experiments indicate that positive emotional reactions can lead to heightened altruism, creativity, and flexible problem solving (see Brief and Weiss 2002 for a review). And as mentioned earlier, the memory of emotions, however inaccurate, often predicts future choices and behaviors better than online emotions (Oishi 2004; Wirtz et al. 2004). Finally, measures of the global judgment stage indicate that it, too, can have predictive power. For example, global life satisfaction judgments have been shown to predict substance abuse (Newcomb et al. 1986; Zullig et al. 2001), suicide (Koivumaa-Honkanen et al. 2001) and deaths due to fatal injuries (Koivumaa-Honkanen et al. 2002). Similarly, global judgments of the workplace can predict job accidents, unit profitability, and productivity (Harter et al. 2002). Thus, all three of the subjective stages are important to understanding and predicting future behavior.

4.4 Implications of the Framework

4.4.1 Personality Influences on the Stages of SWB

One implication of our framework concerns the pronounced effects of individual differences on every stage of the sequential framework. Personality influences on measures of SWB have been found to range from moderate to substantial, and the heritability of SWB has been estimated at about 0.5 (Tellegen et al. 1988). Two of the "Big Five" traits, Extraversion and Neuroticism, have been found to correlate at 0.80 or higher with longterm levels of positive and negative affect, respectively, after controlling for measurement error (Lucas and Fujita 2000; Fujita 1991). Thus, the relation found between various measures of SWB and personality is often higher than that found between situational and demographic variables, and reports of SWB (Diener and Lucas 1999).

As discussed earlier, personality can influence the relation between an individual's objective circumstance and one's emotional reactions. However, evidence indicates that personality can influence all of the stages in the model. People with different temperaments are likely to experience different life events (e.g., Headey and Wearing 1989; Magnus et al. 1993), and a propensity to experience certain events, such as divorce, appears to be partly heritable (Jocklin et al. 1996). People with different personalities react differently to the same events (e.g., Rusting and Larsen 1997) and remember the same emotional reactions differently (e.g., Feldman Barrett 1997). Moreover, the same processes that may be responsible for individual differences in emotional experience may operate within persons as well. For example, Fleeson et al. (2002) found that engaging in extraverted behavior had positive consequences for both introverts and extraverts. Additionally, people with different personalities are likely to select different information when constructing global SWB judgments (Diener et al. 2002). Certain broad personality predispositions to approach versus withdraw (Elliot and Thrash 2002) are likely to influence all stages in our framework. Thus, personality is one of the strongest correlates of reports of affect and life satisfaction probably because it can influence all four stages in the sequence.

4.4.2 Measurement

One of the clearest implications of our model concerns measurement. Because SWB is viewed as an ongoing process, we believe that no single measure is automatically more valid than another measure. Different measures provide information about different stages of SWB, and therefore we strongly advocate multiple measures that tap different stages. When the measures converge, they give greater certainty to the findings. When the measures diverge, however, they can often cast considerable theoretical light on the processes under study. When additional measures are available that help the researcher understand the processes underlying discrepancies between SWB measures (e.g., of norms or self-concept), the researcher can be in an especially strong position to comprehend the processes underlying SWB.

Another implication of our model is that the time when emotion measures are collected can strongly influence the findings. As Kahneman (1999) aptly noted, there can be large differences between predicted, on-line, and recalled emotional experiences. Researchers need to be aware of these differences, and be cognizant of the implications of measurement timing for the results and conclusions of their research.

4.5 Future Research

We have outlined a time-sequential framework for understanding SWB. However, more studies are needed to fully understand and test our framework. First, future research should further examine the relations between different stages in the sequence. We are beginning to understand many of the transition processes that relate one stage to the next, but much more work is needed in this area. Future research should also continue to address the variables that cause dissociations between different stages in the sequence. For example, we know little about the accuracy of recall for moods versus emotions (see Frijda 1993, for a discussion of the distinction between the two). We also know little about how cultural referencing effects (Heine et al. 2002) might influence reports of on-line versus recalled emotions. Schwarz and Strack (1999) suggest that people's evaluations of specific targets, such as marriage or one's car, might depend more on preformed evaluations of the object, whereas evaluations of more global domains might be subject to greater situational influences at the time of measurement. Our framework suggests that measuring on-line versus recalled versus global evaluations of both broad and narrow domains would be a valuable extension of Schwarz and Strack's work.

Future research should also be designed to explore the factors that moderate the relation between the various stages in the SWB sequence. For example, if people have a clear and salient self-concept related to a specific emotion, their recall of it might be less related to their on-line experience of that emotion because they rely heavily on self-concept. Similarly, a person might have a strong belief about the emotions that accompany certain situations, and therefore might rely on situational beliefs when the emotion is recalled. People's memories of their emotions might depend on personality factors such as the stability of self-esteem (Kernis et al. 1998), and stability in emotions might moderate the relation between affect and life satisfaction. Seidlitz and Diener (1998) found that women recall affective experiences more accurately, and that this is probably due to more elaborated cognitions of those experiences. This finding points to the importance of exploring individual and group differences, as well as the social conditions that influence the relation between recalled affect and on-line experience. A factor that might moderate the relation between recalled affect and global judgments of satisfaction is the value that people place on emotions. Thus, our framework points to many interesting research questions about factors that moderate the relation between the sequential stages of SWB.

4.6 Conclusions

In this chapter, we offer an integrative framework of SWB. Our framework is a sequential one that begins with the events that cause emotional experience and ends with broad conclusions people reach in evaluating their lives, based in part on their recall and reconstruction of their emotional experiences. We believe that the framework we present has a number of advantages. First, it covers the entire span of experience, not just the early or late stages. Second, we provide hypotheses and evidence about some of the important transition processes between the phases of the SWB sequence, including how such processes could be influenced by factors such as personality or culture. Third, our framework has clear implications for the theoretical meaning of different measures of SWB. The present framework suggests a new integrative, temporally oriented perspective on SWB, and points to possible limitations of past research.

References

Andrews FM, Withey SB (1976) Social indicators of well-being: America's perception of life quality. Plenum Press, New York

Balatsky G, Diener E (1993) Subjective well-being among Russian students. Soc Indic Res 28:225–243

Baltes PB, Mayer KU (1999) The Berlin aging study: aging from 70–100. Cambridge University Press, Cambridge

Biswas-Diener R, Diener E (2001) Making the best of a bad situation: satisfaction in the slums of Calcutta. Soc Indic Res 55:329–352

Bradburn NM (1969) The structure of psychological well-being. Aldine, Chicago

Brickman P, Campbell DT (1971) Hedonic relativism and planning the good society. In: Appley MH (ed) Adaptation level theory: a symposium. Academic, New York, pp 287–302

Brickman P, Coates D, Janoff-Bulman R (1978) Lottery winners and accident victims: Is happiness relative? J Pers Soc Psychol 36:917–927

Brief AP, Weiss H (2002) Organizational behavior: affect in the workplace. Annu Rev Psychol 53:279–307

Buchanan GM, Seligman MEP (eds) (1995) Explanatory style. Erlbaum, Hillsdale

Cacioppo J, Berntson G, Sheridan J, McClintock M (2000) Multilevel integrative analyses of human behavior: social neuroscience and the complementing nature of social and biological approaches. Psychol Bull 126:829–843

Campbell A, Converse PE, Rodgers W (1976) The quality of American life. Russell Sage, New York

Canli T, Zhao Z, Kang E, Gross J, Desmond JE, Gabrieli JDE (2001) An fMRI study of personality influences on brain reactivity to emotional stimuli. Behav Neurosci 115:33–42

Cantor N, Sanderson CA (1999) Life task participation and well-being: the importance of taking part in daily life. In: Kahneman D, Diener E, Schwarz N (eds) Well-being: the foundations of hedonic psychology. Russell Sage Foundation, New York, pp 230–243

Christianson SA (1992) Remembering emotional events: potential mechanisms. In: Christianson SA (ed) The handbook of emotion and memory: research and theory. Erlbaum, Hillsdale, pp 307–340

Cohen D, Vandello J, Rantilla AK (1998) The sacred and the social: Cultures of honor and violence. In: Gilbert P, Andrews B (eds) Shame: interpersonal behavior, psychopathology, and culture. Series in affective science, Oxford University Press, New York, pp 261–282

Crawford-Solberg E, Diener E, Wirtz D, Lucas RE, Oishi S (2002) Wanting, having, and satisfaction: examining the role of desire discrepancies in satisfaction with income. J Pers Soc Psychol 83:725–734

Csikszentmihalyi M, Larsen R (1978) Intrinsic rewards in school crime. Crime Delinquency 214:322–335

Danner DD, Snowdon DA, Friesen WV (2001) Positive emotions in early life and longevity: findings from the nun study. J Pers Soc Psychol 80:804–813

Dermer M, Cohen SJ, Jacobsen E, Anderson RA (1979) Evaluative judgments of aspects of life as a function for vicarious exposure to hedonic extremes. J Pers Soc Psychol 37:247–260

Diener E (1984) Subjective well-being. Psychol Bull 95:542–575

Diener E, Biswas-Diener R (2002) Will money increase subjective well-being: a literature review and guide to needed research. Soc Indic Res 57:119–169

Diener E, Diener C (1995) The wealth of nations revisited: income and quality of life. Soc Indic Res 36:275–286

Diener E, Fujita F (1995) Resources, personal strivings, and subjective well-being: a nomothetic and idiographic approach. J Pers Soc Psychol 68:926–935

Diener E, Larsen RJ (1984) Temporal stability and cross-situational consistence of affective, behavioral, and cognitive responses. J Pers Soc Psychol 47:871–883

Diener E, Larsen RJ, Emmons RA (1984) Bias in mood recall in happy and unhappy persons. Paper Presented at the 92nd Annual Convention of the American Psychological Association, Toronto

Diener E, Lucas RE (1999) Personality and subjective well-being. In: Kahneman D, Diener E, Schwarz N (eds) Well-being: the foundations of Hedonic psychology. Russell Sage Foundation, New York, pp 213–229

Diener E, Lucas RE, Oishi S, Suh EM (2002a) Looking up and down: weighting good and bad information in life satisfaction judgments. Pers Soc Psychol Bull 28:437–445

Diener E, Nickerson C, Lucas RE, Sandvik E (2002b) Dispositional affect and job outcomes. Soc Indic Res 59:229–259
Diener E, Oishi S, Lucas RE (2003) Personality, culture and subjective well-being: emotional and cognitive evaluations of life. Annu Rev Psychol 59:229–259
Diener E, Scollon CK, Oishi S, Dzokoto V, Suh EM (2000) Positivity and the construction of life satisfaction judgments: global happiness is not the sum of its parts. J Happiness Stud 1:159–176
Diener E, Suh E (1997) Measuring quality of life: economic social, and subjective indicators. Soc Indic Res 40:189–216
Eid M, Diener E Global judgments of subjective well-being: situational variability and long-term stability. In: Zumbo B (ed) Social indicators/quality of life research methods: methodological issues and developments, Kluwer, Dordrecht (in press)
Elliot AJ, Thrash TM (2002) Approach-avoidance maturation in personality: approach and avoidance temperament and goals. J Pers Soc Psychol 82:804–818
Elliot AJ, Chirkov VI, Kim Y, Sheldon KM (2001) A cross-cultural analysis of avoidance (relative to approach) personal goals. Psychol Sci 12:505–510
Emmons RA (1986) Personal strivings: an approach to personality and subjective well-being. J Pers Soc Psychol 51:1058–1068
Emmons RA, Diener E (1985) Factors predicting satisfaction judgments: a comparative examination. Soc Indic Res 16:157–168
Feldman Barrett L (1997) The relationships among momentary emotion experiences, personality descriptions, and retrospective ratings of emotion. Pers Soc Psychol Bull 23:1100–1110
Fleeson W (2001) Toward a structure- and process-integrated view of personality: traits as density distributions of states. Journal of Personality and Social Psychology 80, pp 1011–1027 American Psychological Assn, US
Fleeson W, Malanos AB, Achille NM (2002) An intraindividual process approach to the relationship between extraversion and positive affect: is acting extraverted as good as being extraverted? J Pers Soc Psychol 83:1409–1422
Fredrickson BL (1998) What good are positive emotions? Rev Gen Psychol 2:300–319
Frijda N (1993) Moods, emotion episodes, and emotions. In: Lewis M, Haviland JM (eds) Handbook of emotions. Guilford Press, New York, pp 381–403
Frisch MB, Cornell J, Villanueva M, Retzlaff PJ (1992) Clinical validation of the quality of life inventory. A measure of life satisfaction for use in treatment planning and outcome assessment. Psychol Assess 4:92–101
Fujita FD (1991) An investigation of the relationship between extraversion, neuroticism, positive affect, and negative affect. Unpublished Master's thesis, University of Illinois at Urbana-Champaign
Harker L, Keltner D (2001) Expressions of positive emotion in women's college yearbook pictures and their relationship to personality and life outcomes across adulthood. J Pers Soc Psychol 80:112–124
Harter JK, Schmidt FL, Hayes TL (2002) Business-unit-level relationship between employee satisfaction, employee engagement, and business outcomes: a meta-analysis. J Appl Psychol 87:268–279
Headey B, Wearing A (1989) Personality, life events, and subjective well-being: toward a dynamic equilibrium model. J Pers Soc Psychol 57:731–739
Heine SJ, Lehman D, Peng K, Greenholtz J (2002) What's wrong with cross-cultural comparisons of subjective Likert scales? The reference-group effect. J Pers Soc Psychol 82:903–918
Ito TA, Cacioppo JT (1999) The psychophysiology of utility appraisals. In: Kahneman D, Diener E, Schwarz N (eds) Well-being: the foundations of hedonic psychology. Russell Sage Foundation, New York, pp 453–469
Jackson B, Sellers RM, Peterson C (2002) Pessimistic explanatory style moderates the effect of stress on physical illness. Pers Individ Differ 32:567–573
James W (1884) What is an emotion? Mind 4:188–204

Jocklin V, McGue M, Lykken DT (1996) Personality and divorce: a genetic analysis. J Pers Soc Psychol 71:288–299
Kahneman D (1999) Objective happiness. In: Kahneman D, Diener E, Schwarz N (eds) Well-being: the foundations of hedonic psychology. Russell Sage Foundation, New York, pp 3–25
Keltner D, Kring AM, Bonanno GA (1999) Fleeting signs of the course of life: facial expression and personal adjustment. Curr Dir Psychol Sci 8:18–22
Kernis MH, Whisenhunt CR, Waschull SB, Greenier KD, Keegan D, Berry AJ, Herlocker CE, Anderson CA (1998) Multiple facets of self-esteem and their relations to depressive symptoms. Pers Soc Psychol Bull 24:657–668
King LA, Scollon CK, Ramsey C, Williams T (2000) Stories of life transition: subjective well-being and ego development in parents of children with down syndrome. J Res Pers 34:509–536
Koivumaa-Honkanen H, Honkanen R, Koskenvuo M, Viinamaki H, Kaprio J (2002) Life dissatisfaction as a predictor of fatal injury in a 20 year follow-up. Acta Psychiatr Scand 105:444–450
Koivumaa-Honkanen H, Honkanen R, Viinamaki H, Heikkila K, Kaprio J, Koskenvuo M (2001) Life satisfaction and suicide: a 20-year follow-up study. Am J Psychiatry 158:433–439
Lambert EG, Hogan NL, Barton SM (2001) The impact of job satisfaction on turnover intent: a test of a structural measurement model using a national sample of workers. Soc Sci J 38:233–250
Larsen RJ, Diener E (1987) Affect intensity as an individual difference characteristic: a review. J Res Pers 21:1–39
Larsen RJ, Fredrickson BL (1999) Measurement issues in emotion research. In: Kahneman D, Diener E, Schwarz N (eds) Well-being: the foundations of hedonic psychology. Russell Sage Foundation, New York, pp 40–60
Larsen RJ, Ketelaar T (1991) Personality and susceptibility to positive and negative emotional states. J Pers Soc Psychol 61:132–140
Larsen RJ, Diener E, Cropanzano RS (1987) Cognitive operations associated with individual differences in affect intensity. J Pers Soc Psychol 53:767–774
Larsen RJ, Diener E, Emmons RA (1986) Affect intensity and reactions to daily life events. J Pers Soc Psychol 51:803–814
Lee AY, Aaker JL, Gardner WL (2000) The pleasure and pains of distinct self-construals: the role of interdependence in regulatory focus. J Pers Soc Psychol 78:1122–1134
Levine LJ (1997) Reconstructing memory for emotions. J Exp Psychol Gen 126:165–177
Levine LJ, Prohaska V, Burgess SL, Rice JA, Laulere TM (2001) Remembering past emotions: the role of current appraisals. Cogn Emot 15:393–417
Lucas RE, Fujita F (2000) Factors influencing the relation between extraversion and pleasant affect. J Pers Soc Psychol 79:1039–1056
Lucas RE, Clark AE, Georgellis Y, Diener E (2004) Unemployment alters the set point for life satisfaction. Psychol Sci 15:8–13
Lucas RE, Clark AE, Georgellis Y, Diener E (2003) Re-examining adaptation and the setpoint model of happiness: reactions to changes in marital status. J Pers Soc Psychol 84:537–539
Lucas RE, Diener E, Suh EM (1996) Discriminant validity of well-being measures. J Pers Soc Psychol 71:616–628
Lyubomirsky S, Ross L (1999) Changes in attractiveness of elected, rejected, and precluded alternatives: a comparison of happy and unhappy individuals. J Pers Soc Psychol 76:988–1007
Lyubomirsky S, Tucker KL (1998) Implications of individual differences in subjective happiness for perceiving, interpreting, and thinking about life events. Motiv Emot 22:155–186
Lyubomirsky S, King L, Diener E (2002) Happiness is a good thing: a theory of the benefits of positive affect. Unpublished paper, University of California at Riverside
Magnus K, Diener E, Fujita F, Pavot W (1993) Extraversion and neuroticism as predictors for objective life events: a longitudinal analysis. J Pers Soc Psychol 65:1046–1053

Markus HR, Kitayama S (1994) The cultural construction of self and emotion: implications for social behavior. In: Kitayama S, Markus HR (eds) Emotion and culture: empirical studies of emotional influences. American Psychological Association, Washington, pp 89–131
McFarland C, Ross M, DeCourville N (1987) Women's theories of menstruation and biases in recall of menstrual symptoms. J Pers Soc Psychol 57:522–531
McKnight C, Hebner E, Suldo S (2002) Relationships among stressful life events, temperament, problem behavior, and global life satisfaction in adolescents. Psychol Sch 39:677–687
Newcomb MD, Bentler PM, Collins C (1986) Alcohol use and dissatisfaction with self and life: a longitudinal analysis of young adults. J Drug Issues 63:479–494
Oettingen G, Seligman MEP (1990) Pessimism and behavioral signs of depression in East versus West Berlin. Eur J Soc Psychol 20:207–220
Oishi S (2002) The experiencing and remembering of well-being: a cross-cultural analysis. Pers Soc Psychol Bull 28:1398–1406
Oishi S (2004) On-line versus retrospective recall of emotions in the prediction of the longevity of dating relationships. University of Virginia. Unpublished manuscript
Oishi S, Diener E (2001) Goals, culture, and subjective well-being. Pers Soc Psychol Bull 27:1674–1682
Ortony A, Clore GL, Collins A (1988) The cognitive structure of emotions. Cambridge University Press, New York
Pavot W, Diener E, Colvin R, Sandvik E (1991) Further validation of the satisfaction with life scale: evidence for the cross-method convergence of well-being measures. J Pers Assess 57:149–161
Peterson C, Seligman ME (1984) Causal explanations as a risk factor for depression: theory and evidence. Psychol Rev 91:347–374
Peterson C, Maier SF, Seligman MEP (1993) Learned helplessness: a theory for the age of personal control. Oxford University Press, New York
Reis HT, Gable SL (2000) Event-sampling and other methods for studying everyday experience. In: Reis HT, Judd CM (eds) Handbook of research methods in social and personality psychology. Cambridge University Press, New York, pp 190–222
Reis HT, Gable SL (2003) Toward a positive psychology of relationships. In: Keyes CML, Haidt J (eds) Flourishing: positive psychology and the life well-lived. American psychological association, Washington, pp 129–159
Robinson MD (2000) Running from William James' bear: a review of preattentive mechanisms and their contributions to emotional experience. Cogn Emot 12:667–696
Robinson MD, Clore GL (2002) Episodic and semantic knowledge in emotional self-report: evidence for two judgment processes. J Pers Soc Psychol 83:198–215
Robinson MD, Johnson JT, Shields SA (1998) The gender heuristic and the database: factors affecting the perception of gender-related differences in the experience and display of emotions. Basic Appl Soc Psychol 20:206–219
Ross M, Wilson AE (2000) Constructing and appraising past selves. In: Schacter DL, Scarry E (eds) Memory, brain, and belief. Harvard University Press, Cambridge, pp 231–258
Rozin P, Royzman EB (2001) Negativity bias, negativity domains, and contagion. Pers Soc Psychol Rev 5:296–320
Rusting C, Larsen RJ (1997) Extraversion, neuroticism and susceptibility to positive and negative affect; a test of two theoretical models. Pers Individ Differ 22:607–612
Sandvik E, Diener E, Seidlitz L (1993) Subjective well-being: the convergence and stability of self-report and non-self report measures. J Pers 61:317–342
Schimmack U, Diener E, Oishi S (2002) Life-satisfaction is a momentary judgment and a stable personality characteristic: the use of chronically accessible and stable sources. J Pers 70:345–384
Schimmack U, Oishi S, Diener E, Suh E (2000) Facets of affective experiences: a framework for investigations of trait affect. Pers Soc Psychol Bull 26:655–668
Schwarz N, Strack F (1999) Reports of subjective well-being: judgmental processes and their methodological implications. In: Kahneman D, Di- ener E, Schwarz N (eds) Well-being: the foundations of hedonic psychology, Russell Sage Foundation, New York, pp 61–84

Schwarz N (1996) Cognition and communication: judgmental biases, research methods, and the logic of conversation. Erlbaum, Hillsdale

Schwarz N, Clore GL (1983) Mood, misattribution, and judgments of well-being: informative and directive functions of affective states. J Pers Soc Psychol 45:513–523

Schwarz N, Scheuring B (1988) Judgments of relationship satisfaction: inter- and intraindividual comparisons as a function of questionnaire structure. Eur J Soc Psychol 18:485–496

Schwarz N, Strack F, Kommer D, Wagner D (1987) Soccer, rooms, and the quality of your life: mood effects on judgments of satisfaction with life in general and with specific domains. Eur J Soc Psychol 17:69–79

Scollon CN, Kim-Prieto C, Diener E (2004) Strengths and weaknesses of the experience sampling technique. J Happiness Stud 4:5–34

Seidlitz L, Diener E (1998) Sex differences in the recall of affective experiences. J Pers Soc Psychol 74:262–271

Seligman MEP (1995) The optimistic child. Harper Collins, New York

Seligman MEP (2002) Authentic happiness. Free Press, New York

Smith S, Razzell P (1975) The pools' winners. Calibon Books, London

Smith J, Fleeson W, Geiselmann B, Settersten RA Jr, Kunzmann U (1999) Sources of well-being in very old age. In: Baltes PB, Mayer KU (eds) The Berlin aging study: aging from 70 to 100. Cambridge University Press, New York, pp 450–471

Strack F, Martin L, Schwarz N (1988) Priming and communication: social determinants of information use in judgments of life satisfaction. Eur J Soc Psychol 18:429–442

Suh EM, Diener E, Fujita FD (1996) Events and subjective well-being: only recent events matter. J Pers Soc Psychol 70:1091–1102

Suh EM, Diener E, Oishi S, Triandis HC (1998) The shifting basis of life satisfaction judgments across cultures: emotions versus norms. J Pers Soc Psychol 74:482–493

Tamir M, Robinson M (2004) Knowing good from bad: the paradox of neuroticism, negative affect, and evaluative processing. J Pers Soc Psychol 87:913–925

Tamir M, Robinson M, Clore G (2002) The epistemic benefits of trait- consistent mood states: an analysis of extraversion and mood. J Pers Soc Psychol 83:663–677

Tellegen A, Lykken DT, Bouchard TJ, Wilcox KJ, Segal NJ, Rich S (1988) Personality similarity in twins reared apart and together. J Pers Soc Psychol 54:1031–1039

Tennen H, Affleck G (2002) Benefit-finding and benefit-reminding. In: Snyder CR, Lopez SJ (eds) Handbook of positive psychology. Oxford University Press, New York, pp 584–597

Thomas DL, Diener E (1990) Memory accuracy in the recall of emotions. J Pers Soc Psychol 59:291–297

Veenhoven R (1993) Happiness in nations: subjective appreciation of life in 55 nations 1986–1990. RISBO, Rotterdam

Winkielman P, Knaeuper B, Schwarz N (1998) Looking back at anger: reference periods change the interpretation of emotion frequency questions. J Pers Soc Psychol 75:719–728

Wirtz D, Kruger J, Scollon CN, Diener E (2004) What to do on spring break? Predicting future choice from online versus recalled affect. Psychol Sci 14:520–524

Zelenski JM, Larsen RJ (1999) Susceptibility to affect: a comparison of three personality taxonomies. J Pers 67:761–791

Zullig KJ, Valois RT, Huebner ES, Oeltmann JE, Drane W (2001) Relationship between perceived life satisfaction and adolescents' substance abuse. J Adolesc Health 29:279–288

Chapter 5
Subjective Well-Being, Homeostatically Protected Mood and Depression: A Synthesis

Robert A. Cummins

Abstract This chapter concerns the idea that Subjective Wellbeing (SWB) is managed by a system of psychological devices which have evolved for this purpose. It is proposed that this management is actually directed at the protection of Homeostatically Protected Mood, as the major component of SWB. We normally experience HPMood as a combination of contentment, happiness and arousal. A theoretical description of this construct is offered that can account for many of the commonly observed empirical characteristics of SWB data. It is further proposed that when homeostasis fails, due to the overwhelming nature of a negative challenge, people lose contact with HPMood and experience the domination of negative rather than positive affect. If this condition is chronic, people experience the clinical condition we call depression.

Keywords Subjective wellbeing • HPMood • Depression • Happiness • Homeostasis

5.1 Introduction

The purpose of this chapter is to draw together three threads that have been occupying our research over the past decade or so. The first of these is the composition and character of Subjective Wellbeing (SWB). The second is homeostatic process by which SWB is normally held within a narrow range of values. And the third is the nature of the relationship between SWB, homeostasis and depression. Each of these areas will now be addressed and the nature of their integration explained.

The single most important thing about Subjective Wellbeing is that it is positive. It is normal for people to feel good about themselves. This feature of SWB data is evident in the results of all publications that investigate the construct, and very explicitly in data gathered by the Australian Unity Wellbeing Index project (Cummins et al. 2003). This project measures the SWB of the Australian population several times

R. A. Cummins (✉)
Deakin University, Melbourne, VIC, Australlia
e-mail: cummins@deakin.edu.au

A. Delle Fave (ed.), *The Exploration of Happiness*, Happiness Studies Book Series,
DOI: 10.1007/978-94-007-5702-8_5, © Springer Science+Business Media Dordrecht 2013

each year. Each survey involves a telephone interview of 2,000 new respondents, nation wide. The project commenced in April 2001 and the accumulated data from the 21 surveys conducted to April 2009 provide much of the data for this chapter.

The scale used to measure and conceptualize SWB is the Personal Wellbeing Index (International Wellbeing Group 2006) which has a unique construction. It is designed as the first-level deconstruction of the highly abstract question ‘How satisfied are you with your life as a whole’. In order to achieve this design aim, each of the eight items has two important characteristics. The first lies in the semi-abstract nature of each question, such as ‘How satisfied are you with your relationships’. This format is deliberately non-specific. It allows the response that people give to be dominated by non-specific mood affect (the essence of SWB, see later), slightly flavored with cognitions attached to relationships. A more specific question, such as ‘How satisfied are you with your friends’, would elicit a more cognitively driven response.

The second characteristic of the eight items (domains) that comprise the Personal Wellbeing Index is that when they are regressed together against ‘Satisfaction with life as a whole’, each one contributes unique variance. These matters of theoretical construction are elaborated in the test manual.

Each item is rated on an end-defined 0–10 scale (Jones and Thurstone 1955) that is anchored by ‘completely dissatisfied’ and ‘completely satisfied’ (see Cummins and Gullone 2000 for an argument as to why this form of scale is superior to a Likert scale). The data are then averaged across the eight domains for each respondent and the result transformed onto a 0–100 scale. The cumulative results for the Australian population can be found in Cummins et al. (2009) and show the distribution of SWB in this population. The distribution of SWB is approximately normal within the positive (satisfied) sector of the response scale. The mean is 75 points and only 4.4 % of respondents score 50 or below. It is, thus, normal to feel positive about oneself.

5.1.1 Subjective Wellbeing Stability

The second intriguing feature of SWB is its stability. This can be demonstrated by two kinds of data. One uses the mean scores from population surveys and the other are data obtained from individuals.

To take the population data first, two reports (Cummins 1995, 1998) first demonstrated the extraordinary level of SWB stability, and therefore predictability, of population mean scores. The first of these chapters combined data from population surveys performed in various Western countries. It included highly diverse studies, each one having been conducted by different researchers, using different scales of measurement, at different times over the decades 1970–1990. When the results were transformed onto a 0–100 scale it was found that the mean of the 16 surveys was 75 points and their standard deviation was 2.5. Thus, using two standard deviations on either side of the mean to define a normal range, the SWB mean scores extend between 75 ± 5 or 70–80 points.

Of course, this estimate of the normal range is heavily contaminated with error variance resulting from the many methodological differences between the studies. Much greater stability is revealed by the 21 Australian Unity Wellbeing Index surveys. Over the nine-year period of these surveys (2001–2009) SWB varied over a total range of 3.1 points (73.2–76.3). Using these 21 values as data yields a mean of 74.93 points, a standard deviation of 0.75 and, therefore, a normative range of 73.43–76.43 points. In other words, the mean score of a random survey of people in Australia can be predicted, with 95 % certainty, to lie within a 3.0 % point range. There is no precedent in the literature for such extraordinary stability in measures of SWB.

The above analyses have been based on the use of sample means as data. When measures of SWB from individuals are used, the standard deviation is much larger, but is also very consistent. Using the data from the Australian population (Cummins et al. 2009) the mean is 74.93 points, the standard deviation is 12.36 and so the normal range is 50.21–99.64 points. It can be seen that this range rather neatly fits the positive sector of the distribution, however it is certainly too large to be regarded as the true normal range. This is because the calculation involves the 4.4 percent of people who fall below this range and, as will be argued later, this is considered to indicate the presence of pathology. So, a new range can be calculated omitting these values. This produces a mean of 76.45 and a standard deviation of 10.13. Using these new values, the normal range becomes 56.19–96.71.

A further slight adjustment can be made on the assumption that the true distribution is normal and that the 4.4 % of values that fall below 50 are overly representative of low values within the normative range. This idea is supported by the slightly higher frequency of scores above, compared to below the median of 75 points, over the range of 50–100 (see Cummins et al. 2009). So, if the above calculation is adjusted downward slightly it gives a normal range for SWB between 55 and 95 and a mean of 75 points. Of course, this is only an approximation and requires verification by other methodologies, but it is a reasonable basis for further theory-building.

5.2 How can these Data Patterns be Explained?

It is apparent from these results that SWB is exhibiting some determined characteristics as follows: (1) It is highly stable. (2) It is normally restricted to the positive half of the dissatisfied—satisfied continuum. (3) It shows a normal distribution consistent with what Psychologists refer to as an individual difference and is under strong genetic determination (e.g. Lykken and Tellegen 1996). That is, its distribution is consistent with SWB being an innate personal characteristic.

So what kind of a system might be responsible for such behavior? There is a substantial literature in which researchers describe the models they imagine responsible for SWB. The earliest of these were the 'Physical and Spiritual Model' (Liu 1975), the 'Lewinian Lifespace Model' (Campbell et al. 1976) and the 'Two-Dimensional Conceptual Model' (Andrews and Withey 1976) but all of these were mainly concerned with the composition of Quality of Life into its objective and subjective components. It took more than a decade for researchers to incorporate some of the psychometric characteristics described above into their models.

The first of these pioneers were two Australian researchers, Headey and Wearing (Headey et al 1984a, b; Headey and Wearing 1986, 1987, 1989). Using data from a panel study they observed that people appeared to have a 'set-point' for their SWB. That in the absence of significant life events, people tended to maintain a relatively steady level of SWB, and that if an event caused SWB to change then, over time, it tended to regain its previous level. They called this their 'Dynamic Equilibrium Model' and considered the management of SWB to be vested in a genetically-inbuilt psychological system, based in stable personality characteristics, which had the primary purpose of maintaining self-esteem. They characterized the positive sense of SWB as a 'Sense of Relative Superiority' because it had the consequence of making people feel that their subjective life experience is better than average for the population.

The second researchers to take up this challenge were Stones and Kozma (1991) who proposed their 'Magical Model of Happiness'. Like Headey and Wearing, they depicted SWB as a self-correcting process that maintains stability around set-points that differ between individuals. They also regard SWB stability as a function of a dispositional system (Kozma et al. 2000 now referred to this as the 'Propensity Model'). However, they also found that the propensity for stability could not be entirely explained through personality variables alone, and that the best predictor of future SWB was the level of past SWB.

All of these data are consistent with the idea, also proposed by other authors (Hanestad and Albrektsen 1992; Nieboer 1997; Ormel 1983; Ormel and Schaufeli 1991) that SWB is neurologically maintained in a state of dynamic equilibrium. However, these earlier models did not attempt to account for the nature of the relationship between SWB in dynamic equilibrium, and other demographic and psychological variables. This feature requires that theoretical attention be given to the processes of SWB management, which we call SWB homeostasis.

In 1998, Cummins first used the term 'homeostasis' to describe the basic mechanism underpinning SWB management. The term implies an analogy between the physiological management of internal body states, such as body temperature, and the management of SWB. While the homeostatic management of body temperature lies within the autonomic system, SWB is considered to be managed by dispositional, genetically pre-wired, neurological systems.

The term, 'homeostasis', is charged with meaning. Describing management in these terms makes very clear predictions concerning the relationship between SWB and other variables. The variable being managed, SWB, must conform to the standard performance requirements of homeostatic systems, and these include the three characteristics that have been previously listed. In addition to these, other characteristics should also be displayed if SWB management may be considered homeostatic. These include the following:

1. There must be a threshold value which is being defended by the homeostatic processes. There must also be evidence that, as this value is approached, the

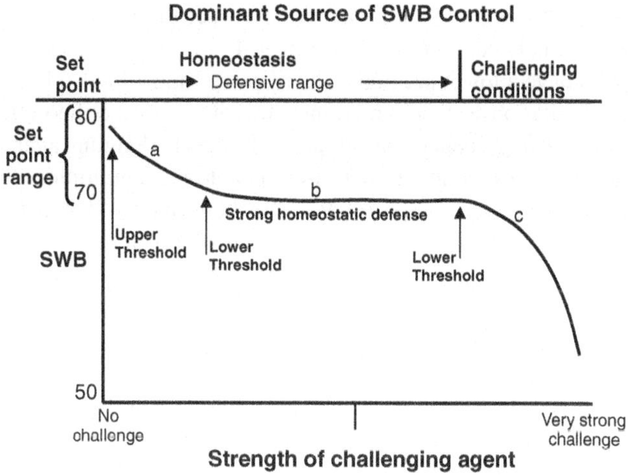

Fig. 5.1 Changing levels of SWB as homeostasis is challenged

system works harder than normal to retain control. Then, as the threshold value is exceeded, there must be evidence that homeostasis has failed and is no longer controlling the level of SWB.

2. Following homeostatic defeat, over time the system should act to regain control. If this is successful, the level of SWB should return to a stable approximation of its set-point.
3. The aim of homeostasis is to maintain the variable it is managing within a narrow range of values. Thus, SWB must evidence a 'set-point-range' which reflects the moment-to-moment range in which SWB will normally be found for each individual. The magnitude of this range may also be an individual difference, with some ranges being more tightly controlled than others.
4. SWB should respond to variables that either enhance or challenge the operation of the homeostatic system. But the nature of the relationship with such variables should be consistent with the operation of a homeostatic system. The implications of these requirements are illustrated with the aid of Fig. 5.1.

This Figure comprises several parts as follows:

1. The vertical axis shows the 0–100 scale of SWB and includes an illustrative set-point-range of 70–80 points.
2. The lower horizontal axis shows the strength of a negative challenge to SWB, such as might be delivered by poverty or anxiety.
3. The upper horizontal axis shows the dominant source of control. The source of control changes depending on whether the strength of the challenging agent is weak or strong.
4. The curving 'response line' depicts the changes in SWB due to changes in the strength of challenge. The upper (80 point) and lower (70 point) margins of the set-point-range are identified as 'thresholds' and indicated by vertical arrows.

5. An important limitation in this depiction is that the position of the response line will vary between people, determined by their set-point-range. Thus, for people who have a lower set-point, the response line will also be lower.
6. A second limitation in this depiction is that it shows the theoretical outcome of the combined influences of supportive and challenging agents acting on the homeostatic system at any one time. Due to such multiple influences, any empirical investigation of the relationship between SWB and its sources of influence can only be expected to approximate the pattern that is shown

The predictions derived from Fig. 5.1 are as follows:

1. Under conditions of zero threat, SWB will average to its set-point, which in this case is 75 points.
2. As mild sources of threat are experienced, the level of SWB will vary within its set-point-range. Moreover, its position within the range will be a probability statement determined by the balance of good and bad momentary experience and the resilience of the homeostatic system. Thus, a sustained environment where good experience dominates, will allow SWB to average within the upper portion of the set-point-range. A sustained challenge will cause SWB to average within the lower portion of the set-point-range. However, the extent of such fluctuations is predicted to be quite modest. Since the magnitude of the set-point-range is calculated to be around 10–12 % points (Cummins et al. 2008, Sect. 3.8.1), the total movement of SWB due to such influences will not be more than a few percentage points on either side of the set-point. This phase is shown in Fig. 5.3a.
3. As the strength of threat intensifies, the strength of the homeostatic defence also increases in an attempt to maintain stable levels of SWB. The result is phase (b) in which homeostasis manages to hold-the-line and prevents SWB from decreasing below its lower threshold value of 70 points. The evidence for this lower threshold to be located at about 70 points, on average, is presented in Cummins (2003). Importantly during this phase (b), the value of SWB is insensitive to changing levels of the challenging agent. That is, although the strength of the challenge is increasing, SWB will be held steady at the value of the lower threshold. This phase will continue as long as the homeostatic system is effective. However, at some higher strength of challenge, homeostasis will be overwhelmed.
4. Once the strength of the challenging agent becomes too strong for homeostatic management, the value of SWB enters phase (c). In this phase the dominant source of control has shifted from homeostatic processes to the challenging agent. Now the value of SWB is sensitive to the strength of the challenging agent and, as the strength of the challenge increases, the value of SWB will sharply fall.

Within this theoretical and predictive background, two kinds of elaboration will now be presented. The first concerns the nature of the homeostatic system itself. The second examines empirical evidence for the proposition that the relationship between SWB and challenging agents conforms to the outcomes predicted by this homeostatic model.

5.3 The Mechanisms of Homeostasis

It is proposed that the mechanism of homeostasis comprises two kinds of buffers as External an Internal. The two major External buffers are wealth and relationships.

5.3.1 The External Buffers

There are serious misconceptions as to what money can and cannot do in relation to personal wellbeing. Most importantly, it cannot shift the set-point to create a perpetually happier person. Set-points for SWB are proposed to be under genetic control (Cummins et al. 2003; Lykken and Tellegen 1996), so in this sense money cannot buy happiness. No matter how rich someone is, their average level of SWB cannot be sustained higher than their set-point range. People adapt readily to luxurious living standards, so genetics trumps wealth after a certain level of income has been achieved.

The real power of wealth is to protect wellbeing through its capacity to be used as a flexible resource to assist homeostasis (Cummins 2000). It does this by allowing people to minimize the unwanted challenges they experience in their daily life. Wealthy people pay others to perform tasks they do not wish to do themselves. Poor people, who lack such financial resources, must fend for themselves to a much greater extent. As a consequence their level of SWB is far more at the mercy of their environment. Because of this influence, SWB rises with income, but only up to a certain level. In Australia SWB rises with gross household income up to about $91,000–$120,000, but at higher incomes no further systematic rise in SWB can be detected (Cummins et al. 2009).

This pattern of the relationship between SWB and wealth is much the same when comparisons are made between countries (e.g World Bank 1997). It is what the economists refer to as Decreasing Marginal Utility; that rising income has its strongest effect to raise wellbeing at low income levels.

This curvilinear, asymptotic relationship is a typical output from a management system that can be saturated. That is, supplying more of some relevant resource (money) may or may not cause an increase in output. The effect of the resource is dependent on the level of deprivation. Thus, for poor people or countries, all other things being equal, increased wealth will increase SWB. But this will continue only up to some ceiling value for SWB (about 80 points), which reflects full and unrestricted functioning of the system in relation to that resource.

These results are also convergent evidence that the power of money lies in its usefulness as a flexible resource, which can be used to diminish the probability of encountering chronic negative life events. In terms of Fig. 5.1, this represents a shift from being dominantly at (c) and (b) to being dominantly at (a) and (b). That is, the resource of money has an effect in two stages. The first is the most obvious. As income rises, fewer people within the sample experience homeostatic defeat due to some factor that can be ameliorated through the resource of money. This represents the significant rise in SWB up to $91,000–$120,000. Above this level of income there will be a continued, but gradual rise in average SWB, as progressively more of the sample experience a lifestyle that allows their SWB to inhabit the upper portion of their set-point-range. However, of course, in any population sample there will always be some people with a level of SWB that lies below its set-point irrespective of the financial situation. The cause will be attributable to situations, such as parenting unpleasant children, which are not amenable to resolution through money.

A further observation from Fig. 5.1 is that SWB plateaus at about 80 points. There are two reasons for this. First it reflects limitations to the upward movement of SWB due to resource saturation of the homeostatic system. Second it reflects the normal distribution of set-points within any population sample.

A second major external resource is a relationship with another adult that involves mutual sharing of intimacies and support. Almost universally, the research literature attests to the power of such relationships to moderate the influence of potential stressors on SWB (for reviews see Henderson 1977; Sarason et al. 1990). It might be expected that the power of the two external buffers to protect SWB is additive, and this is demonstrated by the interaction between income and household structure in Fig. 5.2. These results are drawn from Cummins et al. (2009).

The top line shows the effect of income on the SWB of people living only with their partner. It can be seen that this living arrangement makes people very

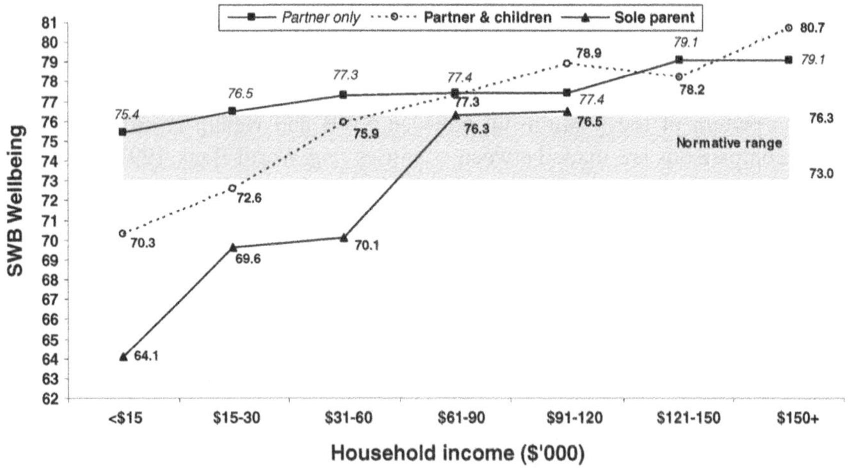

Fig. 5.2 The interaction between income and household composition

resilient. Even at the lowest household income, SWB lies in the middle of the normal range. Notably, it does not change very much as income increases, rising only 3.7 points across the entire income range. This is another example of the ceiling created by homeostasis—that money as a resource cannot be used to chronically increase SWB beyond the set-point range for each individual. Thus, since the mean SWB of this group is already in the normal range at the lowest income level, the only influence of higher income is to increase the probability that SWB lies towards the top of its set-point-range.

The second line in this figure shows partners who are living with one or more children. Their resilience is lower because children drain the emotional and financial resources of their parents. Thus, at the lowest income level, SWB lies well below the normal range. This reflects the demands made by children exceeding the resources available to some parents. However, at a gross household income of $31,000–$60,000 the financial and relationship resources become sufficient for homeostatic control to be returned. Thereafter, rises in income do not statistically differ between the couples with and without children.

The situation for single parents is more extreme. Since they lack the resource of an adult partnership, they require an income of $61,000–$90,000 to regain homeostatic control. It is also informative to observe that the three-person household (partners plus child) on low income has higher SWB than the two-person household (one parent plus child). This is quite the reverse of the relative wellbeing normally assumed by Economists (see Trigger 2003). They usually calculate household wellbeing as income discounted by the number of people in the household. This method is incorrect in relation to SWB. The increased consumption of goods by the additional adult is more than offset by the instrumental and emotional support they are able to provide.

In summary, both income and relationship support are highly effective external buffers for SWB homeostasis, and their combined influence appears to be additive, as expected. Moreover, the relationship between SWB and both of the external buffers conforms fairly well to the predictions of homeostasis. But this is only the external aspects of homeostatic control. There is an additional set of buffers to assist homeostasis that are internal to each person.

5.3.2 *Internal Buffers*

When the external buffers are not strong enough to prevent something bad happening, all is not lost. At the heart of homeostasis is a set of genetically programmed internal buffers. These comprise protective devices that are brought into action because SWB is being threatened. At the simplest level these involve the automatic processes of adaptation and habituation. These act over time to make us less aware of challenging experiences. An example of this phenomenon can be observed in relation to the gradual loss of motor functioning with age. Because people adapt both their behavior and expectations to fit the reality of their diminishing motor capacity, the loss of functioning only weakly engages awareness, and so fails to threaten SWB. The extent to which this can happen is amazing. Many people with Multiple Sclerosis, which induces a gradual loss of motor functioning, report normal levels of SWB even when they lose the capacity to independently breathe and require mechanical ventilation (Bach et al. 1991).

We propose that this kind of adaptation is assisted by a set of cognitive buffers. These use cognition to restructure reality and so to minimize the impact of unavoidable negative experiences. The ways that the cognitive buffers do this are highly varied. For example, one can find meaning in the event ('God is testing me'), fail to take responsibility for the failure ('it was not my fault') or regard the failure [dropping a vase] as useful ('I did not like that old vase anyway and now I can buy another'). There are many such devices that essentially involve maintaining a sense of control, collectively called Secondary Control techniques (Rothbaum et al. 1982).

There are other ways of restructuring reality that do not involve the sense of control. One is protection of self-esteem through 'splintering'. For example, when dropping the vase, one may think 'Well, so I am a bit clumsy, but it doesn't matter because I am so good at [making friends, cooking, writing, etc.]. Here, the cause of the bad event has been relegated to some aspect of performance that the person regards as unimportant to their sense of identity. People may also employ optimistic temporal restructuring, e.g "Well this has been a bad day, but tomorrow will be better". And so on.

No doubt there are many more such cognitive devices but they all serve the same purpose. Some explanation or reason for the negative experience has been found that allows the person to feel that their sense of self and ability to understand the world is intact. Their sense of threat has been dissipated and SWB is assisted to return within its set-point range. A detailed discussion of these internal buffering systems is provided in Cummins and Nistico (2002) and Cummins et al. (2002).

It is important to note, in relation to all this, that the homeostatic system, as described, has the role of maintaining a positive sense of wellbeing that is both non-specific and highly personalized. It is concerned only with the abstract core feelings that the individual has about themselves and only in the most general sense. One consequence of this is to imbue people with a 'positivity bias' in relation to themselves. So, people generally feel they are 'superior' to others, or better than average (Diener et al. 1999; Headey and Wearing 1988, 1989). They believe they are luckier, happier and more moral (Andrews and Withey 1976). This is all part of the general positive bias that is 'value added' by the brain to such thought processes and which leads, under the normal circumstances of living, to a generalized positive self-view (Taylor and Brown 1988; Weinstein 1989).

It is these characteristics that allow the personal sense of wellbeing to be so defendable against the slings and arrows of misfortune. Because these self-beliefs are held at such an abstract level, specific instances of personal bad-luck or incompetence that might otherwise damage the sense of personal wellbeing, can be dismissed by the internal buffers in order to maintain the abstract belief. This general idea is not novel. For example, Tesser et al. (1989) provide empirical support for a model of Self-Evaluation Maintenance, in which the self recognizes good performance on a variety of dimensions, yet aspires to 'be good at' (or personally values) only a few such dimensions. Thus, one's own performance is not threatening to self-evaluation provided that failures are confined to non-valued dimensions in life. Such processes assist people who are deaf, for example, to maintain a positive self-view (Bat-Chava 1994).

So, SWB is heavily defended and this hints at the importance of maintaining positive feelings about the self. But SWB is generally acknowledged to be a mixture of affect and cognition. So is this what homeostasis is actually defending?

5.4 What is Homeostasis Defending?

Most contemporary theorists regard the measurement of SWB, obtained through a verbal or written response, to involve both affective and cognitive processes. This was first recognized by Campbell et al. (1976) who suggested that this amalgam should be measured through questions of 'satisfaction'. This form of question has since become standard for SWB measurement. However, relatively little research has been directed to examining the relative contribution of affect and cognition. Certainly the two components are separable (Lucas et al. 1996) but whether, as claimed by Diener et al. (2004), SWB represents a dominantly cognitive evaluation, is moot. To the contrary, recent research (Davern et al. 2007) points to the essence of SWB as a construct these authors call 'Core Affect'.

The term Core Affect was coined by Russell (2003) to describe a neurophysiological state that is experienced as a feeling and which may be conceptualized as a deep form of trait affect, or mood. He describes it as analogous to felt body temperature in that it is always there, can be accessed when attention is drawn to it, extremes are most obvious, and it exists without words to describe it. Naturally enough, Russell regarded Core Affect in conformity with the circumplex model of affect, comprising a blend of hedonic (pleasant-unpleasant) and arousal values (activation–deactivation).

The reason Davern et al. were attracted to adopt this term was Russell's determined description of Core Affect as a biologically influenced mood, rather than an emotion. Specifically, he made it clear that while the feeling of Core Affect can be consciously accessed, it is not tied to any specific object in the manner of an emotional response. Instead it is a mood-state, which refers to how the individual senses themselves in an abstract but personal way. If the perception of the Core Affect feeling becomes linked to a cause, then the feeling state makes the transition from mood to emotion.

A more recent account of Core Affect, however, has muddied this distinction. Russell (2009) makes it clear that Core Affect may be involved in either moods or emotions. He proposes that Core affect may become directed at something and, indeed, that Core Affect may itself be changed by a variety of other influences. Thus a new term is required that describes the mood affect associated with homeostasis. We propose the term Homeostatically Protected Mood (HPMood) to describe a feeling state with the following characteristics:

1. It is a biologically determined positive mood that comprises the most basic experienced feeling. It is hard-wired for each individual, comprising the tonic state of affect that provides the activation energy, or motivation, for behavior.
2. HPMood is not only the dominant affective constituent of SWB, as determined by Davern et al., but also the basic steady-state, set-point that homeostasis seeks to defend.
3. HPMood perfuses all higher process, including personality (for a review of the neurobiology of personality see Depue and Collins 1999), memory and momentary experience. It perfuses all cognitive processes to some degree, but most strongly the rather abstract notions of self (e.g. I am a good person). These self-perceptions are held at strength of positivity that approximates the set-point HPMood.

Consistent with this fundamental role, we hypothesise that the process of evolution has advantaged the survival of individuals who experience a level of HPMood corresponding to 70–80 points pleasant or positive. Notably, SWB values above and below this range are associated with different forms of cognitive functioning, which each have their own advantages and disadvantages. For example, higher SWB is associated with enhanced friendliness and problem solving (Lyubomirsky et al. 2005), but has the downside of poor information processing, an exaggerated sense of control, and therefore enhanced risk-taking. Lower SWB, on the other hand, leads to more careful information processing (for a review see Forgas 2008) and greater preparedness for threat (Sweeny et al. 2006) but carries the risk of low motivation and even depression if it becomes chronic. Thus, we propose, 75 points is a trade-off between the advantages and disadvantages of higher and lower values. This level then, on average, constitutes the optimum set-point range for SWB, corresponding to the most adaptive range of mood affect.

As measured by Davern et al. (2007), HPMood can be parsimoniously represented as the combined affects of happiness, contentment, and excitement. These represent the activated and deactivated pleasant quadrants of the affective circumplex (for a review of affect see Cropanzano et al. 2003). Davern et al. tested the relative strength of HPMood, cognition, and all five factors of personality, as predictors of SWB. The cognitive component of SWB was measured using 7 items derived from Multiple Discrepancies Theory (Michalos 1985). These items address the perceived gap between what the respondent currently has and general life aspirations, what age-matched others have, the best one has had in the past, expected to have 3 years ago and expects to have after 5 years, deserves and needs.

Consistent with previous research, all three components correlated significantly with SWB and with one another. However, when the variances were controlled by structural equation modelling, it was demonstrated that affect and MDT are the dominant components of SWB. Indeed, after accounting for both of these, personality made only a very small contribution to the explanation of SWB variance. The simplified model from this chapter is reproduced in Fig. 5.3. The personality

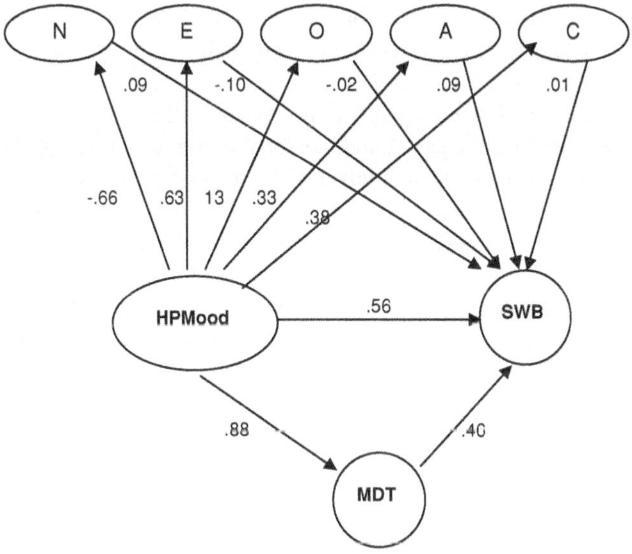

Fig. 5.3 Simplified affective-cognitive model of SWB (Davern et al. 2007)

factors are designated as: N—Neuroticism, E—Extraversion, O—Openness, A—Agreeableness, C—Conscientiousness.

This finding has been replicated using independent data (Blore 2008), from which we deduce that mood is the dominant component of SWB. We also propose HPMood as the driving force behind individual set point levels in SWB homeostasis.

Over the past few years, there have been several critics of set-point theory (e.g. Fujita and Diener 2005; Headey 2008; Lucas 2007) based on observed changes in the SWB of individuals over time. The first two of these chapters report data from the German Socio-Economic Panel Study from 1984 to 2000. For example, Fujita and Diener showed that, over this 16 year period, about 10 % of the sample showed a change in satisfaction of about 30 points. They conclude that SWB "can and does change for some people."

All of these authors interpret changes in SWB over time as indicative that the set-point has changed. However, homeostasis theory and HPMood offers an alternative possibility. We propose that when people report a level of SWB outside their set-point range, they have simply lost contact with their set-point mood-affect. That is, at the time of data collection, their level of SWB was being controlled by a powerful emotional state which overwhelmed homeostasis, and so dominated their awareness. Within this alternative conception, each person's HPMood and set-point remains unaltered and the abnormal level of SWB reflects attention to the dominating emotional state.

This alternative conception also predicts that, over time, external and internal resources will be directed to the restoration of homeostasis, as has been discussed. If these resources are sufficient, they will reduce the perceived level of challenge to the point that that homeostatic control is restored. When this occurs, the person regains contact with their HPMood, and their reported SWB returns to its set-point-range.

An alternative and interesting possibility is that set-points do, in fact, change systematically over the life span (Land, personal communication). Results from the Framingham Heart Longitudinal Study has found that a number of physiological parameters that must be maintained within homeostatic bounds for survival–such as blood pressure–have "optimal" values that change with age. Such changes are adaptive, in that individuals who deviate far from the optimal values are at higher risk of mortality. Through analogy, is possible that SWB set-points also change over the life-span, quite possibly in an upward direction to compensate for functional loss. We certainly find (Cummins et al. 2005) that the highest levels of SWB occur in old age.

5.5 SWB and Depression

From all of the above, SWB can be predominantly characterized as a stable positive mood that is normally held within a narrow range of values for each individual. The level of this set-point-range is genetically determined and a homeostatic system acts to defend our perception of Homeostatically Protected Mood as our normal sense of affective self. SWB is an approximation of HPMood, which is why, under normal conditions, SWB approximates the set-point-range. However, if the level of challenge to SWB becomes too great, homeostasis fails. When this occurs, our affective experience is redirected from HPMood to the dominating emotion, either positive or negative.

Under such conditions, SWB no longer conforms to the set-point-range of HPMood. If it is made to be higher, due to the induction of an acute positive emotion, then the processes of adaptation and habituation soon return the dominant affective experience back to HPMood. Whether, as claimed by Positive Psychology, it is possible to maintain a substantially higher level of positive affect than the set-point-range on a chronic basis is moot. As of this writing no reliable empirical evidence is available to support such a view, which is also counter to homeostatic theory.

If SWB is made to be lower, through the induction of a negative emotion, then the same processes of adaptation and habituation, together with secondary control, will normally allow recovery back to the set-point-range of HPMood. However, if the negative challenge is chronic and strong, recovery may not take place. The homeostatic system has a limited capacity to recover normal functioning and if this capacity is chronically exceeded, recovery will not occur. Under such conditions, homeostasis will be persistently defeated, and the loss of positive affect will remain as the dominating experience. This is the reason that poor countries have such low SWB. They contain a high proportion of their population who are living under conditions of chronic homeostatic defeat. We have recently reported the same phenomenon in Australia through a study of 4,000 people providing care for

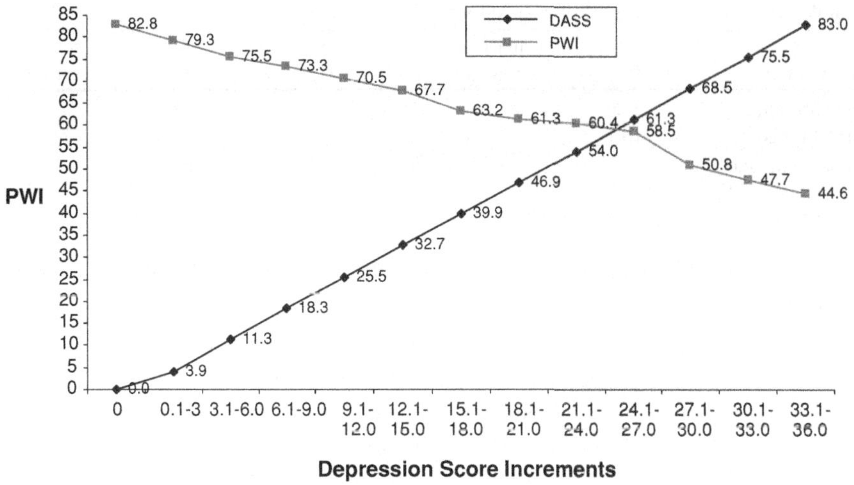

Fig. 5.4 PWI and DASS depression means across increments of depression scores

a disabled family member at home (Cummins et al. 2007). Their mean level of SWB was 59 points.

We propose that this loss of positive mood is the essence of depression. The relationship between SWB and the Depression sub-scale of the Depression, Anxiety and Stress Scale (Lovibond and Lovibond 1995) is shown below using cumulative data from our surveys.

Figure 5.4 is based on DASS increments of 3.0 points. This increment size is the smallest range for our cumulative sample that allows an $N > 20$ per group. The group Ns range from 785 for depression group (0.1–3.0) to 23 for group (33.1–36.0) The Figure reveals a clearly inverse relationship between the falling PWI and rising depression scores. However, two observations pertain. First, the rate of SWB decrease is far less than the rate of depression score increase. This is consistent with resistance to SWB change. Second, the rate at which PWI falls appears to slow at a depression score of 15.1–18 (*moderate*) through to 24.1–27.0 (severe), with these depression categories defined by reference to the scale manual The amount of change between these four contiguous scores, which differ sequentially by <2 points, can be contrasted with the amount of change in the four immediately higher and lower scores, which all differ sequentially by >2 point, as shown below.

Table 5.1 shows the changing rate of PWI decrease and the appearance of the homeostatic plateau over the middle grouping. As the level of challenge (depression score) increases from 0 to 18, the value of SWB moves down in a linear fashion to approximate the start of the homeostatic plateau. This is phase (a) in Fig. 5.1. Then, over the depression rating of 18–27, homeostasis 'holds-the-line' and SWB remains relatively unchanged (Phase b). However, at a depression score of 27 or greater, homeostasis is overwhelmed; control of SWB passes from the homeostatic system to the challenging agent, and SWB drops markedly (Phase c).

Table 5.1 The relative degree of change for the PWI and DASS

Depression increments	6.1—9.0 (normal) to 15.1—18.0 (moderate)	15.1—18 (moderate) to 24.1—27.0 (severe)	24.1—27.0 (severe) to 33.1—36.0 (extreme)
DASS range	21.6	21.4	21.7
PWI range	10.1	4.7	13.9
Phases of change related to Fig. 5.1	(a)	(b)	(c)

A more detailed description of these results in relation to Homeostatic Theory is as follows.

1. In reference to Fig. 5.4, the fact that the highest PWI value corresponds to a depression score of zero is logical. Moreover, the value of 82.8 points is consistent with theory, based on two assumptions, both of which have been previously argued. The first is that the normal range for individual set-points is 55–95, and the second is that the normal set-point-range is 5–6 points on either side of the mean. Then, if zero depression is taken as implying that each SWB value approximates the top of each set-point-range, then this SWB distribution extends from $(55 + 6) = 61$ to $(95 + 6) \approx 100$. The half-way point on this range is 80.5 points, which is a reasonable approximation to the measured value of 82.8 points.
2. The start of the plateau in Fig. 5.4 occurs at a PWI of 63.2 and it ends at 58.5 points. This is also consistent with theoretical prediction. In a previous report using population sample mean scores from 19 different countries as data, the overall mean was found to be 74.4 and the standard deviation 5.1 points (Cummins 2003). It was also calculated that 70 points, corresponding to about one standard deviation below the mean, was the lowest value on the plateau, below which the value SWB fell sharply.

The current data set uses the scores of individuals rather than population mean scores. The overall mean is 73.40 and the standard deviation is much larger as 14.54. One standard deviation below the mean is 58.9 points, which approximates the lower end of the plateau in Fig. 5.4. Thus, the results using either population mean scores as data, or the scores of individuals as data, converge to yield a common finding. This is that SWB values lying one standard deviation below the normative mean approximate the boundary between homeostatic maintenance and homeostatic defeat. Thus, SWB values that lie much further from the normative mean than one standard deviation are likely under the control of the challenging agent rather than homeostasis (refer to Fig. 5.1).

Perhaps the most interesting question raised by these results, is why plotting the PWI against the DASS shows this plateau effect. The DASS items measure the extent of negative affect (down-hearted and blue), life being meaningless, low personal self-worth, etc. In other words, even quite strong negative feelings about the self can co-exist with normal or even high levels of SWB. There is, thus, a degree of disconnection between negative and positive feelings about the self as long as homeostasis is functional. This is highly adaptive in allowing negative feeling to be acknowledged while also maintaining normal levels of SWB. However, once the level of challenge becomes overwhelming, positive feelings about the self evaporate and it is possible that true depression sets-in.

5.6 Summary and Conclusions

It has been argued that Subjective Wellbeing (SWB) is managed by a system of psychological devices which have evolved for this purpose. Further, that this management is actually directed at the protection of Homeostatically Protected Mood, which is the major component of SWB. We experience HPMood as a combination of contentment, happiness and arousal thus giving us a normally positive view of ourselves. It is further proposed that when homeostasis fails, due to the overwhelming nature of a negative challenge, people lose contact with HPMood and experience the dominance of negative rather than positive affect. When this condition is chronic, people experience depression.

Acknowledgments I thank Ann-Marie James for her assistance in the preparation of this manuscript and Australian Unity for their continued support of this research. We also acknowledge the key role played by Renee Bear, Wendy Kennedy and Melissa Weinberg in coining the term Homeostatically Protected Mood.

References

Andrews FM, Withey SB (1976) Social indicators of well-being: American's perceptions of life quality. Plenum Press, New York

Bach JR, Campagnolo DI, Hoeman S (1991) Life satisfaction of individuals with Duchenne Muscular Dystrophy using long-term mechanical ventilatory support. Am J Phys Med Rehabil 70:129–135

Bat-Chava Y (1994) Group identification and self-esteem of deaf adults. Personality Soc Psychology Behav 20(5):494–502

Blore JD (2008) Subjective wellbeing: an assessment of competing theories. Unpublished Doctoral Thesis. Deakin University, Geelong

Campbell A, Converse PE, Rodgers WL (1976) The quality of American life: perceptions, evaluations, and satisfactions. Russell Sage Foundation, New York

Cropanzano R, Weiss HM, Hale JMS, Reb J (2003) The structure of affect: reconsidering the relationship between negative and positive affectivity. J Manage 29(6):831–858

Cummins RA (1995) On the trail of the gold standard for life satisfaction. Soc Indic Res 35:179–200

Cummins RA (1998) The second approximation to an international standard of life satisfaction. Soc Indic Res 43:307–334

Cummins RA (2000) Personal income and subjective well-being: a review. J Happiness Stud 1:133–158

Cummins RA (2003) Normative life satisfaction: measurement issues and a homeostatic model. Soc Indic Res 64:225–256

Cummins RA, Eckersley R, Pallant J, Van Vugt J, Misajon R (2003) Developing a national index of subjective wellbeing: the Australian unity wellbeing index. Soc Indic Res 64:159–190

Cummins RA, Gullone E (2000) Why we should not use 5-point Likert scales: the case for subjective quality of life measurement. In: Paper presented at the second international conference on quality of life in cities. National University of Singapore, Singapore. http://www.deakin.edu.au/research/acqol/instruments/PWI/2000-QOL_in_Cities-Likert_Scales-ss.doc

Cummins RA, Gullone E, Lau ALD (2002) A model of subjective well being homeostasis: the role of personality. In: Gullone E, Cummins RA (eds) The universality of subjective wellbeing indicators: social indicators research series. Kluwer, Dordrecht, pp 7–46

Cummins RA, Hughes J, Tomyn A, Gibson A, Woerner J, Lai L (2007) Australian Unity Wellbeing Index: Report 17.1 The Wellbeing of Australians—Carer Health and Wellbeing. Melbourne: Australian Centre on Quality of Life, School of Psychology, Deakin University. Retrieved 30 June 2009, from http://www.deakin.edu.au/research/acqol/index_wellbeing/index.htm

Cummins RA, Nistico H (2002) Maintaining life satisfaction: the role of positive cognitive bias. J Happiness Stud 3:37–69

Cummins RA, Woerner J, Gibson A, Lai L, Weinberg M, Collard J (2008) Australian Unity Wellbeing Index: Report 19.0. The Wellbeing of Australians—Links with exercise, nicotine and alcohol. Australian Centre on Quality of Life, School of Psychology, Deakin University, Melbourne. ISBN 978 1 74156 113 5. Retrieved 30 June 2009, from http://www.deakin.edu.au/research/acqol/index_wellbeing/index.htm

Cummins RA, Woerner J, Gibson A, Weinberg M, Collard J, Chester M (2009) Australian Unity Wellbeing Index: Report 21.0. The Wellbeing of Australians—Gambling, Chocolate and Swine Flu. Australian Centre on Quality of Life, School of Psychology, Deakin University, Melbourne. ISBN 978 1 74156 125 8. Retrieved 2 Sept 2009, from http://www.deakin.edu.au/research/acqol/index_wellbeing/index.htm

Cummins RA, Woerner J, Tomyn A, Knapp T, Gibson A (2005) Australian unity wellbeing index: Report 14.0—"The Wellbeing of Australians—Personal Relationships". Australian Centre on Quality of Life, School of Psychology, Deakin University, Melbourne. Retrieved, 30 June 2009, from http://www.deakin.edu.au/research/acqol/index_wellbeing/index.htm

Davern M, Cummins RA, Stokes M (2007) Subjective wellbeing as an affective/cognitive construct. J Happiness Stud 8(4):429–449

Depue RA, Collins PF (1999) Neurobiology of the structure of personality: dopamine facilitation of incentive motivation and extraversion. Behav Brain Sci 22:491–569

Diener ED, Napa Scollon CN, Lucas RE (2004) The evolving concept of subjective well-being: the multifaceted nature of happiness. In: Costa PT, Siegler IC (eds) Recent advances in psychology and aging. Elsevier Science BV, Amsterdam, pp 187–219

Diener ED, Suh EM, Lucas RE, Smith HL (1999) Subjective well-being: three decades of progress. Psychol Bull 125(2):276–302

Forgas JP (2008) The strange cognitive benefits of mild dysphoria: on the evolutionary advantages of not being too happy. In: Forgas JP, Haselton MG, von Hippel W (eds) Evolutionary psychology and Social cognition. Psychology Press, New York, pp 107–121

Fujita F, Diener E (2005) Life satisfaction set point: stability and change. J Pers Soc Psychol 88(1):158–164

Hanestad BR, Albrektsen G (1992) The stability of quality of life experience in people with Type 1 diabetes over a period of a year. J Adv Nurs 17:777–784

Headey B (2008) The set-point theory of well-being: negative results and consequent revisions. Soc Indic Res 85(3):389–404

Headey B, Holmstrom E, Wearing A (1984a) The impact of life events and changes in domain satisfactions on well-being. Soc Indic Res 15:203–227

Headey B, Holmstrom E, Wearing A (1984b) Well-being and ill-being: different dimensions? Soc Indic Res 14:115–139

Headey B, Wearing A (1986) The sense of relative superiority—central to well-being. University of Melbourne, Melbourne

Headey B, Wearing A (1987) A theory of life satisfaction and psychological distress. University of Melbourne, Melbourne

Headey B, Wearing A (1988) The sense of relative superiority—central to well-being. Soc Indic Res 20:497–516
Headey B, Wearing A (1989) Personality, life events, and subjective well-being: toward a dynamic equilibrium model. J Pers Soc Psychol 57:731–739
Henderson S (1977) The social network, support and neurosis. the function of attachment in adult life. Br J Psychiatry 131:185–191
International Wellbeing Group (2006) Personal wellbeing index manual. Deain University, Melbourne. Retrieved 30 June 2009, from http://www.deakin.edu.au/research/acqol/instruments/wellbeing_index.htm
Jones LV, Thurstone LL (1955) The psychophysics of semantics: an experimental investigation. J Appl Psychology 39(1):31–36
Kozma A, Stone S, Stones MJ (2000) Stability in components and predictors of subjective well-being (SWB): implications for SWB structure. In: Diener E, Rahtz DR (eds) Advances in quality of life: theory and research. Kluwer Academic Publishers, Great Britain, pp 13–30
Liu B (1975) Quality of life: concept, measure and results. Am J Econ Sociology 34:1–13
Lovibond SH, Lovibond PF (1995) Manual for the depression anxiety stress scales. Psychology Foundation, Sydney
Lucas RE (2007) Adaptation and the set-point model of Subjective Well-Being: Does happiness change after major life events? Curr Directions Psychological Sci 16(2):75–79
Lucas RE, Diener E, Suh E (1996) Discriminant validity of well-being measures. J Pers Soc Psychol 71:616–628
Lykken D, Tellegen A (1996) Happiness is a stochastic phenomenon. Psychol Sci 7:186–189
Lyubomirsky S, King L, Diener E (2005) The benefits of frequent positive affect: does happiness lead to success? Psychol Bull 131(6):803–855
Michalos AC (1985) Multiple discrepancies theory (MDT). Soc Indic Res 16:347–413
Nieboer AP (1997) Life events and well-being: a prospective study on changes in well-being of elderly people due to a serious illness event or death of the spouse. Thesis Publishers, Amsterdam
Ormel J (1983) Neuroticism and well-being inventories. Measuring traits or states? Psychol Med 13:165–176
Ormel J, Schaufeli WB (1991) Stability and change in psychological distress and their relationship with self-esteem and locus of control: a dynamic equilibrium mode. J Pers Soc Psychol 60:288–299
Rothbaum F, Weisz JR, Snyder SS (1982) Changing the world and changing the self: a two-process model of perceived control. J Pers Soc Psychol 42:5–37
Russell JA (2003) Core affect and the psychological construction of emotion. Psychol Rev 110(1):145–172
Russell JA (2009) Emotion, core affect, and psychological construction. Cognition Emotion 23(7): 1259–1283. ISSN: 1464–0600
Sarason IG, Sarason BR, Pierce GR (1990) Social support: the search for theory. J Soc Clin Psychol 9:137–147
Stones MJ, Kozma A (1991) A magical model of happiness. Soc Indic Res 25:31–50
Sweeny K, Carroll PJ, Sheppard JA (2006) Is optimism always best? Future outlooks and preparedness. Curr Directions Psychological Sci 15(6):302–306
Taylor SE, Brown JD (1988) Illusion and well-being: a social psychological perspective on mental health. Psychol Bull 103:193–210
Tesser A, Pilkington CJ, McIntosh WD (1989) Self-evaluation maintenance and the mediational role of emotion: the perception of friends and strangers. J Pers Soc Psychol 57:442–456
Trigger D (2003) Does the way we measure poverty matter? National Centre for Social and Economic Modelling, University of Canberra
Weinstein ND (1989) Optimistic biases about personal risks. Science 246:1232–1233
World Bank (1997) World Values Surveys; GNP/capita purchasing power estimates from World Bank, World Development Report, 1997. Retrieved 30 June 2009, from http://margaux.grandvinum.se/SebTest/wvs/articles/folder_published/article_base_56

Chapter 6
Know Thyself and Become What You Are: A Eudaimonic Approach to Psychological Well-Being

Carol D. Ryff and Burton H. Singer

Abstract In an effort to strengthen conceptual foundations of eudaimonic well-being, key messages from Aristotle's *Nichomacean Ethics* are revisited. Also examined are ideas about positive human functioning from existential and utilitarian philosophy as well as clinical, developmental, and humanistic psychology. How these perspectives were integrated to create a multidimensional model of psychological well-being (Ryff 1989a) is described, and empirical evidence supporting the factorial validity of the model is briefly noted. Life course and socioeconomic correlates of well-being are examined to underscore the point that opportunities for eudaimonic well-being are not equally distributed. Biological correlates (cardiovascular, neuroendocrine, immune) of psychological well-being are also briefly noted as they suggest possible health benefits associated with living a life rich in purpose and meaning, continued growth, and quality ties to others. We conclude with future challenges in carrying the eudaimonic vision forward.

Keywords Autonomy • Environmental mastery • Eudaimonia • Personal growth • Positive relations with others • Purpose in life • Self-acceptance

6.1 Introduction

Eudaimonia, a term that is simultaneously difficult to spell, pronounce, and understand, is the new buzzword in studies of happiness and well-being. I (Ryff) encountered eudiamonia nearly two decades ago and first used the term to challenge

C. D. Ryff (✉)
Institute on Aging and Department of Psychology,
University of Wisconsin-Madison, Madison, MI, USA
e-mail: cryff@wisc.edu

B. H. Singer
Office of Population Research/Institute on Aging,
Princeton University/University of Wisconsin-Madison, Madison, USA

A. Delle Fave (ed.), *The Exploration of Happiness*, Happiness Studies Book Series, DOI: 10.1007/978-94-007-5702-8_6,

prevailing conceptions of subjective well-being focused on assessments of feeling good, contentment, and life satisfaction (Andrews and Withey 1976; Bradburn 1969; Bryant and Veroff 1982; Diener 1984). Drawing on the work of Waterman (1984), I argued that Bradburn's (1969) seminal research on *The Structure of Psychological Well-Being* rested on a mistaken translation of ancient texts, specifically Aristotle's *Nichomachean Ethics*, written in 350 B.C. In these essays, Aristotle stated that the highest of all goods achievable by human action was "eudaimonia." Bradburn, along with others (e.g., utilitarian philosophers from the 19th century) translated the term to mean happiness. Accompanying empirical assessments, as noted above, measured the extent to which people feel good, contented, or satisfied with their lives. The problem with this formulation, however, was that it suggested equivalence between hedonia and eudaimonia, something that was deeply contrary to Aristotle's distinction between the satisfaction of right and wrong desires. Even more troubling was that the essence of eudaimonia—the idea of striving toward excellence based on one's unique potential—was left out. This observation was central to my efforts to articulate a conception of psychological well-being that was explicitly concerned with the development and self-realization of the individual (Ryff 1989a).

Given current interest in the juxtaposition of hedonism and eudaimonism (e.g., Ryan and Deci 2001), it seems wise to revisit the ancients and their descendants in hopes of bringing core meanings of eudaimonia into sharper focus. Thus, in the first section below, we re-examine the writings of Aristotle on the topic of what constitutes the highest of all human goods, and also draw on the work of others who have tried to distill his key messages. In the second section, we discuss "theoretical intermediaries"—namely, other philosophers (existential, utilitarian) or psychologists (developmental, clinical, humanistic) whose work helps to elaborate meanings of positive human functioning. The objective in so doing is to show the various forms that well-being can take, while simultaneously to make clear the full scope of prior thinking that informed the Ryff (1989a) model of psychological well-being.

Following the conceptual recapitulation, we briefly highlight select empirical findings that have emerged from this model of psychological of well-being, with emphasis given to two primary points. The first is that well-being, construed as growth and human fulfillment, is profoundly influenced by the surrounding contexts of people's lives, and as such, that the opportunities for self-realization are not equally distributed. The second point is that eudaimonic well-being may be consequential for health by promoting effective regulation of multiple physiological systems. Finally, we conclude with observations about intellectual tensions in the study of eudaimonic well-being and suggest that finding that which is "intermediate," as advised by Aristotle, may offer a constructive way forward.

6.2 Aristotle and Eudaimonia: Whatever was He Saying?

The *Nichomachean Ethics* (translated by Ross 1925) are replete with strange terms (e.g., "moral incontinence"), grammatical obscurities, digressions and winding argumentative sequences, all of which led Johnston (1997) to wonder whether we are dealing with notes retrieved from the waste basket. Nonetheless, sprinkled along the way sparkling insights and exquisitely distilled thoughts. Many readers may also be sustained by a deep appreciation for how hard Aristotle was thinking in his effort to answer the fundamental question of human existence: how should we live? He refused to rely on cant or religious dogma, and instead, sought to build a reasoned argument with well-articulated propositions and carefully defined terms. This was demanding work, such that even Aristotle occasionally ran out of steam, ending some chapters with phrases like "so much for these questions."

In evaluating the substance of Aristotle's text, it is important to remember that his objective was not to discern the nature of human well-being; rather, it was to formulate an ethical doctrine that would provide guidelines for how to live. As such, some observations are pertinent to the task at hand, while others are not. Clearly, his opening question: "What is the highest of all goods achievable by human action?" is spot on for any examination of what constitutes a well-lived life. And, his opening answer, issued over 2,000 years ago, is remarkably cogent for current inquiries about human well-being:

> Both the general run of men and people of superior refinement say that it [the highest of all goods achievable by action] is happiness, and identify living well and faring well with being happy; *but with regard to what happiness is they differ*, and the many do not give the same account as the wise. For the former think it is some plain and obvious thing, like pleasure, wealth, or honor (Aristotle/Ross 1925, p. 5).

Much of the *Ethics* is then devoted to disabusing the reader of the idea that happiness consists of satisfying appetites, something he likened to a "life suitable to beasts" (p. 6), or of money-making, or political power, or even amusement and relaxation, reminding us that "serious things are better than laughable things" (p. 263). In challenging the mass of mankind which is "quite slavish in their tastes" (p. 6), he spoke of a dramatically different alternative in which the highest human good was "*activity of the soul in accordance with virtue*, and if there be more than one virtue, in accordance with the best and most complete" (p. 11).

This assertion then brought Aristotle to the next point in the argument: what is the nature of virtue? It is here that his answers are particularly trenchant for contemporary scholars of well-being. A first key meaning of virtue in his view is that it is a kind of mean, aiming at what is *intermediate*:

> Both fear and confidence and appetite and anger and pity and in general pleasure and pain may be felt both too much and too little, and in both cases not well; but to feel them at the right times, with reference to the right objects, towards the right people, with the right motive, and in the right way, is what is both intermediate and best, and this is characteristic of virtue (p. 38).

He then elaborates many other examples of the appropriate middle ground in Book II, Chap. 7—with regard to money, we are to avoid excess and tasteless vulgarity at one extreme, but also deficiency and niggardliness at the other; with regard to honor, too much leads to vanity, while too little results in undue humility; with regard to "giving amusement," excess is buffoonery, and the man who falls short is a boor; and with regard to pleasantness toward others, the obsequious flatterer is at one extreme and the quarrelsome, surly person at the other. Thus, virtue for Aristotle was a state of character concerned with choice in which deliberate actions are taken to avoid excess or deficiency.

However, the good life for him was not just about achieving the mean in all modes of conduct. It clearly involved more, and this is where his writings convey the essential message of eudaimonia: "If happiness is activity in accordance with virtue, it is reasonable that it should be in accordance with the *highest virtue; and this will be that of the best thing in us*" (p. 263). These words bring into high relief Aristotle's strongly teleological perspective—namely, the highest human good involves activities that are goal-directed and have purpose. Most importantly, the essential end point (telos) is *to achieve the best that is within us*. As paraphrased by Johnston (1997): "The excellence of the human being is thus going to be associated with growth towards some final realization of his or her true and best nature" (p. 6).

To summarize, Aristotle was clearly not concerned with the subjective states of feeling happy. Rather, his conception of the highest good towards which we all should be reaching was the task of self-realization, played out individually, each according to his or her own disposition and talent. He was also explicitly concerned with action, not just abstract ideas: "we must become just by doing just acts, and temperate by doing temperate acts" (p. 34). A further point is that Aristotle recognized that other needs must be met as well if we are to achieve the best that is within us: "one will also need external prosperity; for our nature is not self-sufficient for the purpose of contemplation, but our body also must be healthy and must have food and other attention" (p. 268). At the same time, he reminded that "we can do noble acts without ruling earth and sea; for even with moderate advantages one can act virtuously" (p. 268). Finally, it should be noted that Aristotle's essays covered many more topics (e.g., justice, intellectual virtues, friendship) than are summarized here.

The most thoroughgoing distillation of Hellenic eudaimonism in contemporary scholarship is David Norton's (1976) *Personal Destinies: A Philosophy of Ethical Individualism*. Norton begins by paying tribute to the Athenians, specifically the "coherent sensibility of that astonishing culture" (p. 31), and then describes eudaimonism as an ethical doctrine wherein each person is obliged to know and live in truth to his *daimon* (a kind of spirit given to all persons at birth), thereby progressively actualizing an excellence (from the Greek word "arête") consistent with innate potentialities. In his words, eudaimonia translates to "meaningful living conditioned upon self-truth and self-responsibility" (p. xi). It is thus the essence of the two great Greek imperatives: first, to "know thyself" (a phrase inscribed on the temple of Apollo at Delphi), and second, to "choose yourself" or "become what you are" (p. 16).

Adopting a critical perspective, Norton also reminds us that the Hellenic scholars did not believe all human beings were invested with potential excellences in the form of daimons. Instead, they exempted several major classes such as slaves, possibly women [he notes Aristotle's approving citation of the line by Sophocles "A modest silence is a woman's crown" (p. 32)], and perhaps artisans and tradesmen. Further, the Hellenic conception did not give all daimons equivalent worth; rather, they were arranged hierarchically, such that in their final perfection, some individuals would be superior to others. Norton's thoughtful book also provides links between eudaimonism, "from its wellspring in ancient Greece" (p. 42) and other philosophical views (Kierkegaard, Nietzsche, Sartre) as well as psychological accounts of self-actualization (Maslow), some of which are elaborated below.

6.3 Theoretical Intermediaries: Elaborating Meanings of Human Fulfillment

Aristotle's central point, namely that the ultimate aim in life is to strive to realize one's true potential, was accompanied by considerably more detail about virtue, defined as finding the middle ground between excess and deficiency, than about virtue, defined as making the most of one's talents and capacities. For the task of articulating substantive specifics of self-realization, I (Ryff) thus drew on my training as a life-span developmental psychologist, wherein numerous accounts of human growth and development were available (Bühler 1935; Bühler and Massarik 1968; Erikson 1959; Neugarten 1968, 1973). These were valuable for describing the developmental tasks and challenges that confront individuals at different life stages. Ideas from existential and humanistic psychology (Allport 1961; Frankl and Lasch 1959/1992; Maslow 1968; Rogers 1962) were also useful for their reminders that finding meaning and purpose in life is sometimes difficult in a world that is seems meaningless, or horrific (e.g., times of war, Nazi concentration camps). Stated otherwise, existential views brought eudaimonia face-to-face with adversity, something on which the *Nichomacean Ethics* was surprisingly silent. Finally, formulations from clinical psychology were incorporated, particularly those few accounts that attempted to define mental health in positive terms rather than focus on dysfunction (Jahoda 1958; Jung 1933).

Other input came from the writings of two utilitarian philosophers, namely, John Stuart Mill and Bertrand Russell, both of whom agreed wholeheartedly with Aristotle that subjective feelings of happiness are not the ultimate target. Mill's (1893/1989, p. 117) message, in fact, was that happiness would never be achieved if made an end in itself:

> Those only are happy, I thought, who have their minds fixed on some object other than their own happiness, on the happiness of others, on the improvement of mankind, even on some art or pursuit, followed not as a means, but as itself and ideal end. Aiming thus at something else, they find happiness by the way.

Russell (1930/1958), in turn, emphasized that happiness is not something that just happens to us, like having repined fruit fall effortlessly into the mouth, but rather is something for which we must strive and work hard, hence his title *The Conquest of Happiness*. For Russell, happiness depended most importantly on

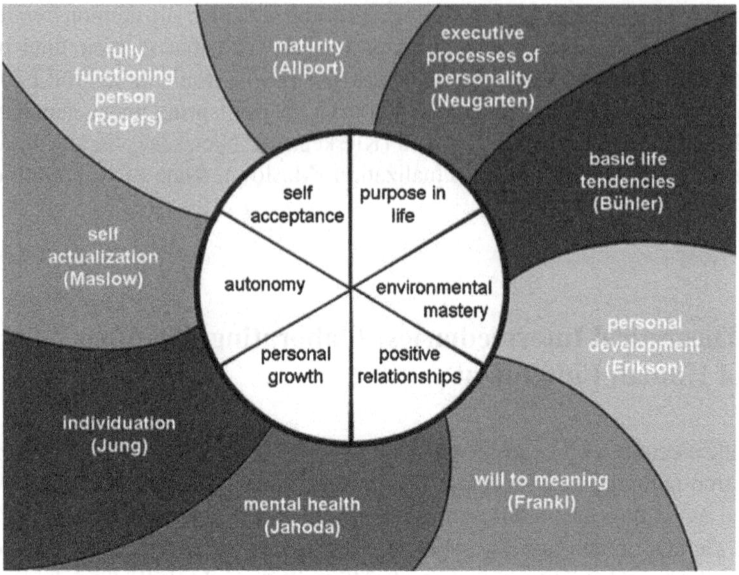

Fig. 6.1 Core dimensions of psychological well-being and their theoretical foundations

"zest," by which he meant having active interest and engagement in life, and by "affection," by which he meant having meaningful bonds of love with significant others.

The central challenge in working with all of the above perspectives was the task of integrating them into some coherent whole. This was a progressive process (see Ryff 1982, 1985, 1989b), wherein the objective was to identify recurrent themes or points of convergence in these many formulations of positive functioning. Figure 6.1 offers a visualization of what resulted from this distillation. In the center of the figure are the six key dimensions of psychological well-being, each of which represent frequently endorsed aspects of what it means to be healthy, well, and fully functioning. Surrounding the six dimensions are their conceptual underpinnings, noted briefly above. How each of the six dimensions grew out of the integration of these prior perspectives is detailed below.

6.3.1 Self-Acceptance

The Greeks admonished that we should know ourselves; that is, strive to accurately perceive our own actions, motivations, and feelings. But many of the above formulations emphasized something more, namely, the need to have positive self-regard. This is defined as a central feature of mental health (Jahoda) as well as a characteristic of self-actualization (Maslow), optimal functioning (Rogers), and maturity (Allport). Life-span theories also emphasized the importance of acceptance of self, including one's past life (Erikson, Neugarten). The process of individuation (Jung) further underscored the need to come to terms with the dark side of one's self (the shadow). Thus, both Erikson's formulation of ego integrity and the Jungian individuation emphasized a kind of self-acceptance that is notably richer than standard views of self-esteem. It is a kind of self-evaluation that is long-term and involves awareness, and acceptance of, both personal strengths and weaknesses.

6.3.2 Positive Relations with Others

All of the above perspectives describe the interpersonal realm as a central feature of a positive, well-lived life. Aristotle's *Ethics,* for example, included lengthy sections on friendship and love, Mill's autobiography offered much detail about the great love of his life, and Russell saw affection as one of the two great sources of happiness. Jahoda, in turn, considered the ability to love to be a central component of mental health, while Maslow described self-actualizers has having strong feelings of empathy and affection for all human beings and the capacity for great love, deep friendship, and close identification with others. Warm relating to others was also posed as a criterion of maturity (Allport). Adult developmental stage theories (Erikson) emphasized the achievement of close unions with others (intimacy) as well as the guidance and direction of others (generativity). Beyond all of these perspectives, philosophical accounts of the "criterial goods" of a well-lived life (Becker 1992) underscored the primacy of love, empathy, and affection. From a cultural perspective, there is near universal endorsement of the relational realm as a key feature of how to live (see Ryff and Singer 1998).

6.3.3 Personal Growth

Of all the aspects of well-being, it is personal growth that comes closest in meaning to Aristotle's eudiamonia, as it is explicitly concerned with the self-realization of the individual. This part of positive functioning is thus dynamic, involving a continual process of developing one's potential. Self-actualization, as formulated by Maslow, and elaborated by Norton, is centrally concerned with realization of personal potential, as is Jahoda's positive conception of mental health. Rogers also described the fully functioning person as having openness to experience in which s/he is continually developing and becoming, rather than achieving a fixed state wherein all problems are solved. Life-span theories (Buhler, Erikson, Neugarten, Jung) also give explicit emphasis to continued growth and the confronting of new challenges at different periods of life.

6.3.4 Purpose in Life

This dimension of well-being draws heavily on existential perspectives, especially Frankl's *search for meaning* vis-à-vis adversity. His logotherapy concerned itself directly with helping people find meaning and purpose in their life travails and suffering. Creating meaning and direction in life is also the fundamental challenge of living authentically according to Sartre. While these views tend to emphasize the will to meaning in the face of what is awful, or absurd in life, themes of purpose are also evident in other literatures less focused on darkness. Russell's emphasis on zest, for example, is fundamentally about actively engaging and having a reflecting stance toward life. Jahoda's definition of mental health gave explicit emphasis to the importance of beliefs that give one a sense of purpose and meaning in life. Allport's definition of maturity included having a clear comprehension of life's purpose, which included a sense of directedness and intentionality. Finally, life-span developmental theories refer to the changing purposes or goals that characterize different life stages, such as being creative or productive in midlife, and turning toward emotional integration in later life.

6.3.5 Environmental Mastery

Jahoda defined the individual's ability to choose or create environments suitable to his/her psychic conditions as a key characteristic of mental health. Life-span developmental theories also emphasize the importance of being able to manipulate and control complex environments, particularly in midlife, as well as the capacity to act on and change surrounding world through mental and physical activities. Allport's criteria of maturity included the capacity to "extend the self," by which he meant being able to participate in significant spheres of endeavor that go beyond the self. Together, these perspectives suggest that active participation in and mastery of the environment are important ingredients of an integrated framework on positive psychological functioning. Although this area of well-being appears to have parallels with other psychological constructs, such as sense of control and self-efficacy, the emphasis on finding or creating a surrounding context that suits one's personal needs and capacities is unique to environmental mastery.

6.3.6 Autonomy

Many of the conceptual frameworks underlying this multidimensional model of well-being emphasize qualities such as self-determination, independence, and the regulation of behavior from within. Self-actualizers, for example, are described as showing autonomous functioning and a "resistance to enculturation" (Maslow). The fully functioning person described by Rogers has an internal locus of evaluation, whereby one does not look to others for approval, but evaluates oneself by personal standards. Individuation is also described as involving a "deliverance from convention" (Jung), in which one no longer belongs to the collective beliefs, fears, and laws of the masses. The existential idea of living in "bad faith" (Sartre 1956) similarly conveys the importance of self-determination and living authentically, rather than following the dogma or dictates of others. Finally, life-span developmentalists (Erikson, Neugarten, Jung) wrote about the importance of turning inward in the later years of life, and relatedly, gaining a sense of freedom of the norms governing everyday life. This aspect of well-being is undoubtedly the most western of all of the above dimensions.

The preceding conceptual distillation required the development of empirical tools to operationalize the aspects of psychological well-being (PWB) described above. The process therein is briefly described below, followed by a select summary of research findings using the PWB assessment scales.

6.4 Empirical Translation: Assessment Tools and Select Findings

6.4.1 Measuring Psychological Well-Being and Evaluating its Validity

The development and evaluation of self-report scales to measure the above six dimensions of well-being was guided by the construct-oriented approach to personality assessment (Wiggins 1980). Of key importance in the empirical translation is the presence of psychological theory that specifies the constructs of interest. Based on such theory, as summarized in the previous section, the first step in the scale construction process is to define high and low scorers on each of the six dimensions. Such definitions are provided in Table 6.1. Multiple independent writers then composed self-descriptive items that fit with these definitions and that could be applicable to both sexes as well as adults of any age. Initial item pools were large (e.g., approximately 80 items for each scale). These were then culled using criteria of face validity (i.e., ambiguity or redundancy of item, lack of fit with scale definition, lack of distinctiveness with items from other scales, inability to produce a variable response, and whether all aspects of the guiding definitions had been covered).

The reduced item pools (32 items per scale, divided between 16 positively and negatively scored items) were then administered to the initial research sample of young, middle, and old-aged adults (Ryff 1989a). Item-to-scale correlations were then computed to refine the item pools. The construct-oriented approach requires that each item correlate more highly with its own scale than another scale. Items

Table 6.1 Definitions of theory-guided dimensions of well-being

Self-acceptance

High scorer: Possesses a positive attitude toward the self; acknowledges and accepts multiple aspects of self including good and bad qualities; feels positive about past life

Low Scorer: Feels dissatisfied with self; is disappointed with what has occurred in past life; is troubled about certain personal qualities; wishes to be different than what he or she is

Positive relations with others

High scorer: Has warm, satisfying, trusting relationships with others; is concerned about the welfare of other others; capable of strong empathy, affection, and intimacy; understands give and take of human relationships

Low scorer: Has few close, trusting relationships with others; finds it difficult to be warm, open, and concerned about others; is isolated and frustrated in interpersonal relationships; not willing to make compromises to sustain important ties with others

Personal growth

High scorer: Has a feeling of continued development; sees self as growing and expending; is open to new experiences; has sense of realizing his or her potential; sees improvement in self and behavior over time; is changing in ways that reflect more self-knowledge and effectiveness

Low scorer: Has a sense of personal stagnation; lacks sense of improvement or expansion over time; feels bored and uninterested with life; feels unable to develop new attitudes or behaviors

Purpose in life

High scorer: Has goals in life and a sense of directedness; feels there is meaning to present and past life; holds beliefs that give life purpose; has aims and objectives for living

Low scorer: Lacks a sense of meaning in life; has few goals or aims; lacks sense of direction; does not see purpose of past life; has no outlook or beliefs that give life meaning

Environmental mastery

High scorer: Has a sense of mastery and competence in managing the environment; controls complex array of external activities; makes effective use of surrounding opportunities; able to choose or create contexts suitable to personal needs and values

Low scorer: Has difficulty managing everyday affairs; feels unable to change or improve surrounding context; is unaware of surrounding opportunities; lacks sense of control over external world

Autonomy

High scorer: Is self-determining and independent; able to resist social pressures to think and act in certain ways; regulates social pressures to think and act in certain ways; regulates behavior from within; evaluates self by personal standards

Low scorer: Is concerned about the expectations and evaluations of others; relies on judgments of others to make important decisions; conforms to social pressures to think and act in certain ways

failing to meet this criterion, or that had low correlations with their own scale, were deleted. This evaluation process was iterative—i.e., items from each scale were eliminated one at a time and then the entire process was repeated, given that each item deletion meant the overall scale had been empirically reconfigured. The process was terminated, when each scale had been reduced to 20 items, divided equally between positively and negatively scored items. Additional psychometric evaluations (e.g., test–retest reliability, internal consistency) were also provided for scales of this length.

Since that original publication, multiple investigations have examined the factorial validity of the theory-based model of PWB. Five such studies (Cheng and Chang 2005; Clarke et al. 2001; Ryff and Keyes 1995; Springer and Hauser 2006; Van Dierendonck 2004), all using confirmatory factor analyses, have shown that the best-fitting model is, in fact, the theory-guided six factor model. Included in this mix are three nationally representative samples, two from the U.S. (MIDUS, Midlife in the U.S.; NSFH, National Survey of Families and Households), and one from Canada (CSHA, Canadian Study of Health and Aging). Other sources of evidence are also relevant for evaluating the validity of the well-being scales, such as how they correlate with other psychological constructs as well as sociodemographic and biological factors, and how they vary over time (longitudinal analyses). Summaries of these findings are available elsewhere (Ryff and Singer 2006). Select findings from this research are briefly discussed below.

6.4.2 Psychosocial and Sociodemographic Correlates of Psychological Well-Being

Social scientists have linked the above aspects of well-being to many psychological constructs, such as identity status (Helson and Srivastava 2001), self-enhancing cognitions (Taylor et al. 2003a, b), emotion regulation (Gross and John 2003), personality traits (Lopes et al. 2003; Schmutte and Ryff 1997), personal goals (Carr 1997; Riediger and Freund 2004), values (Sheldon 2005), coping strategies (Kling et al. 1997), social comparison processes (Heidrich and Ryff 1993; Kwan et al. 2003), and spirituality (Kirby et al. 2004; Wink and Dillon 2003). Others have examined associations between well-being and life experiences, such as early parental loss or parental divorce (Maier and Lachman 2000), growing up with an alcoholic parent (Tweed and Ryff 1991), trauma disclosure (Hemenover 2003), community relocation (Smider et al. 1996), caregiving (Marks 1998), and change in marital status (Marks and Lambert 1998). Collectively, these investigations speak to the diverse interests researchers bring to the topic of well-being, and thereby, to the many factors that may influence positive functioning conceptualized under the eudaimonic umbrella, broadly defined.

We will focus on sociodemographic correlates of well-being, namely, how PWB varies by age and socioeconomic status of respondents. The reasons are to underscore the life course dynamics of well-being as well as the opportunity structures, or lack thereof, surrounding the challenge of "becoming what you are." Both receive insufficient attention in current psychological inquiries. With regard to age, Fig. 6.2 shows cross-sectional age differences in well-being among young, middle, and older aged adults from the Midlife in the U.S (MIDUS) national survey. The age diversity of well-being for both men and women is immediately apparent. Some aspects show incremental profiles with age (e.g., autonomy, environmental mastery), while others show sharply decremental profiles from young adulthood to old age (e.g., purpose in life, personal growth), and still others show little age

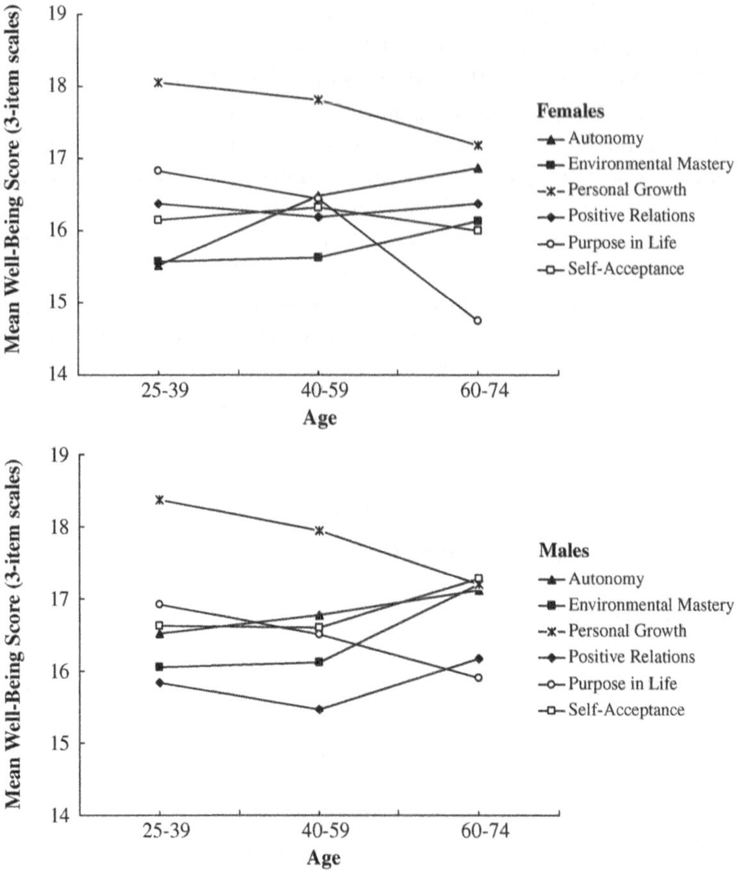

Fig. 6.2 Age differences in psychological well-being (*Source* MIDUS national survey)

variation (e.g., positive relations with others, self-acceptance—only for women). These patterns have been replicated across multiple studies, including those with community samples and nationally representative samples (Ryff 1989a, 1991; Ryff and Keyes 1995) as well as with instruments of dramatically different length (e.g., 3-, 20-item scales).

What is as yet unknown is whether the patterns represent aging changes, or cohort differences, although other longitudinal analyses (over shorter age periods) have documented that psychological well-being does, indeed, change with aging, particularly as individuals negotiate life challenges and life transitions, such as caregiving or community relocation (Kling et al. 1997a, b; Kwan et al. 2003). With regard to the sharply downward trajectories for purpose in life and personal growth, the two most eudiamonic aspects of well-being, we have emphasized current societal challenges in providing older persons with meaningful roles and opportunities for continued growth. Sociologists have termed this the "structural

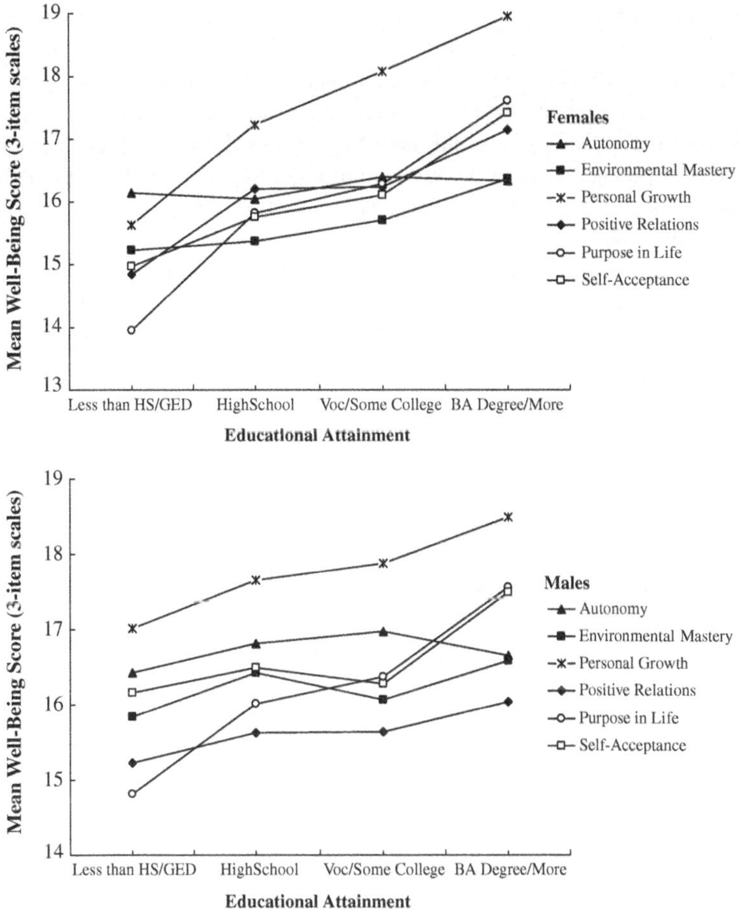

Fig. 6.3 Educational differences in psychological well-being (*Source* MIDUS national survey)

lag" problem, in which contemporary social institutions lag behind the added years of life that many now experience (Riley et al. 1994). Related to such ideas, Greenfield and Marks (2004), using MIDUS data, focused on older persons who occupied few major roles and found that those who engaged in formal volunteering had higher levels of purpose in life than those lacking both major roles and volunteer experiences.

Whether or not the surrounding context nurtures self-realization is partly illuminated by examining how reported well-being varies depending on individuals' socioeconomic status, such as their levels of education, income, or occupational status. Figure 6.3 arrays scores on the six dimensions of well-being among females and males in MIDUS as a function of their educational attainment. The story is clear: psychological well-being and educational standing are strongly positively linked, with the association being especially pronounced for personal growth and purpose in life, the two pillars of eudaimonia. These findings bring into high relief Dowd's (1990) observation that the opportunities for self-realization are not equally distributed, but occur via the allocation of resources, which enable only some to make the most of their talents and capacities.

Aristotle missed this point, although the Greeks did differentiate society into subgroups of people, some of whom were thought to possess the essential daimon, and others not. In the present era, there is greater awareness of problems of social inequality and their implications for health (Adler et al. 1999). Our research on educational disparities in psychological well-being (Marmot et al. 1997, 1998) adds to this literature, by showing that those at the low end of the SES hierarchy are not only more likely to succumb to disease and disability, they also suffer from diminished opportunities to make the most of their lives. As detailed in the biological section below, we see the two as linked—i.e., thwarted self-realization may be a critical part of the complex biopsychosocial processes that contribute to early morbidity and mortality.

Nonetheless, it is important to deviations from these patterns, which *on average,* link higher PWB to higher standing in the social hierarchy. Our work has shown remarkable resilience among some who lack socioeconomic advantage and/or have been confronted with significant life challenges (Markus et al. 2004; Ryff et al. 2004; Singer and Ryff 1997, 1999; Singer et al. 1998). We have also found such resilience among racial/ethnic minorities (Ryff et al. 2003). These studies are valuable for documenting the meaning-making and growth-producing effects of adversity, thus bringing empirical substance to Frankl and Lasch 1959/1992 vision. Regarding Hellenic eudaimonia, such findings challenge the view that realizing the highest human good is the exclusive terrain of privileged segments of society.

6.4.3 *Biological Correlates of Psychological Well-Being: The Positive Health Agenda*

Within moral philosophy, deontological theories rest on principles of obligation (from the Greek word *deon,* meaning duty). Consequentialist theories, in contrast, focus on the outcome or consequences to define right moral action. Aristotle's formulation of the highest human good as eudaimonia may well be primarily deontological; that is, it is a purely conceptual argument.[1] We are, however, intrigued with the idea of bringing empirical defense to the argument that some kinds of human goods are perhaps better than others. One such realm of consequentialist evidence pertains to biology and human health. That is, if eudaimonic well-being truly is the to right way to live, presumably it will benefit their health, both in terms of health behaviors (e.g., those experiencing self-realization may take better

[1] We are grateful to Alan Waterman for pointing out this distinction.

care of themselves), but also with regard to neurobiological processes that underlie their phenomenological experiences of growth and development. This perspective also provides a useful antidote to medical models of health, focused exclusively on illness and disease (Ryff and Singer 1998). Our alternative approach suggests that progress toward understanding *positive* human health follows from first assessing human flourishing (i.e., psychological well-being, as formulated within the eudaimonic tradition) and then probing its neurobiological substrates. The key hypothesis in such inquiry is that having high levels of purpose, growth, and quality ties to others, etc. is part of what keeps people healthy, even in the face of challenge. A first step in testing the hypothesized protective features of psychological well-being is thus to examine its neurobiological correlates.

Our work therein has just begun, but preliminary findings are promising. In a sample of aging women (Ryff et al. 2004) we correlated the six dimensions of PWB with diverse biomarkers (cardiovascular, neuroendocrine, immune) and found evidence of numerous links supporting our guiding predictions. Older women with higher levels of personal growth and purpose in life had, for example, better neuroendocrine regulation—i.e., they started the day with lower levels of salivary cortisol and stayed lower throughout the day, compared to older women with lower levels of growth and purpose. We found that those with higher levels of life purpose had lower inflammatory markers (i.e., sIL-6r, the soluble receptor for interluekin-6). Those with higher levels of environmental mastery, positive relations with others, and self-acceptance, in turn, showed lower levels of glycosylated hemoglobin (a marker for insulin resistance). Personal growth and purpose in life were also significantly positively correlated with HDL cholesterol, the "good" cholesterol. Finally, we included objectively measured sleep assessments and found that those with higher levels of environmental mastery experienced longer periods of REM sleep and faster entry into REM sleep. Longer periods of REM sleep were also evident for those with higher levels of positive relations with others, which along with high purpose in life was also significantly correlated with less body movement during sleep.

Extending these findings, Friedman et al. (2005) has documented the interplay between well-being and sleep in predicting inflammatory factors in older women. Those with both low levels of interpersonal well-being and poor sleep efficiency had the highest levels of interleukin-6, in contrast to those with positive profiles on one or both of these factors. In a sample of midlife adults, Urry et al. (2004) examined the neural correlates of well-being, and found that those with higher levels of PWB (all scales except autonomy) had greater left than right superior frontal activation (referred to EEG asymmetry), compared to those with lower well-being. This pattern of cerebral activation asymmetry has been previously linked to more positive dispositional styles and reduced likelihood of depression. Thus, eudaimonic well-being appears to be tied to more adaptive patterns of brain circuitry. Although limited by small samples and cross-sectional data, the above findings offer promising evidence that eudaimonic well-being is linked with better neuroendocrine regulation, better immune function, lower cardiovascular risk, better sleep, and more adaptive neural circuitry.

6.5 Summary: Constructive Tensions and Finding that Which is Intermediate

Our primary objective in this paper has been to revisit the philosophical and theoretical roots of eudaimonia so as to clarify how its central ideas infuse the study of human well-being. Whether we have done justice to these ideas, or fully utilized them to advance theoretical and empirical understanding of self-realization and human fulfillment is for others to evaluate. Also needed is thoughtful evaluation of how our perspective overlaps with, or is distinctive from, other flowers blooming in psychology's eudaimonic garden (see Ryan and Deci 2001 and other contributors to this special issue).

We conclude with observations about "constructive tensions" that come with the territory of studying human well-being. A central one pertains to the competing pulls of self versus other in formulating what it means to function optimally. In some circles, the human potential movement itself was seen as little more than an arena of narcissistic self-spelunking and ego-diving (see Ryff 1985). Preoccupations with personal growth were depicted as crippling basic social institutions (e.g., the family), and thus ensued countervailing calls to elevate social responsibility and concern for others as the highest good. A further tension inherent in any effort to formulate ultimate ideals for human conduct is the pull between universalism versus relativism (see Ryff and Singer 1998). Are there multiple forms of eudaimonic well-being—distinct varieties of self-realization nurtured by different societal contexts and culturally distinct ways of being? Or, is there a single formulation that applies to our species as a whole?

These challenging questions draw on the values and moral philosophies (implicit or explicit) of those who choose to study, if not, promote, human well-being. In reflecting on these tensions, we were struck anew by Aristotle's admonishment to seek "that which is intermediate." Following such guidance, we should avoid excess and extremes, whether it be a kind of well-being that is so solipsistic and individualist as to leave no room for human connection and the social good, or a version that is so focused on responsibilities and duties outside the self that inherent talents and capacities are neither recognized nor developed. Similarly, we are not well-served by rigid, tightly constrained formulations of how selves are realized any more than we benefit from a relativistic buffet in which any type of well-being goes. Moreover, even with regard to the dimensions of eudaimonic well-being we put forth (e.g., personal growth, self-knowledge, purposeful living), there are possible extremes in which self-realization spins out of control at great cost to others, or where responding to the expectations of others eliminates the capacity for autonomy.

Thus, we close with renewed appreciation for the idea of *balance*, both as a conceptual guide and as an empirical reality that scholars of well-being need to better understand. This will require that we peer deeply into what levels of well-being contribute to flourishing individual lives as well as optimally functioning social institutions. We will thus be required to address issues, such as what constitutes too little, or too much, life purpose? Or, what is too little, or not enough, self-knowledge? Questions such as these could not be more timely for the scientific study of human well-being where current inquiry is now poised to predict important empirical outcomes (e.g., the health of individuals, their families, and their communities) based on reported levels of personal growth and life purpose.

Acknowledgments This research was supported by the National Institute of Mental Health (P50-MH61083), and the National Institute on Aging (P01-AG020166). We are grateful to Emily Greenfield and Alan Waterman for their insightful comments and suggestions on an earlier version of this manuscript.

References

Adler NE, Marmot MG, McEwen BS, Stewart J (1999) Socioeconomic status and health in industrialized nations: social, psychological, and biological pathways, vol 896. New York Academy of Sciences, New York

Allport GW (1961) Pattern and growth in personality. Holt, Rinehart, & Winston, New York

Andrews FM, Withey SB (1976) Social indicators of well-being: America's perception of life quality. Plenum Press, New York

Aristotle (1925) The nicomachean ethics (trans: Ross D). Oxford University Press, New York

Becker LC (1992) Good lives: prolegomena. Soc Philos Policy 9:15–37

Bradburn NM (1969) The Structure of psychological well-being. Aldin, Chicago

Bryant FB, Veroff J (1982) The structure of psychological well-being: a sociohistorical analysis. J Pers Soc Psychol 43:653–673

Bühler C (1935) The curve of life as studied in biographies. J Appl Psychol 43:653–673

Bühler C, Massarik F (eds) (1968) The course of human life. Springer, New York

Carr DS (1997) The fulfillment of career dreams at midlife: does it matter for women's mental health? J Health Soc Behav 38:331–344

Cheng S-T, Chang ACM (2005) Measuring psychological well-being in the Chinese. Pers Individ Differ 38(6):1307–1316

Clarke PJ, Marshall VW, Ryff CD, Wheaton B (2001) Measuring psychological well-being in the Canadian study of health and aging. Int Psychogeriatr 13(Suppl 1):79–90

Diener E (1984) Subjective well-being. Psychol Bull 95:542–575

Diener E, Suh EM (2000) Measuring subjective well-being to compare the quality of life of cultures. In: Diener E, Suh M (eds) Culture and subjective well-being. The MIT Press, Cambridge, pp 3–12

Dowd JJ (1990) Ever since Durkheim: the socialization of human development. Hum Dev 33:138–159

Erikson EH (1959) Identity and the life cycle: selected papers. Psychol Issues 1:1–171

Frankl VE, Lasch I (1992) Man's search for meaning: an introduction to logotherapy. Beacon Press, Boston (Original published 1959)

Friedman EM, Hayney M, Love GD, Urry H, Rosenkranz MA, Davidson RJ, Singer BH, Ryff CD (2005) Plasma interluekin-6 in aging women: links to positive social relationships and sleep quality. Proc Natl Acad sci 102:18757–18762

Greenfield EA, Marks N (2004) Formal volunteering as a protective factor for older adults' psychological well-being. J Gerontol B Psychol Sci Soc Sci 59B(5):S258–S264

Gross JJ, John OP (2003) Individual differences in two emotion regulation processes: implications for affect, relationships, and well-being. J Pers Soc Psychol 85(2):348–362

Heidrich SM, Ryff CD (1993) The role of social comparison processes in the psychological adaptation of elderly adults. J Gerontol Psychol Sci 48:P127–P136

Helson R, Srivastava S (2001) Three paths of adult development: conservers, seekers, and achievers. J Pers Soc Psychol 80(6):995–1010

Hemenover SH (2003) The good, the bad, and the healthy: impacts of emotional disclosure of trauma on resilient self-concept and psychological distress. Pers Soc Psychol Bull 29(10):1236–1244

Jahoda M (1958) Current concepts of positive mental health. Basic Books, New York

Johnston I (1997) Lecture on Aristotle's nicomachaean ethics [electronic version], from http://www.mala.bc.ca/~johnstoi/

Jung CG (1933) Modern man in search of a soul (trans: Dell WS, Baynes CF). Harcourt, Brace & World, New York)

Kirby SE, Coleman PG, Daley D (2004) Spirituality and well-being in frail and nonfrail older adults. J Gerontol B Psychol Sci Soc Sci 59B(3):P123–P129

Kitayama S, Markus HR (2000) The pursuit of happiness and the realization of sympathy: cultural patterns of self, social relations, and well-being. In: Diener E, Suh EM (eds) Culture and subjective well-being. The MIT Press, Cambridge, pp 113–161

Kling KC, Ryff CD, Essex MJ (1997a) Adaptive changes in the self-concept during a life transition. Pers Soc Psychol Bull 23(9):981–990

Kling KC, Seltzer MM, Ryff CD (1997b) Distinctive late-life challenges: implications for coping and well-being. Psychol Aging 12(2):288–295

Kwan CML, Love GD, Ryff CD, Essex MJ (2003) The role of self-enhancing evaluations in a successful life transition. Psychol Aging 18(1):3–12

Lopes PN, Salovey P, Straus R (2003) Emotional intelligence, personality, and the perceived quality of social relationships. Pers Individ Differ 35:641–658

Maier EH, Lachman ME (2000) Consequences of early parental loss and separation for health and well-being in midlife. Int J Behav Dev 24(2):183–189

Marks NF (1998) Does it hurt to care? caregiving, work-family conflict, and midlife well-being. J Marriage Fam 60(4):951–966

Marks NF, Lambert JD (1998) Marital status continuity and change among young and midlife adults: longitudinal effects on psychological well-being. J Fam Issues 19:652–686

Markus HR, Ryff CD, Curhan KB, Palmersheim KA (2004) In their own words: well-being at midlife among high school-educated and college-educated adults. In: Brim OG, Ryff CD, Kessler RC (eds) How healthy are we?: a national study of well-being at midlife. The University of Chicago Press, Chicago, pp 273–319

Marmot M, Ryff CD, Bumpass LL, Shipley M, Marks NF (1997) Social inequalities in health: next questions and converging evidence. Soc Sci Med 44(6):901–910

Marmot MG, Fuhrer R, Ettner SL, Marks NF, Bumpass LL, Ryff CD (1998) Contribution of psychosocial factors to socioeconomic differences in health. Milbank Q 76(3):403–448

Maslow AH (1968) Toward a psychology of being, 2nd edn. Van Nostrand, New York

Mill JS (1989) Autobiography. Penguin, London (Original work published 1893)

Neugarten BL (1968) The awareness of middle age. In: Neugarten BL (ed) Middle age and aging. University of Chicago Press, Chicago, pp 93–98

Neugarten BL (1973) Personality change in late life: a developmental perspective. In: Eisodorfer C, Lawton MP (eds) The pychology of adult development and aging. American Psychological Association, Washington, pp 311–335

Norton DL (1976) Personal destinies: a philosophy of ethical individualism. Princeton University Press, Princeton

Riediger M, Freund AM (2004) Interference and facilitation among personal goals: differential associations with subjective well-being and persistent goal pursuit. Pers Soc Psychol Bull 30(12):1511–1523

Riley MW, Kahn RL, Foner A (1994) Age and structural lag. Wiley, New York

Rogers CR (1962) The interpersonal relationship: the core of guidance. Harvard Educ Rev 32(4):416–429

Russell B (1958) The conquest of happiness. Liveright, New York (Original work published 1930)

Ryan RM, Deci EL (2001) On happiness and human potentials: a review of research on hedonic and eudaimonic well-being. Annu Rev Psychol 52:141–166
Ryff CD (1982) Successful aging: a developmental approach. Gerontologist 22:209–214
Ryff CD (1985) Adult personality development and the motivation for personal growth. In: Kleiber D, Maehr M (eds) Advances in motivation and achievement, vol 4., Motivation and AdulthoodJAI Press, Greenwich, pp 55–92
Ryff CD (1989a) Happiness is everything, or is it? explorations on the meaning of psychological well-being. J Pers Soc Psychol 57(6):1069–1081
Ryff CD (1989b) Beyond ponce de leon and life satisfaction: new directions in quest of successful aging. Int J Behav Dev 12:35–55
Ryff CD (1991) Possible selves in adulthood and old age: a tale of shifting horizons. Psychol Aging 6(2):286–295
Ryff CD, Keyes CLM (1995) The structure of psychological well-being revisited. J Pers Soc Psychol 69(4):719–727
Ryff CD, Singer BH (1998) The contours of positive human health. Psychol Inq 9(1):1–28
Ryff CD, Singer BH (2006) Best news yet for the six-factor model of well-being, Soc Sci Res 35:1103–1119
Ryff CD, Keyes CLM, Hughes DL (2003) Status inequalities, perceived discrimination, and eudaimonic well-being: dDo the challenges of minority life hone purpose and growth? J Health Soc Behav 44(3):275–291
Ryff CD, Singer BH, Love GD (2004a) Positive health: connecting well-being with biology. Philos Trans R Soc Lond B 359:1383–1394
Ryff CD, Singer BH, Palmersheim KA (2004b) Social inequalities in health and well-being: the role of relational and religious protective factors. In: Brim OG, Ryff CD, Kessler RC (eds) How healthy are we?: a national study of well-being at midlife. University of Chicago Press, Chicago, pp 90–123
Sartre JP (1956) Being and nothingness. Philosophical Library, Oxford
Schmutte PS, Ryff CD (1997) Personality and well-being: reexamining methods and meanings. J Pers Soc Psychol 73(3):549–559
Sheldon KM (2005) Positive value change during college: normative trends and individual differences. J Res Pers 39(2):209–223
Singer BH, Ryff CD (1997) Racial and ethnic equalities in health: environmental, psychosocial, and physiological pathways. In: Devlin B, Feinberg SE, Resnick D, Roeder K (eds) Intelligence, genes, and success: scientists respond to the bell curve. Springer, New York, pp 89–122
Singer BH, Ryff CD (1999) Hierarchies of life histories and associated health risks. In: Adler NE, Marmot M (eds) Socioeconomic status and health in industrial nations, vol 896., Social, psychological, and biological pathwaysNew York Academy of Sciences, New York, pp 96–115
Singer BH, Ryff CD (2001) New horizons in health: an integrative approach. National Academy Press, Washington
Singer BH, Ryff CD, Carr D, Magee WJ (1998) Life histories and mental health: a person-centered strategy. In: Raftery A (ed) Sociological methodology. American Sociological Association, Washington, pp 1–51
Smider NA, Essex MJ, Ryff CD (1996) Adaptation to community relocation: the interactive influence of psychological resources and contextual factors. Psychol Aging 11(2):362–372
Springer KW, Hauser RM (2006) An assessment of the construct validity of Ryff's scales of psychological well-being: method, mode, and measurement effects. Soc Sci Res 35:1080–1102
Taylor SE, Lerner JS, Sherman DK, Sage RM, McDowell NK (2003a) Are self-enhancing cognitions associated with healthy or unhealthy biological profiles? J Pers Soc Psychol 85:605–615
Taylor SE, Lerner JS, Sherman DK, Sage RM, McDowell NK (2003b) Portrait of the self-enhancer: well adjusted and well liked or maladjusted and friendless? J Pers Soc Psychol 84(1):165–176

Tweed S, Ryff CD (1991) Adult children of alcoholics: profiles of wellness and distress. J Stud Alcohol 52:133–141

Urry HL, Nitschke JB, Dolski I, Jackson DC, Dalton KM, Mueller CJ et al (2004) Making a life worth living: neural correlates of well-being. Psychol Sci 15(6):367–372

van Dierendonck D (2004) The construct validity of Ryff's scales of psychological well-being and its extension with spiritual well-being. Pers Individ Differ 36(3):629–643

Waterman AS (1984) The psychology of individualism. Praeger, New York

Wiggins JS (1980) Personality and prediction: principles of personality assessment. Addison-Wesley, Menlo Park

Wink P, Dillon M (2003) Religiousness, spirituality, and psychosocial functioning in late adulthood: findings from a longitudinal study. Psychol Aging 18(4):916–924

Chapter 7
Living Well: A Self-Determination Theory Perspective on Eudaimonia

Richard M. Ryan, Veronika Huta and Edward L. Deci

Abstract This article distinguishes between hedonic and eudaimonic approaches to wellness, with the former focusing on the outcome of happiness or pleasure and the latter focusing not so much on outcomes as on the process of living well. We present a model of eudaimonia that is based in self-determination theory, arguing that eudaimonic living can be characterized in terms of four motivational concepts: (1) pursuing intrinsic goals and values for their own sake, including personal growth, relationships, community, and health, rather than extrinsic goals and values, such as wealth, fame, image, and power; (2) behaving in autonomous, volitional, or consensual ways, rather than heteronomous or controlled ways; (3) being mindful and acting with a sense of awareness; and (4) behaving in ways that satisfy basic psychological needs for competence, relatedness, and autonomy. In fact, we theorize that the first three of these aspects of eudaimonic living have their positive effects of psychological and physical wellness because they facilitate satisfaction of these basic, universal psychological needs. Studies indicate that people high in eudaimonic living tend to behave in more prosocial ways, thus benefiting the collective as well as themselves, and that conditions both within the family and in society more generally contribute toward strengthening versus diminishing the degree to which people live eudaimonic lives.

Keywords Autonomy • Awareness • Happiness • Intrinsic aspirations • Mindfulness • Self-determination theory • The good life • Wellness

In both traditional and current views hedonia and eudaimonia are often juxtaposed as opposing perspectives on human wellness. The hedonic approach defines well-being as happiness, interpreted as the occurrence of positive affect and the absence of negative affect (Kahneman et al. 1999). Hedonistic psychology therefore has a clear and measurable target for research, which is one of its major advantages as a

R. M. Ryan (✉) · V. Huta · E. L. Deci
University of Ottawa, Ottawa, ON, Canada
e mail: ryan@psych.rochester.edu

A. Delle Fave (ed.), *The Exploration of Happiness*, Happiness Studies Book Series,
DOI: 10.1007/978-94-007-5702-8_7,

focus for a science of well-being. In contrast, the concept of eudaimonia, generally defined as living a complete human life, or the realization of valued human potentials (Ryan and Deci 2001) has been used in more varied ways, and assessments of eudaimonia have been multiple and not always well coordinated. In short there is a notable imbalance in the exactingness with which hedonic and eudaimonic well-being researchers have specified their targets.

Our principal aim is to articulate a framework for the general study of eudaimonia, and to introduce a specific working model of eudaimonia derived from self-determination theory (SDT; Deci and Ryan 1985; Ryan and Deci 2000), with elements that are amenable to empirically based testing and elaboration. Because eudaimonia refers to living well, any theory of eudaimonia consists of a set of prescriptions and proscriptions. How well the theory fairs in terms of yielding a high quality life is thus an empirical question. In other words, the criteria for judging a theory of eudaimonia rest in its ability to predict, and when implemented, bring about, outcomes that people value deeply and that can be said to represent wellness. In this way, the proposed framework is also intended to connect with the existing bodies of research on values, motives, well-being, and quality of life.

A central premise of our thesis is that hedonic versus eudaimonic psychologies do not in principle constitute a debate about what well-being "feels like" or what "happiness", considered as a state of mind, entails. Rather, eudaimonic conceptions focus on the *content* of one's life, and the *processes* involved in living well, whereas hedonic conceptions of well-being focus on a specific *outcome,* namely the attainment of positive affect and an absence of pain. Thus, in our view, hedonic and eudaimonic perspectives are not distinct because they conceive of different types of well-being states or outcomes but rather because they have altogether different targets. The foci of eudaimonic research are to specify what living well entails and to identify the expected consequences of such living. These consequences may include hedonic satisfactions, but typically eudaimonic theorists have been especially interested in other outcomes indicative of a good life, such as vitality, intimacy, health, and sense of meaning, among others.

By contrast, the focus of hedonic research is on a valued but delimited state, namely pleasure. Although pleasure is often demeaned as an important human outcome, it is in our view a very significant one. Pleasure and positive affect are important human experiences not only because they represent intrinsically preferred states, but also because they can facilitate and support other human functions (Isen 2003; King et al. 2006). More-over, it is clear that pleasure, psychological health, and optimal functioning are inter-correlated.

Accordingly, from our perspective, positive affect and pleasure are both correlates and consequences of living well—of eudaimonia. That is, a person who engages in meaningful endeavors, actualizes potentials, and is "fully functioning"—all characteristics frequently mentioned as hallmarks of eudaimonia—will typically experience considerable happiness and pleasure (Ryan and Deci 2001). Yet antecedents of pleasure can also include goals and lifestyles antithetical to most eudaimonic conceptions, such as living a life of shallow values, greed, or exploitation of others. There are, in short, multiple routes to pleasure, not all of which entail living eudaimonically. The hedonic/eudaimonic distinction is thus neither a trivial nor a simple one.

Defining health and wellness is not only of theoretical interest to researchers but also has substantial applied significance. If one aims to develop interventions one has to know what the target is. In the past, both psychological and medical researchers have often done this negatively—seeing health and wellness as the absence of disease or psychopathology. In the context of modern positive psychology, both hedonic and eudaimonic conceptions of wellness have gained salience, but each may lead to a different set of prescriptions (Ryan and Deci 2001; Maddux 2002).

Because it can be so variously produced, we suggest that a focus on hedonic outcomes cannot by itself reliably lead to either individual or collective well-being. Indeed, in the view we shall propose, the more directly one aims to maximize pleasure and avoid pain the more likely one is to produce instead a life bereft of depth, meaning, and community. Prescriptions based on maximizing pleasure are too often associated with dead-end routes to wellness such as selfishness, materialism, objectified sexuality, and ecological destructiveness, thus demonstrating how easily a map derived from hedonic thinking can mislead. By contrast, specification of eudaimonic living might not only be of value as a guide to a more complete and meaningful life; it should also yield more stable and enduring hedonic happiness (Huta and Ryan 2006).

The distinction between eudaimonia and hedonia is also significant on a broader societal level. Whether one is making comparative national health assessments or actually creating social and economic policies, the kind of good life we are targeting makes a difference. Numerous authors have pointed out that a focus on hedonic happiness is by no means culturally neutral; it is both presupposed by and a reflection of individualistic, market-based economics (e.g. Ferguson 1990; Christopher 1999; Kasser et al. 2007). Focusing instead on broader eudaimonic outcomes may suggest important alternative routes to individual and societal wellness and may play a critical function with respect to economic and social policies.

We begin by briefly reviewing the concept of eudaimonia as formulated by Aristotle, who introduced this seminal idea. We then propose an SDT-based framework for eudaimonia that focuses on intrinsic goals, autonomy, basic psychological need satisfactions, and the connections of these processes with both hedonic phenomena and other, more eudaimonic indicators of well-being. We will also review some of the empirical evidence that supports SDT and its eudaimonic conception.

7.1 Aristotle's Conception of Eudaimonia

The eudaimonic tradition in well-being studies derives from Aristotle's philosophy of happiness, especially as articulated within his *Nicomachean Ethics* (translated by Broadie and Rowe 2002). Therein he sets out a definition of human happiness that is centered on what it means to live a good life, a life representing human excellence. Yet, by beginning with Aristotle we do not suggest that his formulation of eudaimonia is fully definitive. Aristotle had his own historically and culturally shaped ideas of human excellences and the processes of obtaining them that in no way should be taken as the "final word". Indeed, some of his emphases concerning optimal human living match ours, and others do not. Moreover, whereas Aristotle's approach was wholly deductive, our intent is to use a scientific approach that inherently entails openness to what the data tell us about eudaimonia. Nonetheless, insofar as Aristotle supplied the staring point for this school of thinking, his approach merits consideration.

7.1.1 Eudaimonia Defined

In Aristotle's view eudaimonia is the chief human good. He defined eudaimonia as a character of persons that entails living in accordance with reason and moderation, and aiming toward excellence and the realization of a complete human life. This summary definition is quite complex, and has been variously interpreted. Herein we highlight some of its essential features.

7.1.1.1 Feeling Good Versus Living Well

Most importantly, Aristotle distinguished between happiness as experiencing pleasure (i.e. hedonia) versus happiness as living well (i.e. eudaimonia). Broadie and Rowe (2002), in commenting on the *Nicomachean Ethics* state that even Aristotle's use of the word *eudaimonia* implies this distinction. They suggested that an ancient Greek citizen, knowing that someone was in a state of pleasure, would not on that account apply the term eudaimonia to him or her. Eudaimonia is not a "feeling", it is instead a description of character: it is an adjective suggesting an exemplary life. As they stated it: "gluttons smacking greasy lips are happy, but not *eudaimonia.* By contrast, to ascribe eudaimonia is to honor the recipient" (p. 12). Such a person has qualities that characterize an excellent human life, whether or not he or she happens to "feel good". Eudaimonia is thus not conceived of as a mental state, a positive feeling, or a cognitive appraisal of satisfaction, but rather as a way of living.

7.1.1.2 Living Well Means Pursuing the Right Ends

For Aristotle eudaimonic living requires engaging one's best human capacities by actively pursuing virtues and excellences. In this view, as people pursue excellence they are actualizing their most authentic or highest natures (daimon), though not their only natures. Moreover, Aristotle suggested that the pursuit of these excellences is an intrinsically worthy endeavor. It is an end in itself. In contrast, he was particularly critical of the pursuit of wealth or power, because these are ends without inherent value. As he stated it: "wealth is clearly not the good we are looking for, since it is useful, and for the sake of something else" (p. 98). Thus, whereas wealth and power have extrinsic value, the pursuit of human excellences and virtue is intrinsically valued. He went on to suggest that such elevation of means, whether they be power, influence, or material goods, compromises and distracts from eudaimonic living. Aristotle similarly debated whether the pursuit of pleasure per se can be eudaimonic, because pleasure can at times be an end in itself. Yet it became clear that, in his view, it is usually not. Pleasure seeking typically stalls the pursuit of human excellences, reducing individuals to no better than "grazing cattle".

So what ends does the eudaimonic person specifically pursue? Aristotle's model of eudaimonia included a list of specific virtues and excellences that constitute a good life, each of which he defends with extensive arguments. The list includes attributes such as courage, generosity, wisdom, and being fair and just in relation to others. Without doubt, his list contained important human goods, but what attributes it ought to include or exclude is certainly open to debate.

7.1.1.3 Eudaimonia Entails Reflectiveness and Reason

Aristotle explicitly argued that in pursuing the excellent life the eudaimonic person is continuously engaged in reflectivity and deliberation concerning his or her actions and aims. A reflective life, characterized by deliberation and reason, is thus one that both facilitates the development of human excellence and is, he believed, an end in itself that expresses uniquely human capacities. Indeed, for Aristotle, the contemplative or reflective life was considered the most eudaimonic, expressing as it does a uniquely human attribute of the highest intrinsic worth. Philosophically, Aristotle's view represents a self-affirming stance, that would resonate for psychologists such as us who value self-knowledge and awareness.

For Aristotle, application of reason and reflection included seeing what is true and not being self-deceived. As he stated it,

> What most distinguishes the good person is his ability to see what is true in every set of circumstances...but most people are deceived, and the deception seems to come about because of pleasure; for it appears a good thing when it is not. So they choose what is pleasant as something good, and they avoid pain as something bad (p. 129).

He was suggesting that a focus on pleasure and pain, rewards and punishments, can lead people to biased insights, or avoidance of truths, because they bend their perceptions for hedonic purposes.

7.1.1.4 Eudaimonia is Based on Volition and Reflects the Self

We cannot deem a person eudaimonic except insofar as we attribute his or her seeking of excellence and virtues to the person's own volition. As Aristotle put it, the excellences "depend on us and are voluntary" (p. 132). Their pursuit is actively chosen. Thus, external coercion and ignorance were both considered obstacles to voluntary action through which the excellences are pursued. Waterman (1993) highlighted this in his characterization of eudaimonia as *personal expressiveness.*

To summarize, the Aristotelian view of eudaimonia considers well-being not as a state of pleasure versus pain, but as living well. As he put it, "the happy man both lives well and does well" (p. 103). Living well entails actively and explicitly striving for what is truly worthwhile and is of inherent or intrinsic human worth, and it contrasts with the pursuit of crass endeavors such as materialism or pleasure seeking that pulls one away from virtues. Eudaimonia is characterized by reflectiveness and reason. Finally, eudaimonic pursuits are voluntary, and are expressions of the self rather than products of external control or ignorance. Together, Aristotle's eudaimonia is thus characterized as living well, and entails being actively engaged in excellent activity, reflectively making decisions, and behaving voluntarily toward ends that represent the realization of our highest human natures.

7.2 Self-Determination Theory: A Brief Overview of its Development

As already stated, we began with Aristotle's view because he was the originator of the eudaimonic tradition. We culled some of the reasons why he was compelled to distinguish eudaimonic happiness from hedonic happiness, and to denigrate the later. In addition, we highlighted aspects of his conception of living well that entailed pursuit or actualization of intrinsic human excellences, accomplished through mindful reflection and volition.

Many of these elements in Aristotle's conception of eudaimonia are at the core of self-determination theory's (SDT's) conceptions of wellness. SDT began with a focus on *intrinsic motivation,* or the pursuit of an activity because of its inherent interest and enjoyability (e.g. Deci and Ryan 1980). In this research the role of rewards, the importance of competence, and the central role of autonomy in motivation became topics of study. We then shifted attention to *extrinsically motivated* activities, those that are instrumental rather than inherently enjoyable, and to how they are adopted and enacted. We demonstrated that whereas many such activities are regulated by external or introjected controls, others are assimilated and integrated as personal values, and thus are more autonomously pursued. The relative autonomy of extrinsic goals in turn has strong predictive relations for human performance, persistence, and well-being outcomes. The process of *internalization,* through which external regulations and values become integrated to the self, thus became a central focus of SDT (Deci and Ryan 1985; Ryan and Connell 1989).

As we studied intrinsic motivation and internalization processes and their determinants and consequences, it became increasingly clear that there are some necessary conditions for each to flourish, and moreover that these conditions were universally associated with personal and relational well-being. Thus, SDT articulated a theory of *basic psychological needs* that are the foundations of personal growth (as manifest in intrinsic motivation), integrity (as manifest in integrative processes), and well-being (Ryan 1995; Deci and Ryan 2000). Building on this basic needs theory, SDT research began to distinguish the types of goals and aspirations people pursue in terms of their relation to both basic needs and well-being outcomes (e.g. Kasser and Ryan 1996). Intrinsic aspirations, such those for personal growth, deep relationships, and generativity, were empirically distinguished from extrinsic aspirations, such as those for wealth, fame, or image, and shown to have differential relations with psychological and physical wellness, and distinct social antecedents. Most recently, as we explore the impact of varied life goals, need satisfaction, and the social contexts that engender volition and vitality, the central role of mindfulness and awareness in volition and goal adoption has become a salient concern (Brown and Ryan 2003).

Throughout there has also been a practical or applied bent to SDT, stemming from the aim of identifying the factors that facilitate versus thwart motivation and wellness in development in general, and in specific domains such as work, education, sport, parenting, and clinical care.

This brief schematic of developments within SDT thus points to the scope of the theory, and underscores why we can only superficially review elements of the theory in this paper. More importantly it suggests how extensively the foci of SDT research overlap with the themes that occupied Aristotle in his writings on eudaimonia. Our interests in intrinsic versus extrinsic life goals, the basic and universal human needs underlying wellness, the critical role of reflection and awareness, and the centrality of volition all exemplify obvious points of convergence. Thus, we will not review the details of SDT or the empirical findings supporting it. Instead, our aim is to specify a formal model of eudaimonia that builds on our prior work, and to articulate some testable and expandable ideas for future eudaimonic assessments and studies.

7.3 Toward a Formal Theory of Eudaimonia

As we stated at the outset, we conceive of eudaimonia as referring to *a way of living,* not to a psychological state or outcome. Specifically, it is a *way of living that is focused on what is intrinsically worthwhile to human beings.* In stating this we are making a broad claim that there are intrinsic values built into human nature and that these values are universal (Deci and Ryan 2000). Within our formal theory of eudaimonia we specify at least some of these intrinsic values, and at the same time we argue that the list is not in any way closed. In fact, because we argue that intrinsic values have specific attributes and consequences, there may be additional values that can be empirically identified or that fit with the criteria we lay out.

7.3.1 Eudaimonia and the Pursuit of First-Order Outcomes

The concept of intrinsic worth means more than simply that the values in question are inherent or natural to humans. There are, for example, inherent and natural attributes in humans that do not represent intrinsic values. For example it is "natural" to respond to threats with aggression or fear, but aggression and fear are not intrinsically valued. People value these capacities not for their inherent value, but because they can help us survive. Thus, life and survival are inherently valued, but aggression is not. Thus, another attribute of an intrinsic value is that it is a *first-order value* defined as: (1) a value not reducible to other values, and (2) a value that does not exist for the sake of another value. It must be a basic value in its own right.

We illustrate this with an example. First, consider the value of wealth. If we asked a person, "Why are you working so hard?" one common answer might be, "To accumulate money or wealth". If we then asked, "Why do you want wealth?" there again might be various answers. One might be, "because I want to be admired". We would then need to ask, "Why do you want to be admired?" Again, various answers might emerge, because so far we have not reached a "bottom line". But suppose the person answers, "Because I want to feel loved". When we get to this answer we can try again, asking "Why do you want to be loved?" But here our interviewee will likely be puzzled. When it comes to love, we seem to have hit an irreducible. Our subject might say: "I don't know what you mean, everyone wants love;" or "Because love is good". This is not to say that some evolutionary theorists might not see love as instrumental to adaptation, or some health specialists might argue that love promotes immunological responsiveness. But at a fundamental *psychological* level, love is irreducible. It is a good that explains itself. It is a first-order value.

Eudaimonia is therefore a way of living in which intrinsic values predominate in the sense that people are focused on what has inherent worth and on the goals that are by nature first order. We therefore can distinguish a eudaimonic lifestyle from a non-eudaimonic one by the degree to which people's energies and interests are focused on intrinsic values versus second- or third-order values and/or goals whose value is either derivative or unclear.

Indeed, it follows from the above that most second and third- order values will be associated with extrinsic aspirations. The concept of extrinsic has twofold implications in this context: (1) the aspirations will often be instrumental, having their salience because there is something more basic that they serve, even though the person may not be conscious of the connection, and (2) they are goals without inherent value in their own right. In addition, many extrinsic goals (though not all) are not inherent in human nature but are acquired. Thus, a woman stock trader may have wealth and power as primary foci without realizing that they are derivative. For example, she may be unaware that the hyper desire for power is actually driven by a need for autonomy that was thwarted at an earlier age, or that her desire for wealth is driven by a need for love or regards that was similarly not well satisfied. Instead, these motives represent need substitutes based in underlying intrinsic needs that were thwarted (Deci 1980). Put differently, a non-eudaimonic lifestyle is often one in which an individual becomes preoccupied with second- and third-order values or motives that are derivative and now disconnected from intrinsic needs that were unsatisfied.

In a different vein, a man who very highly values a first-order content such as love may find himself overly invested in achieving some greatness, be it material or symbolic, to enhance the lives of those he loves. Yet in so doing, his time and interests are drawn away from *loving*. Although such "sacrifice" may be in some ways admirable, it nonetheless reduces the degree of eudaimonia characterizing the man's life. Such examples show how many instrumental goals in life, even when well intended, can move people away from eudaimonia, because they are engaged in derivative activities that are too infrequently fulfilling. This was an issue about which Aristotle seemed acutely aware.

7.3.1.1 Are Intrinsic Goals Always First-Order Goals?

Previously we argued that intrinsic goals are first-order goals, insofar as they are not reducible to other goals, but are done for their own sake. Typically that is the case. For example, when a person has the goal of intimacy and relatedness, it is nearly always valued in its own right. However, a person might cultivate intimacy with someone in order to get an inheritance. In this case, the "real" goal is money, not intimacy, and that in turn, has its own underlying lower-order goals. Similarly a person could value community contributions in order to impress others, but again that shows that we still have not gotten to the bottom line goal. In other words, an intrinsic goal is really only an intrinsic goal when it is a first-order goal. This bespeaks the importance of a thorough analysis of goal contents.

In most of the empirical investigations of goal contents accomplished within SDT, it is the relative weight given to intrinsic versus extrinsic goals that has been used to predict well-being and mental health outcomes. This relative weight approach, originally developed by Kasser and Ryan (1993, 1996) provides an indication of where the most important emphasis is within a person's configuration of goals, and thus gives an estimate of the degree to which the person is focused on more instrumental, extrinsic goals, or those goal contents that are intrinsically valuable in the manner described by Aristotle.

We have suggested that there are values and goals that can be distinguished as intrinsic and extrinsic in accord with the definitions we provided above. From this it follows that we should be able to distinguish between such values empirically and to establish that they have differential consequences for well-being outcomes. We turn now to each of these issues.

7.3.2 Distinguishing Intrinsic from Extrinsic Aspirations

Kasser and Ryan (1993, 1996) and Kasser (2002) initiated a program of research exploring the distinction between intrinsic and extrinsic aspirations. They specifically proposed that there are significant individual differences in people's focus on intrinsic versus extrinsic aspirations and that these would have a predictable effect on a variety of wellness-relevant outcomes, from subjective happiness, to relationship quality, to physical health.

In their first published study, Kasser and Ryan (1993) found that persons whose aspirations for financial success were strong relative to those for relationships, growth, and community had lower well-being on a number of indicators. Subsequently, Kasser and Ryan (1996) examined seven life goals. They hypothesized that three of them, wealth and material possessions, social recognition and fame, and image or attractiveness, would represent extrinsic goals. Four others were thought to represent intrinsic goals: personal growth, affiliation and intimacy, contributing to one's community, and physical health. Kasser and Ryan found that these aspirations loaded cleanly on two factors. Wealth, fame, and image loaded on a factor they labeled *extrinsic aspirations,* while growth, affiliation, community contribution, and health loaded on an *intrinsic aspirations* factor. Further, results revealed that the strength of intrinsic relative to extrinsic aspirations, as indexed by ratings of goal importance, was positively related to a host of psychological well-being indicators, including self-actualization, positive affect, and vitality, and negatively to indicators of ill-being, including depression, negative affect, anxiety, and physical symptoms.

Similar findings have since been found in a number of diverse cultures, and with working adults as well as college students (e.g. Ryan et al. 1999; Schmuck et al. 2000; Vansteenkiste et al. 2004). Recently, in fact, Grouzet et al. (2005) demonstrated that the intrinsic/extrinsic goal distinction stood up empirically in samples from 15 different cultures, with the two goal types lying on opposite sides of a circumplex model. Of note in this piece is that additional values were placed in the derived map of aspirations. Hedonism, a desire for fun and pleasure, interestingly turned out to fall midway between intrinsic and extrinsic categories. This stands to reason insofar as hedonic pursuits are in many circumstances done for their own sake and worthwhile in terms of a good life. However, they are at other times sought out as distractions, or ways of avoiding responsibilities or anxieties, and in such cases will function more as extrinsic goals. Thus, hedonic goals need to be differentiated for us to understand their contributions to eudaimonia. Similarly, religious aspirations also fell midway between intrinsic and extrinsic poles, representing the well-known fact that religious motivations can be both intrinsic and extrinsic in nature (e.g. Ryan et al. 1993).

An important point here is that the question of how goals align with these conceptual distinctions is today, unlike in Aristotle's time, in part an empirical question that does not depend solely on speculation and argument. The point of an empirical model is to specify criteria by which we can distinguish goals of different types. Studies using this SDT framework have at least some starting methods and criteria to support or disconfirm theoretical proposals.

7.3.2.1 Intrinsic Versus Extrinsic Goal Attainment

Many social-cognitive theorists suggest that people feel good when they achieve their goals and that goal attainment (regardless of content) is beneficial to psychological health (e.g. Bandura 1989; Locke and Latham 1990). However, SDT proposes that such "expectancy" models must be qualified by the content of goals. It is primarily when people achieve intrinsic (rather than extrinsic) aspirations that they should experience greater well-being and less ill-being.

A number of studies have examined this hypothesis. For example, Kasser and Ryan (2001) examined the relation of the attainment of intrinsic versus extrinsic aspirations to various mental health outcomes in two samples. In the first sample, they found that the attainment of intrinsic goals was positively related to a composite index of well-being, whereas attainment of extrinsic goals was not. Moreover, the attainment of both intrinsic and extrinsic aspirations, relative to the attainment of intrinsic aspirations alone, did not additionally contribute to psychological health. Finally, the adjustment of people who attained only extrinsic aspirations was comparable to those who were low in their attainment of both intrinsic and extrinsic aspirations. In another sample, the attainment of intrinsic (relative to extrinsic) aspirations was again associated with higher well-being and more positive relationships. In addition, people high in their attainment of extrinsic aspirations reported lower quality of friendships, relative to those who were high in their attainment of intrinsic and extrinsic aspirations. Sheldon and Kasser (1998) assessed the impact of intrinsic versus extrinsic goal progress on changes in well-being over a several month interval, finding that although progress toward the attainment of all goals positively predicted changes in well-being, these relations were most apparent for intrinsic goals. Finally, Ryan et al. (1999) examined intrinsic and extrinsic aspiration attainments in samples from both the U.S. and Russia. They demonstrated that whereas attainment of extrinsic goals did not predict greater well-being when controlling for intrinsic goal attainment, intrinsic goal attainment predicted enhanced well-being even when controlling for extrinsic attainments. These results suggest that the attainment of intrinsic aspirations is beneficial for well-being and social functioning whereas the attainment of extrinsic aspirations is largely unrelated to psychological health.

7.3.3 Basic Psychological Needs and Intrinsic and Extrinsic Aspirations

Ryan et al. (1996) suggested that the key difference between the intrinsic and extrinsic aspirations, and the reason that the pursuit and attainment of the two groups of aspirations are differentially related to psychological health, is the degree to which they are linked to the satisfaction of the basic psychological needs for autonomy, competence, and relatedness. The *need for autonomy* refers to a sense of choice and volition in the regulation of behavior. The *need for competence* concerns the sense of efficacy one has with respect to both internal and external environments. The *need for relatedness* refers to feeling connected to and cared about by others. According to SDT satisfaction of these basic needs fosters well-being, and support for and satisfaction of each is a necessary condition for a person's growth, integrity, and well-being, both within and across domains. Deci and Ryan (2000) supplied an extensive review of the theory of basic needs and its empirical support. Intrinsic goals and aspirations are particularly apt at satisfying these three psychological needs. For instance, take the example of personal growth. A person who is focused on personal growth, which includes self-development, learning, and assimilation, is likely to a high degree to experience greater competence and to be involved in volitional and social activities. Similarly, community contributions, and altruistic or generative acts more generally, are hypothesized to satisfy all three needs fairly directly. When a person willingly gives to others he or she will exercise autonomy and feel a sense of connection with others. Further, the act of giving is likely to be associated with a sense of competence, as it means that people are in the position of being able to help.

SDT therefore hypothesizes that the attainment of intrinsic goals satisfies these needs, and in turn those attainments should enhance well-being. That is, psychological need satisfaction is specifically hypothesized to mediate between intrinsic goal attainments and well-being. By contrast, extrinsic goals are typically not as well linked with basic need satisfaction, and thus will not typically facilitate greater well-being, even when attained. This proposition was recently tested by Niemiec et al. (2006). They examined the consequences of pursuing and attaining intrinsic versus extrinsic aspirations over a one year period, beginning one year after the participants had graduated from college. Results indicated that although valuing either intrinsic or extrinsic aspirations led to greater attainment of the respective goals, only the attainment of intrinsic aspirations facilitated psychological well-being. In fact, on some measures extrinsic goal attainment was associated with greater ill being. Moreover, the positive relations between intrinsic goal attainment and well-being were mediated by satisfaction of the basic needs for autonomy, competence, and relatedness, which extrinsic attainments did not foster.

7.3.4 The What and Why of Life Goals

Numerous studies have demonstrated the systematic relations between intrinsic and extrinsic goal contents and well-being outcomes. However, SDT also views all behaviors as capable of being regulated by both controlled and autonomous motivations, raising the idea that, beyond goal contents—that is, beyond the "what" of goals—the reasons why the goal was undertaken is also of import in predicting well-being.

Regarding this "why" behind behavior, SDT specifies a continuum of types of regulation that vary along the dimension of autonomy. The most heteronomous form of regulation on this dimension is *external regulation,* which is exemplified by a person acting to avoid punishments or obtain contingent rewards. A somewhat less controlling reason for acting is *introjection,* in which the person acts because of internally controlling states, including contingent self-regard, or avoidance of shame and guilt. Still more autonomous is *identified regulation,* in which the motivation for acting is based on an explicit value for the action and/or its outcomes. One can be even more autonomous if such values are well integrated into one's system of values, which constitutes *integrated regulation.* Finally *intrinsic motivation* also represents a highly autonomous form of regulation. Beginning with Ryan and Connell (1989), dozens of studies accomplished in diverse cultures have shown empirically that this continuum of relative autonomy applies to behaviors in multiple domains (Vallerand 1997; Ryan and Deci 2000).

First, it is noteworthy that several studies have shown that, on average, intrinsic goals tend to be more autonomously enacted than extrinsic goals. That is, people are more likely to enact goals for money, image, or fame because of introjects or external regulations. They feel pressured to make more, look better, or attain recognition. By contrast, relatedness, growth, health, and community contribution all tend to be supported by autonomous reasons, including identified or integrated values, and, in some cases, intrinsic motivation.

Nonetheless, the relative autonomy of a goal can be considered independently of the intrinsic or extrinsic content of the goal, and SDT predicts that each of these issues will bear on well-being. For instance one could give to one's community, a presumably intrinsic goal content, but do so because one feels pressured to do so by others or by one's introjects. Alternatively one could contribute because of an integrated value, and thus the giving would be autonomous. Put differently, SDT predicts that both the "what" (goal contents) and the "why" (the relative autonomy underlying actions) are important to consider in the relations between goals and well-being outcomes. This too has been demonstrated in numerous studies. Perhaps the first was accomplished by Carver and Baird (1998) whose results showed independent variance associated with both the "what" and the "why" of a monetary goal in predicting self-actualization. Sheldon et al. (2004) provided three studies showing the independent contributions of these what and why effects, on a variety of well-being outcomes, which they demonstrated at both within- and between-subject levels of analysis.

Perhaps most impressively, Vansteenkiste and his colleagues have engaged in a series of studies in multiple domains where goal contents and relative autonomy have been experimentally manipulated. Goal contents are manipulated by *goal framing,* in which the focus of the activity is differently introduced. For example, in introducing people to a dietary regimen, they could either be told that it will make them more attractive (an extrinsic goal) or more healthy (an intrinsic goal). They could at the same time be subjected to a more controlling motivational approach ("you should do this") or a more autonomy supportive approach ("it is your choice"). In studies of obesity, learning, exercise, second language learning, ecological behaviors, and job searching, among other goals, Vansteenkiste and his co-workers have consistently demonstrated the significant impact of both the what and the why, not only on well-being outcomes, but also on goal persistence and success (see Vansteenkiste et al. 2006 for a recent review of this body of work).

Furthermore, the measures of both the what and why of goals have been directly linked to measures of eudaimonia. In a study that assessed Aristotle's definition of eudaimonia in relation to people's strivings and actual daily activities, the measures of eudaimonia had moderately positive correlations with indices of both what and why (Huta and Ryan 2006).

7.4 Autonomy and Mindfulness in Eudaimonic Living

Aristotle, as we indicated, depicted a eudaimonic life as one in which the individual is reflective and applies a sense of reason to his or her activities. In line with this we have already highlighted that goals associated with eudaimonia tend to be autonomous, and that autonomy is associated with greater well-ness, as well as more persistence and higher quality performance in what one does. We now briefly consider the issue of autonomy in somewhat more depth, especially its association with mindfulness, or awareness of what is truly occurring.

The term *autonomy* literally means "self-governing" and implies, therefore, the experience of regulation by the self. Its opposite, *heteronomy,* refers to regulation from outside the self, by alien or external forces. An autonomous act is one done freely and willingly by the actor. In the case of intrinsic motivation this is obvious, because intrinsic motivation represents doing an activity because of its inherent satisfactions, which one typically does quite freely. But in the case of activities that are not intrinsically motivated, the issue is not inherent enjoyment, but rather inherent and self-endorsed value. A person who acts autonomously reflectively embraces an activity as his or her own, endorsing it at the highest order of reflection. This idea of reflective endorsement of one's actions is indeed central to nearly all sophisticated philosophical treatments of the concept of autonomy, be they phenomenological (e.g. Ricoeur 1966; Pfander 1967) or analytic (e.g. Dworkin 1988; Friedman 2003). It is especially important to note that autonomy does not require acting in the absence of constraints or demands, nor does acting in opposition to a constraint or demand necessarily imply autonomy. Specifically, if one behaves in accord with constraints or external influences the key issue is whether the person reflectively concurs with them. A person could, for example, pay taxes out of fear of the consequences of not doing so, in which case the behavior would be heteronomous (i.e. controlled) and compliant. But a person could also pay taxes autonomously because he or she concurs with the importance of collecting this revenue for the good of all. Similarly, a person could refrain from paying taxes by cheating because he or she does not care about the needs of the many, in which case the behavior would be heteronomous (i.e. controlled) and defiant. But a person could also honestly withhold a portion of his or her taxes because of a moral objection to the way that portion of the taxes are being used, in which case the action would be autonomous. The point is that autonomy is defined by one's reflective and thoughtful endorsement of actions (whether in accord with or in opposition to a constraint or demand), and heteronomy is defined as action that does not involve a reflective self-endorsement (see Ryan 1993, for a fuller discussion).

This leads to yet a further strong claim: eudaimonia is necessarily rooted in human autonomy, as Aristotle also claimed. One cannot be following one's true self and not be autonomous. Indeed, autonomy is ideally behaving in accord with one's daimon, as Waterman among others has emphasized. Nor can one be eudaimonic and unreflective (Ryan and Deci 2004). It is through reflective consideration of one's goals and activities that one can come to endorse some and reject others. Thus, reflective capacities support the development of autonomy, and vice versa (Ryan 2005). Eudaimonia therefore necessitates the exercise of reflective capacities, in which one considers the meaning and value of one's way of living.

Brown and Ryan (2003) recently began empirically investigating the role of awareness and reflectivity in action through the concept of mindfulness. Mindfulness is defined as awareness of what is occurring in the present moment, and is characterized by an open and receptive processing of events, both internal and external. It is akin to what Aristotle was describing when he said the eudaimonic person sees what is true in every set of circumstances. When mindful people are aware of what is really occurring, and thus they are in a better position to make meaningful choices and to act in an integrated manner.

Evidence from recent research underscores the importance of mindfulness and awareness in promoting both autonomous regulation and enactment of values. Brown and Ryan (2003) showed at both within- and between-person levels of analysis an association between greater mindfulness and autonomous self-regulation. More recently, studies have shown that people who are more mindful are less materialistic, embrace more intrinsic (relative to extrinsic) values, and experience less discrepancy between what they have and what they want (Brown and Ryan 2004). Thus, it seems minimally that mindfulness is characteristic of people who are engaged in eudaimonic living. It is likely, however, that mindfulness actually conduces to eudaimonia, by facilitating awareness of what is worth doing, and doing it well.

7.5 The Outcomes of Eudaimonic Living

A central aspect of our model is that eudaimonia refers to the contents and process of living—to a lifestyle—and is not defined by its specific outcomes. Nonetheless we hypothesize that eudaimonia is predictably associated with numerous outcomes, including varied aspects of psychological well-being, relationship qualities, and one's impact on collective outcomes.

7.5.1 Subjective Well-Being

First, consider subjective well-being (SWB; Diener 1984), conceived of as pleasure and satisfaction in life, which Kahneman et al. (1999) described as hedonic well-being. In our model, both eudaimonic and non-eudaimonic activities can lead to SWB (Ryan and Deci 2001). That is, eudaimonia supplies one route to feeling good, but not an exclusive one. In fact, the direct pursuit of hedonic activities may also be a way of attaining pleasure, especially in the very short run. A person who exploits others, greedily consumes goods, or pursues fun and sensation may not be eudaimonic, but the person may derive pleasure.

Among the benefits of eudaimonic pursuits is that they may yield a more enduring sense of subjective well-being. Recent work by Huta and Ryan (2006) has supported this prediction. They followed students using an experience sampling method. Their results indicated that, at a within-person, momentary, level of analysis, only hedonic activities were consistently positively linked with positive affect and negatively linked with negative affect; eudaimonic activities on average had little relation with these. Yet, at the between-person level, it was people who engaged in a lot of eudaimonic activity or had eudaimonic goals who consistently had high life satisfaction and a high mean level of positive affect. By contrast, people occupied with hedonic activities or goals did not show these enduring benefits. These findings were consistent with the expectation that eudaimonia gradually enhances a person's baseline level of well-being, whereas hedonia has more temporary effects.

7.5.2 Psychological Well-Being

In addition to greater SWB, there are other aspects of well-being that may be more enhanced by eudaimonic than non-eudaimonic ways of living, as revealed by research on both autonomous regulation, and intrinsic and extrinsic goals. Many of these are captured by Ryff and Singer's (1998) dimensions of psychological well-being (PWB), which Ryff and Singer construed as outcomes of a life well lived. Measures of PWB include indicators of personal growth, environmental mastery, positive relationships, life purpose, self-acceptance, and autonomy (conceived of within the PWB model as being primarily independence rather than self-endorsement and volition as in SDT). Moreover, Ryff and Singer have shown that PWB in turn fosters additional outcomes in terms of physical health and wellness.

In terms of the model being proposed in this paper, we construe the dimensions of PWB not as a measure of eudaimonia per se, but rather as indicators that one has been living well. That is, as assessed, PWB is more a measure of a set of outcomes of eudaimonic living rather than a definition of eudaimonia. Accordingly, Huta and Ryan (2006) has shown that her measures of eudaimonia, which assesses striving to be the best one can be, developing one's potential, and having concerns for the greater good, are indeed positively related to most of Ryff and Singer's facets of psychological well-being.

Although we have just portrayed PWB as an outcome of eudaimonic living, it is important to recognize that PWB can, in turn, yield other outcomes such as the presence of healthy psychological and physical functioning and the absence of psychopathology and disease. Indeed, in their paper in this issue, Ryff and Singer reviewed several studies showing that PWB did in fact lead to better physical health. When viewed in this way, PWB can be understood as a set of processes that mediate between the independent variables of intrinsic goals and autonomous regulation on the one hand, and the dependent variables of psychological and physical wellness on the other hand. This would place PWB in the same type of mediating role in which we have placed basic psychological need satisfaction.

7.5.3 Other Outcomes Associated with Eudaimonic Living

7.5.3.1 Meaning

A sense of meaning, which is one of the PWB dimensions mentioned above is also sometimes viewed as an outcome of eudaimonia (e.g. McGregor and Little 1998). In our view, eudaimonic living as represented by a focus on intrinsic goals and a practice of reflection and mindfulness would undoubtedly produce a sense of meaning and a greater sense of purpose in life (Ryan and Deci 2004). Moreover, eudaimonic living as we define it ought to provide a strong elixir against a sense of alienation or lack of life purpose, presumed opposites of finding meaning. Indeed, Huta and Ryan (2006) found that eudaimonic goals and activities were positively related to several measures of meaning in life.

7.5.3.2 Vitality

One interesting variable that we have considered to be enhanced through eudaimonia is *subjective vitality* (Ryan and Frederick 1997). Subjective vitality is defined in terms of a sense of psychological and physical energy that is available to the self for life pursuits. Ryan and Frederick (1997) assessed people's subjective vitality and showed its close associations with autonomy, and Nix et al. (1999) showed in experimental settings how behaviors regulated by external controls reduced vitality relative to comparisons that were not controlled. Numerous studies comparing intrinsic and extrinsic goals have shown greater subjective vitality associated with, or in many cases, brought about by, investment in or attainment of intrinsic goals (e.g. Kasser and Ryan 1996, 2001; Niemiec et al. 2006). Several studies have shown the close association between mindfulness and vitality, such that, when mindful, people experience more available energy (Brown and Ryan 2003). Finally, Huta and Ryan (2006) found that trait eudaimonia had a consistent positive link with vitality. In short, this configuration of distinct variables, namely autonomous regulation, intrinsic goal focus, and mindfulness all enhance subjective vitality, which in turn strongly covaries with an array of mental and physical health outcomes.

7.5.3.3 Physical Health

In some studies of intrinsic goals, autonomous regulation, and mindfulness, physical symptoms and physical health have been assessed and positively related to these independent variables (e.g. Kasser and Ryan 1996; Williams et al. 1998).

Moreover, basic psychological need satisfaction, which in the current model plays a mediational role, also predicts physical symptoms and health outcomes (e.g. Reis et al. 2000). Physical health is a major focus of Ryff and Singer's research, which they have directly related to PWB (see their article in this issue). Some of this body of work makes it plausible that it is eudaimonic living that yields better physical health, such as the within-person approach of Reis et al. (2000) and some of the in-depth studies accomplished by Ryff and colleagues. At the same time, because physical health makes living well more possible, there are undoubted reciprocal relations at work, making for an intriguing area of study. Currently we are working to disentangle relations between mindfulness and health through intervention studies (see Brown and Ryan 2003, for a preliminary study of this kind).

7.5.3.4 Still Other Outcomes

Research has also been initiated to map out additional kinds of well-being to which eudaimonia might be linked. Huta and Ryan (2006) hypothesized that eudaimonia often produces states and outcomes that are subtle or not fully captured by the well-being concepts typically assessed. The researchers showed that eudaimonic individuals: have high levels of inner peace, as well as frequent experiences of moral elevation and deep appreciation of life; feel connected not only with themselves but also with a greater whole that transcends them as individuals; have a sense of where they fit into a bigger picture and are able to put things in perspective; and describe themselves as "feeling right" (as opposed to "feeling good", the state that hedonically oriented individuals seem to pursue). A life of hedonia has in most analyses been unrelated to these outcomes.

7.6 Putting it Together: An Integrative, Yet Open, Empirical Model

To summarize our model, eudaimonia is viewed as living well, defined in terms both of pursuing goals that are intrinsically valued and of processes that are characterized by autonomy and awareness. The ways in which goals, regulatory styles, and capacities for mindfulness operate together has been detailed over many studies, but our major claim here is that they are all aspects of eudaimonic living. A further claim is that eudaimonic living is associated with a wide array of wellness outcomes. Those outcomes include hedonic happiness as typically assessed, but it also produces a fuller, more stable and enduring type of happiness than that obtained when one's goals are more directly hedonistic. Among these enduring positive outcomes are a sense of meaning, subjective vitality, higher quality relationships, and better physical health indicators, especially with respect to symptoms related to stress. Finally we claim that these relations between eudaimonia and well-being outcomes are mediated by satisfaction of the basic psychological needs for autonomy, competence, and relatedness. That is, eudaimonic living fosters well-being because it provides satisfaction of people's most fundamental psychological needs.

7.7 Social Implications of Eudaimonic Living

The starting point for our model of eudaimonia was the question of what constitutes the "good life", or living well. As we have outlined, we consider living well to involve pursing intrinsic goals, acting autonomously and volitionally, and fostering one's own awareness or mindfulness. Considerable research has connected these three motivational processes to psychological and physical health outcomes, and has shown that satisfaction of the basic psychological needs for competence, relatedness, and autonomy mediate the relations between the motivational processes and the wellness outcomes.

We now turn to a consideration of broader issues that address two important and related questions, specifically: (1) what are the implications of eudaimonia for societal and collective well-being; and (2) what are the conditions within a society that conduce toward its members being able to pursue the kind of life represented by eudaimonia?

7.7.1 The Prosocial Nature of People High in Eudaimonia

Given our depiction of people high in eudaimonia as pursuing worthwhile goals and being mindfully self-regulated, it follows that such persons would likely be more socially responsible. The emerging evidence suggests that to be so. For example, Brown and Kasser (2005) found that people embracing the extrinsic goal of materialism consumed more and left bigger environmental footprints. Sheldon and McGregor (2000) used a "tragedy of the commons" paradigm to show that people with more intrinsic goals were less likely to over-consume, and thus were more likely to foster a sustainable environment. McHoskey (1999) demonstrated that people embracing intrinsic goals were less prone to Machiavellian behavior and more prone towards social interests. These and other studies attest to the fact that promotion of eudaimonic living may be better for a society as a whole, insofar as its members show more care, concern, and responsibility in their actions. Waterman (1981) also reviewed studies showing that eudaimonia is positively linked to prosocial concerns.

7.7.2 What Kinds of Families and Societies Foster Eudaimonic Lifestyles

A tougher question concerns what kind of social contexts facilitate people becoming eudaimonic. We can ask that question at the micro level of the family, as well as at the more macro level of cultural and economic conditions. We take each in turn.

Kasser et al. (1995) tapped into an ongoing longitudinal project to examine the antecedents of intrinsic versus materialistic, extrinsic goals in a sample of largely urban 18 year olds. The researchers found that psychological need support—specifically a maternal environment characterized by greater autonomy support and greater warmth—promoted the adoption of less materialistic goals, greater community participation, and in general better mental health. This study employed multiple methods to assess maternal environments and well-being outcomes, including maternal reports, clinical interview ratings, and self-reports from the teens. Moreover, the study showed that these supports for autonomy and relatedness were prospectively predictive of the intrinsic versus extrinsic goal outcomes. Kasser et al. suggested that to the extent children are provided with supports for basic needs they will develop more eudaimonic lifestyles. In contrast those treated in controlling ways, or who experienced coldness or rejection from caregivers were more prone to insecurity and low self-esteem, which in turn appears to have made them more susceptible to extrinsic goals. That is, they seek external trappings of worth to the extent they have felt inwardly unloved or unworthy (see also Ryan et al. 1996; Kasser 2002). A study by Williams et al. (2000) of high school students found that those students whose parents tended to be need thwarting also expressed strong extrinsic aspirations and engaged in high risk behaviors such as using tobacco and alcohol.

On a more societal level it does seem clear that within modern capitalistic societies, which are increasingly dominating the global scene, there are pervasive forces that pull people away from eudaimonic living. Consumerism is prompted by continuous exposure to desire-creating advertisements, which often attempt to promote insecurity in order to create a sense of need. Moreover, the winner take all atmosphere associated with the values of a competitive market economy can crowd out altruism, sense of community, and other prosocial attitudes. It seems that the eudaimonic life is continuously threatened by the individualistic attitudes associated with such economies, whereas hedonic well-being has a much closer fit with the capitalist ethic (Kasser et al. 2007). It is indeed paradoxical that, whereas the capitalistic system provides resources that could facilitate eudaimonic living among those individuals who have not fallen through the bottom of the system, it also has seductive and coercive aspects that undermine the very goals, values, and lifestyles that constitute eudaimonic living.

At the same time, some policy makers and social scholars do seem attuned to the fact that competitive individualism and hedonic happiness for the masses will lead to and ultimately be compromised by an unsustainable environment. Indeed, the tragedy of the commons is ever becoming our real situation, rather than a simulation game. Moreover, there is increasing awareness, in part aided by many of the studies reviewed herein, that materialistic living, even when successfully attained, does not significantly enhance well-being—even hedonic well-being let alone eudaimonic living. Instead, human happiness and quality of life will be facilitated best by policies and structures that allow people to feel both maximal psychological freedom and strong relatedness to one another, neither of which is facilitated by materialism.

As we move further into our new century, it appears that the topic of eudaimonia is ever more relevant and timely. In this respect the study of what constitutes eudaimonia, and what promotes it, are among the most important agendas in contemporary behavioral science, much as it was a critical part of ancient philosophies.

References

Aristotle (2002) Nichomachean Ethics (Trans and commentary: Broadie S, Rowe C). Oxford, New York

Bandura A (1989) Human agency in social cognitive theory. Am Psychol 44:1175–1184

Broadie S, Rowe C (2002) Preface in Aristotle (2002) Nichomachean Ethics (trans: Broadie S, Rowe C). Oxford, New York

Brown KW, Kasser T (2005) Are psychological and ecological well being compatible? The role of values, mindfulness, and lifestyle. Soc Ind Res 74:349–368

Brown KW, Ryan RM (2003) The benefits of being present: mindfulness and its role in psychological well-being. J Pers Soc Psychol 84:822–848

Brown KW, Ryan RM (2004) Fostering healthy self-regulation from within and without: a self-determination theory perspective. In: Linley PA, Joseph S (eds) Positive Psychology in Practice. Wiley, New York, pp 105–124

Carver CS, Baird E (1998) The American dream revisited: Is it what you want or why you want it that matters? Psychol Sci 9:289–292

Christopher JC (1999) Situating psychological well-being: exploring the cultural roots of its theory and research. J Couns Dev 77:141–152

Deci EL (1980) The psychology of self-determination. In: DC Heath, Lexington

Deci EL, Ryan RM (1980) The empirical exploration of intrinsic motivational processes. In: Berkowitz L (ed) Advances in experimental social psychology, vol 13. Academic, New York, pp 39–80

Deci EL, Ryan RM (1985) Intrinsic motivation and self-determination in human behavior. Plenum Publishing Co, New York

Deci EL, Ryan RM (2000) The "what" and "why" of goal pursuits: Human needs and the self-determination of behavior. Psychol Inq 11:227–268

Diener E (1984) Subjective well-being. Psychol Bull 95:542–575

Dworkin G (1988) The theory and practice of autonomy. Cambridge University Press, New York

Ferguson H (1990) The science of pleasure: cosmos and psyche in the bourgeois world view. Routledge, London

Friedman M (2003) Autonomy, gender, politics. Oxford University Press, New York

Grouzet FME, Kasser T, Ahuvia A, Fernandez-Dols JM, Kim Y, Lau S, Ryan RM, Saunders S, Schmuck P, Sheldon K (2005) The structure of goal contents across 15 cultures. J Pers Soc Psychol 89:800–816

Huta VM, Ryan RM (2006) Pursuing pleasure versus virtue: links with different aspects of well-being, University of Rochester, Rochester (unpublished manuscript)

Isen AM (2003) Positive affect as a source of human strength. In: Aspinwall LG, Staudinger UM (eds) A psychology of human strengths: fundamental questions and future directions for a positive psychology. American Psychological Association, Washington, pp 179–195

Kahneman D, Diener E, Schwarz N (1999) Well-being: the foundations of hedonic psychology. Russell Sage Foundation, New York

Kasser T (2002) Sketches for a self-determination theory of values. In: Deci EL, Ryan RM (eds) Handbook of Self-Determination Research. University of Rochester Press, Rochester, pp 123–140

Kasser T, Cohn S, Kanner AD, Ryan RM (2007) Some costs of American corporate capitalism: A psychological exploration of value and goal conflicts. Psychol Inquiry (in press)
Kasser T, Ryan RM (1993) A dark side of the American dream: correlates of financial success as a central life aspiration. J Pers Soc Psychol 65:410–422
Kasser T, Ryan RM (1996) Further examining the American dream: differential correlates of intrinsic and extrinsic goals. Pers Soc Psychol Bull 22:280–287
Kasser T, Ryan RM (2001) Be careful what you wish for: optimal functioning and the relative attainment of intrinsic and extrinsic goals. In: Schmuck P, Sheldon KM (eds) Life goals and well-being: towards a positive psychology of human striving. Hogrefe and Huber Publishers, Goettingen, pp 115–129
Kasser T, Ryan RM, Zax M, Sameroff AJ (1995) The relations of maternal and social environments to late adolescents' materialistic and prosocial values. Dev Psychol 31:907–914
King LA, Hicks JA, Krull JL, Baker AK (2006) Positive affect and the experience of meaning in life. J Pers Soc Psychol 90:179–196
Locke EA, Latham GP (1990) A theory of goal setting and task performance. Prentice-Hall, Englewood Cliffs
Maddux JE (2002) Stopping the "madness": positive psychology and the deconstruction of the illness ideology and the DSM. In: Snyder CR, Lopez SJ (eds) Handbook of positive psychology. Oxford, New York, pp 13–25
McGregor I, Little BR (1998) Personal projects, happiness, and meaning: On doing well and being yourself. J Pers Soc Psychol 74:494–512
McHoskey JW (1999) Machiavellianism, intrinsic versus extrinsic goals, and social interest: a self-determination theory analysis. Motiv Emot 23:267–283
Niemiec CP, Ryan RM, Deci EL (2006) The path taken: consequences of attaining intrinsic and extrinsic aspirations in post-college life, University of Rochester, unpublished manuscript
Nix G, Ryan RM, Manly JB, Deci EL (1999) Revitalization through self-regulation: the effects of autonomous versus controlled motivation on happiness and vitality. J Exp Soc Psychol 35:266–284
Pfander A (1967) Phenomenology of willing and motivation. In: Spiegelberg H (ed) Translator. Northwestern University Press, Evanston (Original work published 1908)
Reis HT, Sheldon KM, Gable SL, Roscoe J, Ryan RM (2000) Daily well-being: the role of autonomy, competence, and relatedness. Pers Soc Psychol Bull 26:419–435
Ricoeur P (1966) Freedom and nature: the voluntary and the involuntary. In: Kohak EV (ed) Translator. Northwestern University Press, Chicago
Ryan RM (1993) Agency and organization: intrinsic motivation, autonomy and the self in psychological development. In: Jacobs J (ed) Nebraska Symposium on Motivation: Developmental Perspectives on Motivation, vol. 40. University of Nebraska Press, Lincoln, pp 1–56
Ryan RM (1995) Psychological needs and the facilitation of integrative processes. J Pers 63:397–427
Ryan RM (2005) The developmental line of autonomy in the etiology, dynamics, and treatment of boderline personality disorders. Dev Psychopathol 17:987–1006
Ryan RM, Chirkov VI, Little TD, Sheldon KM, Timoshina E, Deci EL (1999) The American dream in Russia: extrinsic aspirations and well-being in two cultures. Pers Soc Psychol Bull 25:1509–1524
Ryan RM, Connell JP (1989) Perceived locus of causality and internalization: examining reasons for acting in two domains. J Pers Soc Psychol 57:749–761
Ryan RM, Deci EL (2000) Self-determination theory and the facilitation of intrinsic motivation, social development, and well-being. Am Psychol 55:68–78
Ryan RM, Deci EL (2001) On happiness and human potentials: a review of research on hedonic and eudaimonic well-being. In: Fiske S (ed) Annual review of psychology, vol 52. Annual Reviews Inc., Palo Alto, pp 141–166
Ryan RM, Deci EL (2004) Avoiding death or engaging life as accounts of meaning and culture: a comment on Pyszczynski, Greenberg, Solomon, Arndt, and Schimel. Psychol Bull 130:473–477

Ryan RM, Frederick CM (1997) On energy, personality and health: subjective vitality as a dynamic reflection of well-being. J Pers 65:529–565

Ryan RM, Rigby S, King K (1993) Two types of religious internalization and their relations to religious orientation and mental health. J Pers Soc Psychol 65:586–596

Ryan RM, Sheldon KM, Kasser T, Deci EL (1996) All goals are not created equal: an organismic perspective on the nature of goals and their regulation. In: Gollwitzer PM, Bargh JA (eds) The psychology of action: linking cognition and motivation to behavior. Guilford, New York, pp 7–26

Ryff CD, Singer B (1998) The contours of positive human health. Psychol Inq 9:1–28

Schmuck P, Kasser T, Ryan RM (2000) The relationship of well-being to intrinsic and extrinsic goals in Germany and the US. Soc Indic Res 50:225–241

Sheldon KM, Kasser T (1998) Pursuing personal goals: skills enable progress, but not all progress is beneficial. Pers Soc Psychol Bull 24:1319–1331

Sheldon KM, McGregor HA (2000) Extrinsic value orientation and the tragedy of the commons. J Pers 68:383–411

Sheldon KM, Ryan RM, Deci EL, Kasser T (2004) The independent effects of goal contents and motives on well-being: It's both what you pursue and why you pursue it. Pers Soc Psychol Bull 30:475–486

Vallerand RJ (1997) Toward a hierarchical model of intrinsic and extrinsic motivation. In: Dans Zanna MP (ed) Advances in experimental social psychology, Academic Press, New York, pp 271–360

Vansteenkiste M, Lens W, Deci EL (2006) Intrinsic versus extrinsic goal contents in self-determination theory: another look at the quality of academic motivation. Educ Psychol 41:19–31

Vansteenkiste M, Simons J, Lens W, Sheldon KM, Deci EL (2004) Motivating learning, performance, and persistence: the synergistic effects of intrinsic goal contents and autonomy-supportive contexts. J Pers Soc Psychol 87:246–260

Waterman AS (1981) Individualism and interdependence. Am Psychol 36:762–773

Waterman AS (1993) Two conceptions of happiness: contrasts of personal expressiveness (eudaimonia) and hedonic enjoyment. J Pers Soc Psychol 64:678–691

Williams GC, Cox EM, Hedberg V, Deci EL (2000) Extrinsic life goals and health risk behaviors in adolescents. J Appl Soc Psychol 30:1756–1771

Williams GC, Freedman ZR, Deci EL (1998) Supporting autonomy to motivate glucose control in patients with diabetes. Diabetes Care 21:1644–1651

Chapter 8
The Multiple Determination of Well-Being: Independent Effects of Positive Traits, Needs, Goals, Selves, Social Supports, and Cultural Contexts

Kennon M. Sheldon and Tan H. Hoon

Abstract Although most researchers acknowledge that subjective well-being (SWB) is multiply determined, little research and theory simultaneously considers the effects of many types of determinants, located at many different levels of analysis. Guided by a six-level model of "optimal human being", we tested the hypothesis that psychological need-satisfaction, a positive Big Five trait profile, good personal goal-progress, high self-esteem, positive social support, and a happiness-conducing cultural membership would each uniquely predict SWB. These hypotheses were confirmed, supporting the hierarchical perspective and irreducibility assumption that under-girded the research. Implications for SWB theory and interventions, and for the task of integrating the many different types of personality constructs that exist, are discussed.

Keywords Subjective well-being • Personality hierarchies • Culture

8.1 Introduction

Subjective well-being (SWB) remains a growth industry in the contemporary research scene. As just a sampling of recent activity, research has investigated the psychometric components (Pavot and Diener 2004; Schwarz and Strack 1999), temporal resolution (Sandlik et al. 1993), functional concomitants (Lyubomirsky et al. 2005a, b), longitudinal course (Clark et al. 2003), personality/demographic

K. M. Sheldon (✉)
Psychological Sciences, University of Missouri-Columbia,
McAlester Hall, Columbia, MO 65211, USA
e-mail: sheldonk@missouri.edu

A. Delle Fave (ed.), *The Exploration of Happiness*, Happiness Studies Book Series,
DOI: 10.1007/978-94-007-5702-8_8, © Springer Science+Business Media Dordrecht 2013

correlates (Argyle 1999), and cultural conditionality of SWB (Diener et al. 1995), as well as many other topics. In part spurred by the positive psychology movement (Seligman and Csikszentmihalyi 2000), this work contributes to an increasingly complete picture of the nature and causes of SWB (Pavot and Diener 2004; Ryan and Deci 2000a, b; Sheldon 2004).

However, one topic that has received almost no research attention is the multi-level nature of SWB—that is, the fact that SWB is simultaneously influenced by variables at many different levels of the person and world. Of course, most researchers would agree that SWB is multiply-determined, by factors ranging vertically from biological to cognitive to personality to social (for example, as acknowledged in the chapter organization of the book *Well-being: The foundations of hedonic psychology*, edited by Kahneman et al. 1999). Still, to date, few theoretical or predictive frameworks have attempted to address many of these levels of analysis at the same time. How do they all contribute to influence peoples' experienced mood and sense of satisfaction? Are some levels more important than others, and others less important? More typically, researchers focus on just one level of analysis, elaborating upon ideas and measures located primarily at that level (Staats 1999).

This article proposes a new way to conceptualize and test the multi-determination idea—namely, by measuring representative factors at major levels of organization that influence the human personality (i.e., needs, traits, goals, self-systems, social systems, and cultural systems; explicated below), and comparing their effects upon SWB. Our general hypothesis was that important and previously efficacious predictor variables derived from each level of analysis should, when combined together into a single prediction equation, each have unique main effects upon SWB. This "irreducibility hypothesis" is based on the assumption that the SWB-relevant constructs and processes identified by researchers at each level of human science are all valid—each level provides independent information regarding human thriving, and thus each should uniquely predict SWB. To use a concrete example, the positive effects of social support should not be explainable in terms of a person's positive goals, or his/her positive traits, or his/her high self-esteem; the phenomenon that has been studied by social support researchers is more than these.

An advantage of this multi-systemic approach is that it can provide a tool for evaluating the relative importance of a particular level of analysis, compared to other levels of analysis upon which one might instead focus attention. If the effects of a previously important predictive factor at a particular level of analysis fail to survive in such a "destructive testing" approach (Anderson and Anderson 1996), then one might legitimately question the relevance of that factor and/or level of analysis for understanding that phenomenon—perhaps research attention should focus elsewhere. Conversely, this approach may provide a tool for identifying the most important factors and levels for understanding a particular phenomenon (here, SWB). Which predictors, located at which level of analysis, emerge as most essential? The potential relevance of such data for designing SWB-relevant interventions and public policies should be clear.

8.1.1 Hierarchical Frameworks for Viewing Behavior and Personality

As a framework for the inquiry we drew from the hierarchical model of causal influences upon human behavior and well-being that was proposed by Sheldon (2004). This model formalizes the fact that behavior and feeling can be influenced by manifold levels of reality ranging from atomic to molecular to cellular to organic to neuronal to nervous-systemic to cognitive to personality to social to cultural. Each level of organization was said to emerge from the functioning of the level below, but also to have reciprocal top-down effects upon lower-level functioning (see also Sperry 1993). In his analysis of optimal human being (i.e., the determinants of well-being and thriving), Sheldon (2004) focused primarily on the top three levels of this hierarchy, namely, the personality, social, and cultural levels, in the process identifying the constructs at each level shown to have influence on well-being. Personality processes received special attention, as potentially the most relevant of all for thriving; in particular, universal psychological needs, varying personality traits, varying goals and intentions, and varying self-images and self-concepts, were each the subject of a chapter. Each of these four aspects of personality will be considered in greater detail.

8.1.1.1 The Four Tiers of Personality.

The four aspects of personality depicted in Fig. 8.1 are based on McAdams' (1995, 1996) proposals. McAdams argued that traits/dispositions, goals/motives, and selves/self-narratives are three distinct and important "tiers" of personality theory and organization. Each level addresses issues that the other levels do not. None of them are determined by the others, and thus information from each of the levels is necessary for a complete understanding of a person (i.e., motive effects upon behavior are more than mere trait and self-concept effects, self-concept effects are more than mere trait and motive effects, and so on). Furthermore, McAdams and Pals (2006) argued that the field of personality psychology is no longer well-served by attempts to reduce different aspects of personality to one another, instead calling for simultaneous and integrated consideration of all of them together. One goal of this research is to test McAdams' claim that constructs at these three levels of personality have effects that are independent and

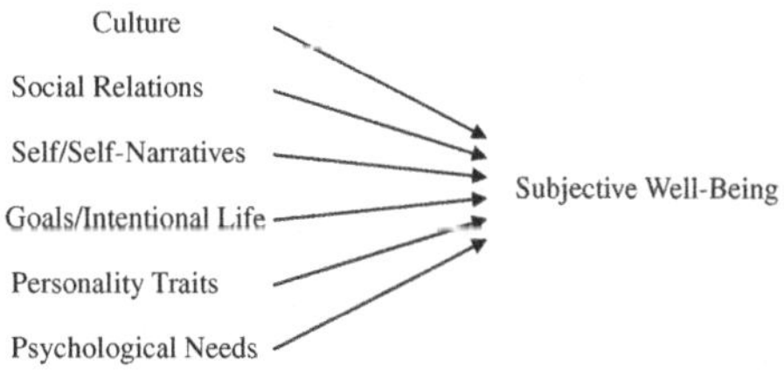

Fig. 1 Six levels of the person relevant to optimal human being (Sheldon 2004)

non-reducible to each other, by hypothesizing that they should all have simultaneous effects upon SWB.

The three levels identified by McAdams (1996) involve domains of individual difference. However, Sheldon (2004) argued that foundational and evolved (i.e. species-typical) human nature also needs to be considered for a complete picture (see McAdams and Pals 1996, for related theorizing). What are the most basic personality processes upon which individual differences rest? In considering this fourth level Sheldon discussed universal biophysical requirements, psychological needs, social-cognitive mechanisms, and socio-cultural practices—all thought to be inborn propensities that do not vary across individuals, although they may of course vary in their expression.

Notably, the four levels of personality presented in Fig. 2 do not necessarily form a functional hierarchy, as in Carver and Scheier's (1982, 1998) control theory model of personality. Thus, traits do not necessarily serve goals, goals do not necessarily serve self-concepts, and self-concepts do not necessarily serve social relations. Neither do the four levels represent a causal sequence, leading in domino sequence from low to high, or from high to low. Thus, for example, we would not expect goal effects to mediate self effects, or self effects to mediate social relation effects. Instead, the levels are merely viewed as distinct facets of the person, each of which contains information that cannot be gotten from the other facets (McAdams 1996, 2000). Thus, the current research is simply an exploration of four important facets of personality, in conjunction with information concerning social and cultural contexts, as predictors of a single construct, namely, SWB.

What personality constructs are most predictive of SWB? In reviewing the corresponding research literatures, Sheldon (2004) concluded that the highest degree of optimality or thriving may occur when a person: (1) experiences much satisfaction of basic psychological needs (at the species-typical or foundation level of personality), (2) evidences low levels of neuroticism and also high levels of other extraversion, agreeableness, conscientiousness, and perhaps openness (at the trait or dispositional level of personality), (3) achieves many of his/her personal goals, especially self-concordant personal goals (at the goal or intentional level of personality), and (4) feels much self-esteem and proximity to desired future selves (at the self and self-concept level of personality).

In the current research we simultaneously compared the associations of all of these constructs upon SWB. We did this in two steps: by first (1) comparing the relative efficacy of two or more candidate constructs *within* each conceptual level for predicting SWB, in order to select the strongest predictor to represent that level of analysis, and then by (2) comparing *between* all of the thereby-designated predictors, one from each level, as simultaneous predictors of global concurrent SWB. Consistent with the "irreducibility hypothesis," we expected that the best predictors within each level would uniquely predict SWB when pitted against the best predictors from the other levels.

Notably, our preliminary step of identifying two candidate predictors at each level and letting them compete for variance might capitalize unduly on chance, or upon data characteristics irrelevant to our conceptual purposes. Nevertheless we took such an approach in the current study, hoping to illustrate a method for beginning to consolidate and prioritize disparate constructs within personality psychology. Although the conclusion that "X is a better predictor of Y than Z" must be taken with caution within any particular study, over time, multiple researchers' reports should cumulate to a clear understanding of the relative importance of various predictors. In short, making initially reasonable choices of constructs to examine, then following through with those comparisons, may ultimately be the best way to bring greater order to the "zoo" of partially overlapping predictors in personality psychology.

8.1.1.2 Two Higher Levels: Social Relations and Cultural Influences.

Again, Sheldon (2004) also considered two trans-personality levels of analysis, namely, social relations and culture. These higher levels of organization emerge from the interactions of multiple personalities, and contain information that goes beyond the properties of the constituent personalities. In order to evaluate the associations of the social relations level of analysis upon SWB, in the current studies we examined participants' perceived social support and autonomy support. Of course, social support has long been known to be important for many kinds of psychological health and coping outcomes (Lakey and Lutz 1996; Sarason et al. 2001). Similarly, the social-level factor of autonomy support, which is the extent that important others grant one choice and input rather than trying to coerce and control one, has been shown to be beneficial for outcomes as diverse as learning, intrinsic motivation, creativity, mood, and psychological vitality (Deci and Ryan 2000; Sheldon et al. 2003). Again, we first compared the predictive efficacy of these two variables, and then moved forward with the strongest predictor to the second, cross-level phase of the analysis.

"Culture" can be defined in terms of the shared norms, traditions, and values of a large group of interacting personalities that have emerged over time (Geertz 1974). Of course, cultural syndromes can have important influence upon many different aspects of human behavior and experience (Markus et al. 1996). In order to address this top level of the Fig. 2 model, we sampled participants in two very different cultures: The U.S. and Singapore. The U.S. is considered to be a prototypically individualist (i.e. modern and individual-centered) culture, whereas Singapore is considered to be a fairly collectivist (i.e., traditional and group-centered) culture (Diener et al. 1995; Triandis 1997). Asian collectivist cultures typically evidence lower mean levels of well-being compared to western cultures, and Diener et al. (1995) showed specifically that national well-being in Singapore is considerably lower than national well-being in the U.S. Consistent with the irreducibility hypothesis and with past SWB findings (Diener et al. 1995), we expected that cultural group would have its own main effects upon SWB, independently of the other five predictors. Based on previous research on the inter-correlations of culture, personality, and well-being (Diener and Suh 1999), cultural membership should still have an effect on SWB even after all of the lower-level effects have been accounted for.

To summarize, even though there is likely some empirical overlap between some of the constructs examined (i.e., competence need-satisfaction is likely correlated with goal progress, and so on), we expected that each identified construct would uniquely predict SWB, because each ultimately refers to a different level of organization within the human personality. To find support for this hypothesis would indicate that goal effects cannot be reduced to need effects, that trait effects cannot be reduced to goal effects, and so on; all of these perspectives will be required for a truly comprehensive model of personality and SWB.

8.1.1.3 The Role of Inter-Level Consistency.

Sheldon (2004) also suggested that SWB is affected not only by the *contents* of (or conditions within) the differing levels of the person, but also, by the *relations between* the levels of the person, independently of their contents. The implication is that one can have a good profile of characteristics at each level but still not achieve optimality because the different levels of oneself are not well-integrated (i.e., a conflicted young woman is pursuing positive goals and self-images that are nevertheless inconsistent with her also-positive traits and social relationships). Conversely, one can be well-integrated between levels, but still not thrive because of what the levels contain (i.e., a sociopath whose personality is well-organized nevertheless suffers because of his many negative personality characteristics). Ideally, one has both factors going for one; i.e., one is both "organismically" and "systemically" integrated (Sheldon and Kasser 1995).

Thus, we asked participants to consider how each level of themselves (needs, traits, goals, selves, and social supports) relates to, or functions with respect to, each other level. We predicted that inter-level consistency would have its own independent main effect upon SWB, above the significant main effects of the predictors at each level of analysis. Again, this would support Sheldon's (2004) contention that SWB is a combination of both the person's profile of characteristics within the different levels of analysis, and, the degree of functional linkage between those levels.

8.2 Methods

8.2.1 Participants and Procedure

Initial participants were 328 introductory psychology students at the University of Missouri (MU) and 237 introductory management students at the National University of Singapore (NUS).[1] Although NUS is somewhat more selective in its

[1] A portion of this dataset was used by Sheldon and Niemiec (in press). However, none of the relations in this article have been reported before.

admission and is located in a larger urban center compared to MU, both universities are large public institutions that draw students from all over their respective nations. Also, both classes were large lecture topic-introductions, attracting a wide variety of students from within each University. Thus, these convenience samples seemed reasonably representative of the two cultures from which they were drawn. Thirty-two participants (22 Americans and 10 Singaporeans) were dropped because there was missing data on at least one of the 15 primary study variables, resulting in a final N of 533 consisting of 306 Americans (114 men and 192 women) and 227 Singaporeans (133 men and 94 women). Because of the differing gender proportions within the two samples, gender will be co-varied out of the primary models below.

U.S. participants completed the survey using a web-based format, and Singaporean participants completed the survey in group testing sessions using a paper-and-pencil format. Although web based survey methodologies are still relatively new, initial research indicates that data from such surveys are largely equivalent to paper-and-pencil data (Birnbaum 2000; Stanton 1998). Both surveys were administered in English, which is the official language of instruction at NUS. The measures were all presented in the same order to Singaporean participants: First, the SWB measures (i.e. the "dependent measures") were presented, followed by the need-satisfaction measures, the personality trait measures, the goal measures, the self measures, and finally the social support measures. Thus, following SWB the order of presentation of the predictor variables moved from low to high in the Fig. 8.1 hierarchy. Approximately half of the U.S. participants also received the measures in this order, and the other half first rated SWB and then rated the predictor variables moving from high to low in the Fig. 8.1 hierarchy. Although it had some main effects, order of measures did not interact with the primary results, below, and will not be considered further.

8.2.2 Measures

8.2.2.1 SWB

SWB was measured by summing positive affect and life-satisfaction and subtracting negative affect (Diener 1994; see Bettencourt and Sheldon 2001; Sheldon and Elliot 1999; Sheldon and Kasser 2001; Sheldon and Krieger 2004; Sheldon et al. 2004). The SWB questions were framed in terms of "how much you feel this way, in general in your life," and administered with a 1 (not at all) to 5 (extremely) scale. Affect was measured via the 20-item Positive affect/negative affect scale (PANAS; Watson et al. 1988); items include "interested," "nervous," "attentive," and "upset." Coefficient alpha for positive and negative affect were 0.75 and 0.81 respectively (0.64 and 0.88 in the U.S. sample, and 0.79 and 0.84 in the Singaporean sample). Life-satisfaction was measured via the 5-item Satisfaction with Life Scale (Diener et al. 1985), using the same scale; an example item is "in most ways, my life is close to my ideal" (alpha = 0.86; 0.85 and 0.83 in the U.S. and Singapore). Supporting the validity of combining the three variables, principal component analysis showed that positive affect, negative affect (recoded) and life-satisfaction loaded on a single factor accounting for 54 % of the variance (loadings = 0.77, 0.62, and 0.81, respectively). Coefficient alpha for the 25-item SWB variable was 0.89.

8.2.2.2 Need-Satisfaction.

As one way of assessing psychological need-satisfaction we employed the Basic Psychological Needs scale (BPNS; Deci et al. 2001). This 21-item scale assesses the extent to which participants feel autonomy, competence, and relatedness, the three primary psychological needs postulated by self-determination theory (Deci and Ryan 2000). The scale contains items such as "I feel free to express my ideas and opinions" (autonomy), "Most days, I feel a sense of accomplishment from what I do" (competence), and "people in my life care about me" (relatedness). In addition, we employed the 9-item need-satisfaction scale used by Sheldon et al. (2001) in their study of "most satisfying events" (MSEs). This scale also assesses autonomy, competence, and relatedness, via items similar to the BPNS. Both scales addressed "life in general." Aggregate autonomy, competence, and relatedness measures were computed by standardizing and averaging the two measures of each construct (alphas = 0.73, 0.79, and 0.74, respectively, for the whole sample; for the U.S. sample, alphas were 0.76, 0.77, and 0.73, and for the Singaporean sample, alphas were 0.69, 0.73, and 0.72).

8.2.2.3 Personality Traits.

Participants were administered two short Big Five measures. One was the Gosling et al. (2003) Ten Item Personality Measure (TIPI), which presents participants with ten pairs of synonymous traits (i.e., "extraverted, enthusiastic" and "sympathetic, warm") and asks them to rate how well the pair applies personally, using a 1 (disagree strongly) to 7 (agree strongly) scale. Two pairs assess each of the Big Five traits, one containing two directly-worded traits and the other two oppositely-worded items. The other short Big Five measure was the set of 15 single trait adjectives (referred to as the STA measure), three for each of the big five traits, that was used by Sheldon et al. (1997) (example adjectives are "orderly," "talkative," and "curious"). This measure was also administered with a 7-point scale. Aggregate extraversion, neuroticism, conscientiousness, agreeableness, and openness measures were computed by standardizing and averaging the two measures of each construct (all alphas were 0.75 or more for the full sample and both sub-samples, except for agreeableness, with alphas of 0.66 in the full sample and 0.62 and 0.69 in the sub-samples).

8.2.2.4 Goals and Intentions.

Positive goal conditions were measured in two ways: by assessing the self-concordance of personal goals (i.e., the extent personal goals are motivated by interests and identifications rather than by internal and external pressures; Sheldon 2004; Sheldon and Elliot 1999), and by assessing the participant's success in achieving those goals. For U.S. participants these ratings were based on a single important self-generated personal goal towards which the participant is striving, and for Singaporean participants these ratings were based on four self-generated personal goals (Emmons 1999). To assess self-concordance, participants rated why they strive, in terms of four reasons: external (because I have to or my situation demands it), introjected (because I'd feel guilty, anxious, or ashamed if I didn't), identified (because I identify with it, even when its not fun and enjoyable), and intrinsic (because it is intrinsically interesting or challenging). As in past research (Sheldon and Elliot 1999; Sheldon and Kasser 1995, 2001), a single self-concordance score was computed by summing the intrinsic and identified ratings and subtracting the external and introjected ratings (see Sheldon 2004, for more discussion of the self-concordance construct). To assess success at goals, participants rated "how well I have done in the past," using a 1 (not at all) to 5 (very much) scale. These ratings constituted the goal-progress variable. Singaporean success ratings were averaged over the four goals (alpha = 0.56); reliabilities were not computed for the goal variables because the U.S. measure was based on only one goal.

8.2.2.5 Self and Self-Feelings.

To assess positive conditions at the self level of personality, we employed two measures. The first was the 10-item Rosenberg self-esteem measure (Rosenberg 1965), which contains items such as "I take a positive attitude toward myself." A 7-point scale was used for this measure (alpha = 0.90; 0.83 and 0.92 in the U.S. and Singapore, respectively). The second measure was based on an assessment of participants' "possible selves" (Markus and Ruvolo 1989). All participants first wrote (or typed) a most desired future possible self (i.e., "an image of yourself in the best possible future") and a most feared future possible self (i.e., "an image of yourself in the worst possible future"). Participants then rated "how close are you already to each possible self," "how likely is it that each self will come to be," and "to what extent do you feel that you can control whether or not you will become each possible self?", using 1 (not very) to 5 (extremely) scales. Preliminary analyses revealed that the ability to control becoming the feared self was uncorrelated with the other five ratings in both samples, thus this item was excluded. After recoding the two remaining feared possible self ratings, a "positive possible self" variable was created for each participant by averaging the five ratings (alpha = 0.68; 0.65 and 0.72 in the U.S. and Singapore, respectively).

8.2.2.6 Social Support.

To assess positive conditions at the social relations (or interpersonal) level of analysis, we also used two measures. One was based on the Sarason et al. (1987) brief social support measure. Specifically, participants rated how satisfied they are with their overall social support regarding six issues, using a 1 (very dissatisfied) to 5 (very satisfied) scale. The six issues included items such as having "People who can distract you from your worries when you feel under stress" and having "People who care about you, regardless of what is happening to you." The six responses were averaged to form a "social support" composite (alpha = 0.90; 0.92 and 0.88 in the U.S. and Singapore, respectively). The second measure was based on the six-item version of the perceived autonomy support scale (Black and Deci 2000; Williams et al. 1999), which assesses the extent to which authorities and other important persons support the participant's right to make their own choices. It contains items such as "this person listens to how I would like to do things" and "this person provides me with choices and options." In the U.S. sample, participants responded with respect to mother, father, and one other influential older adult. In the Singapore sample, participants responded with respect to "two important people who are most involved in your life." A five-point scale was employed. An aggregate "autonomy-support" score was computed by averaging across the six items and persons rated (alphas = 0.91 in both samples).

8.2.2.7 Culture.

The effects of cultural membership were assessed using a dummy variable coded 0 (U.S.) or 1 (Singapore). Notably, our only explicit prediction regarding culture was that Singaporean cultural membership would have a negative main effect upon SWB, which would persist with the other predictors in the equation. However, we also examined the data for other informative patterns consistent with the literature. In addition to being lower on SWB, it seemed likely that Singaporean participants would also evidence lower means on at least some of the predictor variables, particularly need-satisfaction (Sheldon et al. 2001), self-esteem (Heine et al. 2001), and goal self-concordance and progress (Oishi and Diener 2001).

Beyond mean differences, a potentially more important issue for our theoretical approach was, "should cultural membership interact with any of the predictors in relation to SWB?" At first glance it seems that a universalist perspective would say "no;" however, a more differentiated view suggests that different constructs at a particular level of analysis (i.e., self-esteem versus achieved ego-identity, at the self-level of analysis, or conscientiousness versus agreeableness, at the trait level of analysis) might well have different sized (but still significant) effects within different cultures, without invalidating the universalist argument that self-level constructs matter within every culture. Based on past research, it seemed possible that self-esteem (Diener et al. 2003) and goal self-concordance and progress (Oishi and Diener 2001) would have different effects upon SWB in the U.S. versus Singapore. However, because some other studies have not found such differences (Sheldon et al. 2004; Sheldon et al. 2001), we had no firm expectations concerning culture x predictor interactions.

8.2.2.8 Inter-Level Consistency.

Six items were used in order to assess the inter-level consistency of the various aspects of the person. First, participants were presented with brief definitions of traits, goals, selves, and immediate social environment (i.e., "traits" were defined as "your habitual ways of acting and reacting in the world," "goals" were defined as "your conscious values, purposes, and objectives," "selves" were defined as "the dominant self-images and self-concepts you live inside," and "social environment" was defined as "your primary social relationships and social network"). Participants then rated "whether each area of your life is consistent or inconsistent with each of the other areas. Does each particular area of your life, taken as a whole, tend to harmonize with, or conflict with, each other area?" The areas were juxtaposed two at a time, resulting in six items; the scale was 1 ("very different or inconsistent") to 5 ("very similar or consistent"). The items were averaged to create an "inter-level consistency" variable (alpha = 0.82; 0.84 and 0.80 in the U.S. and Singapore, respectively). Notably, we did not ask participants to rate the consistency of the various parts of themselves with foundational psychological needs, because these needs are assumed not to vary across individuals.

8.3 Results

8.3.1 Analysis Plan

After presenting descriptive statistics and preliminary correlational and factor analyses, we first compare the candidate constructs *within* each level as predictors of SWB. That is, at the organismic needs level, which is the strongest predictor—autonomy, competence, or relatedness need-satisfaction? At the trait level, does neuroticism, extraversion, agreeableness, openness, or conscientiousness best predict? Also, does progress or self-concordance best predict at the goal level, does self-esteem or having a positive possible self best predict at the self level, and does general social support or autonomy support best predict at the social relations level? After identifying the best predictor at each level, we then proceed to compare the "winners" as simultaneous predictors of the SWB criterion. Finally, we examine the effects of the inter-level consistency variable, and consider potential interactions.

Table 8.1 Descriptive statistics for major study variables

	Entire sample		U.S. sample	Singaporean sample
	Mean	S.D.	Mean	Mean
SWB	4.74	1.50	5.07	4.29
Autonomy needsat	3.68	0.58	3.80	3.50
Competence needsat	3.64	0.66	3.77	3.46
Relatedness needsat	3.97	0.64	4.12	3.77
Neuroticism	3.30	1.07	3.34	3.27
Extraversion	4.76	1.20	4.90	4.58
Agreeableness	5.21	0.84	5.36	5.02
Conscientiousness	5.25	1.13	5.08	5.38
Openness	5.09	0.99	4.92	5.21
Self-concordance	2.65	2.81	2.98	2.20
Goal-progress	3.90	0.71	4.74	3.28
Self-esteem	5.26	1.06	5.39	5.09
Positive possible self	1.21	1.09	1.97	1.56
Social support	4.15	0.75	4.26	4.00
Autonomy support	4.04	0.66	4.07	4.01
Inter-level consistency	3.80	0.62	3.90	3.67

Note All U.S./Singapore means are significantly different at the 0.01 level or greater, with the exception of autonomy-support and neuroticism

8.3.2 Preliminary Analyses

Table 8.1 contains descriptive statistics for the major study variables, and also presents variable means split by sample. As can be seen, the Singaporean sample was significantly lower on every variable except perceived autonomy-support and neuroticism. Notably, the cultural mean differences in SWB, need-satisfaction, and self-esteem are consistent with previous published research (i.e., Diener et al. 1995; Diener et al. 2003; Heine et al. 2001; Sheldon et al. 2001) and with current study hypotheses.

As a second preliminary analysis we computed the correlations between the major study variables (not tabled). Two patterns were noteworthy. The first concerns the correlations between the 14 predictors and SWB—all 14 correlations were positive (all $rs \geq 0.20$, 12 $rs > 0.40$) and significant (all $ps < 0.01$). Thus, the assumption that all of these predictors should have relevance for SWB (Sheldon 2004) received preliminary support. The second pattern concerns the 91 correlations among the 14 predictors. These correlations were also uniformly positive and mostly significant, suggesting considerable common variance among them.

To evaluate the nature of this overlap, we conducted a principal components analysis of the 14 predictors. Three components with eigenvalues greater than one emerged. After varimax rotation, the first factor was defined by the three need-satisfaction variables, by extraversion, conscientiousness, and neuroticism (reversed), and by self-esteem, goal-progress, and having a positive possible self. Relatedness need-satisfaction cross-loaded on the second factor, which was also loaded upon by agreeableness, social support, and autonomy-support. The third factor was defined by goal self-concordance and openness to experience. The second factor might be interpreted as a "positive sociality" factor and the third factor might be interpreted as a "growth orientation" factor. The first factor is broader, and may represent a group of personality factors that have relevance to positive disposition, optimism, and well-being. Notably, essentially the same factor structure emerged when an oblique rotation was employed, thus we do not present this oblique solution.

8.3.3 Identifying the Best Predictor at Each Level

To evaluate the relative strength of the candidate predictors at each of the five conceptually derived levels of personality, we conducted five analyses in which SWB was regressed upon the predictors at each level. In the need-satisfaction analysis, competence satisfaction was the strongest predictor ($\beta = 0.45$, $p < 0.01$); relatedness ($\beta = 0.26$, $p < 0.01$) and autonomy ($\beta = 0.15$, $p < 0.01$) were also significant, replicating past studies of the simultaneous effects of the three needs (Reis et al. 2000; Sheldon et al. 2001). In the trait analysis, neuroticism was the strongest predictor ($\beta = -0.43$, $p < 0.01$); extraversion ($\beta = 0.20$, $p < 0.01$), conscientiousness ($\beta = 0.21$, $p < 0.01$), agreeableness ($\beta = 0.15$, $p < 0.01$), and openness ($\beta = 0.07$, $p < 0.05$) were also significant, consistent with Sheldon's (2004, p. 186) suggestion that all five traits have relations with SWB. In the goals analysis, progress ($\beta = 0.43$, $p < 0.01$) and self-concordance ($\beta = 0.16$, $p < 0.01$) were both significant, consistent with prior goal research (Sheldon and Elliot 1999; Sheldon and Houser-Marko 2001). In the self analysis, self-esteem ($\beta = 0.60$, $p < 0.01$) and positive possible self ($\beta = 0.22$, $p < 0.01$) were both significant, and in the social relations analysis, social support ($\beta = 0.40$, $p < 0.01$) and autonomy support ($\beta = 0.24$, $p < 0.01$) were both significant. The latter two sets of results are also consistent with prior findings in the literature.

8.3.4 Primary Analysis

In sum, the analyses above suggest that high competence need-satisfaction, low neuroticism, good goal progress, high self-esteem, and high social support, are the best predictors within each level. To test the hypothesis that each would uniquely predict SWB, we next conducted a hierarchical regression analysis. Cultural membership was entered at step 1, and gender at step 2, to ensure that any culture differences are not due to the differing gender compositions in the two samples. The five conceptual predictors were then entered as a block at step 3, followed by the

Table 8.2 Hierarchical regressions predicting SWB

	Entire sample		U.S sample	Singaporean sample
Predictor variables	ß	ΔR²		
Step 1		0.07**		
Cultural membership	−0.26**			
Step 2		0.002		
Cultural membership	−0.25**			
Gender	0.05			
Step 3		0.62**		
Cultural membership	−0.09**			
Gender	0.07**		0.08*	0.05
Competence needsat	0.30**		0.28**	0.28**
Neuroticism	−0.27**		−0.34**	−0.15**
Goal progress	0.08**		0.08*	0.05
Self-esteem	0.23**		0.18**	0.33**
Social support	0.16**		0.14**	0.18**
Step 4		0.01**		
Inter-level consistency	0.09**		0.07***	0.13**

Note *$p < 0.05$, **$p < 0.01$, ***$p < 0.10$

inter-level consistency measure at step 4. Table 8.2 contains the results of the analysis. As can be seen, cultural membership was significant at step 1, an effect which remained significant when gender was controlled at step 2 (gender itself was non-significant). More importantly, all five primary predictors were significant at step 3, uniquely predicting SWB. Finally, at step 4, the inter-level consistency measure was also significant. Notably, all of the earlier predictors remained significant also at step 4. The total variance (R^2) accounted for at step 4 was 0.691, and the R^2 for the number of independent variables in the equation was 0.687.

8.3.5 Supplementary Analyses

8.3.5.1 Omitting the Winnowing Step.

We further considered the possibility of entering all 14 initial predictors into the equation at the same time. We found that neither autonomy nor relatedness need-satisfaction was significant, nor were extraversion, openness, nor conscientiousness. However, agreeableness, goal self-concordance, positive possible self, and autonomy support all made significant contributions, suggesting that the potential positive benefits of the trait, goal, self, and social relations levels are not exhausted by the single representative construct used. Still, the additional variance explained by adding these four constructs was quite modest ($R^2 = 0.71$ vs. 0.69 in the primary model), suggesting that not much was missed by omitting them. Also worthy of note, inter-level consistency remained significant in the 14-predictor analysis.

8.3.5.2 Culture by Predictor Interactions.

Table 8.2 also contains the coefficients that emerged when the analysis was conducted in each country separately. As can be seen, some of the coefficients varied somewhat between the two samples. However, a supplementary analysis entering interaction product terms at a fifth step of the primary regression analysis revealed that there was only one significant culture X predictor interaction: as can be seen in Table 8.2, the negative association of neuroticism with SWB was somewhat smaller in the Singaporean than the U.S. sample ($p < 0.01$). We do not attempt to interpret this potentially chance finding.

8.3.5.3 Predictor by Predictor Interactions.

Further supplementary analyses also examined predictor x predictor interactions. For example, might the combination of high goal progress and high self-esteem be especially beneficial? All possible pairings of the five primary predictors yielded 10 interaction product terms, which were employed in a repetition of the Table 8.2 analysis in which the product terms were entered at a fifth step. However, only one of these 10 effects was significant (namely, the neuroticism x self-esteem coefficient was significant and negative, suggesting that self-esteem is less beneficial when combined with high neuroticism). Overall, however, it appears that the effects of particular constructs do not depend on constructs at the other levels of analysis.

8.4 Discussion

Despite the huge volume of research on SWB that has appeared in the two decades since Diener's (1984) landmark *Psychological Bulletin* article, there have been few attempts to consider many possible determinants of SWB simultaneously. This has left the field in some disarray. How do the large number of constructs and predictors thus far examined relate to each other, relate to SWB itself, and/or moderate each other's influence upon SWB? Does any research area, or type of construct, have the "inside track" to explaining what makes for a happy person? Might some levels of analysis or types of constructs be eliminated as non-essential, or be subsumed by other levels of analysis or types of construct? Questions such as these must be addressed if we are ever to approach an integrated yet parsimonious understanding of human thriving (Staats 1999).

In the current studies we began to address such questions, applying the 6-level model of person-in-context proposed by Sheldon (2004). As depicted in Fig. 8.1, this model asserts that optimality (here, SWB) is multiply determined, by factors at many different levels of the person ranging from biological to cultural. In particular, the model distinguishes between four potentially hierarchical aspects of personality (needs, traits, goals, and selves) and two higher levels of organization within which personality is embedded (the relations between personalities, and membership within a culture; see also McAdams and Pals 2006). Furthermore, the model asserts that all of these levels should have relevance for understanding SWB—none of them are reducible to each other.

The model led us to the testable hypothesis that representative constructs at each level of analysis would uniquely explain SWB. In a preliminary step, the most effective predictor of SWB was identified at the lower five levels of Fig. 8.1: namely, competence need-satisfaction, low neuroticism, good goal-progress, positive self-esteem, and ample social support. In a second and more important step, these five predictors were entered into a competition to predict SWB, along with a sixth factor of cultural membership (U.S. vs. Singapore), along with a measure of inter-level consistency. All of these measures had significant influence; despite the fact that the predictor variables were positively correlated, they nevertheless could each tell us something about SWB that the other variables could not, consistent with McAdams' (1996, 2000, 2006) and Sheldon's (2004) claims regarding the irreducibility of each tier of personality. Thus, for example, the effects of self-level variables cannot be accounted for just by measuring personality traits, goal attainments, need-satisfaction, social relations, and cultural memberships; self-level measures are necessary for a complete picture. The same is true for the other levels.

As expected, the cultural membership effect also remained significant at the last step of the analysis, although its effects were significantly weakened. This finding suggests that culture has irreducible top-down effects upon its members, effects that cannot be completely accounted for by the important personality-level constructs that we examined. It also suggests that east/west cultural differences in SWB represent more than mere response biases, modesty norms, or scale usage differences, since the effects of such differences upon self-report SWB should have been accounted by the inclusion of so many other self-report measures in the equation. Notably, Diener and Suh (1999) have also argued that cross-cultural differences in the desirability and familiarity of SWB constructs do not account for national differences in SWB.

Another finding worthy of comment is that a measure of inter-level consistency had independent effects upon SWB. This supports the idea that the overall self-consistency (or functional integrity) of a person's multi-level system has an influence upon his or her SWB, beyond the effects of positive conditions at each level considered separately (Sheldon and Kasser 1995). This result implies that no matter how positive a person's characteristics, he or she will be even better off if those characteristics are also functionally consistent (i.e., if the formerly conflicted young woman manages to get her positive traits and goals lined up with her positive self-image and social supports). Conversely, having a consistent and coherent system may be less beneficial if the contents that are being integrated are themselves sub-optimal (i.e., the afore-mentioned highly integrated sociopath).

The current results have potentially important implications for SWB and positive psychological interventions (Joseph and Linley 2004; Ruini and Fava 2004). Specifically, they suggest that many levels of the person should be targeted, for maximal effect. Of course, some characteristics may be more modifiable than others. For example, the big five traits may be least susceptible to alteration via interventions, whereas psychological need-satisfaction (i.e., feelings of autonomy, competence, and relatedness in one's daily life) may be more readily modified. Similarly, social supports may be more readily alterable than cultural membership. Another caveat to the "target every level" conclusion is that it may be pragmatically unfeasible to try to change all aspects of a person at once.

Fortunately, effecting change at just one or two levels of a person may often be enough to create cascading positive effects upon other levels of that person. For example, Deci and Ryan (2000) proposed that when psychological needs are satisfied (at the organismic level of personality), people gain the internal resources to make positive changes of many different kinds. Obviously, more research is needed to test the intriguing idea that some levels of personality offer more tractable intervention-targets than others, and the further idea that influencing only one or two levels may sometimes be enough to bring about positive change at other levels.

8.4.1 Limitations.

The studies reported herein have a number of limitations. First, only two cultural groups were examined, one representing individualistic and the other collectivistic cultures. It would be useful to generalize the results to other exemplars of these groups, to further affirm that (1) important constructs at each level of analysis have main effects within every culture, and that (2) cultural membership itself continues to have effects even after lower-level predictors are accounted for. Relatedly, our measures were all "western" in focus, representing prominent constructs that have been researched within the American and European traditions. It would be advantageous to employ alternative measures of SWB which take into account possible differences in the meaning and construction of happiness in different cultures (Diener and Suh 1999). Another limitation is that only a few constructs were employed at each level of analysis, in some ways confounding construct content with construct level; also, in some cases, shortened measures of these constructs were employed. Thus, future research will be required to more confidently identify the most efficacious predictors at each level, and to confirm that their effects hold up to the most-efficacious predictors at other levels. Finally, all constructs were measured by self-report, raising the possibility that common method variance is playing an inordinately strong role. However, we felt it worthwhile to begin this new type of inquiry using the typical self-report scales employed by researchers within each "level." Still, future research should seek to tap alternative sources of information beyond self-report.

8.5 Conclusion

These data support the six-level model of optimal human being presented in Fig. 8.1 (Sheldon 2004), showing that positive need-satisfaction, personality traits, personal goals, self-evaluations, social supports, and cultural membership all make unique contributions to SWB. It appears that none of these effects are reducible to the other effects, just as proponents of the constructs typically assume (McAdams and Pals 2006). The data also indicate that the degree of consistency between the different levels of a person makes a difference for SWB, independently of the contents of each level. Thus, we suggest that the model may provide a useful tool for integrating across theories of personality and social structure, as well as for integrating across diverse theories of SWB.

References

Adams GR, Montemayor R, Callotta TP (eds) (1996) Psychosocial development during adolescence: progress in developmental contextualism. Sage, London

Adams GR, Shea J, Fitch SA (1979) Toward the development of an objective assessment of ego-identity status. J Youth Adolesc 8:223–237

Anderson CA, Anderson KB (1996) Violent crime rate studies in philosophical context: a destructive testing approach to heat and southern culture of violence effects. J Pers Soc Psychol 70:740–756

Argyle M (1999) Causes and correlates of happiness. In: Kahneman D, Diener E, Schwarz N (eds) Well-being: the foundations of hedonic psychology, Russell Sage Foundation, New York, pp 353–373

Baker R, Siryk B (1984) Measuring adjustment to college. J Couns Psychol 31:179–189

Benet-Martinez V, Karakitapoglu-Aygun Z (2003) The interplay of cultural syndromes and personality in predicting life satisfaction: comparing Asian Americans and European Americans. J Cross Cult Psychol 34:38–60

Birnbaum MH (ed) (2000) Psychological experiments on the internet. Academic, San Diego

Black A, Deci E (2000) The effects of instructors' autonomy support and students' autonomous motivation on learning organic chemistry: a self-determination theory perspective. Sci Educ 84:740–756

Cohen J, Cohen P (1983) Applied multiple regression/correlation analysis for the behavioral sciences. Erlbaum, Hillsdale

Costa PT Jr, McCrae RR (1992) NEO-PI/FFI manual supplement. Psychological Assessment Resources, Odessa

Deci EL, Ryan RM (2000) The "what" and "why" of goal pursuits: Human needs and the self-determination of behavior. Psychol Inq 11:227–268

Deci EL, Ryan RM, Gagne M, Leone DR, Usunov J, Kornazheva BP (2001) Need satisfaction, motivation, and well-being in the work organizations of a former Eastern bloc country: a cross-cultural study of self-determination. Pers Soc Psychol Bull 27:930–942

Diener E (1984) Subjective well-being. Psychol Bull 95:542–575

Diener E (1994) Assessing subjective well-being: progress and opportunities. Soc Indic Res 31:103–157

Diener E, Diener M, Diener C (1995) Factors predicting the subjective well-being of nations. J Pers Soc Psychol 69:851–864

Diener E, Emmons R, Larsen R, Griffin S (1985) The satisfaction with life scale. J Pers Assess 47:1105–1117

Diener E, Oishi S, Lucas RE (2003) Personality, culture, and subjective well-being: emotional and cognitive evaluations of life. Annu Rev Psychol 54:403–425

Diener E, Suh EM (1999) National differences in subjective well-being. In: Kahneman D, Diener E, Schwarz N (eds) Well-being: the foundations of hedonic psychology. Russell Sage Foundation, New York, pp 434–452

Emmons RA (1999) The psychology of ultimate concerns. Guilford, New York

Gosling SD, Rentfrow PJ, Swann WB Jr (2003) A very brief measure of the big five personality domains. J Res Pers 37:504–528

Grolnick WS, Deci EL, Ryan RM (1997) Internalization within the family: the self-determination theory perspective. In: Grusec JE, Kuczynski L (eds) Parenting and children's internalization of values: a handbook of contemporary theory. Wiley, New York, pp 135–161

Heine SJ, Kitayama S, Lehman DR (2001) Cultural differences in self-evaluation: Japanese readily accept negative self-relevant information. J Cross Cult psychol 32:434–443

Heine SH, Lehman DR, Markus HR, Kitayama S (1999) Is there a universal need for positive self-regard? Psychol Rev 106:766–794

Joseph S, Linley A (2004) Positive therapy: a positive psychological theory of therapeutic practice. In: Linley PA, Joseph S (eds) Positive psychology in practice. Wiley, Hoboken, pp 354–370

Kahneman D, Diener E, Schwarz N (eds) (1999) Well-being: the foundations of hedonic psychology. Russell Sage Foundation, New York

Keyes CLM, Shmotkin D, Ryff CD (2002) Optimizing well-being: the empirical encounter of two traditions. J Pers Soc Psychol 82:1007–1022

Lakey B, Lutz CJ (1996) Social support and preventive and therapeutic interventions. In: Pierce GR, Sarason BR (eds) Handbook of social support and the family. Plenum series on stress and coping, Plenum Press, New York, pp 435–465

Lyubomirsky S, King LA, Diener E (2005a) Is happiness a good thing? the benefits of long-term positive affect. Psychol Bull 131:803–855

Lyubomirsky S, Sheldon K, Schkade D (2005b) Pursuing happiness: the architecture of sustainable change. Rev Gen Psychol 9:111–131

Marcia JE, Waterman AS, Matteson DM, Archer SL, Orlofsky J (1993) Ego identity: a handbook for psychosocial research. Springer, New York

Markus H, Ruvolo A (1989) Possible selves: personalized representations of goals. In: Pervin L (ed) Goal concepts in personality and social psychology. Erlbaum, Hillsdale, pp 211–241

McAdams DP (1995) What do we know when we know a person? J Pers 63:365–396

McAdams DP (1998) Ego, trait, identity. In: Westenberg PM, Blasi A (eds) Personality development: theoretical, empirical, and clinical investigations of Loevinger's conception of ego development. Lawrence Erlbaum Associates, Mahwah, pp 27–38

McAdams DP (1996) Personality, modernity, and the storied self: a contemporary framework for studying persons. Psychol Inq 7:295–321

McAdams DP, Pals J (2006) A new big five: fundamental principles for an integrative science of personality. Am Psychol 61:204–217

McGregor I, Little B (1998) Personal projects, happiness, and meaning: on doing well and being yourself. J Pers Soc Psychol 74:494–512

Oishi S, Diener E (2001) Goals, culture, and subjective well-being. Pers Soc Psychol Bull 27:1674–1682

Pavot W, Diener E (2004) Findings on subjective well-being: applications to public policy, clinical interventions, and education. In: Linley PA, Joseph S (eds) Positive psychology in practice. Wiley, Hoboken, pp 679–692

Robbins RJ (1994) An assessment of perceptions of parental autonomy support and control: child and parent correlates. Unpublished Doctoral Dissertation, Department of Psychology, University of Rochester

Rosenberg M (1965) Society and the adolescent self-image. Princeton University Press, Princeton

Ruini C, Fava GA (2004) Clinical applications of well-being therapy. In: Linley PA, Joseph S (eds) Positive psychology in practice. Wiley, Hoboken, pp 371–387

Ryan RM, Deci EL (2000) On happiness and human potentials: a review of research on hedonic and eudaimonic well-being. Annu Rev Psychol 52:141–166 (Annual Reviews, Inc, San Diego, CA)

Ryan RM, Deci EL (2000b) Self-determination theory and the facilitation of intrinsic motivation, social development, and well-being. Am Psychol 55:68–78

Sandvik E, Diener E, Seidlitz L (1993) Subjective well-being: the convergence and stability of self-report and nonself-report measures. J Pers 61:317–342

Sarason BR, Sarason IG, Gurung RAR (2001) Close personal relationships and health outcomes: a key to the role of social support. In: Sarason BR, Duck S (eds) Personal relationships: implications for clinical and community psychology. Wiley, New York, pp 15–41

Sarason IG, Sarason BR, Shearin EN, Pierce GR (1987) A brief measure of social support: practical and theoretical implications. J Soc Pers Relat 4:497–510

Schwarz N, Strack F (1999) Reports of subjective well-being: judgmental processes and their methodological implications. In: Kahneman D, Diener E, Schwarz N (eds) Well-being: the foundations of hedonic psychology. Russell Sage Foundation, New York, pp 61–84

Seligman MEP, Csikszentmihalyi M (2000) Positive psychology: an introduction. Am Psychol 55:5–14

Sheldon KM (2004) Optimal human being: an integrated multi-level perspective. Erlbaum, Mahwah

Sheldon KM The interface of motivational science and personality: self-concordance, quality motivation, and multi-level personality integration. To appear in Shah J, Gardner W (eds) Handbook of motivational science. Guilford (in press)

Sheldon KM, Elliot AJ (1999) Goal striving, need-satisfaction, and longitudinal well-being: the self-concordance model. J Pers Soc Psychol 76:482–497

Sheldon KM, Elliot AJ, Kim Y, Kasser T (2001) What's satisfying about satisfying events? comparing ten candidate psychological needs. J Pers Soc Psychol 80:325–339

Sheldon KM, Elliot AJ, Ryan RM, Chirkov V, Kim Y, Wu C, Demir M, Sun Z (2004) Self-concordance and subjective well-being in four cultures. J Cross Cult Psychol 35:209–233

Sheldon KM, Houser-Marko L (2001) Self-concordance, goal-attainment, and the pursuit of happiness: can there be an upward spiral? J Pers Soc Psychol 80:152–165

Sheldon KM, Kasser T (1995) Coherence and congruence: two aspects of personality integration. J Pers Soc Psychol 68:531–543

Sheldon KM, Kasser T (2001) Getting older, getting better? personal strivings and personality development across the life-course. Dev Psychol 37:491–501

Sheldon KM, Krieger L (2004) Does law school undermine law students? examining changes in goals, values, and well-being. Behav Sci Law 22:261–286

Sheldon KM, Niemiec C (2006) Its not just the amount that counts: balanced need-satisfaction also affects well-being. Manuscript under review

Sheldon KM, Ryan RM, Rawsthorne L, Ilardi B (1997) "True" self and "trait" self: cross–role variation in the big five traits and its relations with authenticity and well–being. J Pers Soc Psychol 73:1380–1393

Sheldon KM, Ryan RM, Reis HR (1996) What makes for a good day? competence and autonomy in the day and in the person. Pers Soc Psychol Bull 22:1270–1279

Sperry RW (1993) The impact and promise of the cognitive revolution. Am Psychol 48:878–885

Staats AW (1999) Unifying psychology requires new infrastructure, theory, method, and a research agenda. Rev Gen Psychol 3:3–13

Stanton JM (1998) An empirical assessment of data collection using the internet. Pers Psychol 51:709–725

Triandis H (1997) Cross-cultural perspectives on personality. In: Hogan R, Johnson J, Briggs S (eds) Handbook of personality psychology. Academic, San Diego, pp 440–465

Watson D, Tellegen A, Clark L (1988) Development and validation of brief measures of positive and negative affect: the PANAS scales. J Pers Soc Psychol 54:1063–1070

Williams GC, Cox EM, Kouides R, Deci EL (1999) Presenting the facts about smoking to adolescents: the effects of an autonomy supportive style. Arch Pediatr Adolesc Med 153:959–964

Chapter 9
Orientations to Happiness and Life Satisfaction: The Full Life Versus the Empty Life

Christopher Peterson, Nansook Park and Martin E. P. Seligman

Abstract Different orientations to happiness and their association with life satisfaction were investigated with 845 adults responding to Internet surveys. We measured life satisfaction and the endorsement of three different ways to be happy: through pleasure, through engagement, and through meaning. Each of these three orientations individually predicted life satisfaction. People simultaneously low on all three orientations reported especially low life satisfaction. These findings point the way toward a distinction between the full life and the empty life.

Keywords Empty life • Eudemonia • Flow • Full life • Hedonism • Life satisfaction • Meaning

9.1 Introduction

Philosophers and psychologists have long been concerned with the good life and how it can be achieved (Guignon 1999; Russell 1930, 1945). Often they propose a sovereign principle to be followed in order to be happy. So, the doctrine of *hedonism*—maximizing pleasure and minimizing pain—was articulated thousands of years ago by Aristuppus (435–366 BCE) who championed immediate sensory gratification (Watson 1895). Hedonism was elaborated by Epicurus (342–270 BCE) into the edict of ethical hedonism, which holds that our fundamental moral obligation is to maximize our experience of pleasure. Early Christian

C. Peterson (✉) · N. Park
Department of Psychology, University of Michigan, 525 East University,
Ann Arbor, MI 48109-1109, USA
e-mail: chrispet@umich.edu

M. E. P. Seligman
Department of Psychology, University of Pennsylvania, Philadelphia,
PA 19104, USA

A. Delle Fave (ed.), *The Exploration of Happiness*, Happiness Studies Book Series,
DOI: 10.1007/978-94-007-5702-8_9,

philosophers denounced hedonism as inconsistent with the goal of avoiding sin, but Renaissance philosophers such as Erasmus (1466–1536) and Thomas Moore (1478–1535) argued that it was God's wish that people be happy, so long as they did not become preoccupied with "artificial" ways of achieving pleasure. Later British philosophers like David Hume (1711–1776) and Jeremy Bentham (1748–1832) used the doctrine of hedonism to lay the foundation for utilitarianism, which was ushered into psychology as the underpinning of psychoanalysis and all but the most radical of the behaviorisms. Hedonism is alive and well today in the name of a new field—hedonic psychology (Kahneman et al. 1999). At least in the modern Western world, the pursuit of pleasure is widely endorsed as a way to achieve satisfaction: "Don't worry—be happy."

Standing in contrast to hedonism is another venerable tradition that can be traced to Aristotle's (384–322 BCE) notion of *eudemonia*—being true to one's inner self (demon). According to this view, true happiness entails identifying one's virtues, cultivating them, and living in accordance with them (Aristotle 2000). Aristotle considered sensual pleasure as touted by the hedonists to be vulgar. Similar positions were advanced by John Stuart Mill (1806–1873) and Bertrand Russell (1872–1970) and undergird more modern psychological notions such as Rogers' (1951) ideal of the fully-functioning person, Maslow's (1970) concept of self- actualization, Ryff and Singer's (1996) vision of psychological well-being, and Deci and Ryan's (2000) self-determination theory. Uniting eudemonic emphases is the premise that people should develop what is best within themselves and then use these skills and talents in the service of greater goods—including in particular the welfare of other people or humankind writ large. Again, in the modern world, the pursuit of a meaningful life is widely endorsed as a way to achieve satisfaction: "Be all that you can be," and "Make a difference."

As implied, different psychological traditions have respectively addressed these two principles of achieving satisfaction. Often these traditions have proceeded independently from one another, with confusion introduced by the tendency of those working within each tradition to claim "happiness" as a label for their subject matter and to deny—if only implicitly—its use by those in the other camp.[1] Sometimes the debate becomes explicit, and we see investigators playing off the merits of pleasure and meaning as routes to the psychological good life (e.g., Compton et al. 1996; Waterman 1993). Research suggests that both points of view can be supported by data (Ryan and Deci 2000).

We extend this line of work by simultaneously examining the pursuit of pleasure and the pursuit of meaning as different routes to happiness. The unique contribution of our research is to consider a third orientation to happiness: the pursuit of *engagement* (Seligman 2002). Here we have been influenced by Csikszentmihalyi's (1990)

[1] In the present chapter, we use "happiness" in its broadest sense to include hedonic features but also fulfillment and contentment (cf. Myers 1992; Seligman 2002). We follow Diener's (1984) lead in defining "life satisfaction" as a summary appraisal of the quality of one's life regardless of how it is achieved (cf. Pavot and Diener 1993).

writings on flow: the psychological state that accompanies highly engaging activities. Time passes quickly. Attention is focused on the activity. The sense of self is lost. The aftermath of the flow experience is invigorating.

In his studies of eudemonia, Waterman (1993) initially equated the flow state with eudemonia (which he termed personal expressiveness) but then concluded from his data that flow represented an "amalgam" of hedonic and eudemonic features. We suggest instead that flow is distinct. Flow is not the same as sensual pleasure. Indeed, flow is nonemotional and arguably nonconscious. People may describe flow as enjoyable, but this is an after-the fact summary judgment; "joy" is not immediately present during the activity itself. So, flow differs from hedonism, in which positive emotional experience is front-and-center (Csikszentmihalyi 1999). At least at any given point in time, flow and pleasure may even be incompatible.

Although the pursuit of a meaningful life can at times produce flow for some individuals—e.g., those volunteering in a hospice or a soup kitchen—not all flow-producing activities are meaningful in the sense of connecting an individual to a greater good (consider playing bridge or Scrabble), and not all meaningful activities entail the total absorption that defines flow. For example, each of us does committee work at our university. At its best, this work is meaningful, but we have yet to lose ourselves in its performance.

We report here an empirical investigation of these three ways of being happy. The following questions guided our inquiry:

- Are these three orientations to happiness empirically distinguishable individual differences;
- Is an orientation to pleasure incompatible with an orientation to engagement, as implied by the characterization of the flow state as noncognitive and nonemotional, or is it possible for the same person to pursue these different ways of being happy;
- Do these three orientations each contribute to life satisfaction, or are some more important than others; and
- Are there interactions between or among these orientations with respect to life satisfaction; that is, does their joint presence predict more life satisfaction than expected from the individual components, and, conversely, does their joint absence predict less than expected life satisfaction?

9.2 Method

9.2.1 Participants

Research participants were two groups of adult volunteers who completed measures on-line. During initial instrument development, 180 respondents participated, and for the main study, 845 respondents participated. Demographic characteristics of these two samples are summarized in Table 9.1.

Table 9.1 Demographic characteristics of samples

	Instrument development sample (n = 180) (%)	Main sample (n = 845) (%)
Age (years)		
18–20	27	15
21–24	15	10
25–34	18	19
35–44	17	21
45–54	16	24
55–64	6	8
65+	1	3
Gender		
Male	38	28
Female	62	72
Education		
<High school	1	1
High school graduate	5	9
Some college	44	31
Associates degree	5	6
Baccalaureate	17	24
>Baccalaureate	28	29
Marital status		
Married/living as	31	45
Single	58	39
Widowed	1	1
Divorced	10	15
Ethnicity		
African American	4	3
Asian American	3	3
Latino/a	3	2
White	82	86
Other	8	6
U.S. citizen	76	85
Town of residence		
Farm	1	1
Country	6	12
Suburban	19	26
Small city (<50 K)	16	17
Medium city (<100 K)	15	15
Large city (<500 K)	16	16
Very large city (>500 K)	27	13
Political leaning		
(1 = liberal, 7 = conservative)	M = 3.55 (SD = 1.85)	M = 3.37 (SD = 1.84)

9.2.2 Measures

9.2.2.1 Orientations to Happiness

To develop the Orientations to Happiness measure used in this study, 12 face-valid items reflecting each of the three orientations were initially drafted by the authors and refined in a focus group of college students ($n = 15$) enrolled in a positive psychology class at the University of Pennsylvania. Each item required a respondent to answer on a 5-point scale the degree to which the item applied ("1 = very much unlike me" through "5 = very much like me"). Items tapping pleasure and meaning resemble those used in previous research contrasting hedonic versus eudemonic orientations (cf. King and Napa 1998; McGregor and Little 1998). Items measuring engagement were based on Csikszentmihalyi's (1990) characterization of the flow state as self-less absorption in ongoing activity.

Along with demographic questions, the initial 36-item Orientations to Happiness measure was placed on the Internet and completed by participants in the instrument development sample ($n = 180$). Internal consistencies of the three subscales formed by averaging the respective items, were satisfactory (pleasure $\alpha = 0.84$, flow $\alpha = 0.77$, and meaning $\alpha = 0.88$) and exceeded the subscale inter-correlations, which nonetheless were of moderate magnitude (mean $r = 0.51$). These results suggested that the three orientations to happiness are distinguishable but related.

To sharpen the distinctions among the subscales, the six items in each subscale with the highest item-total correlations were chosen, and a revised 18-item measure was created and placed online along with demographic questions to be completed by participants in the main study ($n = 845$). The revised version of this scale is presented in Table 9.2. Subscale means were calculated by averaging the relevant items.

9.2.2.2 Satisfaction with Life Scale

The satisfaction with life scale (SWLS) (Diener et al. 1985) consists of five items which measure the individual's evaluation of satisfaction with life in general (e.g., "I am satisfied with my life," and "If I could live my life over, I would change almost nothing"). Respondents select one of seven options (ranging from "strongly disagree" to "strongly agree") for each question. Responses were averaged to provide a total life satisfaction score. Research has established acceptable psychometric properties for the SWLS (Diener 1994). In the current study, the SWLS was skewed toward the right, meaning that most respondents were relatively happy (cf. Diener and Diener 1996; Myers and Diener 1995).

Table 9.2 Orientations to happiness subscale items and factor loadings ($n = 845$)

Eigenvalue	Factor 1	Factor 2	Factor 3
	4.96	2.80	1.60
% of variance	28	16	9
Life of meaning			
02. My life serves a higher purpose	**0.75**	0.01	0.08
05. In choosing what to do, I always take into account whether it will benefit other people	**0.54**	0.01	0.32
11. I have a responsibility to make the world a better place	**0.79**	−0.01	0.05
12. My life has a lasting meaning	**0.82**	0.01	0.17
14. What I do matters to society	**0.73**	0.01	0.11
17. I have spent a lot of time thinking about what life means and how I fit into its big picture	**0.57**	0.11	0.01
Life of pleasure			
03. Life is too short to postpone the pleasures it can provide	0.22	**0.68**	0.12
08. I go out of my way to feel euphoric	0.12	**0.60**	0.36
13. In choosing what to do, I always take into account whether it will be pleasurable	0.00	**0.75**	0.01
15. I agree with this statement: "Life is short—eat dessert first"	−0.01	**0.71**	−0.01
16. I love to do things that excite my senses	0.16	**0.74**	0.01
18. For me, the good life is the pleasurable life	−0.01	**0.79**	0.00
Life of engagement			
01. Regardless of what I am doing, time passes very quickly	0.23	0.00	**0.48**
04. I seek out situations that challenge my skills and abilities	0.40	0.12	**0.51**
06. Whether at work or play, I am usually "in a zone" and not conscious of myself	0.00	0.01	**0.75**
07. I am always very absorbed in what I do	0.13	0.01	**0.78**
09. In choosing what to do, I always take into account whether I can lose myself in it	0.16	0.41	**0.49**
10. I am rarely distracted by what is going on around me	0.12	0.00	**0.61**

Note Numbers in front of items correspond to order in the final Orientations to Happiness measure. Entries in bold represent the factor on which item loaded most highly

9.2.3 Procedure

All measures were placed online at www.positivepsychology.org/ strengths along with demographic questions (age; gender; education; marital status; ethnicity; U.S. citizenship; size of one's town of residence, from 1 = farm through 7 = very large city; and liberal-versus-conservative political leaning assessed by a single 7-point scale, from 1 = liberal to 7 = conservative). On the first page of the web site, a short description of the study including its purpose and its approximate time commitment was provided.

This web site also includes other psychological measures and provides individualized feedback about an individual's top scores on these other measures upon completion of all measures (feedback on the Orientations to Happiness measure was not provided). The feedback feature is apparently attractive to potential respondents and may explain why we did not need to advertise the survey. To preserve respondent anonymity, we did not track how individuals came across our survey on the Internet. They may have learned about it by following a link on the Positive Psychology Webpage, by following links on other webpages, or by hearing about it from previous respondents or from our media interviews.

According to a recent study of Internet users by the UCLA Center for Communication Policy (Lebo 2003), more than 70 % of Americans use the Internet. Although certain limitations exist, Internet surveys provide researchers with the opportunities to recruit efficiently large and diverse samples at relatively little cost (Birnbaum 2000, 2004; Kraut et al. 2004; Schonlau et al. 2002).

9.3 Results

For the main sample ($n = 845$), a principal components analysis of the 18 items in the revised Orientations to Happiness measure, using varimax rotation, provided strong support for the a priori assumption that it assessed three different orientations to the good life. Three factors were identified with eigen-values greater than 1.00, and each of the 18 items loaded most strongly on a factor along with the other items intended to assess the same orientation (Table 9.2). Consistent with this analysis, internal consistencies of the three subscales were satisfactory and exceeded the scale intercorrelations (Table 9.3). Subscale means, created by averaging the appropriate items, could range from 1 to 5. Each had a slight skew. Nevertheless, each subscale yielded a range of scores.

There were no significant demographic variations in life satisfaction other than being married (Table 9.3). However, several modest demographic correlates of the Orientations to Happiness subscales were found. Those who were younger, less educated, or unmarried were somewhat higher in their endorsement of an orientation to pleasure—as Aristotle might have predicted. Ethnic minorities, chiefly African Americans and Asian Americans, scored somewhat higher than Whites on orientation to meaning.

Considered individually, each of the orientations to happiness predicted life satisfaction, from small (pleasure) to moderate (engagement, meaning) degrees (Table 9.3). A hierarchical multiple regression predicting life satisfaction was then computed (Table 9.4), entering in the first step the demographic variables (age, education, gender [1 = male, 2 = female], marital status [married = 1 or not = 0], politics [1 = conservative, 7 = liberal], US citizenship [yes = 1 or no = 1], size of home town [1 = farm, 7 = very large city], and ethnicity [White = 1 versus

Table 9.3 Intercorrelations among measures ($n = 845$)

	Pleasure	Engagement	Meaning	Life satisfaction
Pleasure	–			
Engagement	0.31*	–		
Meaning	0.18*	0.46*	–	
Life satisfaction	0.17*	0.30*	0.26*	–
Age	−0.22*	0.07	0.00	−0.09
Gender (1 = male, 2 = female)	0.09	−0.06	−0.03	0.06
Politics (1 = conservative, 7 = liberal)	−0.02	−0.08	−0.10	−0.05
Education	−0.19*	0.05	0.08	−0.01
Married (0 = no, 1 = yes)	−0.17*	0.01	−0.03	0.17*
Home town size	0.07	0.05	0.05	−0.05
White (0 = no, 1 = yes)	−0.07	−0.11	−0.18*	−0.06
U.S. citizen (0 = no, 1 = yes)	−0.03	−0.10	−0.08	0.01
M	3.20	3.05	3.42	4.93
SD	0.84	0.72	0.88	1.37
α	0.82	0.72	0.82	0.90
Skew	−0.09	0.08	−0.32	−0.73

*$p < 0.001$

Table 9.4 Hierarchical multiple regression predicting life satisfaction ($n = 845$)

	β
Step 1	
Age	−0.17*
Education	0.01
Gender (1 = male, 2 = female)	0.08**
Politics (1 = conservative, 7 = liberal)	−0.05
Home town size	−0.06
U.S. citizen (0 = no, 1 = yes)	0.02
Married (0 = no, 1 = yes)	0.24*
White (0 = no, 1 = yes)	−0.01
	$R^2 = 0.066$**
Step 2	
Pleasure	−0.11**
Engagement	−0.24*
Meaning	−0.17*
	$\Delta R^2 = 0.116$*
Step 3	
Pleasure × engagement	−0.04
Pleasure × meaning	−0.03
Meaning × engagement	0.00
	$\Delta R^2 = 0.004$
Step 4	
Pleasure × engagement × meaning	−2.50**
	$\Delta R^2 = 0.006$**

Note Predictors in steps 1 and 2 were normalized (see text). β weights are for the final model
*$p < 0.001$; **$p < 0.05$

not = 0]), in the second step by the subscales measuring the three orientations to happiness, in the third step the two-way product terms between the orientations (i.e., all possible pairs of three orientations), and in the last step the three-way product (pleasure × engagement × meaning).

Following the guidelines of Aiken and West (1991), we centered the predictors in the first two blocks by normalizing them and computed interactions by multiplying the relevant normalized scores, but we did not center these product terms or the criterion. Multicollinearity diagnostics were well within acceptable limits. The overall regression was significant ($R^2 = 0.19$, $F\ [15,829] = 13.15$, $p < 0.001$). Above and beyond the influence of demographic variables, the "main" effects of the three orientations (all of which were significant predictors in the final model), and the two-way interactions (none of which was statistically significant), the three-way interaction—entered in the last step—was statistically significant, although small in its absolute effect.

We therefore limited our attention to the three-way interaction. To interpret it, we grouped the respondents in various ways on each of the three subscales (e.g., low versus high, low versus medium versus high, quartiles, quintiles, deciles, and so on) and graphed life satisfaction scores as a joint function of these groupings. No matter how we grouped the respondents, the same patterns emerged: (a) somewhat higher life satisfaction scores for respondents simultaneously near the top of all three Orientations to Happiness subscales; and (b) notably lower life satisfaction scores for respondents simultaneously near the bottom of all three subscales. Figure 9.1 is a representative composite, where respondents simultaneously low on all three orientations (who have what might be called the "Empty Life") reported the least life satisfaction, whereas those simultaneously high on all three orientations (who have what can be identified as the "Full Life") reported the greatest life satisfaction.

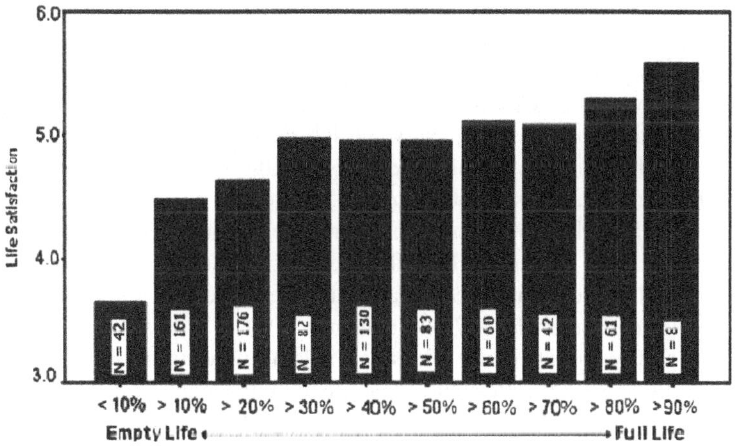

Fig. 9.1 Mean life satisfaction scores along the continuum of the empty life versus the full life. Groups were created by identifying respondents simultaneously in the top 90 % of each of the three subscales, simultaneously in the top 80 % of each, and so on

9.4 Discussion

Drawing on past theory and research, we distinguished three possible orientations to happiness (Seligman 2002). The present study found that these orientations are distinguishable, that they are not incompatible and thus able to be pursued simultaneously, and that each is individually associated with life satisfaction. As previous research has shown, either hedonism or eudemonia can accompany a satisfying life, and so too can engagement.

Our interest was in people's endorsement of these orientations to happiness, and we did not ascertain whether those who said they believe in pursuing pleasure actually have more sensually gratifying experiences than those who do not, whether those who supported engagement as an orientation to happiness more frequently lose themselves in highly absorbing activities, or whether those who agreed with items reflecting a life of meaning are more likely to perform service to others. We intend to pursue such questions in further research, using a version of Waterman's (1993) procedure that asks respondents to report on "activities of importance" and their features.

We also intend to study these orientations and their relationship to life satisfaction over time. We assume that given orientations shape conduct and thereby produce more or less happiness, but the cross-sectional design of the present study does not allow this notion to be tested. In particular, we need to investigate the alternative interpretation of our data that a satisfying life leads to a diverse behavioral repertoire that includes pleasurable, engaging, and meaningful activities (cf. Fredrickson 2001). Although only trends in the present sample, we found it interesting that the respondents with the fullest life were more likely than those in other groups to be older, to be married, and to be more highly educated—all factors that arguably open doors to diverse and satisfying experiences.

The present research nonetheless extends theory in several ways, suggesting in particular that an orientation to engagement differs from orientations to pleasure or to meaning. Also, an orientation to pleasure is not as strong an individual predictor of life satisfaction as orientations to engagement or to meaning. But neither is pleasure irrelevant to life satisfaction, because it represents value added to a life rich in engagement and meaning and value subtracted from a life deficient in these respects. The Full Life as we have defined it predicts life satisfaction somewhat beyond the sum of its parts, and the Empty Life predicts notably less.

Many psychologists who study pleasure seem unconvinced that it can be increased, positing a genetically influenced set point of affectivity to which most of us return following hedonically laden experiences, either good or bad (Brickman and Campbell 1971; Kahneman 1999). Perhaps the immutability of our ability to experience pleasure explains why its pursuit can be futile (Csikszentmihalyi 1999). In contrast, a life of engagement seems more under deliberate control (Massimini and Delle Fave 2000), as does a life of meaning (Frankl 1963). As positive psychology turns its attention to interventions that cultivate the good life, perhaps interventions that target engagement and meaning will prove most fruitful (Linley and Joseph 2004). However, we would not want to rule out all attempts to increase pleasure, and perhaps the way to boost pleasure is to follow one implication of the present results that pleasure-enhancing techniques like savoring be incorporated into those that increase engagement and meaning (Linville and Fischer 1991). Perhaps increased pleasure can occur as a happy by-product of such interventions.

Besides our cross-sectional design, let us note an additional limitation of our research, specifically our strategy of obtaining research participants. Although increasingly common in psychological research, samples obtained from the World Wide Web are often criticized because of the special characteristics of respondents. Individuals need to have access to a computer and the ability to use it. They need to be interested enough to spend time answering questions. But contrast our web sample with those obtained from typical psychology subject pools and ask which provides a sounder basis for generalization. Our respondents ranged across the adult years and different levels of formal education. Men and women were represented. Many were married. They lived in all parts of the United States or came from many different countries. Our main sample included more than 100 (14 %) non-White respondents. Respondents fell at all points along the conservative-liberal political spectrum. Without belaboring the point, we observe that Internet samples are at least as diverse as those recruited from psychology subject pool samples at colleges or universities (Birnbaum 2000, 2004; Kraut et al. 2004; Lebo 2003; Lenhart 2000; Schonlau et al. 2002).

Many of the individuals who simultaneously scored low on all three orientations were likely depressed, anxious, or otherwise distressed. These are the people that clinical psychology has studied for 50 years, grouping everyone else together as "normal" (Seligman and Csikszentmihalyi 2000). We suggest that a distinction can be made along the continuum from the mere normal to the supernormal. Investigating those people who have particularly high life satisfaction may well reveal ways of improving the well-being of all of us (Diener and Seligman 2002).

Acknowledgments We acknowledge the support of the Manuel D. and Rhoda Mayerson Foundation in creating the Values in Action Institute, a nonprofit organization dedicated to the development of a scientific knowledge base of human strengths.

References

Aiken LS, West SG (1991) Multiple regression: testing and interpreting interactions. Sage, Thousand Oaks

Aristotle (2000) Nicomachean ethics (trans: Crisp R). Cambridge University Press, Cambridge

Birnbaum MH (ed) (2000) Psychological experiments on the Internet. Academic Press, San Diego

Birnbaum MH (2004) Human research and data collection via the Internet. Annu Rev Psychol 55:803–832

Brickman P, Campbell DT (1971) Hedonic relativism and planning the good society. In: Appley MH (ed) Adaptation-level theory. Academic, New York, pp 287–305

Compton WC, Smith ML, Cornish KA, Qualls DL (1996) Factor structure of mental health measures. J Pers Soc Psychol 71:406–413
Csikszentmihalyi M (1990) Flow: the psychology of optimal experience. HarperCollins, New York
Csikszentmihalyi M (1999) If we are so rich, why aren't we happy? Am Psychol 54:821–827
Deci EL, Ryan RM (2000) The "what" and "why" of goal pursuits: human needs and the self-determination of behavior. Psychol Inq 11:227–268
Diener E (1984) Subjective well-being. Psychol Bull 95:542–575
Diener E (1994) Assessing subjective well-being: progress and opportunities. Soc Indic Res 31:103–157
Diener E, Diener C (1996) Most people are happy. Psychol Sci 7:181–185
Diener E, Seligman MEP (2002) Very happy people. Psychol Sci 13:80–83
Diener E, Emmons RA, Larsen RJ, Griffin S (1985) The satisfaction with life scale. J Pers Assess 49:71–75
Frankl VE (1963) Man's search for meaning: an introduction to logo- therapy. Washington Square Press, New York
Fredrickson BL (2001) The role of positive emotions in positive psychology: the broaden-and-build theory of positive emotions. Am Psychol 56:218–226
Guignon C (ed) (1999) The good life. Hackett, Indianapolis
Kahneman D (1999) Objective happiness. In: Kahneman D, Diener E, Schwarz N (eds) Well-being: the foundations of hedonic psychology. Russell Sage, New York, pp 3–25
Kahneman D, Diener E, Schwarz N (eds) (1999) Well-being: the foundations of hedonic psychology. Russell Sage, New York
King LA, Napa CK (1998) What makes life good? J Pers Soc Psychol 75:156–165
Kraut R, Olson J, Banaji M, Bruckman A, Cohen J, Couper M (2004) Psychological research online: report of board of scientific affairs' advisory group on the conduct of research on the Internet. Am Psychol 59:105–117
Lebo H (2003) The UCLA Internet report: surveying the digital future-year- three. University of California Regents, Los Angeles. Retrieved 31 July 2003 from http://www.ccp.ucla.edu/UCLA-Internet-Report-Year-Three.pdf
Lenhart A (2000) Who's not online: 57% of those without Internet access say they do not plan to log on. Pew Internet & American Life Project, Washington. Retrieved 31 July 2003 from http://www.pewinter-net.org/reports/toc.asp?Report_21
Linley PA, Joseph S (eds) (2004) Positive psychology in practice. John Wiley and Sons, New York
Linville PW, Fischer GW (1991) Preferences for separating or combining events. J Pers Soc Psychol 60:5–23
Maslow AH (1970) Motivation and personality, 2nd edn. Harper & Row, New York
Massimini F, Delle Fave A (2000) Individual development in a biocultural perspective. Am Psychol 55:24–33
McGregor I, Little BR (1998) Personal projects, happiness, and meaning: on doing well and being yourself. J Pers Soc Psychol 74:494–512
Myers DG (1992) The pursuit of happiness: who is happy—and why. William Morrow, New York
Myers DG, Diener E (1995) Who is happy? Psychol Sci 6:10–19
Pavot W, Diener E (1993) Review of the satisfaction with life scale. Psychol Assess 5:164–172
Rogers CR (1951) Client-centered therapy: its current practice, implications, and theory. Houghton Mifflin, Boston
Russell B (1930) The conquest of happiness. Liveright, New York
Russell B (1945) A history of western philosophy, and its connection with political and social circumstances from the earliest times to the present day. Simon & Schuster, New York
Ryan RM, Deci EL (2000) On happiness and human potentials: a review of research on hedonic and eudaimonic well-being. Annu Rev Psychol 52:141–166
Ryff CD, Singer B (1996) Psychological well-being: meaning, measurement, and implications for psychotherapy research. Psychother Psychosom 65:14–23

Schonlau M, Fricker RD, Elliott MN (2002) Conducting research surveys via e-mail and the web. RAND, Santa Monica

Seligman MEP (2002) Authentic happiness. Free Press, New York

Seligman MEP, Csikszentmihalyi M (2000) Positive psychology: an introduction. Am Psychol 55:5–14

Waterman AS (1993) Two conceptions of happiness: contrasts of personal expressiveness (eudaimonia) and hedonic enjoyment. J Pers Soc Psychol 64:678–691

Watson J (1895) Hedonistic theories from Aristippus to Spencer. Macmillan, New York

Chapter 10
The Pleasant Life, the Engaged Life, and the Meaningful Life: What About the Balanced Life?

M. Joseph Sirgy and Jiyun Wu

Abstract Martin Seligman, in his very popular book *Authentic Happiness* (Seligman 2002), argued that authentic happiness is derived from three major sets of experiences in life, namely experiencing pleasantness regularly (the pleasant life), experiencing a high level of engagement in satisfying activities (the engaged life), and experiencing a sense of connectedness to a greater whole (the meaningful life). In this chapter, we maintain that balance in life contributes significantly to subjective well-being. Balance contributes to subjective well-being because of the satisfaction limit that people can derive from a single life domain. People have to be involved in multiple domains to satisfy the full spectrum of human development needs. Different life domains tend to focus on different human developmental needs. More specifically, balance contributes to subjective well-being because subjective well-being can only be attained when both survival and growth needs are met. High levels of subjective well-being cannot be attained with satisfaction of basic needs or growth needs alone. Both needs have to be met to induce subjective well-being.

Keywords Balanced life • Life satisfaction • Subjective well-being • Happiness • Balance • Need satisfaction • Survival versus growth needs

Recently, Seligman and Royzman (2003) have argued that authentic happiness is grounded in three traditional theories, namely hedonism theory (the pleasant life), desire theory (the engaged life), and objective list theory (the meaningful

M. Joseph Sirgy (✉)
Department of Marketing, Virginia Polytechnic Institute and State University, Blacksburg, VA 24061-0236, USA
e-mail: sirgy@vt.edu

J. Wu
Management and Marketing Department, School of Management, Rhode Island College, Providence, RI 02908, USA
e-mail: JWU@ric.edu

A. Delle Fave (ed.), *The Exploration of Happiness*, Happiness Studies Book Series, DOI: 10.1007/978-94-007-5702-8_10,

life). Happiness, based on Seligman's interpretation of *hedonism*, is a matter of maximizing feelings of pleasure and minimizing feelings of pain. Hedonism has its modern conceptual roots in Bentham's utilitarianism (Bentham 1978) and its manifestation in American consumerism. More recently, according to Seligman and Royzman, the research by Danny Kahneman—the Nobel Prize winner in economics—conceptualized happiness through momentary experiences of pleasures. Kahneman uses the Experience Sampling Method (ESM) to measure happiness (Kahneman 1999). This method involves having researchers beep their subjects at random during the day and asking how much pleasure or pain they are experiencing at the moment. Based on these momentary perceptions of positive and negative affect, Kahneman extrapolates approximate total happiness points over the week. Thus, happiness as "objective happiness" for a given time period is computed by adding up subjects' on-line hedonic assessments of all the individual moments that comprise that period. Seligman's theory of authentic happiness (Seligman 2002) takes into account hedonism in that part of what makes a happy life a pleasant life. Happiness in the present involves paying attention to bodily pleasures and enhancing these pleasures. Seligman provides good advice on how people can enhance their pleasures through habituation (i.e., spreading out the events that produce pleasure far enough to generate a craving), savoring (i.e., indulging the senses), and mindfulness (i.e., becoming acutely aware of the surrounding).

Desire theory (the engaged life) focuses on gratification, not pleasure. It goes beyond hedonism. Desire theory holds that happiness is a matter of getting what you want (Griffin 1986), with the content of the want left up to the person who does the wanting. Desire theory subsumes hedonism when what we want is lots of pleasure and little pain. However, desire theory holds that fulfillment of a desire contributes to one's happiness regardless of the amount of pleasure (or displeasure). Desire may be in the form of wanting truth, illumination, and purity. These desires are very different from bodily pleasures. The desire theory criterion for happiness moves from hedonism's amount of pleasure felt to the somewhat less subjective state of how well one is engaged/absorbed and how well one's desires are satisfied. Seligman (2002) provides plenty of advice to his readers on how to enhance gratification by engaging in activities that generate flow experience (cf. Csikszentmihalyi 1999). Thus, in addition to experiencing pleasure (the pleasant life), people can experience desire fulfillment through engagement (the engaged life).

Objective List theory (Nussbaum 1992; Sen 1985) maintains that happiness consists of a human life that achieves certain things from a list of worthwhile pursuits such as career accomplishments, friendship, freedom from disease and pain, material comforts, civic spirit, beauty, education, love, knowledge, and good conscience. Thus, leading a meaningful life is key to happiness. The meaningful life is not necessarily subjective as is the pleasant life (and the engaged life). Leading a meaningful life is at least objective. The person who lives a meaningful life is one that serves what is larger and more worthwhile than just the self's pleasures and desires.

Thus, Seligman (2002) holds that there are three distinct kinds of happiness: the Pleasant Life (pleasure), the Engaged Life (engagement), and the Meaningful Life (virtue). Seligman's theory of authentic happiness attempts to synthesize all three theories of happiness. The Pleasant Life is about happiness in hedonic sense. The Engaged Life is about happiness through engagement, and the Meaningful Life is about happiness by achieving virtue. Seligman and his colleagues (Peterson et al. 2005) conducted two studies to test the notion that people who score highly on the three dimensions of authentic happiness (life of pleasure, life of engagement, and life of meaning) score high on traditional measures of life satisfaction, and vice versa. The first study involved 180 adult volunteers who participated in a on-line survey. The goal of that study was to develop the measures capturing the three dimensions of authentic happiness. The second study involved 845 respondents who completed an on-line survey. The results of this study show that respondents scoring simultaneously high on all three dimensions reported significantly higher life satisfaction than those who scored low on the same dimensions. Thus, these results provided some support for Seligman's theory of authentic happiness.

The attempt in this chapter is to argue that Seligman's theory of authentic happiness misses another important criterion of happiness, namely achieving balance in life. That is, to achieve "authentic happiness," people have to experience a pleasant life, a good life, a meaningful life, *plus* a balanced life. Thus, the attempt described in this chapter can be described as *developing a foundation for a theory of the balanced life.*

10.1 Balance and Imbalance

Imbalance is defined as *a state reflecting satisfaction or fulfillment in a focused domain (e.g., work, family) that ultimately leads to negative affect in other domains*. Consider the following scenario involving a career woman only a few years out of college. She received a degree in accounting and joined a major consulting firm. To prove herself to her employer, she worked more than 60 h a week. She did not have much of a social life. Then she dated her college friend, and a year-and-a-half later they got married and started a family. Currently, she has a 6 months baby girl, and she remains devoted to her job. She puts the same number of hours in her job as she did before giving birth. Lately, she realizes that she is failing as a mother and wife too. Her job is consuming more time at the expense of her family. Although she feels good about her job, she feels a great deal of stress related to her role as mother and wife. This is a classic situation of imbalance between work and family life. Of course, balance is restored between work and family life if our subject decides to take action and engage in activities allowing her to experience a reasonable amount of satisfaction from both work and family domains.

We define *balance as a state reflecting satisfaction or fulfillment in several important domains with little or no negative affect in other domains.* Research on imbalance between work and family roles has shown that work-family role conflict is associated with life dissatisfaction (e.g., Bedeian et al. 1988; Collins and Killough 1989; Edwards and Rothbard 2000; French and Caplan 1973; Fu and Shaffer 2001; Holaham and Gilbert 1979; Lewis and Cooper 1987; Parasuraman et al. 1992; Sekaran 1986; Sturges and Guest 2004; Wiley 1987) as well as low martial and family satisfaction and symptoms of low mental and physical well-being (e.g., Bedeian et al. 1988; Buell and Breslow 1960; Caplan et al. 1975; French and Caplan 1973; Parasuraman et al. 1992; Sekaran 1986; Steffy and Ashbaugh 1986; Wiley 1987; Zohman 1973). The family-work conflict occurs when one domain consumes resources needed for another domain.

With respect to balance, there is some evidence suggesting that people are more satisfied with life when the source of the satisfaction derives from *multiple* life domains than a single domain. For example, Marks and McDermid (1996) described a theory of role balance that suggests that people who have well-balanced role systems, which they conceptualize as full engagement in and enjoyment of all roles, have higher levels of well-being. Using a sample of employed mothers, they showed that those who were more "role balanced" and enjoyed "every part of their life equally well" reported less role overload, had higher self-esteem, and lower depression levels. Bhargava (1995) conducted a study in which subjects were asked to discuss life satisfaction of others. Most subjects inferred life satisfaction of others as a direct function of their satisfaction in *multiple* domains. They calculated happiness by summing satisfaction across several important domains—the more positive affect in multiple domains, the higher the subjective well-being. Additional evidence comes from a study conducted by Chen (1996) who found that those who believe they will achieve some of their goals (and receive satisfaction from *multiple* domains) report higher levels of life satisfaction than those who do not believe that they will achieve these goals.

This balance phenomenon has several implications. First, the strategy implies that "putting all your eggs in one basket" may not be effective in enhancing subjective well-being. That is, one should not allow one life domain to overwhelm one's satisfaction or dissatisfaction with life. It is best to be invested emotionally in several domains. Doing so allows one to compensate for the dissatisfaction of some domains with satisfaction of other domains.

Frisch (2006, Chaps. 3 and 4) has addressed the issue of "putting all your eggs in one basket" by recounting the story of a patient named Carol. Carol put all her energy into caring for her children. She did not do anything significant in terms of leisure and recreation. She hardly saw any adult friends, although her friends were very important at one point in her life. Frisch assessed Carol's situation as putting all her emotional eggs in the one basket of family life. This is a dangerous strategy because if things go wrong in Carol's family life, she is likely to feel depressed. And this is exactly what happened. She over-invested herself in the family domain.

To overcome this problem, Frisch's recommends the use of the "happiness pie" and "vision quest" techniques (Frisch 2006, Chaps. 3 and 4). These techniques are methods to allow psychotherapy clients to establish some meaningful goals and priorities in their lives. The therapist asks the client to draw a picture of his or her life in terms of a pie chart. Overall happiness is the pie composed of particular slices that make up overall happiness. Some slices are larger than others because they are more important. The therapist instructs the client to think about 16 areas of life, namely physical health, self-esteem, philosophy of life, standard of living, work, recreation, learning, creativity, helping activities, love relationship, friendships, relationships with children, relationships with relatives, home, neighborhood, and community. The therapist then asks the client to "draw a picture of what areas seem to dominate your life most now. In other words, where is most of your time and mental energy going?" If the picture drawn turns out to be a pie with one or two life domains (e.g., work), then the therapist guides the client to do some soul searching and develop a new pie that reflects new priorities concerning what the client really wants out of life. The therapist is guided by the balance principle—the more balanced the pie is, the more likely that the client can experience life satisfaction and happiness.

The *vision quest technique* is used as a follow-up to the *happiness pie exercise*. The goal here is to clarify the client's goals and priorities in life. The client is instructed to go over each of the 16 life domains and identify goals the person would like to achieve during one's "limited time on earth." After doing so, the client is urged to select about five goals that are considered to be the most important lifetime goals. For example, Frisch cites how one client identified specific lifetime goals in the area of health, play and friendship, love, work, self-esteem, and spiritual life. The client started out by admitting that the only life domain that really mattered was work, work, and more work.

A social psychologist and happiness researcher recommends: "don't let your entire life hinge on one element" (Niven 2000, p. 71). He asserts: "Your life is made up of many different facets. Don't focus on one aspect of your life so much that you can't experience pleasure if that one area is unsettled. It can become all you think about, and it can deaden your enjoyment of everything else—things you would otherwise love (p. 71)."

Based on the preceding discussion, we develop our first theoretical postulate. It can be stated as follows:

Postulate 1 People who have balance in their lives (life satisfaction stemming from multiple life domains) are likely to experience higher levels of subjective well-being than those who have imbalance (life satisfaction stemming from a single life domain).

10.2 How do People Achieve Balance in Their Lives?

We identified a major pathway that people experience to achieve balance. This pathway involves need satisfaction limits and satisfaction of survival plus growth needs (see Fig. 10.1). We will describe these concepts of balance in some detail next.

The two concepts of balance to subjective well-being (need satisfaction limits and satisfaction of survival plus growth needs) are all grounded in the need satisfaction approach to subjective well-being (e.g., Kosenko et al. 1990; Sirgy

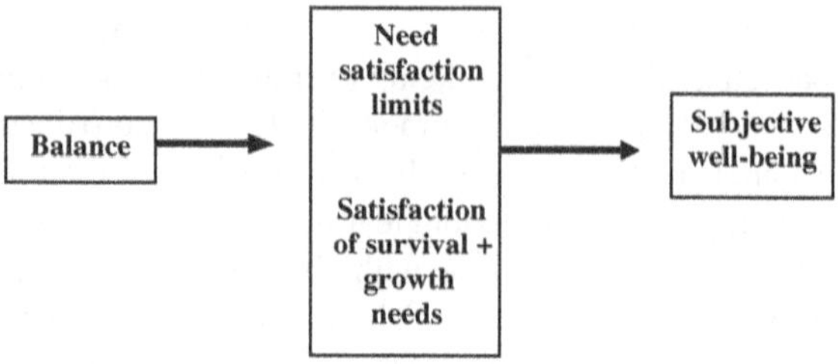

Fig. 10.1 How balance contributes to subjective well-being

2002, pp. 34–36; Sirgy et al. 1995). This approach is developed using concepts propagated by Maslow (1954, 1970), McClelland (1961), Herzberg (1966), and Alderfer (1972). For an excellent review of the research using the need satisfaction approach in organizational psychology and management, see O'Brien (1986), Roberts and Glick (1981), and Salanick and Pfeffer (1977).

10.3 Need Satisfaction Limits

We believe that the psychological explanation of how balance contributes to subjective well-being is directly related to the principle of *need satisfaction limits.* We maintain that satisfaction from one life domain can contribute only a limited amount (a quota) of positive affect to subjective well-being. The basic tenet of the need satisfaction approach (e.g., Alderfer 1972; Herzberg 1966; Maslow 1954, 1970; McClelland 1961) is that people have a variety of developmental needs they seek to fulfill (developmental needs such as biological, safety, social, esteem, self-actualization, knowledge, and beauty-related needs), and the more they satisfy these needs the more they feel good about their lives. That is, those who are more successful in satisfying their developmental needs are likely to experience greater happiness and life satisfaction than those who are less successful. Those who are more successful do so because they are effective in organizing their lives in manageable domains (e.g., work life, family life, leisure life, love life) and participate actively in these domains.

How do people organize their lives to fulfill their developmental needs? To satisfy their biological needs, people engage in a variety of activities such as eating right, exercising regularly, having regular check-ups, having regular sex, and so on. The events related to those activities and their outcomes generate a certain amount of satisfaction and dissatisfaction. These affective reactions are organized and stored in memory in certain life domains such as health, love, residential, and family (see Table 10.1). When a person is asked how he feels about his health life, it is likely that he will reflect on his affective experiences in relation to health-related activities such as eating right, exercising regularly, having regular check-ups, and so on. When the same person is asked about his love life, he reflects about his affective experiences related to love, romantic relationships, and sex. When asked about his residential life, he reflects on those experiences related to the use of his residence, his neighborhood, and community.

Table 10.1 Developmental needs satisfied through activities organized in terms of life domains

	Health life	Love life	Residential life	Family life	Social life	Leisure life	Work life	Education life	Spiritual life
Biological needs	Most	Most	Most	Most	Some	Some	Most	Least	Least
Safety needs	Most	Most	Most	Some	Some	Some	Some	Least	Least
Social needs	Some	Most	Some	Some	Most	Most	Some	Some	Some
Esteem needs	Least	Some	Some	Least	Some	Some	Most	Some	Some
Actualization needs	Least	Some	Least	Least	Least	Some	Some	Most	Most
Knowledge needs	Least	Least	Least	Least	Least	Some	Some	Most	Most
Aesthetics needs	Least	Least	Least	Least	Some	Most	Some	Most	Most

Notes "Most," "some," and "least" indicate the extent to which those activities in a specific life domain are successful in satisfying a specific developmental need. For example, the table shows that safety needs can be "most" satisfied through the health, love, and residential life domains and "least" satisfied in the educational life domain

Social psychologists such as Lewin (1951) and organizational psychologists (e.g., Danna and Griffin 1999; Rice et al. 1985; Seeman 1967) have long recognized that affective experiences are segmented in "life spheres," or what QOL researchers refer to as *life domains*. Thus, a person may have affective experiences segmented in relation to education, family, health, job, friends, and romantic relationships, among others. Memory (conscious, subconscious, and unconscious) is likely to be divided into life domains, and within each domain the person has deep-seated cognitions reflecting affective experiences in that domain.

Note that although most life domains are organized and structured around one focal set of needs (biological, safety, social, etc.), they reflect affective experiences related to satisfaction of other needs. For example, many think leisure life involves a set of activities dealing with one's social needs. Those activities serve not only to satisfy one's social needs but also a variety of other needs such as the need for aesthetics and creativity (see Table 10.1). Developmental needs (biological, safety, social, etc.) are satisfied through activities engaged in certain life domains. The life domains shown in the table are for illustrative purposes only. They are not meant to capture all life domains. It should be noted that different people segment their affective experiences differently. For example, a person actively engaged in political activities may have a "political life," which may be absent for many others.

This is an important point that brings us back to the notion that subjective well-being is not simply cumulative positive minus negative affect—irrespective of the source. It is the satisfaction of human developmental needs, the full range of needs—not a handful of selected needs. One cannot substitute positive affect related to one need with another need. To illustrate the satisfaction limit with an arithmetic example, suppose that a woman's level of subjective well-being is 50 (on a scale varying from −100 to +100). This means that she is relatively happy with life. The source of this moderate degree of happiness comes from five key domains—work, leisure, family, community, and neighborhood. Now let us focus on work life. She has +15 points of satisfaction. The satisfaction limit in the work domain is +10. In other words, only 10 out of the 15 could contribute to subjective well-being. She is +5 over the limit in her work domain. Only so much of that satisfaction can contribute to her overall life satisfaction. Why? Because satisfaction from work life may reflect the satisfaction of only a subset of human developmental needs, not the full range of these needs.

There are a number of measures of subjective well-being that are based on the notion that life satisfaction is the sum of the satisfaction of various life domains and possibly moderated by the salience of these domains (e.g., Alfonso et al. 1996; Andrews and Withey 1976; Campbell et al. 1976; Frisch 2006; Hall 1976). For example, Alfonso et al. produced an Extended Satisfaction with Life Scale (ESWLS), using five items for each eight domains (social, sex, self, family, relationships, work, physical, and school). The sum composite of all the domain satisfaction correlated highly with general life satisfaction. The nomological validity of these measures provides evidence to the theoretical notion of need satisfaction limits.

Furthermore, evidence of the need satisfaction limits comes from a body of evidence showing that materialism is negatively correlated with life satisfaction (see Wright and Larsen 1993, for a meta-analysis of the research findings). Here, materialistic people can be viewed as imbalanced in that they regard wealth and material possessions to be most important in life. Materialistic people who are successful hoarding material wealth may feel successful and happy with their material life. But there is so much happiness that can be extracted from the material domain. Placing undue emphasis on making money is likely to lead them to neglect their family, their place in the community, their social life, and so forth. This neglect is likely to create negative affect in family, neighborhood, social, leisure, and spiritual life. Negative affect from these other domains, in turn, adversely affects subjective well-being. The overall result is that materialistic people are less happy than their less materialistic counterparts.

Additional evidence for the need satisfaction limits comes from a longitudinal study involving several hundred Harvard graduates over a forty-year period. The study showed that happiness, external play, objective vocational success, mature inner defenses, good outward marriage, all correlate highly (Valliant 1977). In other words, those who are happy the most seem to be satisfied with multiple life domains in which each domain contributes to the satisfaction with different developmental needs. External play reflects satisfaction with social, esteem, intellectual, and aesthetics needs; objective vocational success reflects satisfaction with basic economic needs as well as family, safety, esteem, and self-actualization needs; mature inner defenses may relate to esteem and self-actualization needs; and good outward marriage relate to biological, family, safety, and social needs. Thus, happy people are likely to have their development needs more met than the less happy.

As a sign of acceptance of the notion of satisfaction with the full spectrum of human developmental (=QOL) are policies developed by the United Nations Development Programme(UNDP). The UNDP develops policies based on the concept of human development that reflects basic and higher-order needs *a la* Maslow (United Nations Development Programme 1998). The UNDP's Human Development Index (HDI) is based on this concept. The HDI measures the overall achievements in a country along three dimensions of human development: longevity, knowledge, and a decent standard of living.

Based on the preceding discussion, we develop our second theoretical postulate. It can be stated as follows:

Postulate 2 Balance contributes to subjective well-being because of the satisfaction limit that people can derive from a single life domain. People have to be involved in multiple domains to satisfy the full spectrum of human development needs. Different life domains tend to focus on different human developmental needs.

10.4 Satisfaction of Survival Plus Growth Needs

One can argue that high levels of life satisfaction or subjective well-being cannot be achieved by satisfying only survival needs or growth needs. Balance is achieved when both sets of needs are sufficiently met.

Fredrickson and Losada (2005) have empirically demonstrated that people who flourish (have a high level of subjective well-being) tend to experience a ratio of 4.3 of positive to negative affect, whereas normal people average a 2.5 ratio. People who languish (low levels of subjective well-being) have a much lower ratio of positive to negative affect. The authors argue that positive emotions are evolved psychological adaptations that increased human ancestors' odds of survival and reproduction. In contrast, negative affect narrows behavioral urges toward specific actions that were life-preserving for human ancestors (e.g., fight and flight responses). Positive affect widens the array of thoughts and action such as play and exploratory behavior, which in turn contributes to generativity and behavioral flexibility. In other words, negative emotions serve the survival needs (e.g., biological, safety, and economic needs), whereas positive emotions serve higher-order (growth) needs such as social, esteem, self-actualization, knowledge, and aesthetics needs. Survival needs are associated with negative than positive affect. Conversely, growth needs are associated with positive than negative affect. Human flourishing is associated with high ratio of positive to negative affect. Both positive and negative affect are necessary because positive affect reflects the satisfaction of growth needs and negative affect reflects the satisfaction of survival needs.

Much research has been done to demonstrate this principle in the context of organizational psychology and management (e.g., Herzberg 1966; O'Brien 1986; Roberts and Glick 1981; Salanick and Pfeffer 1977). For example, the two-factor theory (Herzberg 1966) posits that job satisfaction is affected by two sets of factors, namely hygiene and motivation factors. Hygiene factors are related to survival needs (e.g., pay, working conditions, collegiality, and corporate policies). In contrast, motivation factors are related to growth needs (e.g., achievement programs, recognition awards, career advancement opportunities, corporate ownership and profit sharing). The two-factor theory argues that job satisfaction can be enhanced by developing conditions and programs at work that serve to satisfy *both* survival needs (e.g., biological, safety, and economic needs) and growth needs (e.g., social, esteem, self-actualization, knowledge, and aesthetics needs). For excellent reviews of much of the research in this area, see O'Brien (1986), Roberts and Glick (1981) and Salanick and Pfeffer (1977).

Additional evidence of this principle comes from research in industrial/organizational psychology on work-life balance. For example, research in that area has found that organizational values supportive of work-family balance and organizational work-family balance programs can bring about balance between work and family life (e.g., Burke 2001, 2003; Ezra and Deckman 1996; Madsen 2003). Work-family balance programs include alternative work schedules, telecommuting, wellness classes, and caregiver services. Furthermore, factors in the family domain (e.g., spousal support) were found to play a significant role in reducing work-family conflict (Bedeian et al. 1986). The basic idea here is that subjective well-being can be significantly enhanced through successful performance at work (satisfaction of higher-order needs). However, employees cannot be highly successful if they neglect their health and their family responsibilities. Health and family responsibilities are related to lower-order needs. Therefore, work-life balance programs are designed to enhance subjective well-being by helping employees become successful at work while helping them take care of their health and family responsibilities.

Additional suggestive evidence of the viability of the principle of satisfaction of survival plus growth needs come from cultural psychology. Consider the notion of the Ying and Yang, which is popular in East Asian cultures. The Ying and Yang concept posits that subjective well-being can be achieved by keeping a good balance between positive and negative emotions (Kitayama and Markus 2000). The adage is to remain calm, undisturbed, and not agitated. Thus, the Ying and Yang is balance between fulfillment of physical (lower-order needs) and spiritual needs (higher-order ones). Kitayama and Markus report findings from Japan about correlations between positive and negative affect. These correlations were mostly positive and significant (in contrast to negative correlations among U.S. subjects).

Further cross-cultural evidence of the combined effect of both lower- and higher-order needs on subjective well-being comes from studies that examined the relationship between income and happiness. For example, Veenhoven (1995) hypothesized that money enhances happiness when it contributes to the satisfaction of basic needs (e.g., food, shelter, and clothes). Study findings indicate that within societies there is a relationship between income and satisfaction at the lower end of the scale only, and that relationship is strong in poorer countries and weak in rich countries. Oishi et al. (1999) found that satisfaction with self-esteem and with freedom were stronger correlates of life satisfaction in richer nations.

Based on the preceding discussion, we develop our third theoretical postulate. It can be stated as follows:

Postulate 3 Balance contributes to subjective well-being because of subjective well-being can only be attained when both survival and growth needs are met. High levels of subjective well-being cannot be attained with satisfaction of basic needs or growth needs alone. Both needs have to be met to induce subjective well-being.

10.5 Toward a Program of Research of Balance

The three postulates about balance and how it affects subjective well-being can be viewed as a foundation for a possible theory of balance. Readers may ask why we do not report an empirical study to provide direct evidence of our theoretical model. Our response is that we have provided much "suggestive" evidence of three postulates to help researchers conduct a formal program of research in this area. Direct evidence cannot come from one study but from a program of research involving many studies conducted in a variety of contexts with a variety of populations in a variety of cultures and countries. To do so, we would like to offer suggestions that can help formalize this program of research.

10.6 Developing Hypotheses and Suggesting Methods and Measures for Testing

We theorized that people who have balance in their lives (life satisfaction stemming from multiple life domains) are likely to experience higher levels of subjective well-being than those who have imbalance (life satisfaction stemming from a single life domain) [*Postulate 1*]. That balance contributes to subjective well-being because of the satisfaction limit that people can derive from a single life domain. People have to be involved in multiple domains to satisfy the full spectrum of human development needs. Different life domains tend to focus on different human developmental needs [*Postulate 2*]. Furthermore, balance contributes to subjective well-being because of subjective well-being can only be attained when both survival and growth needs are met. High levels of subjective well-being cannot be attained with satisfaction of basic needs or growth needs alone. Both needs have to be met to induce subjective well-being [*Postulate 3*]. These theoretical postulates can be stated in terms of testable hypotheses as follows: *People experiencing high levels of satisfaction from multiple life domains are likely to report higher levels of subjective well-being than people experiencing high levels of satisfaction stemming from a single domain.* However, this hypothesis does not account for the affect in the remaining life domains. Hence we need to qualify the hypothesis as follows: *People experiencing high levels of satisfaction from multiple life domains (with the remaining domains reflecting neutral affect) are likely to report higher levels of subjective well-being than people experiencing high levels of satisfaction stemming from a single domain (with the remaining domains reflecting neutral affect).* Note that the first theoretical postulate does not address the issue of compensatory mechanism among various life domains. The notion of compensation refers to the process by which people sum the positive and negative evaluations of the various life domains to arrive at an overall evaluation of life. Thus, any negative evaluations of certain domains can be neutralized (or compensated) by positive evaluations in other domains (e.g., Andrews and Withey 1976; Campbell et al. 1976). The reader should note that we do no assume a compensatory mechanism in achieving balance. In other words, the theory does not address what happens when the remaining life domains have significant amounts of negative affect. We only assume neutrality.

But then one can argue that the effect may be simply due to the accumulation of positive affect. Positive affect from multiple domains should produce greater subjective well-being than positive affect from a single domain. Again, this may occur as a direct function of compensation (e.g., Andrews and Withey 1976; Campbell et al. 1976). And again, the reader should note that our first postulate of balance does not address this notion of cumulative affect. To rule out the effect of cumulative affect, we rephrase the hypothesis as follows: *People experiencing moderate levels of satisfaction from multiple life domains (with the remaining domains reflecting neutral affect) are likely to report higher levels of subjective well-being than people experiencing high levels of satisfaction stemming from a single domain (with the remaining domains reflecting neutral affect)*. Note that the way we phrased this hypothesis implies that the sum of the positive affect in multiple domains in question should be equivalent to the positive affect score from a single domain. Thus, we should phrase the hypothesis in a way to control for the possible confound of cumulative affect. Furthermore, our first theoretical postulate implies that people who experience high levels of satisfaction in a single domain versus multiple domains regard those domains as highly salient. Therefore, we need to further rephrase the hypothesis as follows:

Hypothesis 1 People experiencing moderate levels of satisfaction from multiple life domains (regarded as highly salient, with the remaining domains reflecting neutral affect) are likely to report higher levels of subjective well-being than people experiencing high levels of satisfaction stemming from a single domain (regarded as highly salient, with the remaining domains reflecting neutral affect).

Suggestive evidence to the hypothesis comes from a study conducted by Diener et al. (1985) that demonstrated small doses of positive affect (low in intensity) contributed more to subjective well-being than infrequent but large doses of positive affect (high in intensity). However, Diener et al. did not use the balance concept to explain the study findings.

Given our statement of Hypothesis 1 as the most concrete and operational form of Postulate 1, how do we go about empirically testing this hypothesis? This hypothesis can be tested using measures sensitive enough to capture the level of intensity of positive affect in a variety of life domains with additional measures capturing the perception of salience of these domains. Of course, the dependent measure should capture subjective well-being, life satisfaction, or overall happiness. The data have to be based on several large-scale samples to ensure wide variability of scores in positive affect and domain salience. The samples have to involve different populations from different cultures and countries. The demographic profile of these samples have to be representative of their respective populations, and the samples' demographics have to equivalent across cultures and countries. The survey items have to be constructed in such a way to avoid the response bias commonly found in life satisfaction surveys in which respondents report higher levels of positive affect than normal (e.g., Schwarz and Strack 1999).

With respect to Postulate 2, we theorized that people who have balance in their lives (life satisfaction stemming from multiple life domains) are likely to experience higher levels of subjective well-being than those who have imbalance (life satisfaction stemming from a single life domain). *That balance contributes to subjective well-being because of the satisfaction limit that people can derive from a single life domain. People have to be involved in multiple domains to satisfy the full spectrum of human development needs.* Different life domains tend to focus on different human developmental needs. How do we operationalize this theoretical postulate in terms of a concrete hypothesis? The emphasis of this postulate is the notion that satisfaction in multiple domains ensures the satisfaction of a variety of human developmental needs than satisfaction in a single domain. Hence, we can put forth a mediating hypothesis as follows:

Hypothesis 2a People experiencing moderate levels of satisfaction from multiple life domains (regarded as highly salient, with the remaining domains reflecting neutral affect) are likely to experience satisfaction of a wide range of human developmental needs (e.g., biological, economic, family, safety, social, esteem, actualization, aesthetic, and intellectual needs). In contrast, people experiencing high levels of satisfaction from a single domain (regarded as highly salient, with the remaining domains reflecting neutral affect) are likely to experience satisfaction of a small range of needs.

Hypothesis 2b People experiencing satisfaction of a wide range of human developmental needs (e.g., biological, economic, family, safety, social, esteem, actualization, aesthetic, and intellectual needs) are likely to experience higher levels of subjective well-being than people experiencing satisfaction of a small range of needs.

Testing hypotheses 2a and 2b require the use of additional measures related to satisfaction of human developmental needs *al la* Maslow. One particular measure we can recommend is the Sirgy et al. (1995) measure of life satisfaction that is conceptualized in terms of Maslow's need hierarchy theory.

With respect to Postulate 3, we theorized that balance contributes to subjective well-being *because subjective well-being can only be attained when both survival and growth needs are met.* High levels of subjective well-being cannot be attained with satisfaction of basic needs or growth needs alone. Both needs have to be met to induce subjective well-being. We can operationalize Postulate 3 by fine tuning Hypothesis 2b as follows:

Hypothesis 3 People experiencing satisfaction of both lower- (e.g., biological, economic, family, and safety needs) and higher (e.g., social, esteem, actualization, aesthetic, and intellectual needs)—order human developmental needs are likely to experience higher levels of subjective well-being than people experiencing satisfaction of with either lower-order or higher-order needs solely. This hypothesis can easily be tested by grouping satisfaction of the human developmental needs in terms of lower-order versus higher-order need satisfaction.

10.7 Conclusion

To reiterate, Seligman (2002), argued that authentic happiness is derived from three major sets of experiences in life, namely experiencing pleasantness regularly (the pleasant life), experiencing a high level of engagement is satisfying activities (the engaged life), and experiencing a sense of connectedness to a greater whole (the meaningful life). We posed the question: what about the balanced life? We maintain that balance in life contributes significantly to authentic happiness, subjective well-being, or life satisfaction.

We introduced in this chapter the concept of balance and its role in subjective well-being. We argued that people who have balance in their lives (life satisfaction stemming from multiple life domains) are likely to experience higher levels of subjective well-being than those who have imbalance (life satisfaction stemming from a single life domain). That balance contributes to subjective well-being because of the satisfaction limit that people can derive from a single life domain. People have to be involved in multiple domains to satisfy the full spectrum of human development needs. Different life domains tend to focus on different human developmental needs. Furthermore, balance contributes to subjective well-being because of subjective well-being can only be attained when both survival and growth needs are met. High levels of subjective well-being cannot be attained with satisfaction of basic needs or growth needs alone. Both needs have to be met to induce subjective well-being.

Although research evidence was cited to support many of the theoretical notions involving the balanced life, we encourage happiness researchers to subject all of the theoretical propositions to rigorous, empirical tests. We suggested specific hypotheses translated from the theoretical postulates that can aid researchers conduct empirical testing. We also offered some methodological suggestions. Only through good science and empirical research can we come closer to understanding the true dimensions of authentic happiness.

References

Alderfer CP (1972) Existence, relatedness, and growth: human needs in organizational settings. The Free Press, New York

Alfonso VC, Allinson DB, Rader DE, Gorman BS (1996) The extended satisfaction with life scale: development and psychometric properties. Soc Indic Res 38:275–301

Andrews FM, Withey SB (1976) Social indicators of well-being: America's perception of life quality. Plenum Press, New York

Bedeian AG, Mossholder KW, Touliatos J (1986) Individual propensities for emotional supportiveness within a dual-career context: work and non-work reactions. Int J Manpow 7(4):7–12

Bedeian AG, Burke BG, Moffett RC (1988) Outcomes of work-family conflict among male and female professionals. J Manag 14:475–491

Bentham J (1978) The principles of morals and legislation. Prometheus, Buffalo

Bhargava S (1995) An integration-theoretical analysis of life satisfaction. Psychol Stud 40:170

Buell P, Breslow L (1960) Mortality from coronary heart disease in California men who work long hours. J Chronic Dis 11:615–626

Burke RJ (2001) Organizational values, work experiences and satisfactions among managerial and professional women. J Manag Dev 20(4):346–353

Burke RJ (2003) Organizational values, work experiences, and satisfactions among Australian psychologists. Int J Organ Analysis 11(2):123–135

Campbell A, Converse PE, Rodgers WL (1976) The quality of American life. Sage, New York

Caplan RD, Cobb S, French JRP, VanHarrison R, Pinnean SR (1975) Job demand and worker health: main effect and occupational differences. U.S. Government Printing Office, Washington

Chen N (1996) Individual differences in answering the four questions of happiness. Ph.D. dissertation, University of Georgia, Athens

Collins KM, Killough LN (1989) Managing stress in public accounting. J Account 167(5):92–96

Csikszentmihalyi M (1999) If we are so rich, why aren't we happy? Am Psychol 54:821–827

Danna K, Griffin RW (1999) Health and well-being in the workplace: a review and synthesis of the literature. J Manag 25(3):357–384

Diener E, Larsen R, Levine S, Emmons R (1985) Intensity and frequency: dimensions underlying positive and negative affect. J Pers Soc Psychol 48:1253–1265
Edwards JR, Rothbard NC (2000) Mechanisms linking work and family: clarifying the relationship between work and family constructs. Acad Manag Rev 25:178–199
Ezra M, Deckman M (1996) Balancing work and family responsibilities: flextime and child care in the federal government. Public Adm Rev 56(2):174–179
Fredrickson BL, Losada MF (2005) Positive affect and the complex dynamics of human flourishing. Am Psychol 60(7):678–686
French JRP, Caplan RD (1973) Psychosocial factors in coronary heart disease. Ind Medicine 39:383–397
Frisch MB (2006) Quality of life therapy: interventions to improve the quality of life of patients with emotional or physical problems. Wiley, New York
Fu CK, Shaffer MA (2001) The tug of work and family—direct and indirect domain-specific determinants of work-family conflict. Pers Rev 30(5–6):502–522
Griffin J (1986) Well-being: its meaning, measurement, and moral importance. Clarendon Press, Oxford
Hall J (1976) Subjective measures of quality of life in Britain, 1971 to 1975: some developments. Soc Trends 7:47–60
Herzberg F (1966) Work and the nature of man. World, Cleveland
Holaham CK, Gilbert LA (1979) Interrole conflict for working women: career versus jobs. J Appl Psychol 64:86–90
Kahneman D (1999) Objective happiness. In: Kahneman D, Diener E, Schwarz N (eds) Well-being: the foundations of hedonic psychology. Russell Sage, New York, pp 3–25
Kitayama S, Markus HR (2000) The pursuit of happiness and the realization of sympathy: cultural patterns of self, social relations, and well-being. In: Diener E, Suh EM (eds) Culture and subjective well-being. The MIT Press, Cambridge, pp 113–161
Kosenko R, Sirgy MJ, Efraty D (1990) A life satisfaction measure based on need hierarchy theory. In: Meadow HL, Sirgy MJ (eds) Quality-of-life studies in marketing and management. International Society for Quality-of-Life Studies, Blacksburg, Virginia, pp 657–667
Lewin K (1951) Field theory in social science. Harper & Row, New York
Lewis SC, Cooper CL (1987) Stress in two-earner couples and stage of the life cycle. J Occup Psychol 60:289–303
Madsen S (2003) The effects of home-based teleworking on work-family conflict. Hum Resource Dev Q 14(1):35
Marks SR, McDermid SM (1996) Multiple roles and the self: a theory of role balance. J Marriage Fam 58:417–432
Maslow AH (1954, 1970) Motivation and personality. Harper, New York
McClelland DC (1961) The achieving society. The Free Press, New York
Niven D (2000) The 100 simple secrets of happy people: what scientists have learned and how you can use it. Harper San Francisco, New York
Nussbaum M (1992) Human functioning and social justice: in defense of Aristotelian essentialism. Political Theory 20:202–246
O'Brien GE (1986) Psychology of work and unemployment. Wiley, New York
Oishi S, Diner E, Lucas RE, Suh EM (1999) Cross-cultural variations in predictors of life satisfaction: perspectives from needs and values. Pers Soc Psychol Bull 25:980–990
Parasuraman S, Greenhhaus JH, Granrose CS (1992) Role stressors, social support, and well-being among two-career couples. J Organ Behav 13(4):339–356
Peterson C, Park N, Seligman MEP (2005) Orientations to happiness and life satisfaction: the full life versus the empty life. J Happiness Stud 6:24–41
Rice RW, McFarlin DB, Hunt RG, Near JP (1985) Organizational work and the perceived quality of life: toward a conceptual model. Acad Manag Rev 10:296–310
Roberts KH, Glick W (1981) The job characteristics approach to task design: a critical review. J Appl Psychol 66:193–217

Salanick GR, Pfeffer J (1977) An examination of need-satisfaction models of job attitudes. Adm Sci Q 23:224–253
Schwarz N, Strack F (1999) Reports of subjective well-being: judgmental processes and their methodological implications. In: Kahneman D, Diener E, Schwarz N (eds) Well-being: the foundations of hedonic psychology. Russell Sage Foundation, New York, pp 61–84
Seeman M (1967) On the personal consequences of alienation and job satisfaction. Ind Labor Rev 23:207–219
Sekaran U (1986) Dual-career families. Jossey-Bass, San Francisco
Seligman MEP (2002) Authentic happiness: using the new positive psychology to realize your potential for lasting fulfillment. The Free Press, New York
Seligman MEP, Royzman E (2003) Happiness: the three traditional theories. Authentic happiness newsletter, July 2003 (http://www.authentichappiness.org/news/news6.html)
Sen A (1985) Commodities and capabilities. North-Holland, Amsterdam
Sirgy MJ (2002) The psychology of quality of life. Kluwer Academic Publishers, Dordrecht
Sirgy MJ, Cole D, Kosenko R, Meadow HL, Rahtz D, Cicic M, Jin GX, Yarsuvat D, Blenkhorn DL, Nagpal N (1995) Developing a life satisfaction measure based on need hierarchy theory. In: Sirgy MJ, Samli AC (eds) New dimensions of marketing and quality of life (. Greenwood Press, Westport, pp 3–26
Steffy BD, Ashbaugh D (1986) Dual-career planning, marital satisfaction, and job stress among women in dual-career marriages. J Bus Psychol 1(2):114–121
Sturges J, Guest D (2004) Working to live or living to work? Work/life balance early in the career. Hum Resource Manag J 14(4):5
United Nations Development Programme (1998) Human development report 1998. Oxford University Press, New York
Valliant G (1977) Adaptations to life. Little Brown, Boston, p 373
Veenhoven R (1995) The cross-national pattern of happiness: test of predictions implied in three theories of happiness. Soc Indic Res 34:33–68
Wiley DL (1987) The relationship between work/nonwork role conflict and job-related outcomes: some unanticipated findings. J Manag 13:467–472
Wright N, Larsen V (1993) Materialism and life satisfaction: a meta-analysis. J Consumer Satisf Dissatisfaction Complain Behav 6:158–165
Zohman BL (1973) Emotional factors in coronary disease. Geriatrics 28:110–119

Part II
Socio-Economic and Cultural Issues

Chapter 11
The Four Qualities of Life Ordering Concepts and Measures of the Good Life

Ruut Veenhoven

Abstract The terms 'quality-of-life', 'well-being' and 'happiness' denote different meanings; sometimes they are used as an umbrella term for all of value, and at other times to denote special merits. This paper is about the specific meanings of the terms. It proposes a classification based on two bi-partitions; between life 'chances' and life 'results', and between 'outer' and 'inner' qualities. Together these dichotomies imply four qualities of life: (1) livability of the environment, (2) life-ability of the individual, (3) external utility of life and (4) inner appreciation of life. This fourfold matrix is applied in three ways: firstly to place related notions and alternative classifications, secondly to explore substantive meanings in various measures for quality of life and thirdly to find out whether quality-of-life can be measured comprehensively. This last question is answered in the negative. Current sum-scores make little sense. The most inclusive measure is still how long and happily people live.

Keywords Quality of life • Utility • Happiness • Well-being

There are many words that are used to indicate how well we are doing. Some of these signify overall thriving; currently the terms 'quality of life' and 'well-being' are used for this purpose, and sometimes the word 'health'.[1] In the past the terms 'happiness' and 'welfare' were more commonly used. There are several problems with these terms.

One problem is that these terms do not have an unequivocal meaning. Sometimes they are used as an umbrella for all that is good, but on other occasions they denote specific merit. For instance: the term 'well-being' is used to

[1] The World Health Organization defines health as "a state of complete physical, mental and social well-being".

R. Veenhoven (✉)
Erasmus University Rotterdam, P. O. Box 1738, 3000 Rotterdam, The Netherlands
e-mail: veenhoven@fsw.eur.nl

R. Veenhoven
North-West University, Mmabatho 2745, South Africa

A. Delle Fave (ed.), *The Exploration of Happiness*, Happiness Studies Book Series,
DOI: 10.1007/978-94-007-5702-8_11, © Springer Science+Business Media Dordrecht 2013

denote the quality of life-as-a-whole and to evaluate life-aspects such as dwelling conditions or employment chances. Likewise, the phrase 'quality-of-life' refers in some contexts to the quality of society and in other instances to the happiness of its citizens. There is little view on a consensus on the meaning of these words; the trend is rather to divergence. Over time, connotations tend to become more specific and manifold. Discursive communities develop their own quality-of-life notions.

The second problem is in the connotation of inclusiveness. The use of the words as an umbrella term suggests that there is something as 'overall' quality of life, and that specific merits can be meaningfully added in some wider worth; however, that holistic assumption is dubious. Philosophers have never agreed on one final definition of quality-of-life, and in the practice of empirical quality-of-life measurement we see comparisons of apples and pears.

The above problem of many meanings is partly caused by the suggestion of inclusiveness. One of the reasons why the meanings become more specific is that the rhetoric of encompassingness crumbles when put to practice. The broad overall meaning appears typically unfeasible in measurement and decision making. Hence connotations tend to become more specific and diverse. As a result, rhetoric denotation of the overall good requires new terms periodically. New expressions pop up as against more narrow meanings. For instance, in the field of healthcare the term 'quality of life' emerged to convey the idea that there is more than mere quantity of survival time. Likewise, the word 'well-being' came into use in contrast to sheer economic 'welfare'.[2] Yet, in the long run these new term fall victim to their success. Once they are adopted as a goal for policy, analysts and trend watchers start extracting palpable meanings and make the concepts ever more 'multi-dimensional'.

Obviously, this communicative practice causes much confusion and impedes the development of knowledge in this field. In reaction, there have been many proposals for standard definitions.[3] Unfortunately, this has not really helped. Firstly, such scientific definitions hardly affect the common use of language. Secondly, they add to the confusion, because scholars are not able to agree on one meaning either, for instance, McCall (1975) defines quality-of-life as 'necessary conditions for happiness', while Terhune (1973) defines it as subjective satisfaction itself. Likewise, Colby (1987) describes well-being as 'adaptive potential', whereas Jolles and Stalpers (1978, p. 31) define it as 'basic commend

[2] In the Netherlands in the 1970s, the 'limits to growth' movement used the slogan 'not welfare, but well-being' (In Dutch: Geenwelvaartmaarwelzijn). In this context, the capriciousness of the term is emphasized. Interestingly, the term was soon taken over by social workers, who came to call their services 'well-being work'. Hereby, the term well-being came to denote a very limited meaning, in fact far more limited than economic welfare, which denotes all goods and services produced in society. Still the suggestion of encompassivenes remained, much to the pleasure of the profession.

[3] For an overview of the various definitions of 'quality of life' see: Fernandez-Ballesteros (1996). A review of definitions of happiness canbe found with Veenhoven (1984, pp. 16–17).

to life'. Elsewhere I have listed fifteen definitions of happiness (Veenhoven 1984, pp. 16–17). Recently Noll (1999) listed many meanings of quality of life in nations.

Since we cannot really force the use of words, we can better try to clarify their meanings. An analytic tool for this purpose is proposed in this article. First a four-fold classification of qualities of life is presented (Sect. 11.1). By means of this taxonomy common terms and distinctions are placed (Sect. 11.2). The matrix is then used to chart substantive meanings in common measures of the good life (Sect. 11.3). Next the question is raised whether we can meaningfully speak about comprehensive quality of life (Sect. 11.4).

11.1 Grouping Qualities of Life

Terms like 'quality of life', 'well-being' and 'happiness' denote evaluations. When sorting out what kind of evaluation they aim at, we must establish what *thing* is evaluated by what *standard.*

11.1.1 Quality of What Life?

In the case of 'quality of life' the object of evaluation is 'life'. Mostly that life is an individual life, the quality of life of a person. Yet the term is also used for aggregates, for instance when we speak about the quality-of-life of women. In that case the term refers usually to the average of individuals. Sometimes the term is used in reference to humanity as a whole. In this context the object of evaluation is mostly the average individual, and the long-term destiny of the species. The evaluation then concerns 'human life', rather than 'human lives'.

The term 'quality of life' does not refer exclusively to human life. It is also used for animals, for instance in discussions about conditions of slaughter cattle. At a higher level of abstraction it is also used for all life. Quality of life is then the condition of the entire ecosystem. Ecological propagandists like this confusion of object matter, because it suggests that protection of endangered species is also good for the individual human.

The terms 'well-being' and 'happiness' denote even more varied objects of evaluation, because they are also used in reference to social systems. When speaking about the 'public well-being' or the 'happiness of the nation' we often aim at the collective level, how well society functions and maintains itself. Propagandists also exploit this ambiguity, in this case as a means to disguise differences in interest between individuals and society.

In this paper I focus on the quality of *individual human lives.* As we will see, that is difficult enough.

11.1.2 What Quality of Life?

The aim of this paper is to chart the specific meanings denoted by terms like 'quality-of-life', so we must explore what qualities are implied by the term quality. This requires an exploration of the 'varieties of the good'.

A classic distinction is between 'objective' and 'subjective' quality of life. The first refers to the degree that a life meets explicit standards of the good life, as assessed by an impartial outsider. For instance the result of a medical examination. The latter variant concerns self-appraisals based on implicit criteria, for example, someone's subjective feeling of health. These qualities do not necessarily correspond; someone may be in good health by the criteria of his doctor, but nevertheless feel bad. On the basis of this distinction, Zapf (1984, p. 25) has proposed a fourfold classification of 'welfare' concepts. When conditions of life score well on objective measures and subjective appreciation of life is positive, he speaks of 'well-being'; when both evaluations are negative he speaks of 'deprivation'. When objective quality is good, but subjective appreciation is negative, the term 'dissonance' is applied, and the combination of bad conditions and positive appreciation is labeled 'adaptation'.

Though elegant, these distinctions have not proven particularly useful. The taxonomy does not explain much. The main reason is that the difference is more in observation than in substance. Objective health-assessment aims at the same qualities as subjective appraisals, though by different means. Further the labeling gives rise to misunderstanding. The word 'objective' suggest indisputable truth, whereas the term 'subjective' is easily interpreted as a matter of arbitrary taste. This suggestion is false, the fact that income can be measured objectively does not mean that its value is beyond question.

11.1.2.1 Chances and Outcomes

A substantively more relevant distinction is between opportunities for a good life and the good life itself. This is the difference between potentiality and actuality. I refer to this as 'life-chances'[4] and 'life-results'. Opportunities and outcomes are related, but are certainly not the same. Chances can fail to be realized, due to stupidity or bad luck. Conversely, people sometimes make much of their life in spite of poor opportunities.

This distinction is quite common in the field of public-health research. Preconditions for good health, such as adequate nutrition and professional care are seldom mixed up with health itself. Much research is aimed at assessing the relationships between these phenomena; for instance by checking whether common nutritional advice really yields extra years lived in good health.

[4] In sociology, the term 'life-chances' is used in the more limited meaning of access to scarce resources in society.

Yet in social policy discussions means and ends are less well distinguished. For instance, in the Netherlands the term 'well-being' is used for both social services, i.e. state pensions, as well as for the expected effects, satisfied citizens. This is not just sloppy thinking, it is also an expression of the ideology that there is quality to be found in the welfare society.

11.1.2.2 Outer and Inner Qualities

A second difference is between 'external' and 'internal' qualities. In the first case the quality is in the environment, in the latter it is in the individual. Lane (1994) made this distinction clear by telling 'quality of society' from 'quality of persons'. Likewise Musschenga (1994, p. 182) discerned 'quality of the conditions for living' from 'the quality of being human'.

This distinction is also quite commonly made in public health. External pathogens are distinguished from inner afflictions, and researchers try to identify the mechanisms by which the former produce the latter, and the conditions in which this is more and less likely. Yet again this basic insight is lacking in many social policy discussions. For instance, in the current discourse on city renewal the word 'quality-of-life' is used both for clean streets and feelings of being home in the neighborhood. All the research that found negligible relationships has not changed this use of words.

11.1.3 Four Qualities of Life

The combination of these two dichotomies yields a fourfold matrix. This classification is presented in Scheme 11.1. The distinction between chances and results is presented vertically, the difference between outer and inner qualities horizontally.

RUUT VEENHOVEN

	Outer qualities	*Inner qualities*
Life chances	Livability of environment	Life-ability of the person
Life results	Utility of life	Appreciation of life

Scheme 11.1 Four qualities of life

11.1.3.1 Two Kinds of Life Chances

In the upper half of the scheme we see two variants of potential quality of life, with next to the outer opportunities in one's environment, the inner capacities to exploit these. The environmental chances can be denoted by the term *livability*, the personal capacities with the word *life-ability*. This difference is not new. In sociology the distinction between 'social capital' and 'psychological capital' is sometimes used in this context. In the psychology of stress the difference is labeled negatively in terms of 'burden' and 'bearing power'.

Livability of the Environment. The left top quadrant denotes the meaning of good living conditions. Often the terms 'quality-of-life' and 'well-being' are used in this particular meaning, especially in the writings of ecologists and sociologists. Economists sometimes use the term 'welfare' for this meaning. Another term is 'level of living'.

'Livability' is a better word, because it refers explicitly to a characteristic of the environment and does not have the limited connotation of material conditions. One could also speak of the 'habitability' of an environment, though that term is also used for the quality of housing in particular. Elsewhere I have explored that concept of livability in more detail (Veenhoven 1996, pp. 7–9).

Life-Ability of the Person. The right top quadrant denotes inner life-chances. That is: how well we are equipped to cope with the problems of life. This aspect of the good life is also known by different names. The words 'quality of life' and 'well-being' are also used to denote this specific meaning, especially by doctors and psychologists. There are more names however. In biology the phenomenon is referred to as 'adaptive potential'. On other occasions it is denoted by the medical term 'health', in the medium variant of the word,[5] or by psychological terms such as 'efficacy' or 'potency'. Sen (1992) calls this quality of life variant 'capability'. I prefer the simple term 'life-ability', which contrasts elegantly with 'livability'.

11.1.3.2 Two Kinds of Life-Results

The lower half of the scheme is about the quality of life with respect to its outcomes. These outcomes can be judged by their value for one's environment and value for oneself. The external worth of a life is denoted by the term 'utility of life'. The inner valuation of it is called 'appreciation of life'. These matters are of course related. Knowing that one's life is useful will typically add to the appreciation of it. Yet not all useful lives are happy lives and not every good-for-nothing really cares. This difference has been elaborated in discussions on utilitaristic moral philosophy, which praises happiness as the highest good. Adversaries of that view hold that there is more worth to life than just pleasures and pains. Mill (1863) summarized that position in his famous statement that he preferred an unhappy Socrates to a happy fool.

[5] There are three main meanings of health: The maxi variant is all the good (WHO definition), the medium variant is life-ability, and the mini-variant is absence of physical defect.

Utility of Life. The left bottom quadrant represents the notion that a good life must be good for something more than itself. This presumes some higher values. There is no current generic for these external turnouts of life. Gerson (1976, p. 795) referred to these kinds as 'transcendental' conceptions of quality of life. Another appellation is 'meaning of life', which then denotes 'true' significance instead of mere subjective sense of meaning. I prefer the more simple 'utility of life', admitting that this label may also give rise to misunderstanding.[6] Be aware that this external utility does not require inner awareness. A person's life may be useful from some viewpoints, without them knowing.[7]

Appreciation of Life. Finally, the bottom right quadrant represents the inner outcomes of life. That is the quality in the eye of the beholder. As we deal with conscious humans this quality boils down to subjective appreciation of life. This is commonly referred to by terms such as 'subjective well-being', 'life-satisfaction' and 'happiness' in a limited sense of the word.[8] Life has more of this quality, the more and the longer it is enjoyed. In fairy tales this combination of intensity and duration is denoted with the phrase 'they lived long and happily'.

11.1.4 Similar Distinctions in Other Disciplines

This categorizing can be clarified using some analogies. Similar conceptual distinctions can be found in biology, economics and systems theory.

11.1.4.1 Biology

In evolutionary biology, external living conditions are referred to as the 'biotope' or 'habitat'. A biotope can be more or less suitable (livable) for a species, depending on e.g. availability of food, shelter and competition. Inner capabilities to survive in that environment are called 'fitness'. This latter term acknowledges that capabilities must meet (fit) environmental demand. Unlike moral philosophers, biologists see no quality in capacity that is not functional.

This chance-constellation is seen to result in 'adaptation', and good adaptation is seen to manifest in 'survival'. As evolutionary biologists focus on species rather than on individual specimen, they mean mostly survival of the species. Hence the success of an individual life is mainly judged by its procreation. Once genes have been passed on, the external utility of an individual life is often little more than that of a prey for another creature.

---

[6] A problem with this name is that the utilitarians used the word utility for subjective appreciation of life, the sum of pleasures and pains.

[7] Frankl's (1946) logo-therapy aims to make people believe in meanings of their life they do not see.

[8] This quality-of-life is the subject of the Journal of Happiness Studies.

	Outer quality	*Inner quality*
Life chances	Biotope	Fitness
Life results	Adaptation: Continuation of species	Adaptation: Long and happy life

	Outer quality	*Inner quality*
Chances	Market	Capital
Results	Public wealth	Private profit

	Outer quality	*Inner quality*
Chances	Input	Throughput
Results	Output: External effects (input for other systems)	Output: Feedback (for system maintenance)

Scheme 11.2 Comparable concepts in **a** biology, **b** economics, **c** system theory

At the individual level good adaptation is seen to manifest in a relatively long life. An organism that perishes prematurely has adapted less well than the one that completed its programmed lifetime. In higher animals, good adaptation also reflects in hedonic experience. Continuous stress and pain is indicative of poor adaptation. As humans are capable of reflecting on their experiences, their feelings of pleasure and pain condense into overall appraisals of happiness. So, human adaptation manifests in long *and* happy living. Though inner experience is no great issue in biology, this idea is implied in its logic.

These biological concepts are summarized in Scheme 11.2a.

11.1.4.2 Economics

In economic thought, the equivalent of the life situation for a person is the market for a business. As a person's situation can be more or less livable, so a market can be more or less exploitable. Successful exploitation of market chances requires 'capital', both financial capital to buy materials and machinery and human capital to run the enterprise. Capital is, for a business, what 'capability' is for an individual. These chances can result in economic success. At the business level this is 'profit', which is analogous to an individual's 'appreciation of life'.[9] At the societal level business success can contribute to public wealth, and thereby to social and cultural evolution. This is analogous to an individual's 'utility of life'. These economic analogies are presented in Scheme 11.2b.

11.1.4.3 System Theory

Finally there is also an analogy with system theory, the main concepts of which are 'input', 'throughput' and 'output'. In this thinking, 'input' is the system's environment, in particular the things the system can extract from that environment. Without any input, the system cannot function and perishes. The richer the input is, the better, and the more in line it is with the system's needs. Good input for a system is what a 'livable' situation is for an individual.

System theory acknowledges that environmental supply alone is not enough to keep the system going. The system must actively process the input. This is commonly called 'throughput'. The capacity to do this job is an inner quality of the system. This system capability is analogous to 'life-ability' of a person.

In system theory the term 'output' denotes all results of system activity. Part of that output is external and serves as input for other systems. This is analogous to the 'utility of life'. Another part of the output is used for system preservation. This concerns inner effects and belongs to the right bottom quadrant.

For an individual, system maintenance involves first of all survival. Since biological organisms cannot live forever, that boils down to living a relatively long life. In higher organisms, system-preservation also manifests in how well they feel. As noted above, affective appraisals function as feedback mechanisms in

[9] This analogy fits to the extent that the profit of a firm also reflects the degree to which functional demands for the business are met. Yet unlike functional needs for human functioning these demands are not fixed genetically and nor are they linked so closely to affect-like signals.

	Outer qualities	*Inner qualities*
Life chances	**Livability of environment** ∘ Ecological e.g. moderate climate, clean air, spacious housing, ∘ Social e.g. freedom, equality and brotherhood ∘ Economical e.g. wealthy nation, generous social security, smooth economic development ∘ Cultural e.g. flourishing of arts and sciences, mass education ∘ Etc...	**Life-ability of the person** ∘ Physical health negative: free of disease positive: energetic, resilient ∘ Mental health negative: free of mental defects positive: autonomous, creative ∘ Knowledge e.g. literacy, schooling ∘ Skills e.g. intelligence, manners ∘ Art of living e.g. varied lifestyle, differentiated taste ∘ Etc...
Life results	**Objective utility of life** ∘ External utility e.g. For intimates: rearing children, care for friends e.g. For society: being a good citizen e.g. for mankind: leaving an invention ∘ Moral perfection e.g. authenticity, compassion, originality ∘ Etc...	**Subjective appreciation of life** ∘ appraisal of life-aspects e.g. Satisfaction with job e.g. satisfaction with variety ∘ Prevailing moods e.g. Depression, ennui e.g. zest ∘ Overall appraisals Affective: general mood-level Cognitive: contentment with life

	Outer quality	*Inner quality*
Chances	**Objective quality** Life meets normative ideals	
Results		**Subjective quality** life meets preferences life is enjoyed

	Outer quality	*Inner quality*
Chances	Conditions for happiness • General happiness requisites • Idiosyncratic happiness requisites	
Results		Happiness

◀ **Scheme 11.3** Some sub-meaning within quality-quadrants. 2.1. **a** Fit with Brock's classification. **b** Fit with McCall's classification

higher animals, positive affect typically signaling that things are going well. In humans these appraisals are condensed into estimates of overall 'happiness'. So, in humans, good output manifests at the individual level in long and happy living. These parallel notions are presented in Scheme 11.3.

11.2 Ordering Concepts of the Good Life

With the help of this matrix we can now place the various notions about the good life. I will start with an overview of concepts that neatly fit the quality quadrants (Sect. 11.2.1). Next I will mention some common notions that overlap quadrants (Sect. 11.2.2). Finally I confront the matrix with some other classifications of qualities of life (Sect. 11.2.3).

11.2.1 Meanings Within Quality-Quadrants

Most discussions of the good life deal with more specific values than the four qualities of life discerned here. Within each of the quadrants there is a myriad of sub-meanings, most of which are known under different names. It would need a voluminous tome to record all the terms and meanings used in the literature. I present some of the main variants below. The main points are summarized in Scheme 11.3.

11.2.1.1 Aspects of Livability

Livability is an umbrella term for the various qualities of the environment, which seem relevant for meeting human needs. In rhetoric use, the word refers mostly to specific kinds of qualities which typically root in some broader perception of the good society. The circumstantial qualities that are emphasized differ widely across contexts and disciplines.

Ecologists see livability in the natural environment and describe it in terms of pollution, global warming and degradation of nature. Currently, they associate livability typically with environmental preservation. City planners see livability in the built environment and associate it with sewer systems, traffic jams and ghetto formation. Here the good life is seen as a fruit of human intervention.

In the sociological view society is central. Firstly, livability is associated with the quality of society as a whole. Classic concepts of the 'good society' stress material welfare and social equality, sometimes equating the concept more or less with the welfare state. Current notions emphasize close networks, strong norms and active voluntary associations. The reverse of that livability concept is 'social fragmentation'. Secondly, livability is seen in one's position in society. For long the emphasis was on 'under-class' but currently attentions shifts to 'outer-class'. The corresponding antonyms are 'deprivation' and 'exclusion'.

11.2.1.2 Kinds of Life-Ability

The most common depiction of this quality of life is absence of functional defects. This is 'health' in the limited sense, sometimes referred to as 'negative health'. In this context doctors focus on unimpaired functioning of the body, while psychologists stress the absence of mental defects. In their language, quality of life and well-being are often synonymous with mental health. This use of words presupposes a 'normal' level of functioning. Good quality of life is the body and mind working as designed. This is the common meaning used in curative care.

Next to absence of disease one can consider excellence of function. This is referred to as 'positive health' and associated with energy and resilience. Psychological concepts of positive mental health involve also autonomy, reality control, creativity and inner synergy of traits and strivings. A new term in this context is 'emotional intelligence'. Though originally meant for specific mental skills, this term has come to denote a broad range of mental capabilities. This broader definition is the favorite in training professions.

A further step is to evaluate capability in a developmental perspective and to include acquisition of new skills for living. This is commonly denoted by the term 'self-actualization'; from this point of view a middle-aged man is not 'well' if he behaves like an adolescent, even if he functions without problems at this level. Since abilities do not develop in idleness, this quality of life is close to the 'activity' in Aristotle's concept of eudaimonia (Ostenfelt 1994). This quality concept is also currently used in training professions.

Lastly, the term 'art of living' denotes special life-abilities; in most contexts this quality is distinguished from mental health and sometimes even attributed to slightly disturbed persons. Art of living is associated with refined tastes, an ability to enjoy life and an original style of life.

11.2.1.3 Criteria for Utility of Life

When evaluating the external effects of a life, one can consider its functionality for the environment. In this context, doctors stress how essential a patient's life is to its intimates. The life of a mother with young children is valued as higher than the life of a woman of the same age without children. Likewise, indispensability at the workplace figures in medical quality of life notions.

At a higher level, quality of life is seen in contributions to society. Historians see quality in the addition an individual can make to human culture, and rate for example the lives of great inventors higher than those of anonymous peasants. Moralists see quality in the preservation of the moral order, and would deem the life of a saint to be better than that of a sinner.

In this vein the quality of a life is also linked to effects on the ecosystem. Ecologists see more quality in a life lived in a 'sustainable' manner than in the life of a polluter. In a broader view, the utility of life can be seen in its consequences for long term evolution. As an individual's life can have many environmental effects, the number of such utilities is almost infinite.

Apart from its functional utility, life is also judged on its moral or esthetic value. Returning to Mill's statement that he preferred an unhappy Socrates to a happy fool, Mill did not say this just because Socrates was a philosopher whose words have come down to us; it was also because he admired Socrates as an outstanding human being. Likewise, most of us would attribute more quality to the life of Florence Nightingale than to that of a drunk, even if it appeared that her good works had a negative result in the end. In classic moral philosophy this is called 'virtuous living', and is often presented as the essence of 'true happiness'.

This concept of exemplaric utility sometimes merges with notions of inner life-ability, in particular in the case of self-actualization.

Self-development is deemed good, even if it might complicate life. In some philosophies of life, reaching a state of enlightenment is more important than departing from it.

This quality criterion is external; the individuals need not be aware of their perfection or may actually despise it. It is an outsider that appraises the quality of the individual's life on the basis of an external criterion. In religious thinking such a judgement is made by God on the basis of eternal truth, in post-modern thought it narrated by self-proclaimed experts on the basis of local conviction.

Clearly, the utility of life is not easy to grasp; both the criteria and those who would judge are multifarious. Later we will see that this prohibits comprehensive measurement of this quality of life. This quadrant is typically the playground of philosophers.

11.2.1.4 Appreciation of Life

Humans are capable of evaluating their life in different ways. As already noted, we have in common with all higher animals that we can appraise our situation affectively. We feel good or bad about particular things and our mood level signals overall adaptation. As in animals these affective appraisals are automatic, but unlike other animals humans can reflect on that experience. We have an idea of how we have felt over the last year, while a cat does not. Humans can also judge life cognitively by comparing life as it is with notions of how it should be.

Most human evaluations are based on both sources of information, that is: intuitive affective appraisal and cognitively guided evaluation. The mix depends mainly on the object. Tangible things such as our income are typically evaluated by comparison; intangible matters such as sexual attractiveness are evaluated by how it feels. This dual evaluation system probably makes the human experiential repertoire richer than that of our fellow-creatures.

In evaluating our life we typically summarize this rich experience in overall appraisals. For instance we appreciate domains of life. When asked how we feel about our work or own marriage, we will mostly have an opinion. Likewise, most people form ideas about separate qualities of their life, for instance how challenging their life is and whether there is any meaning in it. Such judgments are made in different time-perspectives, in the past, the present and in the future. As the future is less palpable than the past and the present, hopes and fears depend more on affective inclination than on cognitive calculation.

Mostly such judgments are not very salient in our consciousness. Now and then they pop to mind spontaneously, and they can be recalled and refreshed when needed. Sometimes however, life-appraisals develop into pervasive mental syndromes such as depression or ennui.

Next to aspects of life we also evaluate life-as-a-whole. Jeremy Bentham (1789) thought of this form of evaluation as a type of 'mental calculus', and currently most scholars in the field also see it as a cognitive operation. For instance Andrews and Withey (1976) suggest that individuals compute a weighed average of earlier life-aspect evaluations, while Michalos' (1985) multiple discrepancy theory presumes comparisons of life as it is with various standards of how it should be. Many philosophers see it as an estimate of success in realizing one's life-plan (e.g. Nordenfelt 1989).

Yet there are good reasons to assume that overall life-satisfaction is mostly inferred from affective experience (Veenhoven 1997, pp. 59–61). One reason is that life-as-a-whole is not a suitable object for calculative evaluation. Life has many aspects and there is usually not one clear-cut ideal model to compare with. Another reason seems to be that affective signals tend to dominate, seemingly cognitive appraisals are often instigated by affective cues (Zajonc 1980). This fits the theory that the affective system is the older in evolutionary terms, and that cognition works as an addition to that navigation system rather than as a replacement.

This issue has important consequences for the significance of subjective appreciation as a criterion for quality-of-life. If appreciation is a matter of mere comparison with arbitrary standards, there is little of value in a positive evaluation; dissatisfaction is then an indication of high demands. If, however, happiness signals the degree to which innate needs are met, life-satisfaction denotes how well we thrive.

Whatever the method of assessment, the fact that we are able to come to an overall evaluation of life is quite important. Later on we will see that this is the only basis for encompassing judgments of the quality of life.

11.2.2 Meanings in Broader Words for the Good Life

With the help of the taxonomy given above, we can now clarify the substantive meaning of several further terms. This enumeration is not exhaustive; the goal is to illustrate this approach.

11.2.2.1 Adjustment

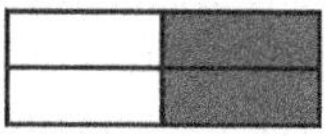

This term came into use in the 1960s, in particular in gerontologic studies of 'adjustment to old age', and was used interchangeably with 'adaptation'. These words were soon ousted by phrases like 'morale', 'psychological well-being' and 'life-satisfaction'. The term referred to personal qualities; hence it belongs in the right side of our matrix. Adjustment denotes how well a person deals with life, and refers both to equipment and success. Hence the concept does not fit one quadrant, but covers both life-abilities and life-appraisals. In the diagram this is indicated by two equally dark quadrants.

11.2.2.2 Art of Living

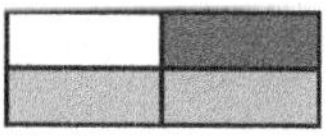

The expression 'art of living' refers, first of all, to a person's life-ability and therefore belongs in the right-top quadrant. As noted above, the term depicts mostly the quality of a life-style, typically refined Epicurianism, but sometimes the wisdom of simple living is also valued as artistry. This main meaning is reflected in the dark colored quadrant. Yet the term bears other connotations, capacity is often associated with its intended results, hence art of living tends to be equated with happiness, or at least with sensorial gratification. Further, the life of a life-artist is sometimes valued as a piece of art in itself, which has some external utility. For instance, we see quality in the life of Casanova, even though the man himself seems not to have been particularly happy. The adjunct connotations of the word are indicated in gray.

11.2.2.3 Deprivation

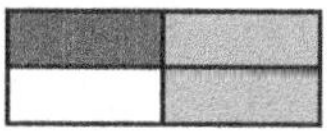

The word 'deprivation' refers to shortfall of something. When used in an absolute sense it means failure to meet basic human needs, when used in a relative sense it means being less well off than others. The word is typically used in the latter meaning, while suggesting the former. Current specifications of this notion are 'poverty' and 'social exclusion'.

In most contexts the lack is in external conditions of life, and concerns access to income, power and prestige. In social policy this kind of deprivation is typically met with redistribution of these scarce resources. This main meaning belongs in the livability quadrant.

Sometimes the word also refers to deficiency in ones capacity to stand up for oneself. The political cure for this problem is 'empowerment', common ingredients of which are general education, political training and boosting of self-esteem. The latter adjunct definition belongs in the life-ability quadrant.

Usually these conditions are associated with the expected outcome for individuals, that is with 'happiness'. Hence measures of deprivation often include items on dissatisfaction, depression and suicidal ideation. Enjoyment of life in spite of objective deprivation is seen as an anomaly. As we have seen above, in Zapf's conceptual schema it is labeled 'resignation'.

11.2.2.4 Happiness

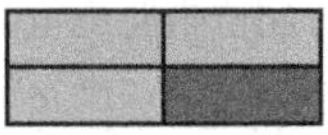

I will now continue the earlier discussion on the connotations of the word 'happiness'. As noted in the introduction of this paper, the word has often been used as a generic term for all worth and is in this sense synonymous with comprehensive 'quality-of-life' or 'well-being'. In the later discussion of inner outcome notions, the word came back in two, more narrow forms, first as a label for all subjective appraisals of life, and second, as the overall evaluation of life as a whole. The latter use of the word is most common in present day 'social indicators research'.

Beyond this main denotation of the word, there are still further adjunctive uses of the term. This appears for example in the well known definition of happiness given by Tatarkiewicz (1975, p. 16) as "...*justified* satisfaction with life". The adjective 'justified' means that mere enjoyment of life does not constitute (true) happiness if it occurs in objective situations, for example a prisoner cannot be really happy. Similarly Tatarkiewicz would not call someone happy when the evaluation is based on misperception, such as in the case of the simpleton 'Happy Hans', or when the enjoyment is derived from a useless life. The word happiness is also used to denote desirable living conditions (top left) and for personal qualities such as health and resilience (top right). So all the other quadrants are marked grey.

11.2.3 Difference with Other Classifications of Qualities of Life

This is of course not the first attempt to chart concepts of the good life. A few examples will show how this matrix differs from other taxonomies.

Philosopher Dan Brock (1993, pp. 268–275) also tried to grasp "the broadest conception of.. what makes a life go best". He distinguishes three main concepts: (1) the degree to which life fits current values and ideals, (2) the degree to which life fits the individuals preferences, and (3) the degree to which the individual enjoys life subjectively. He denotes the first concept as 'objective' and the other two as 'subjective'. Brock insists on the difference between satisfaction of preferences (contentment in my terminology) and hedonic enjoyment (mood level).

These meanings are plotted in Scheme 11.4a using our matrix. The difference is not so much in the appreciation quadrant, but in the other three. Brock's classification is less differentiated, and shovels all the objective meanings onto one heap. As he is mainly concerned with health care, one can imagine that he leaves out societal livability. Yet he does not distinguish either between 'capability for life' and 'utility of life', though this distinction is quite relevant for medical decisions.

Sandoe (1999) proposes a similar classification, which also separates realization of preferences and hedonic experience. The difference is that his 'objective' qualities limit to the development of potentials. His refers to that quality as 'Perfectionism'. This is what I referred to as 'self-actualization'. In the matrix it is a part of the life-ability quadrant.

Storrs McCall (1975) also distinguishes two main concepts of quality of life. Next to happiness itself he emphasizes conditions for happiness. In his view life has also quality if the necessary social conditions are available, even if an individual fails to exploit these chances or opts not to use them. Happiness is seen to result from need-gratification, and hence the necessary conditions are linked to basic human needs. In this concept human nature is the major yardstick, and not normative ideals. Consequently, the utility quadrant remains empty in this case. Since McCall does not distinguish between external and internal requisites, the two top quadrants are merged. See Scheme 11.4b.

11.3 Ordering Measures of the Good Life

The last decades have witnessed a surge in empirical research on the good life, in particular in the fields of social indicators research and medical quality of life assessment. This has produced a wealth of measures. Testbanks contain hundreds of them. See for instance Cummins (1994), Spilker (1996) and Veenhoven (2000a).

Most of these measures are 'multi-dimensional' and are used to assess different qualities of life. Typically, the scores on the different qualities are presented separately in a 'quality-of-life *profile*'. Often they are also summed in a 'quality-of-life *score*' Next, there are also 'uni-dimensional' measures, which focus on one specific quality. Such single qualities are often measured by single questions. For instance, the condition of cancer patients is also measured by simply asking them where they stand between the best and worst they have ever experienced (Bernheim and Buyse 1983).

A lively discussion about the pros and cons of these measures is still going on. This discussion is dominated by psychometricians, who focus very much on factor loadings, reliability issues and inter-test correlations. There is less attention for matters of substance, so there is no clear answer to the question of what these measures actually measure. One of the reasons for this deficiency is a lack of a clear taxonomy of the qualities of life.

Now we have a classification of meanings, we can give it another try. Below I will first outline which of these qualities figure in measures that claim to cover the good of life inclusively (Sect. 11.3.1). Next I will explore whether there are measures that fit one of the four qualities of life separately (Sect. 11.3.2).

THE FOUR QUALITIES OF LIFE

	Outer quality	*Inner quality*
Life-chances		No limitations to work and social functioning Not nervous Energetic General health good
Life results		No pain No bad feelings Happy person

	Outer quality	*Inner quality*
Life-chances	Income, possessions Social contacts Social position (Safety) Opportunities	Health Productivity Autonomy
Life results	(Productivity) (Social responsibility)	*Satisfaction with:* Material life Social contacts Social position Safety Freedom

	Outer quality	*Inner quality*
Life-chances	Income (h) Housing (h) Political support (h) Social relations (l)	Health (h) Education (h)
Life results	Irreplaceable (b)	Doing interesting things (b) Life-satisfaction (b)

THE FOUR OUALITIES OF LIFE

	Outer quality	*Inner quality*
Life-chances	Material wealth Gender equality Income equality	Education
Life results		Life-expectancy

◀ **Scheme 11.4** Meanings measured by **a** Ware's SF 36 Health Survey, **b** Cummins' 'Comprehensive quality of life scale', **c** Allardt's 'Dimensions of Welfare': having, loving, and being, **d** the UNDP's 'Human Development Index'

11.3.1 Meanings in Comprehensive Measures of Quality of Life

As there are so many measures of the good life, I cannot review them all. Four examples must suffice to illustrate the approach. The examples are taken from different research fields: (a) medical 'quality of life' research, (b) psychological 'well-being' research, (c) sociologically oriented research on 'welfare' and (d) socio-economic studies of national 'development'.

a. *Example of a Medical Quality of Life Index*
One of the most common measures in medical quality of life research is the 'SF-36 Health Survey' (Ware 1996). It is a questionnaire on the following topics:

- physical limitations in daily chores (10 items)
- physical limitations to work performance (4 items)
- bodily pain (2 items)
- perceived general health (6 items)
- vitality (4 items)
- physical and/or emotional limitations to social functioning (2 items)
- emotional limitations to work performance (3 items)
- self characterizations as nervous (1 item)
- recent enjoyment of life (4 items)

Ratings on the first four topics are grouped in a 'Physical Component Subscore', ratings on the last four topics in a 'Mental Component Sub-score'. These components are added into a 'Quality of life Total score'.

Most elements of this scale refer to performance potential and belong in the life-ability quadrant right top. This will be no surprise, since the scale is aimed explicitly at health. Still, some of the items concern outcomes rather than potency, in particular the items on recent enjoyment of life (last on the list). Pain and bad feelings are typically the result of health defects. Happiness is clearly also an outcome. As a proper health measure, the SF-36 does not involve outer qualities. So the left quadrants in Scheme 11.4a remain empty.

Several other medical measures of quality of life do involve items about environmental conditions that belong in the livability quadrant. For instance, the 'Quality Of Life Interview Schedule' by Ouelette-Kuntz (1990) is about availability of services for handicapped persons. In this supply centered measure of the good life, life is better the more services are offered and the more greedily they are used. Likewise, the Quality of Life Index for cancer patients (Spitzer et al. 1981) lists support by family and friends as a quality criterion. Some medical indexes also include outer effects that belong to the utility quadrant. Some typical items are: continuation of work tasks and support provided to intimates and fellow patients.

b. *Example of a Psychological Well-Being Scale*
Cummins (1993) sees quality of life (QOL) as an aggregate of 'objective' and 'subjective' components. Each of these components is divided into the following seven domains:

- material well-being: measured by income, quality of house and possessions.
- health: measured by number of disabilities and medical consumption.
- productivity: measured by activities in work, education and leisure
- intimacy: contacts with close friends, availability of support
- safety: perceived safety of home, quality of sleep, worrying
- place in community: social activities, responsibilities, being asked for advice
- emotional well-being: opportunity to do/have things wanted, enjoyment of life

Overall QOL is measured using a points system, objective QOL using simple scores, subjective QOL using satisfaction with domains weighted by perceived importance of domains. Finally the scores on objective and subjective QOL are added.

The objective scores of this list represent typically life-chances, though the safety items are subjective appraisals. This item is therefore placed between brackets in Scheme 11.4b. Most of the items concern environmental chances and are placed in the livability quadrant left top. Two items concern inner capabilities and are placed in the life-ability quadrant top right.

The subjective scores all refer to how the individual appreciates these aspects of life, and belong in the enjoyment quadrant bottom right. The Cummins scale has no items on overall satisfaction with life. The logic of his system produces the somewhat peculiar item 'How satisfied are you with your own happiness?' (item 7 SQOL).

The bottom left quadrant remains empty in this interpretation; however, some of the life-chance items can also be seen as indicative of outer results. The measures of 'place in community' imply not only better access to scarce resources, but can also denote contribution to society. Likewise, the productivity item may not only tap ability to work, but also the results of it. For this reason these items are placed in brackets in the meaning quadrant.

c. *Example of a Sociological Measure of Individual Quality of Life*
One of the first attempts to chart quality of life in a general population was the made in the Scandinavia 'Study of comparative welfare' under the direction of Erik Allardt (1976). Welfare was measured using the following criteria:

- income
- housing
- political support
- social relations
- being irreplaceable
- doing interesting things
- health
- education
- life-satisfaction

Allardt classified these indicators using his, now classic distinction, between 'having', 'loving' and 'being'. This labeling was appealing at that time, because it expressed the rising conviction that welfare is more than just material wealth, and because it fitted modish notions drawn from humanistic psychology. Though it is well known, the classification has not proven to be very useful.

These indicators can also be ordered in the fourfold matrix proposed here. See Scheme 11.4c. Most of the items belong in the left-top quadrant because they concern pre-conditions for a good life rather than good living as such, and because these chances are in the environment rather than in the individual. This is the case with income, housing, political support and social relations. Two further items also denote chances but these are internal capabilities. This is the health factor and level of education. These items are placed in the top-right quadrant of personal life-ability. The item 'being irreplaceable' belongs in the utility bottom left quadrant. It denotes a value of life to others. The last two items belong in the enjoyment bottom right quadrant. 'Doing interesting things' denotes appreciation of an aspect of life,[10] while life-satisfaction concerns appreciation of life as a whole.

d. *Example of a Measure of Socio-Economic Development* Lastly an illustration using measures used in cross-national comparisons of quality of life. The most commonly used indicator in this field is the 'Human Development Index'. This index was developed for the United Nations Development Program which describes the progress in all countries of the world in its annual 'Human Development Reports' (UNDP 1990). The Human Development Index is the major yardstick used in these reports. The basic variant of this measure involves three items; note that we deal now with scores drawn from national statistical aggregates instead of individual responses to questionnaires:
   - public wealth, measured by buying power per head.
   - education, as measured by literacy and schooling.
   - life-expectancy at birth

Later variants of the HDI involve further items:

- gender-equality measured by the so-called 'Gender empowerment index' which involves male–female ratios in literacy, school enrolment and income.
- poverty measured by prevalence of premature death, functional illiteracy and income deficiencies.

In a theoretical account of this measure the UNDP says to focus on how development enlarges people's choice, and there by their chances for leading long, healthy and creative lives (UNDP 1990, p. 9).

When placed in our fourfold matrix, this index can be seen to have three meanings. See Scheme 11.4d. Firstly, it is about living conditions, in the basic variant of material

[10] 'Doing interesting things' can also be seen as a quality in itself, especially when the person does not like it. In this interpretation this item should be placed in the utility quadrant, because it represents some kind of perfection.

	Outer quality	*Inner quality*
Life-chances	*Quality of society* Livability scores *Position within society* Deprivation indexes	Impairment indexes Positive health inventories Capability tests Educational grades
Life-results	?	Satisfaction summations Self-ratings of happiness Happy life-years

Scheme 11.5 Inclusive measures for specific qualities of life

affluence in society, and in the additions also of social equality. These items belong in the top left quadrant. In the case of wealth it is acknowledged that this environmental merit is subject to diminishing utility, however, this is not so with the equalities.

Secondly, the HDI includes abilities. The education item belongs in the top right quadrant. Though a high level of education does not guarantee high mental health or art of living, it means that many citizens at least have basic knowledge. Lastly, the item 'life-expectancy' is an outcome variable and belongs in the bottom right quadrant. The bottom left quadrant remains empty. The UNDP's measure of development does not involve specific notions about the utility of life.

The HDI is the most concise measure of quality of life in nations. Extended variants in this family provide more illustration; for instance, Naroll's (1984, p. 73) 'Quality of Life Index' includes contributions to science by the country, which fits the utility quadrant. The index also includes suicide rates, which belong to the appreciation quadrant.

11.3.2 Measures for Specific Qualities of Life

Next to these encompassing measures of quality of life there are measures that denote specific qualities. These indicators can also be mapped on the matrix. Again some illustrative examples will suffice. Scheme 11.5 presents are overview.

11.3.2.1 Measures of Livability

Environmental life-chances are measured in two ways, by the possibilities embodied in the environment as a whole, and by relative access to these opportunities. The former measures concern the livability of societies, such as nations or cities. These indicators are typically used in developmental policy. The latter are about relative advantage or deprivation of persons in these contexts, and are rooted mostly in the politics of redistribution. These chance estimates are seldom combined.

Contents. Measures of livability of society concern first nations; an illustrative example is Estes' (1984) 'Index of Social Progress'. This measure involves aspects such as wealth of the nation, peace with neighbors, internal stability and democracy. The physical habitability of the land is also acknowledged. There are similar measures for quality of life in cities (e.g. Kunz and Siefer 1995) and regions (e.g. Korczak 1995). There are also livability counts for more or less 'total' institutions such as army bases, prisons, mental hospitals and geriatric residences.

Measures of relative deprivation focus on differences among citizens for such things as income, work and social contacts. Differences in command of these resources are typically interpreted as differential access to scarce resources (e.g. Townsend 1979).

All these measures work with points systems and summate scores based on different criteria in some way. A part of the measures is based on objective assessments and is typically derived from social statistics. Others also include self-reports about living conditions and depend for this purpose on survey data.

Limitations. These inventories cannot really measure livability comprehensively. Firstly the two kinds are seldom combined; secondly both labor under serious limitations.

Limitation number one is that the topics in these inventories do not exhaustively cover environmental conditions. The indexes consist of some tens of topics that are deemed relevant and happen to be measurable. The inventories obviously lack sections on conditions we do not know of as yet. Note for example, that the list of environmental pathogens is growing each year. Further, not all the conditions we are aware of are measurable. For instance, there are no measures for highly valued qualities like 'social solidarity' and 'cultural variety'.

Problem number two is the significance of topics that are included. Since there is no complete understanding of what we really need, we can only guess at the importance of a topic. Though it is evident that we need food and shelter, it is questionable whether we need holidays and a welfare state. The choice of topics to include in a livability index is not based on evidence that we cannot thrive without something, but on the researcher's preconceptions of the good life. Elsewhere I have proposed gauging the significance of livability topics by their observed effects on health and happiness (Veenhoven 1996). The case of the welfare state can be used to illustrate that point. Several livability inventories include expenditures on social security, e.g. Naroll's (1984, p. 73) 'Quality of Life Index'. Yet people appear not to thrive any better in nations with high social security expenditures than in comparable nations where state social security is modest (Veenhoven 2000b). Freedom appears to add more to happiness, in particular economic freedom (Veenhoven 2000c).

Problem number three is the degree of opportunities required, how many should an environment provide to be livable? With respect to food and temperature we know fairly well what amounts we need minimally and what we can use maximally. Yet, on matters of safety, schooling, freedom and wealth we know little about minimum and possible maximum needs. Lacking this knowledge, most indexes assume that more is better.

Problem number four is that the significance of opportunities is not the same for everybody, but depends on capabilities. For instance, freedom in nations appears to add to happiness only when people are well educated (Veenhoven 2000c). This means that topics should be given weights according to conditions. In practice that is hardly feasible.

Lastly there is the problem of aggregation. The aim is inclusion of all relevant opportunities, but the practice is a summing of a few topics. The assortment of topics differs considerably across inventories, and it is not clear whether one collection is better than another. In fact each ideology of the good life can compose its own livability index.

Together this means that inclusive assessment of livability is not feasible. The best we can do is to make *profiles* of conditions deemed promising. Livability sum-scores make little sense.

11.3.2.2 Measures of Life-Ability

Capabilities for living are also measured in different ways. First, there is a rich tradition of health measurement, which roots the healing professions. Second, there is a trade in skill measurement, which serves selection within education and at work. Thirdly, capacities are also measured by performance at school and work.

Contents. Measures of health are, for the greater part, measures of negative health. There are various inventories of afflictions and functional limitations, several of which combine physical and mental impairments. Assessments are based on functional tests, expert ratings and self-reports. The above mentioned SF-36 is an example of the latter kind of measure. In the self-report tradition general health is also measured by single questions. For an overview of these health measures see Spilker (1996). Next there are also some inventories for positive health, mainly self-report questionnaires in the tradition of personality assessment. Jahoda (1958) made the first selection of healthy traits. Verba (1988) reports a later attempt.

Measures of skillfulness concern mostly mental abilities, many of which are parts of so called 'intelligence tests'. Performance tests can be considered to be 'objective' assessment. A new offspring of this tradition is testing for 'emotional intelligence' (Mayor and Salovy 1993),[11] which is mostly a matter of 'subjective' self-reporting. Next there are numerous tests for proficiency at work and in leisure, such as laying bricks or playing cards.

Lastly, many abilities manifest in real life success. School success is measured in years schooling and by the level of schooling achieved. People who do badly at school or received no formal education in all probability lack several necessary abilities. In developing nations literacy is a common topic. Life-ability is also inferred from apparent success at work and in love.

[11] The well known Bar-on (1997) EQ-tests measures positive mental health.

Limitations. As in the case of livability, these measures do not provide a complete estimate of life-ability. Again the measures are seldom combined, and we meet the same fundamental limitations.

Firstly, we cannot grasp all human capabilities; there are limitations to what we can conceive and what we can measure. Possibly the current measurement repertoire misses some essential talents, in particular aptitudes required for new challenges.

Secondly, we are again uncertain about the significance of topics in the inventories. Possibly some of the things we learn in school are irrelevant. Valued positive mental health traits may actually be detrimental for coping with the problems of life. Unlike the case of livability, there is some significance testing in this field. Intelligence tests in particular are gauged by their predictive value for success at school and at work. Yet this validation criterion is not the most appropriate in this context, because success at school and work does not guarantee a happy life. Many of the other ability-tests available lack any validation.

Thirdly, it is typically unclear how much of the ability is optimal, more is not always better. As there are limitations to skill acquisition, it is the right mix that counts.

Fourthly, the functionality of abilities is contingent to the situation and fit with other traits. For instance, assertiveness is more functional in an individualistic society than in a collectivist culture, and fits better with an autonomous personality than in a dependent character.

Lastly, we cannot adequately estimate general ability by adding up test-scores. Though psychometrists dream about a general ability factor, this seems to be a statistical epi-phenomenon rather than a reality. So, also in this case we had better limit ourselves to quality profiles.

11.3.2.3 Measures for Utility of Life

There are many criteria for evaluating the usefulness of a life, of which only a few can be quantified. When evaluating the utility of a persons life by the contribution that life makes to society, one aspect could be good citizenship. That quality can be measured by criteria such as law abidance and voluntary work. I have not yet seen examples of such measures. When the utility of a life is measured with its effect on the environment, consumption is a relevant aspect. There are several measures of 'green living'. It is less easy to quantify moral value. Though it is not difficult to see that some people's lives stand out, there are no tools to rate the common man.

On some criteria we have better information at the aggregate level. Wackernagel et al. (1999) measure of ecological footprint indicates the degree to which citizens in a country use irreplaceable resources. Patent counts per country give an idea of the contribution to human progress and state participation in UN organizations could be seen as an equivalent of good citizenship.

Unlike the foregoing qualities of life, there have been no attempts to measure utility comprehensively. The obvious reason is that the criteria are too vague and varied. Utility is easier to conceive than to measure.

Comprehensiveness is less of a problem when utility is measured subjectively. We can then assess the degree to which someone thinks of their life as useful. There are several questionnaires that measure subjective sense of meaning. Chamberlain and Zika (1988) review some of these. These questionnaires do not measure actual usefulness of life, but rather the person's satisfaction with his perception of the matter. Though these feelings may have some reality basis, the measures say more about the subjective appreciation of life; because the utility of one's life is so difficult to grasp, judgment is easily overshadowed by how much one likes or dislikes life.[12]

11.3.2.4 Measures of Appreciation of Life

It is easier to measure the subjective enjoyment of life. Since this is something people have in mind, we can simply ask them.[13] Interrogation is mostly done by direct questioning via an interview or a written questionnaire. Since the focus is on 'how much' the respondent enjoys life rather than 'why', the use of qualitative interview methods is limited in this field. Most assessments are self-reports in response to standard questions with fixed response options. There are various questionnaires, as well as numerous single items. Incidentally, subjective well-being is assessed by less obtrusive methods, such as analysis of diaries and projective tests.

Contents. Many of these measures concern specific appraisals such as satisfaction with one's sex life or perceived meaning of life. As in the case of life-chances, these aspects cannot be meaningfully added in a whole, firstly, because satisfactions cannot be assessed exhaustively and secondly, because satisfactions differ in significance. Yet humans are also capable of overall appraisals. As noted earlier, we can estimate how well we feel generally and report on that. So, encompassive measurement is possible in this quality quadrant.

There are various ways to ask people how much they enjoy their life-as-a-whole. One way is to ask them repeatedly how much they enjoy it right now, and to average the responses. This is called 'experience sampling'. This method has many advantages, but is quite expensive. The other way is to ask respondents to estimate how well they feel generally or to strike the balance of their life. Almost all the questions ever used for this purpose are stored in the 'Catalog of Happiness Measures', which is part of the 'World Database of Happiness' (Veenhoven 2000a).

---

[12] This is commonly referred to as the 'top-down' effect in evaluations of life. e.g. Diener (1984).

[13] Subjective well-being is also inferred from non-verbal cues, such as smiling, and from signs of despair such as suicide and excessive risk taking. Unfortunately, these 'objective' indicators appear to fit subjective reports rather badly. Physical measures are not available; the 'hedometer' still waits for invention.

Questions on enjoyment of life typically concern the current time. Most questions refer to happiness 'these days' or 'over the last year'. Obviously the good life requires more than this, hence happiness must also be assessed over longer periods. In several contexts we must know happiness over a lifetime, or better, how long people live happily. Remember the above discussion of this criterion in the context of biology and system theory.

At the individual level it is mostly difficult to assess how long and happily people live, because we know only when they are dead. However, at the population level the average number of years lived happily can be estimated by combining average happiness with life-expectancy. For details of this method see Veenhoven (1996).

Limitations? There are doubts about the value of these self-reports, in particular about interpretation of questions, honesty of answers and interpersonal comparability. Empirical studies, however, show reasonable validity and reliability, for the details see Veenhoven (1996, pp. 19–22; 1998) and Schyns (in preparation).

There are also qualms about comparability of responses across cultures, and hence about the above-mentioned estimate of happy years of life. It is claimed that questions are differently understood and that response bias differs systematically in countries. These objections have also been checked empirically and appeared not to carry any weight. Many of these checks are reported in Veenhoven (1993).

In this case there is no problem of summation, the answer to the question about appreciation of life-as-a-whole suffices.

11.4 Can Quality of Life be Measured Inclusively?

As noted in the introduction, terms like 'quality-of-life' and 'well-being' were circulated to denote *overall* worth of life. Hence the introduction of these terms was followed by attempts to measure the goodness of life comprehensively. We have considered the meanings addressed by these inventories in Sect. 11.2.1. All assess overall quality of life by summing different merits and in these summations the qualities discerned are merged. This adding of apples and pears yields a great variety of fruit salads, each with their special flavor and devotees. Unfortunately this trade makes little sense.

Why Cross-Quadrant Sum-Scores Make No Sense

Firstly, three of the four separate qualities in my scheme cannot be measured comprehensively. Above I have argued that exhaustive assessment is not possible in the cases of livability, life-ability and utility of life. Only happiness can be measured completely, because it is an overall judgment in itself. Where most of the components are incomplete, the sum cannot be complete either. Hence, sum-scores are always selective, and therefore say more about *a* good life than about *the* good life.

Secondly, one cannot meaningfully add 'chances' and 'outcomes'. A happy and productive life is no better when lived in a perfect environment by a well-endowed person, than when realized in difficult circumstances by someone who is handicapped.

Thirdly, sum-scores fail to appreciate the functional relationships between the qualities of life discerned. The value of environmental opportunities depends on personal capacities. An orchestra may be well equipped with violins, but if its members are horn players the musical performance will still be poor. Likewise, the worth of life-abilities depends on the environmental challenges for which they are needed. It is their fit that counts, rather than the mere amounts.

These contingencies are acknowledged in some concepts, for instance, Gerson (1976) defines quality-of-life as 'harmony' of self-interest and transcendent utility. Yet this is easier said than measured. Firstly, such harmony can hardly be quantified, for instance, the fit of individual and environmental potentialities cannot be observed as such, at best we can infer fit from resulting enjoyment of life. Secondly, there is mostly not one best fit, but several fitting configurations, for example collectivist and individualistic arrangements can be equally harmonious but still represent quite different qualities.

The above problems could partly be met if one restricts oneself to the few conditions and capabilities of which the mutual fit can be estimated, for instance if we focus on sheer material subsistence. This is close to the 'basic needs approach', which is said to have formed the basis of the Human Development Index (UNDP 1990). Yet the HDI does not really solve the problem either.

11.4.1 Why There is Most in Happiness

When human capacities fit environmental demands, there is a good chance that human needs are gratified. Only bad luck or willful deprivation can block that outcome. Gratification of basic needs will manifest in a stream of pleasant experiences. Biologically this is a signal that we are in the 'right pond'. In human consciousness this manifests in good mood, and subsequently in satisfaction with life as a whole.

So, happiness is both a merit in itself, and indicative of good life-chances. Subjective happiness implies two things: firstly that the minimal conditions for humans thriving are apparently met, secondly that the fit between opportunities and capacities must be sufficient. Hence happiness says more about the quality of life-chances than the sum-scores do.

This means that at least three of the four qualities of life can be meaningfully summarized by the degree and duration of happiness. This is how the good life is characterized in the closing sentence of many fairy tales: "They lived happily ever after".

11.4.2 Why Happiness is Not All

The proposed fourfold matrix visualizes the main limitation of that view: ignoring the utility quadrant. As noted above, a life can be happy but not useful or useful but not happy. Though these qualities often go together, they do not necessarily so.

11.5 Discussion

This exercise started with a discussion of the confusion surrounding words for 'the good life'. As a remedy I proposed a fourfold matrix classification of the qualities of life. This taxonomy was used to clarify the substantive meanings denoted by current words and measures. This worked, though it was often not possible to place current notions in one particular quadrant. One can see this as a weakness, i.e. the scheme does not fit current concepts, or as strength, it denotes new meanings.

Now there are more classifications of quality of life, which are also used to structure this complex field. In Sect. 11.2.3 we have reviewed a few. Is this one any better? It would be too much to review all the alternative classifications. Let it suffice to note that the major distinctions in the field are between 'objective' and 'subjective' qualities and along disciplinary kinds; e.g. economic, social and psychological well-being. A great advantage of the proposed fourfold matrix is that it makes more sense theoretically. The distinction between 'chances' and 'results' positions the merits in a functional perspective, the distinction between 'livability' and 'life-ability' brings the contingencies to mind. As such, this taxonomy helps us to see that overall quality of life cannot be seen as summed merits, but must rather be conceived as merit-configurations.

11.5.1 Elusive Utilities

In this taxonomy the 'utility' quadrant is the most problematic. The criteria are quite diverse and elusive. One can see use in anything. Contrary to happiness there is no link with demands of human nature. The matter is in fact unmeasurable.

In an earlier paper on this subject I therefore left the category out. This left me with a simpler three-step scheme of (1) livability, (2) life-ability and (3) life appreciation (Veenhoven 2000d). This is in line with the utilitarian idea that the ultimate value is in the greatest happiness of the greatest number. Bentham will nod in his glass case.

Though clear cut, that 3-step scheme misses an important class of qualities. That is, the values that override sheer functionality and enjoyment. It is not possible to weave these meanings in as contributions to the happiness of other people, because many of them have no effect on happiness. The best I can do is acknowledge the existence of these many qualities, and mark the morass on my map. Without forewarning we get stuck in it over and over again.

11.5.2 Significance of Happiness

I concluded that the most comprehensive measure for quality of life is how long and happy a person lives. Though happiness was not proclaimed as the only quality criterion, it was presented as the best available summary indicator. Note that this is not a statement of belief, but a conclusion based on assumptions about the nature of happiness.

I acknowledge that subjective appreciation of life is not all, because happiness does not guarantee that other possible values are met. That latter position must be nuanced in two ways: both in favor and against.

The favorable nuance is that happiness and utility do go together quite often. Both outcomes draw on the same opportunities. Useful living also requires tolerable environmental conditions and fair individual capabilities, in many cases similar ones to happiness. Further, objective utility is at least partly reflected in subjective awareness, and as such is part of the appraisal of life as-a-whole.

In contrast, subjective enjoyment of life is not always appropriate in the given conditions. Though happiness works as a compass, it is not always an infallible tool for orientation. I do not deny that happiness results sometimes from cognitive distortion or chemical intoxication. Still, this is the exception rather than the rule, and in the long run dysfunctional happiness will destroy itself. So this problem applies more to short term happiness than to happy life years.

11.5.3 Guide for Research

The taxonomy does more than just map different qualities of life. It can also be used to help explore their interrelations. The first step is to distinguish qualities of life as different phenomena; the next steps will be to chart causal effects. As such the scheme suggests interesting research lines. One thing we can determine is those conditions for happiness that also promise desirable external effects. Since there are probably more ways to happiness, we can then select the most 'useful' one.

11.6 Conclusion

One cannot meaningfully speak about 'quality of life' at large. It makes more sense to distinguish four qualities: (1) livability of the environment, (2) life-ability of the person, (3) utility of life for the environment, and (4) appreciation of life by the person. These qualities cannot be added, hence sum-scores make little sense. The best available summary indicator is how long and happily a person lives.

Acknowledgments I thank the following colleagues for their helpful comments: Ruud Abma, Joop Ehrhardt, Henk DeHeer, Ems Lans, Roelof Hortulanus, Jan Ott, K. Schinkel, Peggy Schyns and Theo VanWilligenburg.

References

Allardt E (1976) Dimensions of welfare in a comparative scandinavian study. Acta Soc 19:227–239

Andrews F, Withey S (1976) Social indicators of wellbeing: American perceptions of quality of life. Plenum Press, New York

Bar-On R (1997) BarOn emotional quotient inventory: a measure of emotional intelligence. Multi-Health Systems Inc., Toronto

Bentham J (1789) An introduction into the principles of morals and legislation. In: The collected works of jeremy bentham. Clarendon Press, Oxford, 1983

Bernheim JL, Buyse M (1983) The anamnestic comparative self-assessment for measuring subjective quality of life for cancer patients. J Psycho-Social Oncol 1:25–38

Brock DW (1993) Life and death: philosophical essays in biomedical ethics. Cambridge University Press, New York

Chamberlain K, Zika S (1988) Measuring meaning in life, examination of three scales. J Pers Individ Differ 9:589–596

Colby BN (1987) Well-being: a theoretical program. Am Anthropologist 87:874–895

Cummins RA (1993) Comprehensive quality of life scale for adults. Manual ComQol-A4, Deakin University, School of Psychology, Australia

Cummins RA (1997) Dictionary of instruments to measure quality of life and cognate areas. Deakin University, School of Psychology, Australia

Diener E (1984) Subjective well-being. Psychol Bull 95:542–575

Estes R (1984) The social progress of nations. Preager, New York

Fernandez-Ballesteros R (1996) Quality of life: concept and assessment. Paper presented at the 26th international congress of psychology, Montreal

Frankl V (1946) Man's search for meaning, an introduction to logo-therapy. Beacon Press, Boston

Gerson EM (1976) On quality of life. Am Sociol Rev 41:793–806

Jahoda M (1958) Current concepts of positive mental health. Basic Books, New York

Jolles HM, Stalpers JA (1978) Welzijnsbeleid en Sociale Wetenschappen Deventer, van Loghem Slaterus

Korczak D (1995) Lebensqualität Atlas. Westdeutscher, Germany

Kunz M, Siefer W (1995) Wo Sie am besten leben, FOCUS, Lebensqualitä- tatlas. Available: www.genios.de/cgi-bin

Lane RE (1994) Quality of life and quality of persons. Anew role for government? Polit Theor 22:219–252

Mayer JD, Salovy P (1993) The intelligence of emotional intelligence. Intelligence 17:433–442

McCall S (1975) Quality of life. Soc Indic Res 2:229–248

Michalos A (1985) Multiple discrepancy theory (MDT). Soc Indic Res 16:347–413

Mill JS (1863) Utilitarianism. 20th impression by Fontana Press, London, 1990

Musschenga AW (1994) Quality of life and handicapped people. In: Nordenfelt L (ed) Concepts and measurement of quality of life in health care. Kluwer Academic Publishers, Dordrecht, pp 181–198

Noll H-H (1999) Konzepte der Wohlfahrtsentwicklung: Lebensqualitat und 'neue' WohlfahrtsKonzepte. Euro-reporting paper nr. 3, ZUMA, Mannheim, Germany

Nordenfelt L (1989) Quality of life and happiness. In: Bjork S, Vang J (eds) Assessing quality of life, health service studies nr. 1. Samhall, Klintland, Sweden

Ostenfelt E (1994) Aristotle on the good life and quality of life. In: Nordenfelt L (ed) Concepts and measurement of quality of life in health care. Kluwer Academic Publishers, pp 19–34

Ouclette-Kuntz H (1990) A pilot study in the use of the quality of life interview schedule. Soc Indic Res 23:283–298

Sandoe P (1999) Quality of life, three competing views. Ethical theory and moral practice 2, pp 11–23

Schyns P Subjective well-being: concepts, measurability and cross-national com-parability. (in preparation)
Sen A (1992) Capability and well-being. In: Sen A, Nussbaum M (eds) The quality of life. Clarendon Press, Oxford, pp 30–53
Spilker B (ed) (1996) Quality of life and pharmaco-economics in clinical trials. Lippincott-Raven Publishers, Philadelphia
Spitzer WO, Dobson AJ, Hall J, Chesterman E, Levi J, Shepherd R (1981) Measuring the quality of life of cancer patients. J Chronical Dis 34:585–597
Tatarkiewicz W (1975) Analysis of happiness. Martinus Nijhoff, The Hague
Terhune KW (1973) Probing policy relevant questions on the quality of life. In: The quality of life concept. Environmental Protection Agency, Washington, USA
Townsend P (1979) Poverty in the UK: a survey of household resources and standards of living. Penguin, Hammondsworth
United Nations Development Program (UNDP) (1990, 1998) Human development report. Oxford University Press, New York
Veenhoven R (1984) Conditions of happiness. Kluwer Academic Publishers, Dordrecht
Veenhoven R (1988) The utility of happiness. Soc Indic Res 20:333–354
Veenhoven R (1996) Happy life-expectancy. Soc Indic Res 39:1–58
Veenhoven R (1997) Progres dans la comprehension du bonheur, Revue Quebecoise de Psychologie 18, pp 29–74. Available in English, advances in the understanding of happiness. http://www.eur.nl/fsw/research/happiness/files/wdhrev.zip
Veenhoven R (1998) Vergelijkenvangeluk in landen. Sociale Wetenschappen 42:58–84
Veenhoven R (2000a) Catalog of happiness measures. World database of happiness. http://www.eur.nl/fsw/research/happiness
Veenhoven R (2000b) Well-being in the welfare state: level not higher, distribution not more equitable. J Comp Policy Anal 2:91–125
Veenhoven R (2000c) Freedom and happiness. In: Diener E, Suh E (eds) Subjective well-being across cultures. MIT-press, Boston
Veenhoven R (2000d) Quality of life and happiness, not quite the same. In: DeGirolamo G (ed) Health and quality of life. Il Pensierro Scientifico, Rome
Verba SK (1988) Measurement ofpositive mental health, some theoretical and practical considerations. Int J Clin Psychol 15:6–11
Wackernagel M, Onisto L, Callejas Linares A, Susana I, Falfan L, Mendez Garcia J, Suarez Guerrero AI, Suarez Guerrero MG (1999) National natural capital accounting with the ecological footprint concept. Ecol Econ 29:375–390
Ware JE Jr (1996) The SF-36 health survey. In: Spilker B (ed) Quality of life and pharmacoeconomics in clinical trials. Lippincott-Raven Publishers, Philadelphia, pp 337–345
Zajonc RB (1980) Feeling and thinking: preference needs no inference. Am Psychol 35:151–175
Zapf W (1984) Individuelle Wohlfahrt: Lebensbedingungen und wahrgenommene Lebensqualität. In: Glatzer W, Zapf W (eds) Lebensqualitat in der Bundesrepublik. Objective Lebensbedingungen und subjectives. Wohlbefinden, Campus Verlag, Frankfurt am Main, pp 13–26

Chapter 12
The Mixed Blessings of Material Progress: Diminishing Returns in the Pursuit of Happiness

Richard Eckersley

Abstract The progress of nations is widely believed to enhance the happiness of their people. However, whether progress, as currently defined and derived, is increasing happiness and well-being in rich nations is problematic. The paper explores the relationship between economic growth and human development and the use of subjective measures of both life satisfaction and social quality of life as indicators of progress, noting the complex nature of well-being and the differences between personal and social perspectives. It questions whether widely used, simple measures are adequate, and whether greater happiness should, in any case, be regarded as the ultimate goal of progress.

Keywords Happiness • Life satisfaction • Progress • Quality of life • Subjective well-being

12.1 Introduction

Notions of progress are closely linked to notions of happiness. The Western worldview is dominated by these concepts, which are becoming increasingly global in their influence. Progress is about making life better, and a happier life is an important ingredient of a better life. Progress can take many forms: better health and education, greater equality and freedom, more choice and opportunity, less conflict and suffering, for example. However, progress in the modern era is principally defined in material terms—a rising standard of living—and measured as growth in per capita Gross National Product (GNP) or Gross Domestic Product (GDP).

This paper is not primarily concerned with the nature of happiness. Rather it focuses on the measurement of progress, and the use for this purpose of measures

R. Eckersley (✉)
23 Garland Rd, Bundanoon, NSW 2578, Australia
e-mail: richard@richardeckersley.com.au

A. Delle Fave (ed.), *The Exploration of Happiness*, Happiness Studies Book Series,
DOI: 10.1007/978-94-007-5702-8_12, © Springer Science+Business Media Dordrecht 2013

of happiness and life satisfaction—and related (but not identical) qualities such as subjective well-being (SWB) and quality of life (QoL).

There are good grounds for equating progress with economic growth. On the face of it, many aspects of human development appear to be closely associated with material progress. For example, in a study of 101 nations, Diener and Diener (1995) found that wealth was significantly correlated with 26 of 32 indices of QoL, chosen to reflect a wide range of universal human values (including happiness, equality, human rights and social justice). Only two—suicide and carbon dioxide emissions (an environmental indicator)—were adversely associated with wealth. The correlation between per capita GDP and total QoL (the mean value of the 32 QoL variables) was 0.79 ($p < 0.001$). Almost two-thirds (62 %) of the variance in the total QoL of nations could be explained by income. In another study, Diener and Suh (1997) noted that per capita purchasing power of nations was so closely related to a composite Advanced QoL Index (made up of variables such as physicians per capita, savings rate, income equality and environmental treaties) ($r = 0.91$, $p < 0.001$), that many would be led to 'accept the notion that economic indicators are sufficient and that we do not need any further indicators'.

By the standard of material progress the world has done extraordinarily well over the past two centuries. Economic growth has been a global phenomenon since the early 19th century, raising living standards and life expectancy in all continents (Maddison 1995, 2000). The average annual growth in world per capita real income has been about 20 times greater since 1820 than it was in the preceding eight centuries. Average world GDP per capita increased 8-fold between 1820 and 1992.

However, growth has been much faster in the West than in 'the Rest' (Maddison 1995). Since 1820, per capita income has increased 13-fold in Western Europe, 17-fold in its Western offshoots (US, Canada, Australia and New Zealand), 10-fold in Southern Europe, 6-fold in Eastern Europe (where income fell after the collapse of communism), 7-fold in Latin America, 6-fold in Asia and Oceania, and 3-fold in Africa. Africa's average per capita income was about the same in 1992 as that in Western Europe in 1820. There are, of course, marked differences between countries within the same region; Japan's per capita income rose almost 28-fold between 1820 and 1992 to rank third behind the United States and Switzerland.

It is in this pattern of growth that a fundamental problem with material progress emerges—growing global inequality. According to Maddison (1995, 2000), the economic 'edge' the West had over 'the Rest' was about 2:1 in 1820 and it has continued to grow since. The ratio of incomes between the richest and poorest regions was less than 3:1 in 1820, and grew steadily to 16:1 in 1992. The long-term divergence between the richest and poorest countries is even greater, increasing from over 3:1 to 72:1.

This pattern of unequal progress has two important global implications for QoL. The first is environmental: along with population growth, the major causes of global environmental degradation are extreme poverty, on the one hand, and excessive consumption, on the other (World Commission on Environment and Development 1987, pp. 1–23). The environmental sustainability of economic progress is important for long-term QoL. A wide range of indicators shows that, globally, we are still moving away from ecological sustainability, not towards it (Eckersley 1998a).

For example, the Living Planet Index of the World Wide Fund for Nature (1998), based on an assessment of forest, freshwater and marine ecosystems, declined by about 30 % between 1970 and 1995, 'meaning that the world has lost nearly a third of its natural wealth in that time'. WWF also says that, globally, consumption pressure, a measure of the impact of people on natural ecosystems based on resource consumption and pollution data, is increasing by about 5 % a year. At this rate, consumption pressure will double in about 15 years. The United Nations Environment Program (1997), in its first review of the global environmental outlook, says that the earth's environment is continuing to degrade. 'Significant environmental problems remain deeply embedded in the socio-economic fabric of all societies in all regions. Progress towards a global sustainable future is just too slow.'

The second point about the current global pattern of growth is its striking inappropriateness given the evidence that material progress continues to have much to offer poorer nations, but appears to be increasingly irrelevant, even hostile, to well-being in rich nations. For example, Wilkinson (1994, 1998, 1999) has shown that in rich nations, health is influenced more by income distribution than average income levels. Diener and Diener (1995) found a 'ceiling effect' with many of their QoL variables, with increasing income conferring large benefits at low income levels, but little if any benefit at high income levels. Max-Neef (1995) has proposed a 'threshold hypothesis' for the relationship between economic growth and human welfare: for every society there seems to be a period in which economic growth (as conventionally measured) brings about an improvement in QoL, but only up to a point—the threshold point—beyond which, if there is more economic growth, QoL may begin to deteriorate.

Further evidence of a weakening nexus between growth and well- being comes from the development of new measures of progress, such as the Index of Sustainable Economic Welfare (ISEW) and Genuine Progress Indicator (GPI), that adjust GDP for a range of social, economic and environmental factors that GDP either ignores or measures inappropriately (Eckersley 1998a; Halstead 1998; Hamilton 1998). These include income distribution, unpaid housework and voluntary work, loss of natural resources, and the costs of unemployment, crime and pollution. These 'GDP analogues' show that trends in GDP and social welfare, once moving together, have diverged since the 1970s in all (Western) countries for which they have been constructed. While per capita GDP has continued to climb, the GPI and ISEW have levelled off or fallen.

In contrast with this situation of developed nations, UNICEF says that for at least one billion people in the developing world, material progress holds out the hope of adequate food, clean water, safe sanitation, decent housing, reliable health care, and at least a basic education (Adamson 1993). 'This is a definition of progress which remains entirely valid', it says. 'And it is one with which the rest of the world must keep faith.' UNICEF says efforts by governments to meet basic human needs have been less than all-out. And yet by any realist standard, the progress made in the developing world in the last 40 years has been remarkable.

In little more than one generation, average real incomes have more than doubled; child death rates have been more than halved; malnutrition rates have been reduced by about 30 %; life expectancy has increased by about a third; the proportion of children enrolled in primary school has risen from less than a half to more than three-quarters; and the percentage of rural families with access to safe water has risen from less than 10 % to more than 60 %. The task to meet minimum human needs is, UNICEF says, more achievable now than ever before.

However, there are important qualifications to this conventional picture of the benefits of material progress:

- Not all the gains are a product of increasing wealth. Many social changes have accompanied economic growth, but have not necessarily been a direct consequence of growth, or have had impacts independent of growth. These include the growth of scientific knowledge, technological innovation, advances in social justice and equality, and an expanded role of government in improving living conditions (in health, hygiene, education and welfare support, for example). These changes contributed greatly to increasing human well-being.
- Some of the improvements in health and well-being have become cheaper with time as knowledge has increased and technology improved. Extra years of life cost less now than they used to (Wilkinson 1998). Furthermore, it can take only a little wealth to produce improvements in health and education standards, as the oft-cited example of the Indian State of Kerala shows (Sen 1993). Despite a low per capita GDP, Kerala has substantially increased life expectancy and literacy and reduced birth rates through a strong commitment to public health and education.
- Periods of rapid economic growth can be associated with diminished QoL, even in early stages of development. In a study of England during the Industrial Revolution, Szreter (1997) demonstrates that rapid economic growth, far from leading inevitably to development, can result in the 'four Ds' of disruption, deprivation, disease and death, because of its impact on social and political stability and order.

Some of these (and other) considerations are reflected in a study by Easterly (1997), using 95 QoL indicators covering seven areas—individual rights and democracy, political instability and war, education, health, transport and communication, class and gender inequality, and 'bads' such as crime and pollution—over up to four time periods from 1960 to 1990. Easterly wanted to see if, as he expected, 'life during growth gets better'. Consistent with other research, virtually all the indicators showed QoL across nations to be positively associated with per capita income. However, when he analysed the data further to take account of various 'country effects', he found growth had an impact on QoL that was significant, positive and more important than exogenous shifts for only a few of the 95 indicators. While Easterly speculates that the most plausible explanation is that there are long and variable time lags that prevented the detection of the 'true' relationship between growth and improvements in life, he admits disappointment: 'For the large majority of indicators, I am unable to detect a medium- run improvement in life during growth'. Life is getting better, he says, not primarily because of growth, but because of time.

This said, my central concern in this paper is not to challenge concepts of progress as may be evident in differences between developing and developed nations today, or between developed nations 200 years ago and now. It is to examine whether the current dominant strategy of Western nations of continuing to base progress so fundamentally on economic growth is the best approach to improving human welfare.

Economic growth is the driving dynamic of modern societies. Current government policy is underpinned by the belief that wealth creation comes first because it increases our capacity to meet other, social objectives. This is a model of progress as a pipeline: pump more wealth in one end and more welfare or well-being flows out the other. However, any consideration of progress must address the core issue of whether, where and in what ways economic growth, as currently defined and derived, is making people happier. It must also ask if the pursuit of happiness is, in itself, a sufficient goal of progress.

Within this broad context of material progress, the paper examines in detail two different subjective measures of QoL—personal and social—and how they are shaped by objective social conditions. QoL relates to total well-being, the condition or state of being well, contented and satisfied with life. Personal QoL (or SWB) reflects an individual's cognitive and affective evaluation of his or her life. Social QoL, however, may be a more diffuse perception, reflecting people's assessment of average personal QoL and/or how social conditions are affecting personal QoL—that is, how well society and social institutions are meeting human needs and desires. Social QoL might combine, say, a judgement of whether people in general are more satisfied with an observation on whether the gap between rich and poor is widening, or whether people are working harder, which will then affect people's personal QoL.

12.2 Subjective Personal Quality of Life

Given that QoL includes how people think and feel about their lives, it has been argued that attempts to measure well-being must include people's own subjective judgement as well as the objective factors that influence QoL (Diener and Suh 1997; Diener et al. 1999). As already noted, many QoL indices are correlated to economic performance indicators. However, the correlations are much stronger for objective QoL measures than for subjective measures. Indeed, one of the most striking findings of research into SWB is the often small correlation with objective resources and conditions (Diener and Suh 1997; Diener et al. 1999). One recent estimate is that external circumstances account for only about 15 % of the variance in SWB (Diener et al. 1999).

This applies to income: there does not appear to be strong causal connection between income and happiness (Myers and Diener 1995, 1996; Diener et al. 1999).

Thus, the proportion of people in developed nations who are happy or satisfied with their lives has remained stable over the past several decades, even though they have become, on average, much richer. Only in the poorest countries is income a good indicator of SWB. In most nations the correlation is small, with even the very rich being only slightly happier than the average person. People in rich countries are happier than those in poor nations, but the differences may be due, at least in part, to factors other than wealth, such as literacy, democracy and equality. Increased income matters to SWB when it helps people meet basic needs; beyond that the relationship becomes more complex.

In a recent review of research on SWB, Diener et al. (1999) conclude that there is no simple answer to what causes happiness. Instead, there is a complex interplay between genes and environment, between life events and circumstances, culture, personality, goals and various adaptation and coping strategies. QoL has been defined as 'the gap between a person's expectations and achievements' (Calman, cited in Katschnig et al. 1997, p. 10). The evidence suggests that people adjust goals and expectations and use illusions and rationalisations to maintain overtime a relatively stable, and positive, rating of life satisfaction or QoL. In other words, as Cummins (1998, 2000a; Cummins and Nistico, under review) argues, life satisfaction is held under homeostatic control. This does not mean that social, economic and political developments do not affect SWB, but that the relationship between the objective and subjective realms is not linear. For example, Cummins (2000b, c) has shown that under normal conditions there is only a very weak relationship between income or health and SWB. However, under adverse conditions such as sustained financial hardship or chronic, serious ill health, homeostasis breaks down and SWB falls to below-normal levels.

The nature of SWB presents an important limitation on the use of standard measures of happiness or life satisfaction as a way of assessing and comparing national performance and progress: the measures represent a 'buffered' view of reality and so present a false, or at least incomplete, picture of social conditions (note how often the word 'illusion' occurs in this discussion). A detailed critique of the measures is beyond the scope of this paper. Veenhoven (for example, 1991, 1996, 1999) has presented a cogent and comprehensive defence of measures of life satisfaction and happiness as social indicators. However, I want to give several, different illustrations of their limitations as measures of progress.

Pusey (1998) asked 'middle Australians', who were the winners and losers from 'the economic change that Australia has experienced over the last 15 years or so'. The proportion saying 'people like me' were losers was considerably smaller than that for 'ordinary people generally', 'people in the middle' or 'wage and salary earners', while the proportion saying 'people like me' were winners was correspondingly higher than for the other categories. In other words, people responded more positively when they were asked to classify themselves as winners or losers.

Surveys of people's perceptions of health services consistently reveal widespread satisfaction (like surveys of life, about 80 % claim to be satisfied). Yet qualitative studies have shown that many people mitigate negative experiences, which are then translated into expression of satisfaction, and so remain effectively hidden in patient satisfaction surveys (Williams 1994; Williams et al. 1998). Many surveys of health services, Williams (1994) argues, provide only an illusion of consumer satisfaction, 'producing results which tend only to endorse the status quo'. Are surveys of life satisfaction doing the same?

The positive bias in life satisfaction measures is also evident if we compare satisfaction levels with other survey findings, including of mental health. Public surveys in Australia consistently indicate that about 5 % of people, or less, say they are unhappy or dissatisfied with their lives (Eckersley 2000a). Yet in other surveys, about 20 % of people agreed their lives were 'coming apart at the seams'—a rather stronger statement about QoL than admitting to dissatisfaction, one would think (Eckersley 1988). Mental health surveys show that almost 20 % of Australians experienced mental health problems in previous 12 months (Australian Bureau of Statistics 1998).

To take another example, this time focusing on young people, a recent survey found 89 % per cent of students aged 13–15 in Victoria, Australia, were satisfied with 'their life in general these days' (Gatehouse Project, Centre for Adolescent Health, Melbourne; personal communication with George Patton). However, another study, again in Victoria and undertaken at about the same time, found 25–40 % of students 11–18 experienced in the previous 6 months feelings of depression, worries about weight, worries about self-confidence, troubles sleeping, and not having enough energy (Waters et al. 1999). A survey of students aged 11–15 in 28 mostly European countries reported similar findings: while the vast majority (over 90 % in many nations) reported feeling healthy and happy, significant minorities (reaching majorities for some countries, ages and complaints) admitted to 'feeling low' and having headaches and stomach aches at least once a week, and to feeling tired most days of the week (Currie et al. 2000). To take 15-year-old American and Swedish girls as examples, 49 % and 45 %, respectively, reported feeling low at least once a week, 38 and 32 % feeling tired in the morning four or more times a week, and 57 and 53 % having a headache at least once a week.

In contrast to the findings of the stability of life satisfaction over time, there is good evidence that psychosocial problems including substance abuse, depression and suicidal behaviour have increased among young people in almost all Western nations over the past 50 years (Rutter and Smith 1995). Some of these increases are large by epidemiological standards. In Australia, for example, the male youth suicide rate has more than tripled and the rate of drug-overdose deaths has increased more than six-fold over recent decades (Eckersley 1997, 1998b). Implicit in notions of progress is the expectation that the young are the major beneficiaries; the evidence suggest they are, instead, paying most of the price.

The comparison between health and SWB can be taken further. The two conditions are related, but while it is, by definition, impossible to measure SWB objectively, this is possible with health. This gives us an insight into how and why subjective responses can differ from objective measures of the same thing. In general population samples, SWB correlates significantly with self-reported health, but not objective health (Diener et al. 1999). And subjective health does not necessarily correlate well with objective health.

People will claim good health even in the face of chronic illness and severe disability (Blaxter 1997). Indigenous Australians report similar or better health than other Australians, but their death rates are about three times higher and their average life expectancy is 20 years lower (Mathers and Douglas 1998). In the 1991–1993 World Values Survey, 79 % of people in the US rated their health as good or very good; in Japan, only 44 % did (Basanez et al. 1998; variable 83). Yet the Japanese have a life expectancy about four years longer than Americans, placing them at opposite ends of the life-expectancy spectrum of developed nations. Self-reported health can vary across cultures and over time because of differences in perceptions and expectations of health, making comparisons between different populations problematic.

Beyond—or perhaps part of—the illusions and other cognitive devices we use to maintain life satisfaction is the 'mask' we all present to the outside world—the public face which hides a different private person. This mask may conceal most in those individuals who outwardly appear happiest and most successful, those whom modern society most celebrates and holds up for admiration. A review of a biography of the famous American entertainer, Danny Kaye, described the book as 'a thorough study of a cruelly mean-spirited, sadly insecure manic depressive who came across to the world at large as a generous, outgoing, happy and well-adjusted fellow' (Gottfried 1995).

Erikson Bloland (1999), in a study of her famous father, the celebrated psychologist Erik Erikson, contrasts the public man—charismatic, confident, concerned, compassionate, an authority on the psychological development of children and adolescents—with the private person—insecure, vulnerable, plagued by feelings of self-doubt and inadequacy, stricken by his inability to soothe and comfort his own children. She notes how often fame and success mask a sense of personal failure and isolation, and are driven by a longing for human connection and intimacy. Erikson Bloland (a psychoanalyst) discusses the psychology of the need to idealise others as well as the need to be idealised. She suggests people hide behind the illusion that they are larger than life out of fear of acknowledging to others how needy and inadequate they sometimes feel. 'The need to appear larger than life—like the need to believe in the superhuman status of others—helps us to cope in a frightening universe, but it also limits our capacity for intimacy.' The difference between the public and private person raises an interesting question: if we measured, say, Danny Kaye's or Erik Erikson's SWB or happiness, which person would we be measuring?

I want to stress that my intention in raising these matters is not to argue that standard measures of happiness or life satisfaction are invalid or meaningless. The contrasting findings cited above are not necessarily incompatible. Life satisfaction is only one dimension of SWB, distinct from pleasant and unpleasant affect (moods and emotions) which are, in turn, partly independent of each other (Myers and Diener 1995; Diener et al. 1999). So the studies are not measuring the same quality.

Another factor is that life satisfaction surveys are measuring point prevalence, the mental health studies 12 or 6-month prevalence. A third consideration is that, given that relatively high SWB is normal, we may need to regard the group in the middle of life satisfaction scales (5–15 % of people), not just those who are unequivocally unhappy or dissatisfied, as being psychologically vulnerable. Nonetheless, the comparisons show that measures of personal QoL do not present a complete and accurate picture of the relationships between social conditions and well-being.

In summary then, there are several aspects of measures of SWB or happiness that present a problem for their use as indicators of progress—of whether life is getting better or worse. These are the relative stability of SWB despite dramatic social, cultural and economic changes in recent decades; the complex, non-linear relationship between objective conditions and subjective states; and the positive biases in measures of SWB.

12.3 Subjective Social Quality of Life

The concerns about the use of personal QoL to measure national progress point to the need for other subjective measures of QoL. Social (or societal) QoL relates to people's perceptions, not of their own lives, but of life in their community or nation, of how they think people in general are faring. I have argued elsewhere that this is a quite different category of measurement (Eckersley 1999a, 2000a). Subjective measures of social QoL appear to have been used much less often than personal measures such as life satisfaction and happiness.

Because it is an attempt to assess progress, the central questions about social QoL have been framed to identify trends, not states. This may be a crucial difference: we are not attempting to measure how full a glass of water is, but whether the level is rising or falling. This is what matters in seeking to evaluate progress. It is also an easier judgement to make because the question includes a benchmark or standard—QoL at some time in the past—which is usually absent in questions about states.

In marked contrast to studies of how people feel about their own lives, polls of how they feel about social trends yield much more negative findings. A June 1997 national poll found that 52 % of Australians believed 'the overall quality of life of people in Australia, taking into account social, economic and environmental conditions and trends' was getting worse. Only 13 % thought life was getting better; 33 % said it was staying about the same and 2 % did not know or did not answer (Eckersley 1998a, 1999a, 2000a). In a May 1999 poll, the proportion of people saying life was getting better increased to 24 % and that saying it was staying about the same rose to 38 %, while the percentage saying it was getting worse fell to 36 %; 2 % did not know or answer (Eckersley 1999a, 2000a). Demographic differences, small in 1997, also widened in some cases—for example, differences between low and high income groups in the percentage saying life was getting better rose from 10 to 21 % points (see Fig. 12.1).

The same question was asked again in January 2000, this time by *The Australian* newspaper (personal communication with Mike Steketee, national affairs editor, *The Australian,* Sydney; *The Weekend Australian*, 17–18 June 2000, p. 22). The

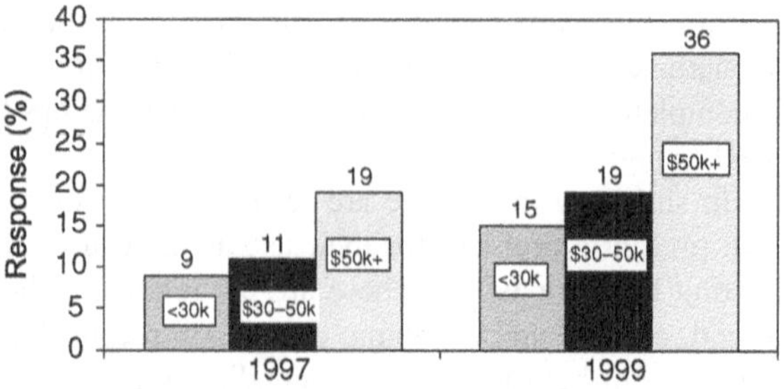

Fig. 12.1 Percentage saying life is getting better, by household income (Eckersley 1999a)

percentage saying life was getting better had again risen, to 31 %. The percentage choosing worse was almost unchanged at 34 %, while that saying life was about the same fell to 34 %; 1 % were uncommitted. The same market research company, Newspoll, conducted all three QoL polls, using a random telephone survey of 1,200 Australians aged 18 and over in all Australian States and in both city and country areas. The results were weighted to reflect the population distribution.

In a follow up to the QoL trend question in the 1999 poll, people were asked 'in about what decade do you think overall quality of life in Australia has been at its highest': 24 % chose the 1990s, 25 % the 1980s, 23 % the 1970s, 13 % the 1960s, 6 % the 1950s, and 2 % before the 1950s. Not surprisingly, the results were strongly age-related, with people tending to spread their choice over the decades they have personally experienced (see Fig. 12.2). There was a good fit between the responses to the two questions: most of those who choose the 1990s as the best decade also thought life was getting better; those who choose the 1980s as the best decade were most likely to think QoL was staying about the same; and most of those who thought the 1970s or earlier were the best time believed QoL was declining (see Table 12.1).

As already noted, QoL questions based on a social, rather than personal, perspective appear to be rare. The only comparable question I have found so far was used in the US in 1999 as part of a wide-ranging survey of Americans' views on the last and next century (Pew 1999). Despite a generally upbeat mood, only a minority (44 %)said life in America had got better since the 1950s (30 % worse, 26 % same/don't know). Consistent with general differences between personal and social perspectives, however, 63 % said their own lives were better than the lives of their families in the 1950s.

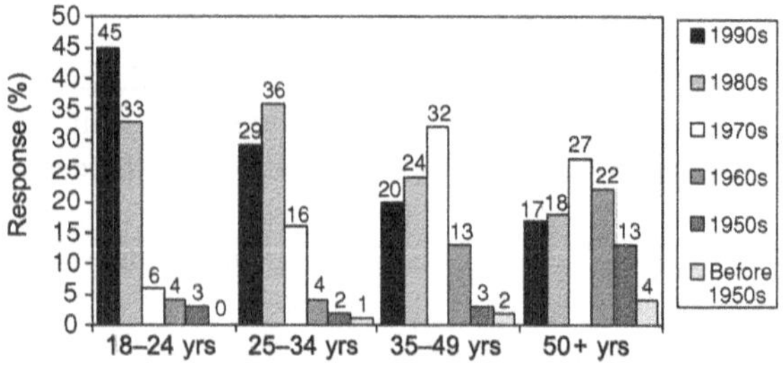

Fig. 12.2 Choice of decade of highest quality of life, by age (Eckersley 1999a)

Table 12.1 Perceptions of quality of life and best decade, 1999

Decade Response (%)	1990s	1980s	1970s	1960s	1950s	Before 1950s
Better	51	18	11	14	10	11
Same	40	47	34	33	33	21
Worse	9	34	54	50	55	66
None/don't know	1	1	2	4	3	2

Percentage choosing each decade who think life is getting better, worse or staying the same (Eckersley 1999a)

While the Australian polls do not offer an explanation for the improvement in public mood in the past 2–3 years, the result is consistent with other recent survey findings (Eckersley 1999a). Electoral anger and resentment, pronounced in the mid-1990s, appear to have abated, turning instead into indifference. The public standing of different occupations suggests that trust in those with financial and political power and influence—politicians, lawyers, business executives, bank managers and journalists—bottomed in 1997–1998 and is now rising again.

Mackay (1999) says that, superficially Australians are quite chirpy, but the mood is fragile and co-exists with a pessimism that still runs deep in the national psyche. He attributes the better spirits to a tendency to disengage from a difficult and complex national agenda and focus on the personal domains of life; an adaptation to the changes reshaping Australian society; the long-awaited pull of the new millennium; and Australia's continuing strong economic performance. These trends could explain, not only the overall lift in social QoL, but also the widening income gap in perceptions, with those who are well-off showing less concern for the worse-off, better able to enjoy the 'good life', and reaping more benefits from the economic changes taking place.

The improvement in public perceptions between mid-1999 and early 2000 could reflect a continuation of the longer-term trend and/or the effect on people's mood of the holiday season and celebration of the new century and millennium. The 2000 poll was conducted on 14–16 January, in the middle of Australia's summer holiday season, which extends from Christmas to Australia Day on 26 January. It is a time when Australians focus on the beach, parties, international cricket tests, the Australian Open tennis competition and other pleasant distractions from the business of life (so reinforcing the trend Mackay has detected).

To summarise, it would appear that questions about social QoL are tapping public perceptions about long-term trends. However, people's opinions are influenced by personal attributes and circumstances and relatively short-term shifts in social conditions and public mood. Ideally, we would like to measure some 'baseline' perception about social QoL that does not fluctuate too much over the short term. But perhaps there is no such thing, and subjective assessments of overall QoL are just that, with people's views of the long term varying over the short term as their moods and perceptions alter. Only a long time series will allow us to determine if there is a long-term change in perceptions.

12.4 Social Quality of Life and Progress

While subjective measures of personal QoL are biased towards the positive, it is possible those of social QoL are biased in the other direction (Eckersley 1999a, 2000a). Perceptions of social QoL could reflect a worldview jaundiced by dystopian images of the future, the media's focus on bad news, and a tendency to take improvements in QoL for granted and to focus instead on aspects of life that have deteriorated or have not met rising expectations. Nevertheless, there is evidence that perceptions of social QoL are grounded in changes in the nature of modern life, both fundamental and specific, objective and subjective. Even the often dark visions many people have of humanity's future could be, in part, an expression of anxieties about the present which may be ill-defined, but nonetheless deeply felt; by projecting these concerns into the future, they can described in fictional, more concrete forms (Eckersley 1999b).

Diener and Suh (1997) note that the central elements of well-being are based on the context of people's most important values and goals: 'SWB is most likely to be experienced when people work for and make progress towards personal goals that derive from their important values.' Similarly, perceptions about social QoL appear to be fundamentally about values, priorities and goals—both personal and national—and the degree of congruence between them. The relationship between social QoL and values emerges from both quantitative and qualitative research in Australia and the US, which I have described elsewhere (Eckersley 1999a, 2000a).

Some research makes this link explicit; more usually it is implicit in people's unease about the moral state of modern society. The research suggests a deep tension between people's professed values and the lifestyle promoted by modern Western societies. Many people are concerned about the greed, excess and materialism they believe drive society today, underlie many social ills, and threaten their children's future. They are yearning for a better balance in their lives, believing that when it comes to things like freedom and material abundance, they don't seem to 'know where to stop' or now have 'too much of a good thing'.

Recent polling in the US has added to this picture of moral angst (Gallup 1999). It found that 49 % of Americans believed there was a moral crisis in the US, while another 41 % believed there were major moral problems. Asked about the changes in moral and cultural values since the 1960s, 32 % thought that on the whole the changes had been good because the country had become more tolerant, while 64 % thought they were bad because it had become too permissive. Only 23 % admitted to being optimistic about future moral and ethical standards in the US, while 43 % were pessimistic. Another survey, of Americans' assessment of the last and next centuries, also found that their misgiving about their country today were focused on the moral climate, 'with people from all walks of life looking sceptically on the ways in which the country has changed both culturally and spiritually' (Pew 1999).

These concerns persist despite a more buoyant public mood in the US today compared to the mid-1990s—71 % of Americans were satisfied 'with the way things are going in the US at this time' in February 1999, an all-time high and up from 24 % in January 1996 (by May 1999, the proportion had dropped to 51 %, but rose again to 69 % in January 2000) (Gallup 1998–2000). There is a prevailing sense that the past century has been one of economic and technological triumph for America, and an optimism that this will continue in the century ahead (Pew 1999).

The moral qualms may not, however, be new. The Gallup data suggest that moral pessimists have always outnumbered optimists, at least as far back as the 1970s, although the gap between them has widened (Gallup 1999). And while, in another survey, only 32 % professed to be satisfied with the honesty and standards of behaviour of American s, and 63 % were dissatisfied, the results do not reveal a marked shift in sentiment between the early 1960s and late 1990s (Washington Post/Kaiser/Harvard 1998). On the other hand, in the same survey, the 1950s easily top scored as the decade, between the 1920s and 1990s, in which people thought American values and morals were particularly good: 28 % chose the 1950s, with nominations declining on either side (only 3 % chose the 1990s). And asked if young people today had as strong a sense of right and wrong as they did, say, 50 years ago, 78 % of Americans said 'no' in 1998, compared to only 34 % in 1952.

A confounding influence on these results is that most people tend to see themselves as more moral than other people (Halpern 1995; see Eckersley 2000a, for examples of this). When they see others transgress, they tend to hold them morally responsible; when they themselves transgress, they tend to blame the circumstances, and to regard the transgression as an exception rather than a 'falsification' of their values. Halpern says this tendency might help to explain the historical tendency of most generations to see the world in a state of moral decline. This illusion—perhaps another of those used to maintain SWB—could be an important source of negative bias in social QoL. Nevertheless, the moral trends that worry people, such as increasing consumerism and individualism, are also real.

So if perceptions about QoL are linked to perceptions about morality and ethics, and while survey results indicate a widespread dismay about moral standards today, the evidence is mixed about whether this dismay is increasing. We also have to remember that being subjective assessments, the benchmarks are also likely to change over time: what is considered moral today is not necessarily what was considered moral in the past. Indeed, given the general trend towards greater moral autonomy, plurality and tolerance, we might have expected perceptions of moral standards to have improved (that they haven't might be further evidence of a negative bias in moral judgments about society).

Beyond the abstract dimension of morality, surveys reveal more tangible dimensions to people's concerns about 'progress' and its impact on QoL, both personal and social. These are consistent with findings about perceived overall social QoL, but are not apparent in the trends in personal QoL.

The 1999 survey of QoL in Australia asked people to rate the importance of several factors in improving their own personal QoL (Eckersley 1999a). It found that 75 % rated as very important 'being able to spend more time with your family and friends' and 66 % 'having less stress and pressure in your life'. Only 38 % rated as very important 'having more money to buy things' and 36 % feeling they were 'doing more for the community'. The 2000 survey by *The Australian* newspaper framed this question in a different way, asking people if there was more or less of these factors in people's lives now compared to ten years ago (Steketee, personal communication). Despite the festive season, 91 % said there was more stress and pressure; 68 % said people had less time to spend with family and friends; 51 % said there was less caring for the needs of the community; but 49 % said people had more money to buy things (see Table 12.2).

In response to other questions in *The Australian* poll, 55 % said the distribution of wealth in Australia was less fair now than 10 years ago (10 % more fair, 28 % no difference); 83 % agreed the rich were getting richer and the poor poorer (13 % disagreed); 57 % said there was a greater proportion of rich people in Australia now compared to ten years ago and 70 % a greater proportion of poor people; 70 % said they would prefer 'the gap between the rich and the poor to get smaller' over 'the overall wealth of Australia to grow as fast as possible' (28 % preferred growth); 79 % said Australians workers were less secure in keeping their jobs compared to ten years ago (10 % more secure, 9 % no difference).

There are other streams of research that also raise, although more indirectly, questions about contemporary social conditions and trends and whether they represent 'progress'. Modern western culture is characterised by individualism, consumerism, economism and the 'postmodern' qualities of relativism, pluralism, transience, ambivalence, ambiguity, fragmentation and contingency. Many of these characteristics would appear, on the basis of the psychological literature, to be harmful to well-being through their influence on values, goals, expectations and other qualities important to well-being such as hope, purpose, meaning, belonging, predictability and coherence (Eckersley 1999a, 2000b).

Arguably, modern Western culture promotes inappropriate and conflicting values and goals, encourages unrealistic expectations, and makes other qualities

Table 12.2 Perceptions of trends in QoL factors over last 10 years

Response	Stress and pressure in people's lives	Money to buy things	Caring for the Needs of the community	Time to spend with family and friends
Lot more	66	16	10	7
Little more	25	33	24	14
Total more	91	49	34	21
Little less	1	20	24	34
Lot less	2	19	27	34
Total less	3	39	51	68
Uncommitted	6	12	15	11

Percentage saying there is more or less of each factor in Australia now compared to ten years ago (Mike Steketee, The Australian, Sydney; personal communication)

harder to achieve. As consumerism (which drives economic growth) reaches increasingly beyond the acquisition of things to the enhancement of the person, the goal of marketing becomes not only to make people dissatisfied with what they have, but also with who they are. A great deal of consumption today (beyond meeting basic needs) is morally located within what have traditionally and universally been regarded as vices: pride (self-centredness), envy and avarice, to say nothing of lust and anger. Virtues such as moderation, patience, prudence (good sense) and compassion have little place in a world of hyper-consumerism.

Kasser and Ryan (1993, 1996; Kasser in press) have shown that people for whom 'extrinsic goals' such as fame, fortune and glamour are a priority in life tend to experience more anxiety and depression and lower overall well-being than people oriented towards 'intrinsic goals' of close relationships, self-acceptance and contributing to the community. People with extrinsic goals tend to have shorter relationships with friends and lovers, and relationships characterized more by jealousy and less by trust and caring. Referring to 'a dark side of the American dream', the authors say that the culture in some ways seems to be built on precisely what turned out to be detrimental to mental health.

In more recent research, Kasser and a colleague have also demonstrated significant correlations between materialistic values and social alienation (Khanna and Kasser, in preparation; personal communication with Tim Kasser, Knox College, Illinois). One of the two measures of alienation they used was a 12-item scale that included statements such as, 'In order to relate to others, I often have to put on a mask', and 'I'm not in tune with most people around me'. Similarly, Saunders and Munro (2000) found consumerism and materialism were positively correlated with depression, anxiety and anger; materialism was also negatively correlated with life satisfaction. While these correlations do not prove that materialism and related values cause a deterioration in well-being, they do suggest their cultural promotion is not conducive to it. The cause-effect relationship is likely to be complex and two-way. In any event, these findings are hard to reconcile with the belief that material progress in already rich nations is improving QoL.

There is often an assumption, explicit or implicit, in the SWB literature that happiness is an unqualified good, and the more happiness the better. While the desire for happiness seems to be part of human nature, the importance attached to happiness, what we believe it to be and how it is found are shaped by culture. The Greek philosopher, Epicurus, and later philosophers such as John Locke, stressed the importance of prudence to happiness. Today, as Csikszentmihalyi (1999) observes, our notion of a happy life 'amounts to little more than a thoughtless hedonism, a call to do one's thing regardless of consequences, a belief that whatever feels good at the moment must be worth doing'. Even if this is not the path to 'true' happiness, there can be no denying the power of the deception. And even if we accept that the pursuit of happiness is a legitimate goal, we should still question the extent to which we focus on maximised happiness (like maximised wealth) as the bottom line of progress, the supreme good.

Part of the conflict inherent in modern notions of progress concerns the social contract on which all societies rely—the ever-present tension between individual and social goals, between private and public good. From a social perspective, for example, is the individual pursuit of happiness compatible with the preservation of liberty, the price of which, the proverb tells us, is eternal vigilance? Democratic freedom relies on a sense of collective, not individual, agency, on pursuing a common vision based on shared values, not maximising individual choice in order to maximise personal satisfaction.

Individualism is closely correlated with SWB (Veenhoven 1999). But while individualism can be personally liberating and socially invigorating, taken far enough it can also be personally isolating and socially fragmenting. Balance is crucial for optimal social functioning: individual freedoms, rights and privileges, however much they might contribute to personal happiness, need to be balanced by social bonds, obligations and responsibilities.

The tension between happiness and other qualities is also apparent at the individual and species level. Consider some of the qualities associated with SWB and happiness (Myers and Diener 1995, 1996; Diener et al. 1999; Cummins and Nistico, under review). From an evolutionary perspective, if happiness is the goal towards which we strive, and if it is as closely related to extroversion as research suggests, why aren't we all highly extroverted? Conversely, given that neuroticism makes us unhappy, why wasn't it selected out of human nature long ago? Clearly introversion and neuroticism—characterised by a more cautious, questioning, doubting, brooding, worrying approach to life—have survival value. Self-esteem, optimism and autonomy—all associated with SWB and happiness—can become counter-productive or dysfunctional when they become too detached from the realities of life and an individual's abilities and circumstances; they need to be kept in check. The depressive phase of bipolar depression is undoubtedly debilitating; but the mania, with its wildly exaggerated self-regard, can be even more destructive to individuals and those close to them.

Headey and Wearing (1988) argue that a sense of relative superiority appears to be a normal and important aspect of human psychology, crucial to well-being. However, they note that it can have costs as well as benefits in that people might filter out information about poor performance and consequently fail to take corrective action. They point out that research has found that depressed people are more realistic in assessing their own performance than people who are not depressed. Diener et al. (1999) cite a range of research that links SWB to positive illusions such as self-deceptions, excessive optimism and over-estimated personal control. It seems, then, that life demands we maintain a balance between a realistic and fantastic view of ourselves. We should be sceptical of any notion that doing 'the right thing'—for oneself, for others, or for society as a whole—is always compatible with wanting to be happy.

In summary, social QoL measures appear to reflect social conditions and trends that personal measures of SWB tend to mask. These broader issues are relevant to measuring national performance and progress. The marked difference between the personal and social measures does, presumably, tell us something important. While people's perceptions of social QoL may be distorted by media and other influences, the evidence suggests they are not distant and detached, but reflect deeply felt concerns about modern life.

The short-term fluctuations may limit the usefulness of social QoL as a measure of long-term progress; only further research will answer this question. However, it is worth noting that the volatility is less marked than with the question about satisfaction 'with the way things are going in the US', mentioned above. The effect of asking about QoL trends, as opposed to states, also warrants examination. Finally, the broader view of QoL represented by the social perspective raises the issue of whether greater happiness is, in itself, an adequate goal of progress.

12.5 Conclusion

Surveys of people's attitudes highlight different dimensions of public perception depending on their focus and the wording of the questions asked. How people feel about their own lives is different from how they feel about society in general. Views on trends can differ from those on states. Some attitudes to life are remarkably stable, changing little over decades; others are volatile, swinging from troughs to peaks in cycles of a few years, even less. Public opinion can reflect people's personal resilience, adaptability and capacity to find a measure of fulfillment and satisfaction whatever their circumstances; it can also reveal their tendency to 'edit' what they will admit about themselves—even to themselves.

There may not be a simple, easy way of measuring QoL in a way that allows us to say whether, on the whole or all things considered, life is getting better or worse. GDP does not do it, nor life expectancy. Subjective measures are important, supplying a crucial dimension missing from objective indicators, but we need to be very clear about what they are measuring. The standard questions about life satisfaction and happiness tell us something—but not everything we need to know. Asking about overall social QoL, as distinct from personal QoL, may be useful, but this remains to be established.

Modern notions of progress centre around economic growth. The problems with growth, as it is currently measured and derived, are that it is increasing inequality among nations; it is environmentally unsustainable; and, contrary to its central objective, it does not seem to be making people happier, at least in nations that are already rich. Measuring progress needs to take many things into account: economic gains must be assessed against environmental losses; issues of equity between and within nations and generations need to be addressed; measures of personal happiness and SWB should be weighed against perceptions of social conditions and trends; a path of progress that is appropriate and beneficial at one stage of human development can be inappropriate and costly at another.

At a time when governments the world over seem to be captive to an ideology of growth, this is an important message to heed.

References

Adamson P (1993) Keeping faith with progress. The Progress of Nations 1993. United Nations Children's Fund (UNICEF), New York, pp 3–5

Australian Bureau of Statistics (1998) Mental health and wellbeing: profile of adults, Australia 1997. ABS catalogue no. 4326.0. Australian Bureau of Statistics, Canberra

Basanez M, Inglehart R, Moreno A (1998) Human values and beliefs: a cross–cultural sourcebook. University of Michigan Press, Ann Arbor

Blaxter M (1997) Whose fault is it? People's own conceptions of the reasons for health inequalities. Soc Sci Med 44(6):747–756

Csikszentmihalyi M (1999) If we are so rich, why aren't we happy? Am Psychologist 54(10): 821–827

Cummins R, Nistico H Maintaining life satisfaction: the role of positive cognitive bias. Clin Psychology Rev (under review)

Cummins R (1998) The second approximation to an international standard for life satisfaction. Soc Indic Res 43:307–334

Cummins R (2000a) Normative life satisfaction: measurement issues and a homeostatic model. In: Zumbo B (ed) Methodological developments and issues in quality of life research. Kluwer, Dordrecht, Netherlands. (in press)

Cummins R (2000b) Objective and subjective quality of life: an interactive model. Soc Indic Res (in press)

Cummins R (2000c) Personal income and subjective well-being: a review. J Happiness Stud (in press)

Currie C, Hurelmann K, Settertobulte W, Smith R, Todd J (eds) (2000) Health and behaviour among young people. Health Behaviour in School-aged Children: a WHO Cross-National Study (HBSC) international report. World Health Organization Regional Office for Europe, Copenhagen

Diener E, Diener C (1995) The wealth of nations revisited: income and quality of life. Soc Indic Res 36:275–286

Diener E, Suh E (1997) Measuring quality of life: economic, social and subjective indicators. Soc Indic Res 40:189–216

Diener E, Suh E, Lucas R, Smith H (1999) Subjective well-being: three decades of progress. Psychol Bull 125(2):276–302

Easterly W (1997) Life during growth. World Bank, Oct (preliminary report), www.worldbank.org

Eckersley R (1988) Casualties of change: the predicament of youth in Australia. Australian Commission for the Future, Melbourne

Eckersley R (1997) Psychosocial disorders in young people: on the agenda but not on the mend. Med J Aust 166:423–424

Eckersley R (1998a) Perspectives on progress: economic growth, quality of life and ecological sustainability. In: Eckersley R (ed) Measuring progress: is life getting better?. CSIRO Publishing, Collingwood

Eckersley R (1998b) Redefining progress: shaping the future to human needs. Family Matters (51): 6–12 (Spring/Summer)

Eckersley R (1999a) Quality of life in Australia: an analysis of public perceptions. Discussion paper no. 23, Sept. The Australia Institute, Canberra

Eckersley R (1999b) Dreams and expectations: young people's expected and preferred futures and their significance for education. Futures 31:73–90

Eckersley R (2000a) The state and fate of nations: implications of subjective measures of personal and social quality of life. Soc Indic Res 52:3–27

Eckersley R (2000b) Killer cults and the search for meaning. Aust Q 72(1): 16–19 (Feb–Mar)

Erikson Bloland S (1999) The price of fame. Aust Financial Rev 12 November, Review, 1,2,8,9. Reprinted from The Atlantic Monthly)

Gallup (1998) Haves and have-nots: perceptions of fairness and opportunity 1998. Gallup Poll Social Audit. The Gallup Organization, Princeton. Some details of the audit and updated results of the 'satisfaction with the US' question can be obtained from Gallup's website, www.gallup.com

Gallup (1999) Politics and moral values. Gallup social and economic indicators. The Gallup Organization, Princeton, www.gallup.com

Gottfried M (1995) Nobody's fool. Simon and Schuster. The review, few skips in Kaye's unfortunate Life, was published in The Bulletin, 9 May 1995, p 91

Halpern D (1995) Values, morals and modernity the values, constraints and norms of European youth. In: Rutter M, Smith D (eds) Psychosocial disorders in young people time trends and their causes. Wiley for Academia Europaea, Chichester

Halstead T (1998) The science and politics of new measures of progress: a United States perspective. In: Eckersley R (ed) Measuring progress is life getting better? CSIRO Publishing, Collingwood

Hamilton C (1998) Measuring changes in economic welfare the genuine progress indicator for Australia. In: Eckersley R (ed) Measuring progress: is life getting better? CSIRO Publishing, Collingwood

Headey B, Wearing A (1988) The sense of relative superiority—central to well-being. Soc Indic Res 20: 497–516

Kasser T, Ryan RM (1993) A dark side of the American dream: correlates of financial success as a central life aspiration. J Personality Soc Psychol 65(2): 410–422

Kasser T, Ryan RM (1996) Further examining the American dream: differential correlates of intrinsic and extrinsic goals. Personality Soc Psychol Bull 22(3): 280–287

Kasser T (in press) Two versions of the American dream: which goals and values make for a high quality of life? In: Diener E, Rahtz D (eds) Advances in quality of life theory and research. Kluwer, Dordrecht

Katschnig H, Freeman H, Sartorius N (eds) (1997) Quality of life in mental disorders. Wiley, Chichester

Mackay H (1999) Mind and mood '99. The Mackay Report, June. Mackay Research, Sydney

Maddison A (1995) Monitoring the World Economy 1820–1992. Development Centre Studies. OECD, Paris

Maddison A (2000) Economic progress: the last half century in historical perspective. In: Castles I (ed) Facts and fancies of human development. Occasional Paper Series 1/2000. Academy of the Social Sciences in Australia, Canberra. These data will also be in a forthcoming book, Contours of the World Economy

Mathers C, Douglas R (1998) Measuring progress in population health and well-being. In: Eckersley R (ed) Measuring progress: is Life Getting Better?. CSIRO Publishing, Collingwood

Max-Neef M (1995) Economic growth and quality of life: a threshold hypothesis. Ecol Econ 15:115–118

Myers D, Diener E (1995) Who is happy? Psychol Sci 6(1):10–19

Myers D, Diener E (1996) The pursuit of happiness. Sci Am 274(5): 54–56 (May)

Pew Research Centre (1999) Technology triumphs, morality falters: public perspectives on the American century. 1999 Millennium Surveys. The Pew Research Centre, www.people-press.org

Pusey M (1998) Incomes, standards of living and quality of life: preliminary findings of the Middle Australia Project. In: Eckersley R (ed) Measuring progress: is life getting better? CSIRO Publishing, Collingwood

Rutter M, Smith DJ (eds) (1995) Psychosocial disorders in young people: time trends and their causes. Wiley for Academia Europaea, Chichester

Saunders S, Munro D (2000) The construction and validation of a consumer orientation questionnaire (SCOI) designed to measure Fromm's (1995) 'marketing character' in Australia. Soc Behav Personality 28(3) (in press)

Sen A (1993) The economics of life and death. Sci Am 268(5): 18–25 (May)

Szreter S (1997) Economic growth, disruption, deprivation, disease and death: on the importance of the politics of public health for development. Population Dev Rev 23(4):693–728
United Nations Environment Program (1997) Global environment outlook 1997: Executive summary, global overview, www.unep.ch/earthw/assess.htm
Veenhoven R (1991) Is happiness relative? Soc Indic Res 24:1–34
Veenhoven R (1996) Developments in satisfaction research. Soc Indic Res 37:1–46
Veenhoven R (1999) Quality of life in individualistic society. Soc Indic Res 48:157–186
Washington Post/Kaiser/Harvard Survey Project (1998) American Values: 1998 Survey of Americans on values. Kaiser Family Foundation, www.kff.org
Waters E, Wake M, Toumbourou J, Wright M, Salmon L (1999) Prevalence of emotional and physical health concerns among young people in Victoria. J Paediatr Child Health 35:28–33
Wilkinson R (1994) The epidemiological transition: from material scarcity to social disadvantage? Daedalus 123(4): 61–77 (Fall)
Wilkinson R (1998) Equity, social cohesion and health. In: Strickland S, Shetty P (eds) Human biology and social inequality. Society for the study of human biology, symposium, series: 39. Cambridge University Press, Cambridge
Wilkinson R (1999) Putting the picture together: prosperity, redistribution, health, and welfare. In: Marmot M, Wilkinson R (eds) Social determinants of health. Oxford University Press, Oxford
Williams B (1994) Patient satisfaction: a valid concept? Soc Sci Med 38(4):509–516
Williams B, Coyle J, Healy D (1998) The meaning of patient satisfaction: an explanation of high reported levels. Soc Sci Med 47(9): 1351–1359
World Commission on Environment and Development (1987) Our common future. Oxford University Press, Oxford
World Wide Fund for Nature (1998) Living planet report 1998. WWF, Gland

Chapter 13
Searching for Happiness: The Importance of Social Capital

Ambrose Leung, Cheryl Kier, Tak Fung, Linda Fung and Robert Sproule

Abstract After four decades of research, scholars of happiness continue to debate its causes. While it is generally agreed that a combination of internal and external factors play a role, predicting happiness well remains a challenge. Recent research has proposed that social capital may be a vital factor that has been overlooked. This paper attempts to address that omission. According to Coleman's (Am J Sociol 94:S95–S120, 1988) seminal work, three dimensions of social capital exist: (1) trust and obligations, (2) information channels, and (3) norms and sanctions. Using bootstrap hierarchical regression on data from the Canadian General Social Survey of Social Engagement Cycle 17 (2003), we identified blocks of social capital variables described by Coleman, as well as an additional factor of belongingness. Even after controlling for major demographic and individual characteristics, the majority of these blocks show significant relationships with happiness. Our findings support social capital as an important piece in predicting happiness.

Keywords Happiness • Social capital • Trust • Obligations • Information channel

A. Leung (✉)
Department of Policy Studies, Mount Royal University, Calgary, AB, Canada
e-mail: acleung@mtroyal.ca

C. Kier
Psychology Centre, Athabasca University, Athabasca, AB, Canada

T. Fung
Information Technologies, University of Calgary, Alberta, Canada

L. Fung
Statcomp Consulting Services Ltd, Calgary, AB, Canada

R. Sproule
Department of Economics, Bishop's University, Sherbrooke, QC, Canada

A. Delle Fave (ed.), *The Exploration of Happiness*, Happiness Studies Book Series, DOI: 10.1007/978-94-007-5702-8_13, © Springer Science+Business Media Dordrecht 2013

13.1 Introduction

The pursuit of happiness is an important personal goal that has attracted the attention of many social scientists across various disciplines around the world. In 1967, Warner Wilson summarized the characteristics of a happy person as follows: 'young, healthy, well-educated, well-paid, extroverted, optimistic, worry-free, religious, married, with high self-esteem, high job morale, modest aspirations, of either sex and of a wide range of intelligence' (p. 294). Wilson's observations have led to four decades of research on happiness. Many researchers have re-examined the factors suggested by Wilson (Argyle 2001; Diener et al. 1999; Frey and Stutzer 2002). Recent research has proposed that social capital may be a vital factor that has been overlooked (Diener and Oishi 2004; Helliwell 2006). Social capital refers to individual resources accumulated through interpersonal activities that help to develop a strong social network and ties among individuals and their community (Leung 2002).

The purpose of this paper is to examine the relationship between happiness and different forms of social capital. A review of the happiness literature will identify important correlates of happiness. The literature on social capital will then be examined. Finally, extant literature on the potential relationship between happiness and social capital will be presented to construct a theoretical framework and to generate hypotheses about the relationship between happiness and social capital. Following Bjornskov (2003) and Frey and Stutzer (2002), we use the terms 'happiness', 'life satisfaction', and 'well-being' interchangeably. However, it is acknowledged that each of these terms can be defined in different ways and may contain a variety of components.

13.2 Review of Literature

13.2.1 Correlates of Happiness from Previous Research

Most research on happiness has focused on the relationship between external factors and the level of happiness as summarized by Argyle (2001), Diener et al. (1999), Dolan et al. (2008), and Frey and Stutzer (2002). Aside from the basic demographic factors such as age, race, and sex that are commonly discussed, happiness has been found to have significant relationships with other external factors such as having a job, being married (rather than being single, divorced, or separated), good health, and having a religion. Education has a small but significant correlation with happiness. Associations between the above demographics and external factors and happiness, however, fail to fully account for why people are happy. "[T]heories that focus only on external influences on SWB [Subjective Well Being] ignore a substantial source of variation in happiness reports" according to Diener et al. (1999, p. 227). Diener et al. (1999) cited studies that revealed demographic variables such as age, sex, income, race, education, and marital status accounted for only 8–20 % of the variance in explaining happiness. Diener et al. (1999, p. 294) concluded, "The past 30 years of research have shown that all of the demographic factors taken together do not account for much variance in SWB".

Furthermore, individual factors such as genetics (Lykken and Tellegen 1996 as cited in Argyle 2001), optimism, a sense of personal control, self-esteem, and extraversion (Myers and Diner 1995) have also been found to be related to happiness; while neuroticism appears to be associated with unhappiness (Argyle 2001). However, even after the inclusion of individual factors along with demographic and external factors described above, researchers still cannot fully account for what contributes to happiness. Some other important component(s) remain missing. Despite of the suggestion by some researchers (e.g., Diener and Oishi 2004 Helliwell 2006) that social capital may be an important missing variable to explain happiness, hardly any research has examined this in an organized fashion.

13.2.2 Social Capital

Social capital is "the idea that individuals and groups can gain resources from their connections to one another (and the type of these connections)" (Paxton 1999, p. 89). Most research on social capital stems from Coleman's (1988) seminal work (Furstenberg 2005; Paxton 1999), suggesting three major forms of social capital: (1) trust and obligations; (2) information channels; and (3) norms and sanctions.

Coleman initially suggested that trust was based on the understanding help received from other people is like a "credit slip" issued to the helper and that an obligation on the part of the person who received help is implied. Coleman believed trust will vanish if the expected obligation is not fulfilled.

More recent literature suggests Coleman's category of trust may be defined too narrowly. Allum et al. (2012), Paldam (2000) argued that the dimension of trust actually consists of two dimensions: generalized trust (trust in people in general) and special trust (trust in known people or particular institutions). Paxton (1999) also suggested that trust was not a single dimension but consisted of trust in individuals and trust in institutions. There is support in the literature to distinguish the two types of trust. Hudson (2006), for instance, found evidence among Europeans of a positive relationship between people's well-being and trust in institutions. Rus and Iglic (2005) found that entrepreneurs in Slovenia relied more on institutional trust while business relationships in Bosnia centred on interpersonal trust.

As a second form of social capital, Coleman suggested that information channels involve an individual gaining more information by knowing more people and developing closer ties with others. Coleman gave a couple of general examples to show how social relations can be used to obtain information (1988). The literature has elaborated on Coleman's idea and suggested two main forms of information channels: social relationships through contacts with family and friends (e.g., Lelkes 2006; Powdthavee 2008); and civic engagement such as participation in a sports organization or a professional association, and membership in voluntary organizations (e.g., Bjornskov 2006; Putnam 2000).

The third major form of Coleman's social capital consists of effective norms and sanctions that can promote actions beneficial for common goals, and constrain actions not desired by society. For example, Coleman suggested "effective norms that inhibit crime make it possible to walk freely outside at night in a city…" (1988, p. 104) There is very little in the literature assessing this form of social capital, although Bjornskov (2006) measured social norms by asking respondents whether behaviour such as accepting bribes and cheating on taxes can be justified. The theoretical construction of norms and sanctions appears to be the most abstract amongst the dimensions of social capital postulated by Coleman.

13.2.3 Happiness and Social Capital

The literature has provided evidence that there may be relationships between happiness and social capital, although no study has investigated all three types of social capital as defined by Coleman.

13.2.3.1 Trust and obligations

Trust, measured in a variety of ways such as trusting most other people and trusting public institutions, was strongly related to happiness in a review of over 100 happiness studies by Dolan et al. (2008). Bjornskov (2006), using an international sample of more than 80 countries, found a positive relationship between generalized social trust ("In general, do you think that most people can be trusted, or can't you be too careful?") and life satisfaction. Hudson (2006) found a positive relationship between well-being and trust in institutions such as the law, the national government, and the UN among EU member countries. Empirical relationships between happiness and obligations have yet to be explored. We believe we may be the first to examine this.

13.2.3.2 Information Channels

There are correlations with happiness for the social type of information channels. Time spent seeing family and friends (Lelkes 2006; Powdthavee 2008), and talking to neighbours (Peasgood 2007) have been found to be positively associated with happiness. Socializing with people was also related to happiness in the review by Dolan et al. (2008), although one study (Martin and Westerhof 2003, as cited in Dolan et al. 2008) found that socializing with family was related to life satisfaction but socializing with friends was not.

Since Coleman's work on information channels, Putnam (2000) distinguished two forms of civic engagement which he named civic participation (membership in organizations) and political participation (voting, following political discussion, signing petitions, etc.). In the review by Dolan et al. (2008), belonging to organizations and engaging in volunteer work was correlated with higher levels of happiness in some studies but not others. Although Bjornskov (2006) included an indicator for civic participation to examine its relationship with well-being and found a negative association, the relationship between happiness and political participation has not been explored. This will be examined in the present study.

13.2.3.3 Norms and Sanctions

The theoretical construction of norms and sanctions appears to be the most abstract amongst the dimensions of social capital postulated by Coleman, so empirical approximations have been more difficult to create. The only study of which we are aware that empirically examined the relationship between norms and happiness was Bjornskov (2006). As proxies for social norms, Bjornskov used questions about whether dishonest behaviour such as bribery or cheating on taxes can ever be justified, and found no significant relationship between such norms and happiness.

13.2.3.4 Sense of Belonging

After Coleman's initial work, the literature discussed a sense of belonging as a form of social capital. For example, this has been explored in relation to health outcomes (Fujiwara and Kawahi 2008a; Maycock and Howat 2007) and children's school achievement (Clift Gore 2005; Maeroff 1998). However, minimal effort can be found in the literature to examine the relationship between happiness and sense of belonging as a form of social capital. An exception is the study by Fujiwara and Kawachi (2008b) who found a significant negative relationship between depression and sense of belonging to one's community. To our knowledge, the relationship between happiness and sense of belonging measured at different levels has not been discussed in the literature.

13.2.4 Bjornskov's Study: Critique

The only study of which we are aware that attempted to investigate all three forms of social capital in relation to happiness was provided by Bjornskov (2006). Using data from a number of countries, Bjornskov identified three dimensions of social capital consistent with Coleman's theory, which he named social trust, associational activities, and social norms. Bjornskov's regression analysis showed that social trust was the only factor to have a significant positive relationship with life satisfaction. Associational activities (which can be considered information channels in Coleman's words) had an unexpected negative relationship with life satisfaction, while the social norms factor had no significant relationship.

Although Bjornskov's use of empirical variables to represent each of the three forms of social capital suggested by Coleman was very informative, his study did not take into account certain important dimensions of social capital. For example, Bjornskov used only a single survey question to represent social trust with no indicator for institutional trust. Furthermore, his study provided no measure of obligations, which has been considered an important aspect of social capital (Dasgupta 2005; Parks-Yancy et al. 2008). As for information channels, although Bjornskov discussed the relationship between life satisfaction and organization membership (civic participation), he examined neither political participation nor contacts with family and friends.

There is clearly a need for more research to investigate the relationship between different forms of social capital and happiness. The aim of this study is to conduct such an examination, encompassing measures for all three facets of social capital and building upon work conducted by Bjornskov (2006) and others.

13.3 Method

13.3.1 Participants

For Statistics Canada's 2003 general social survey (GSS), Cycle 17 (2004), 24,951 individuals aged 15–80 or over were interviewed. The greatest percentage of participants was aged 40–44, with 50.8 % female participants, and 60.8 % currently married. Most participants came from Ontario (38.5 %), 7.6 % came from the Atlantic regions, 24.0 % from Quebec, and 16.5 % from the Prairie provinces. Household income ranged from less than $5,000 to over $100,000, with a mean of between $50 and 60,000. 12.4 % of participants experienced unemployment in the past year. The sample was chosen to reflect the total population of Canada. The data reported here use the sample weights provided by Statistics Canada which reflect the population distribution (Statistics Canada 2004) to ensure accurate estimation of population parameters. After accounting for missing observations, the sample size is 15,660.

13.4 Measures

13.4.1 General Social Survey on Social Engagement, 2003

The present study uses data collected by Statistics Canada in 2003 from the general social survey (GSS) cycle 17. The focus of this survey was social engagement, involving 24,951 participants who are 15 years of age and older across the 10 Canadian provinces, excluding residents of Northwest Territories, Yukon, and Nunavut, and full-time residents of institutions (Statistics Canada 2004). Questions from GSS cycle 17 covered a wide range of topics about age, sex, marital status, well-being, cultural background, social participation, political participation, education, activities, and housing characteristics.

13.4.1.1 Survey Questions: Variables to Measure Social Capital

Questions were selected from the GSS survey to assess the social capital variables described above. Seven questions were used to represent two forms of trust: social trust (trust in family members, neighbours, and strangers), and institutional trust (confidence in the police, the health care system, banks, and business). Fourteen of the survey questions were used to proxy for obligations: six different forms of help received, and eight different forms of help given. Questions related to information channels were divided into four groups: contact with relatives, contact with friends, political participation, and civic participation. Four questions were used to approximate social norms, including feeling safe to walk alone after dark, feeling safe to be home alone after dark, trusting someone living close by to return a lost wallet, and trusting a stranger to return a lost wallet. Questions on sense of belonging (to the community, to the province, and to Canada) were also considered. See "Appendix A" for a list of the original survey questions.

13.5 Results

Bootstrap hierarchical regression (based on Statistics Canada's original method of bootstrapping) was used to assess whether social capital variables were related to happiness. These regression analyses control for the influence of all other blocks when assessing a particular block. Eight control variables were included as a block, as previous research has found them to be associated with happiness: age, sex, region of residence, marital status, unemployment status, household income, self-assessed health, and score on mastery scale. In addition, ten blocks of variables representing the social capital items were entered into the regressions. These were social trust, institutional trust, obligations (help received), obligations (help given), information channels (relatives), information channels (friends), information channels (political participation), information channels (civic participation), norms and sanctions, and sense of belongingness. The variables that make up each of these blocks can be seen in Table 13.1.

Results for the block of control variables indicated a significant effect, $F(11, 189) = 106.95$, $p < 0.001$, supporting previous work that these variables are indeed important to consider in predicting happiness.

Regression results for the block consisting of social trust reached significance, $F(3,197) = 9.00$, $p < 0.001$. Trust in family was significant, $t = 4.58$, $p < 0.001$, but trust in neighbours, $t = 1.54$, NS and trust in strangers, $t = -1.61$, NS were not. This suggests that the more a person trusts family, the higher the happiness level. Trust in others does not seem to factor into one's happiness.

For institutional trust there was a significant effect, $F(4,196) = 16.72$, $p < 0.001$. This was accounted for by a significant effect for confidence in police, $t = 4.05$, $p < 0.001$, confidence in the health care system, $t = 2.72$, $p = 0.007$, confidence in banks, $t = 2.83$, $p = 0.005$, and a non-significant tendency to have confidence in businesses, $t = 1.92$, $p = 0.056$. In all cases, greater trust was associated with greater happiness.

Table 13.1 Summary statistics of weighted variables

Variable blocks	Variable names	Continuous and ordinal variables		Standard error	Binary variables
		Mean	Scale		% of yes
Dependent variable	Happiness	4.40	1–5	0.005	
Control variables	Age	7.33	1–15	0.001	
	Male				49.2
	Married				60.8
	Atlantic				7.6
	Quebec				24.0
	Ontario				38.5
	Prairies				16.5
	Health	3.74	1–5	0.007	
	Income	8.82	1–12	0.019	
	Unemployed				12.4
	Mastery_scale	18.78	0–28	0.029	
Social trust	Trust_family	4.76	1–5	0.004	
	Trust_neighbourhood	3.73	1–5	0.007	
	Trust_stranger	2.23	1–5	0.008	
Institutional trust	Trust_police	3.20	1–4	0.005	
	Trust_healthcare	2.87	1–4	0.006	
	Trust_banks	2.87	1–4	0.006	
	Trust_business	3.05	1–4	0.005	
Obligations: help received	Rhelp_chores				22.4
	Rhelp_transportation				25.5
	Rhelp_childcare				10.8
	Rhelp_teaching				29.1
	Rhelp_emotion				41.5
	Rhelp_other				7.3
Obligations: help given	Ghelp_chores				37.2
	Ghelp_transportation				44.7
	Ghelp_childcare				24.1
	Ghelp_teaching				43.0
	Ghelp_emotion				56.0
	Ghelp_other				12.8
	Ghelp_volunteer				33.6
	Ghelp_donate				73.3
Information channels: relatives	Relative_see	2.98	1–5	0.009	
	Relative_phone	3.51	1–5	0.008	
	Relative_close	3.13	1–5	0.009	
Information channels: friends	Friend_close	3.05	1–5	0.008	
	Friend_other	4.48	1–5	0.010	
	Friend_see	3.64	1–5	0.007	
	Friend_phone	3.56	1–5	0.008	

(continued)

Table 13.1 (continued)

Variable blocks	Variable names	Continuous and ordinal variables		Standard error	Binary variables
		Mean	Scale		% of yes
Information channels: political participation	Search_political				26.1
	Volunteer_political				3.0
	Contact_newspaper				12.7
	Sign_petition				28.0
	Boycott_product				20.1
	Attend_meeting				21.7
	Participate_demonstration				6.3
Information channels: civic participation	Member_proforg				25.1
	Member_political				4.7
	Member_sports				29.0
	Member_education				17.9
	Member_religious				16.8
	Member_school				16.6
	Member_service				8.0
	Member_other				5.7
Norms and sanctions	Walk_alone	4.06	1–5	0.007	
	Home_alone	2.83	1–4	0.003	
	Wallet_close	3.09	1–4	0.007	
	Wallet_stranger	1.87	1–4	0.007	
Belonging-ness	Belong_community	3.49	1–5	0.010	
	Belong_province	3.87	1–5	0.009	
	Belong_Canada	4.21	1–5	0.009	

Results for the block of obligations (help received) reached significance, $F(6,194) = 5.20$, $p < 0.001$, but the block of obligations (help given) did not, $F(8,192) = 1.35$, NS. Examining the individual variables reveals that receiving help in domestic chores did not reach significance, $t = 1.17$, NS, nor did receiving help with transportation, $t = 0.30$, NS, nor receiving help with childcare, $t = 0.06$, NS Receiving teaching help from someone was not significant, $t = 0.97$, NS, nor was receiving other help not listed, $t = -0.54$, NS. The only significant individual help received variable was receiving emotional support, $t = -4.87$, $p < 0.001$. This means that people who received emotional help were less happy than those who did not. Other types of help received did not relate to level of happiness.

Turning to information channels, contact with relatives reached significance, $F(3, 197) = 17.98$, $p < 0.001$ as did contact with friends, $F(4, 196) = 10.37$, $p < 0.001$. This was accounted for by having relatives one feels close to, $t = 7.19$, $p < 0.001$ but not the amount of contact one had with relatives by phone, $t = -1.06$, NS. For friends, there was a significant effect for the number of close friends, $t = 2.58$, $p = 0.011$, for the number of non-close friends, $t = 2.12$, $p = 0.035$ and frequency of seeing friends, $t = 3.91$, $p < 0.001$, but not for frequency of phoning friends, $t = 0.50$, NS.

Table 13.2 *F*-statistics of variable blocks: bootstrap hierarchical regression model

Variable blocks	*F* statistics	Prob > *F*
Control variables	$F(11, 189) = 106.95$	0.0000
Social trust	$F(3, 197) = 9.00$	0.0000
Institutional trust	$F(4, 196) = 16.72$	0.0000
Obligations: help received	$F(6, 194) = 5.20$	0.0001
Obligations: help given	$F(8, 192) = 1.35$	0.2228
Information channels: relatives	$F(3, 197) = 17.98$	0.0000
Information channels: friends	$F(4, 196) = 10.37$	0.0000
Information channels: political participation	$F(7, 193) = 2.40$	0.0223
Information channels: civic participation	$F(8, 192) = 1.39$	0.2009
Norms and sanctions	$F(4, 196) = 2.46$	0.0468
Belongingness	$F(11, 189) = 63.74$	0.0000

As for political participation information channels, there was a significant effect, $F(7, 193) = 2.40$, $p = 0.022$. This was accounted for by a significant effect of searching for information about a political issue, $t = -2.08$, $p = 0.039$. There was a non-significant trend for contacting a newspaper to express one's views, $t = -1.84$, $p = 0.068$, but none of the other individual variables were significant: for volunteering for a political group or party, $t = 1.27$, NS, for signing a petition, $t = 0.17$, NS, for boycotting a product, $t = -1.17$, NS, for attending a public meeting, $t = -1.46$, NS, and for taking part in a demonstration, $t = -0.23$, NS. This suggests that having searched for information on a political issue and having expressed one's view by contacting a newspaper are negatively correlated with happiness. The other variables do not seem to be related to happiness level.

People who engaged in civic participation information channels (e.g., were members of political, religious, or educational organizations) were no more happy than people who did not engage in such behaviour, $F(8, 192) = 1.39$, NS.

The block measuring norms and sanctions was borderline significant, $F(4, 196) = 2.46$, $p = 0.047$. There was a significant effect for feeling safe walking alone, $t = -2.08$, $p = 0.039$ and a non-significant trend for feeling safe being home alone, $t = 1.94$, $p = 0.054$. The safer a person felt walking alone after dark the less happy the person reported being. The less worried a person was about being home alone the happier he/she felt. Believing that a lost wallet would be returned by someone who lived close by, $t = 1.34$, NS or by a stranger, $t = 0.95$, NS were not significant.

Having a sense of belonging (to the community, the province, and to Canada) was found to be a significant predictor of happiness, $F(3,197) = 63.74$, $p < 0.001$. This was accounted for by a significant effect of feeling one belongs to one's community, $t = 11.31$, $p < 0.001$ and of a feeling of belonging to Canada, $t = 3.14$, $p = 0.002$. There was no significant effect for a feeling of belonging to one's province, $t = 1.26$, NS The stronger the sense of belonging to the community and to Canada, the higher the reported happiness.

Table 13.2 shows the *F*-statistics of the different blocks of variables. Coefficients and t-statistics of each variable are contained in "Appendix B".

13.6 Discussion

The goal of this project was to assess whether social capital has a role in explaining people's happiness. We found significant relationships between happiness and each of three types of social capital suggested by Coleman (1988), namely trust and obligations, information channels, and norms and sanctions. Furthermore, we identified sense of belonging as an additional form of social capital that can predict happiness.

Trust is one of the defining elements of social capital (Coleman 1988; Putnam 1995), and our findings support Bjornskov's (2006) conclusion that trust is an essential element of life satisfaction. Our work goes beyond Bjornskov's study by illustrating that both trust in people and trust in institutions are independently related to happiness. Institutional trust in the police, the health care system, banks, and business people are all shown to be positively related to happiness, implying an important relationship between the well being of citizens and their level of trust in both the public and private sectors of society, as also reported by Hudson (2006) and Rus and Iglic (2005).

In terms of social and personal trust, our analysis showed that this has an important relationship with happiness, but only trust in people within one's family was significant. Family likely plays an important role in better living within Canadian society, but the fact that trust in neighbours and strangers doesn't play a role may support Putnam's argument that people are feeling disconnected (Putnam 2000).

According to Coleman (1988), trust is built upon people's obligations for each other through help given and received. While help given appeared to have no significant relationship with happiness, help received was shown to have a significant negative relationship with happiness in the form of emotional support received. Perhaps a person who has received emotional support has experienced difficult times in life, and is likely to be less happy. The fact that people did not feel especially happy giving help to others begs the question of the truth of an oft-repeated notion that being altruistic is actually a rational or selfish way to make oneself feel good (e.g., Cialdini et al. 1997). For instance, some research in public economics has proposed that acts of charity and gift-giving generate a "warm glow" and are done in order for the givers to feel good about themselves (e.g., Allgood 2009, Mayo and Tinsley 2009). The empirical results from our study cast some doubt over this suggestion. More research is needed to further explore the potentially complex relationship between obligations and happiness.

Three of the four forms of information channels included in our analysis were found to have significant relationships with happiness. Consistent with most of the findings from the literature about time spent seeing friends (Lelkes 2006; Powdthavee 2008; cf Martin and Westerhof 2003, as cited in Dolan et al. 2008), our results showed that a strong social network of friends appeared to be an important factor related to one's happiness, including seeing friends and having more friends. Furthermore, having more relatives that a person feels close to was also found to be positively related to happiness. This supports both Coleman's (1988) and Putnam's (2000) contentions about the importance of social connections. Being involved in political activities was related to happiness, but in a negative direction. The people who searched for information about a political issue reported less happiness than those who didn't get involved. A possible explanation for this result is that people who actively searched for political issues may have become more aware of problems around the world, hence are likely to be less happy. Another possibility is that people do not search for information about a particular political issue unless they feel worried or discontented about it, otherwise they just do not bother getting involved. If this were the case, it would support Putnam's (2000) idea that on the whole, today's citizens are apathetic about the world around them. This interpretation may be further supported by our finding that organizational membership is not related to level of happiness, and Bjornskov's (2006) finding of a negative relationship between happiness and organizational membership.

Another category of social capital defined by Coleman is social norms and sanctions. Bjornskov used questions about whether dishonest behaviour such as cheating on taxes can ever be justified as proxies for norms and sanctions, and found no significant relationship with life satisfaction. Unlike Bjornskov's finding, the block of norms and sanctions variables in our analysis was found to have a significant correlation with happiness. Feeling safe alone in one's home was associated with feeling happier. However, counter intuitively, feeling safe walking alone correlated with feeling less happy. We believe this is due to multicollinearity and is an artefact of the statistical process. Perhaps controlling for all other variables previously entered in the hierarchical regression rendered feeling safe walking alone non-significant. This explanation is supported by the finding that when examined in separate analyses including only the four norms and sanctions factors, the variable feeling safe walking alone was a significant positive predictor of happiness.

A form of capital suggested by the literature is sense of belonging (e.g., Clift Gore 2005; Maeroff 1998; Maycock and Howat 2007; Morrow et al. 2002). Our results showed a positive relationship between happiness and sense of belonging to one's local community and to Canada (but not to one's province). Sense of belonging appears to be an important dimension of social capital to complement Coleman's original suggestions and needs to be further explored.

In short, this study has identified measures for social capital in the forms of trust and obligations, information channels, norms and sanctions, and belongingness that are related to happiness. Our results confirm our hypothesis that social capital is a vital piece of information for predicting happiness. While people may not be able to change their internal or external characteristics, some aspects of their social may be modifiable. In addition to demographic and individual factors such as age, income, and health conditions, future research should include variables representing social capital when exploring what accounts for happiness.

Acknowledgments We would like to thank Christopher T. Carlyle and Timothy G.A. McLean for capable research assistance.

Appendix A: Description of Variables

Dependent variable

Happiness

1 very unhappy
2 somewhat unhappy
3 no opinion
4 somewhat happy
5 very happy

Control variables

Age

1 15–17
2 18–19
3 20–24
4 25–29
5 30–34
6 35–29
7 40–44
8 45–49
9 50–54
10 55–59
11 60–64
12 65–60
13 70–74
14 75–79
15 80 years and over

Male

1 male
0 female

Married

1 married or living common law
0 otherwise

Atlantic

1 living in Atlantic
0 otherwise

Quebec

1 living in Quebec
0 otherwise

Ontario

1 living in Ontario
0 otherwise

Prairie

1 living in Prairie
0 otherwise

Health

In general, would you say your health is…?

1 poor
2 fair
3 good
4 very good
5 excellent

Income

Annual personal income of the respondent

1 no income
2 less than $5,000
3 $5,000–$9,999
4 $10,000–$14, 999
5 $15,000–$19,999
6 $20,000–$29, 999
7 $30,000–$39, 999
8 $40,000–$49, 999
9 $50,000–$59, 999
10$60,000–$79, 999
11$80,000–$99, 999
12$100,000 or more

Unemployed

Unemployed at any time in the past 12 months?

1 yes
0 no

Mastery_scale
A 28-point ascending scale to indicate the amount of control over life as perceived by the respondent

Social trust

How much do you trust each of the following group of people?
People in your family
People in your neighbourhood
Strangers

1 cannot be trusted at all
2
3
4
5 can be trusted a lot

Institutional trust

How much confidence do you have in:

…the police?
…the health care system?
…banks?
…local merchants and business people?

1 No confidence at all
2 Not very much confidence
3 Quite a lot of confidence
4 A great deal of confidence

Obligations: help received

In the past month did anyone help you:

by doing domestic work, home maintenance or outdoor work?
by providing transportation or running errands?
by helping with child care?
by teaching, coaching or giving you practical advice?
by giving you emotional support?
by helping you in some other way?

Obligations: help given

In the past month did you help anyone:

by doing domestic work, home maintenance or outdoor work?
by providing transportation or running errands?

by helping with child care?
by teaching, coaching or giving you practical advice?
by giving someone emotional support?
by helping a person in some other way?
did you do unpaid volunteer work for any organization?
did you donate money or goods to any organization or charity?

1 yes
2 no

Information channels: relatives

In the last month, how often did you see relatives (outside of people you live with)?

In the last month, did you communicate with relatives by telephone?

1 not in the last month
2 once a month
3 a few time a month
4 a few times a week
5 every day

How many relatives do you feel close to?

1 1 or 2
2 3–5
3 6–10
4 11–20
5 more than 20

Information channels: friends

How many close friends do you have?
How may other friends do you have who are not relatives or close friends?

1 1 or 2
2 3–5
3 6–10
4 11–20
5 more than 20

In the last month, how often did you see your friends?
In the last month, how often did you communicate with your friends by telephone?

1 not in the last month
2 once a month
3 a few time a month
4 a few times a week
5 every day

Information channels: political participation

In the past 12 months, have you done any of the following activities:

…searched for information on a political issue?
…volunteered for a political party?
…expressed your views on an issue by contacting a newspaper or a politician?
…signed a petition?
…boycotted a product or chose a product for ethical reasons?
…attended a public meeting?
…participated in a demonstration or march?

1 yes
2 no

Information channels: civic participation

In the past 12 months, were you a member or participant in:

a union or professional association?
a political party or group?
a sports or recreation organization (such as hockey league, health club, golf club)?
a cultural, education or hobby organization (such as theatre group, book club, or bridge club)?
a religious-affiliated group (such as church youth group, choir)?
a school group, neighbourhood, civic or community association (such as PTA, alumni, block parents, neighbourhood watch)?
a service club or fraternal organization (such as Kiwanis, Knights of Columbus, the Legion)?
any other type of organization that you have not mentioned?

1 yes
0 no

Norms and sanctions

How safe do you feel from crime walking alone in your area after dark?

1 very unsafe
2 somewhat unsafe
3 reasonably safe
4 does not walk alone
5 very safe

When alone in your home in the evening or at night, do you feel:

1 very worried
2 somewhat worried

3 never alone
4 not at all worried

If you lost a wallet or purse that contained two hundred dollars, how likely is it to be returned with the money in it if it was found:

by someone who lives close by?
by a complete stranger?

1 not at all likely
2 don't know
3 somewhat likely
4 very likely

Belongingness

How would you describe your sense of belonging to:
...your local community?
...your province?
...Canada?

1 very weak
2 somewhat weak
3 don't know
4 somewhat strong
5 very strong

Appendix B: Coefficients and Standard Errors of Bootstrap Hierarchical Regression Model

Variables	Coef.	Std. err.	t	P > |t|	Conf interval	
Age	−0.0101439	0.002236	−4.54	0	−0.01455	−0.00574
Male	−0.0437977	0.01512	−2.9	0.004	−0.07361	−0.01398
Married	0.1682807	0.013712	12.27	0	0.141242	0.195319
Atlantic	0.0005923	0.018215	0.03	0.974	−0.03533	0.036511
Quebec	−0.013001	0.021074	−0.62	0.538	−0.05456	0.028555
Ontario	−0.0242927	0.01726	−1.41	0.161	−0.05833	0.009743
Prairie	−0.0274024	0.01942	−1.41	0.16	−0.0657	0.010893
Health	0.1285453	0.007092	18.13	0	0.114561	0.14253
Income	0.0044611	0.002752	1.62	0.107	−0.00097	0.009889
Unemployed	−0.0248472	0.018304	−1.36	0.176	−0.06094	0.011247
Mastery_scale	0.031246	0.001811	17.26	0	0.027676	0.034816
Trust_family	0.0624439	0.01364	4.58	0	0.035546	0.089341

Variables	Coef.	Std. err.	t	P > |t|	Conf interval	
Trust_neighbour hood	0.0112093	0.00728	1.54	0.125	−0.00315	0.025564
Trust_stranger	−0.010892	0.006762	−1.61	0.109	−0.02423	0.002442
Trust_police	0.0400792	0.009892	4.05	0	0.020573	0.059586
Trust_healthcare	0.0241841	0.0089	2.72	0.007	0.006635	0.041734
Trust_banks	0.0235579	0.008325	2.83	0.005	0.007142	0.039974
Trust_business	0.0214546	0.011182	1.92	0.056	−0.00059	0.043504
Rhelp_chores	0.0157004	0.013369	1.17	0.242	−0.01066	0.042064
Rhelp_ transportation	0.0042811	0.014273	0.3	0.765	−0.02386	0.032427
Rhelp_childcare	0.0008789	0.01598	0.06	0.956	−0.03063	0.032391
Rhelp_teaching	−0.0149689	0.01544	0.97	0.333	−0.04541	0.015475
Rhelp_emotion	−0.0672723	0.013823	−4.87	0	−0.09453	−0.04001
Rhelp_other	−0.0116746	0.021439	−0.54	0.587	−0.05395	0.030601
Ghelp_chores	0.0026329	0.012383	0.21	0.832	−0.02178	0.027051
Ghelp_ transportation	0.0110134	0.012106	0.91	0.364	−0.01286	0.034886
Ghelp_childcare	0.0244669	0.013143	1.86	0.064	−0.00145	0.050385
Ghelp_teaching	0.0075806	0.01401	0.54	0.589	−0.02005	0.035207
Ghelp_emotion	−0.0201869	0.013653	−1.48	0.141	−0.04711	0.006736
Ghelp_other	−0.0312004	0.016897	−1.85	0.066	−0.06452	0.002119
Ghelp_volunteer	0.0079876	0.014288	0.56	0.577	−0.02019	0.036163
Ghelp_donate	−0.0070713	0.015085	−0.47	0.64	−0.03682	0.022676
Relative_see	0.0043683	0.006127	0.71	0.477	−0.00771	0.01645
Relative_phone	−0.0077681	0.007298	−1.06	0.288	−0.02216	0.006624
Relative_close	0.0397616	0.005531	7.19	0	0.028856	0.050668
Friend_close	0.0178798	0.00693	2.58	0.011	0.004214	0.031546
Friend_other	0.0136832	0.006443	2.12	0.035	0.000978	0.026388
Friend_see	0.026618	0.006807	3.91	0	0.013194	0.040042
Friend_phone	0.0037556	0.00747	0.5	0.616	−0.01098	0.018486
Search_political	−0.0288868	0.013917	−2.08	0.039	−0.05633	−0.00144
Volunteer_political	0.0484995	0.038122	1.27	0.205	−0.02668	0.123674
Contact_ newsppaper	−0.0365304	0.019897	−1.84	0.068	−0.07577	0.002705
Sign_petition	0.0022113	0.013377	0.17	0.869	−0.02417	0.02859
Boycott_product	−0.0177564	0.015198	−1.17	0.244	0.04773	0.012214
Attend_meeting	−0.0207156	0.014142	−1.46	0.145	−0.0486	0.007173
Partcipate_ demonstra	−0.0053966	0.023462	−0.23	0.818	−0.05166	0.040869
Member_proforg	−0.0299317	0.011586	−2.58	0.01	−0.05278	−0.00709
Member_political	0.0405098	0.028646	1.41	0.159	−0.01598	0.096998
Member_sports	0.002438	0.012828	0.19	0.849	−0.02286	0.027734
Member_ education	−0.0092161	0.01514	−0.61	0.543	−0.03907	0.020639
Member_religious	0.0177512	0.015761	1.13	0.261	−0.01333	0.048831
Member_school	−0.0110948	0.01585	−0.7	0.485	−0.04235	0.020161
Member_service	0.0018436	0.021482	0.09	0.932	−0.04052	0.044206

Variables	Coef.	Std. err.	t	P > |t|	Conf interval	
Member_other	0.006251	0.024377	0.26	0.798	−0.04182	0.054321
Walk_alone	−0.0131691	0.006327	−2.08	0.039	−0.02565	−0.00069
Home_alone	0.0350363	0.018074	1.94	0.054	−0.0006	0.070677
Wallet_close	0.0097042	0.00723	1.34	0.181	−0.00455	0.023962
Wallet_stranger	0.0060467	0.006336	0.95	0.341	−0.00645	0.018541
Belong_community	0.064539	0.005706	11.31	0	0.053287	0.075791
Belong_province	0.0082137	0.006538	1.26	0.21	−0.00468	0.021107
Belong_Canada	0.0195731	0.006226	3.14	0.002	0.007297	0.03185
Constant	1.970661	0.095658	20.6	0	1.782028	2.159294

Number of observations = 15,660; Population size = 15,961,659; Replications = 200; Design df = 199; $F(61,139)$ = 34.10; Prob > F = 0.0000; R-squared = 0.1977

References

Allgood S (2009) Charity, impure altruism, and marginal redistributions of income. National Tax J 62:219–235

Allum N, Patulny R, Read S, Sturgis P (forthcoming) (2012) Re-evaluating the links between social trust, institutional trust and civic association in Europe. In: Stillwell J (ed) Understanding population trends and processes. Springer, New York

Argyle M (2001) The psychology of happiness, 2nd edn. Routledge, New York

Bjornskov C (2003) The happy few: cross-country evidence on social capital and life satisfaction. Kyklos 56:3–16

Bjornskov C (2006) The multiple facets of social capital. Eur J Polit Econ 22:22–40

Cialdini RB, Brown SL, Lewis BP, Luce C, Neuberg SL (1997) Reinterpreting the empathy-altruism relationship: when one into one equals oneness. J Pers Soc Psychol 73:481–494

Clift Gore E (2005) A place to belong: student agency in the social capital of a magnet high school. J Curriculum Supervision 20:271–297

Coleman JM (1988) Social capital in the creation of human capital. Am J Sociol 94:S95–S120

Dasgupta P (2005) Economics of social capital. Econ Rec 81:S2–S21

Diener E, Oishi S (2004) The nonobvious social psychology of happiness. Psychol Inq 16:162–167

Diener E, Suh EM, Lucas RE, Smith HL (1999) Subjective well-being: three decades of progress. Psychol Bull 125:276–302

Dolan P, Peasgood T, White M (2008) Do we really know what makes us happy? a review of the economic literature on the factors associated with subjective well-being. J Econ Psychol 29:94–122

Frey BS, Stutzer A (2002) What can economists learn from happiness research. J Econ Lit 40:402–435

Fujiwara T, Kawachi I (2008a) Social capital and health: a study of adult twins in the U.S. Am J Prev Med 35:139–144

Fujiwara T, Kawachi I (2008b) A prospective study of individual-level social capital and major depression in the United States. J Epidemiol Community Health 62:627–633

Furstenberg FF (2005) Banking on families: how families generate and distribute social capital. J Marriage Fam 67:809–821

Helliwell JF (2006) Well-being, social capital and public policy: what's new? Econ J 116:C34–C35

Hudson J (2006) Institutional trust and subjective well being across the EU. Kyklos 59:43–62
Lelkes O (2006) Knowing what is good for you: empirical analysis of personal preferences and the "objective good". J Socio-Economics 35:285–307
Leung A (2002) Delinquency, social institutions, and capital accumulation. J Inst Theor Econ 158:420–440
Maeroff GI (1998) Altered destinies: making life better for children in need. Phi Delta Kappan, Bloomington, 79:424–432
Maycock BR, Howat P (2007) Social capital: implications from an investigation of illegal anabolic steroid networks. Health Educ Res 22:854–863
Mayo J, Tinsley CH (2009) Warm glow and charitable giving: why the wealthy do not give more to charity? J Econ Psychol 30:490–499
Morrow V, Christensen P, O'Brien M (2002) Improving the neighbourhood for children. In: Christensen P, O'Brien M (eds) Children in the city: home, neighbourhood and community. Routledge Education, Milton Park, pp 162–183
Myers DG, Diener E (1995) Who is happy? Psychol Sci 6:10–19
Paldam M (2000) Social capital: one or many? definition and measurement. J Econ Surv 14:629–653
Parks-Yancy R, DiTomaso N, Post C (2008) Reciprocal obligations in the social capital resource exchanges of diverse groups. Humanity Soc 32:238–262
Paxton P (1999) Is social capital declining in the United States? a multiple indicator assessment. Am J Sociol 105:88–127
Peasgood T (2007) Does talking to our neighbours enhance our satisfaction with life? In: Proceedings of the paper presented at the meeting of the international conference of policies for happiness. Certosa di Pontignano, Siena
Powdthavee N (2008) Putting a price tag on friends, relatives, and neighbours: using surveys of life satisfaction to value social relationship. J Socio-Economics 37:1459–1480
Putnam RD (1995) Bowling alone: America's declining social capital. J Democracy 6:65–78
Putnam RD (2000) Bowling alone: the collapse and revival of American community. Simon and Schuster, New York
Rus A, Iglic H (2005) Trust, governance and performance: the role of institutional and interpersonal trust in SME development. Int Sociol 20:371–391
Statistics Canada (2004) General social survey 2003, Cycle 17—survey on social engagement in Canada: public use microdata file documentation and user's guide (Catalogue no. 12M0017GPE). Minister of Industry, Ottawa
Wilson W (1967) Correlates of avowed happiness. Psychol Bull 67:294–306

Chapter 14
Cultural Constructions of Happiness: Theory and Empirical Evidence

Yukiko Uchida, Vinai Norasakkunkit and Shinobu Kitayama

Abstract In a review of recent cross-cultural evidence on happiness and well-being, the authors identified substantial cultural variations in (1) cultural meanings of happiness, (2) motivations underlying happiness, and (3) predictors of happiness. Specifically, in North American cultural contexts, happiness tends to be defined in terms of personal achievement. Individuals engaging in these cultures are motivated to maximize the experience of positive affect. Moreover, happiness is best predicted by self-esteem. In contrast, in East Asian cultural contexts, happiness tends to be defined in terms of interpersonal connectedness. Individuals engaging in these cultures are motivated to maintain a balance between positive and negative affects. Moreover, happiness is best predicted by perceived embeddedness of the self in a social relationship. Directions for future research are discussed.

The present chapter is concerned with cross-cultural variations and similarities of happiness and subjective well-being. In the contemporary literature, subjective well-being is typically defined as an overall cognitive appraisal of the quality of one's own life (see e.g., Diener 2000 for a review). Happiness is an emotional concomitant to this overall judgment. Defined in this general way, happiness is likely to be universal and more or less equally valued across different cultures (e.g., Ryan et al. 1996; Ryff and Keyes 1995). Indeed, people everywhere are likely to prefer the desirable over the undesirable and the pleasant over the unpleasant (Diener et al. 1995a; Michalos 1991; Veenhoven 1991). However, it is also likely that exactly what constitutes the good and the valuable varies substantially across

Y. Uchida (✉)
Graduate School of Human and Environmental Studies,
Kokoro Research Center, Kyoto University, Sakyo-ku, Kyoto 606-8501, Japan
e-mail: yuchida@umich.edu; yukikou@educ.kyoto-u.ac.jp

V. Norasakkunkit
Minnesota State University, Mankato, MN, USA
Gonzaga University, Spokane, WA, USA

S. Kitayama
University of Michigan, Ann Arbor, MI, USA

A. Delle Fave (ed.), *The Exploration of Happiness*, Happiness Studies Book Series,
DOI: 10.1007/978-94-007-5702-8_14,

cultures (Diener and Suh 2000; Kitayama and Markus 2000). As a consequence, we may expect considerable cross-cultural variations in meanings of happiness (i.e., what might constitute happiness), motivations underlying happiness (i.e., what people might try to do to achieve happiness), and predictors of happiness (i.e., what factors might predict happiness).

14.1 Theory: Culture and Happiness

14.1.1 Cultural Perspective

In psychology, emotions have often been seen as universal and biologically determined (Ekman 1992). More recently, however, a number of culturally oriented psychologists have emphasized the critical role of public meanings (folk theories and common- sense) and practices (daily routines and scripts) in shaping emotions (Benson 2000; Bruner 1990, 1996; Kitayama 2002; Markus and Kitayama 1991a; Shweder and Sullivan 1993). These meanings and practices constitute local "ways of life", which as a whole define a culture (Bruner 1990).

These culturally oriented theorists have argued that emotions are not the direct outcome of physiological or neurological mechanisms. Rather, emotions are always situated and embedded in specific cultural contexts. Accordingly, they are fully saturated with cultural meanings (Kitayama et al. 2004b). This analysis implies, for example, that what happiness means might vary considerably across cultures (Diener and Suh 2000; Kitayama and Markus 2000). Thus, people in different cultures might categorize quite different sorts of positive events and experiences as instances of happiness. Underlying this cross-culturally divergent construal and experience of emotion is a set of culturally shared ideas about personhood—namely, these about what is the self, what self one would hope to be, and what social relations one should have with other selves.

14.1.2 Happiness in East and West

Markus and Kitayama (1991a, 2004; Kitayama and Markus 2000) have called ideas about personhood the cultural models or construals of self, and suggested that these models of self are implicated in all aspects of psychological processes evoked in social life including cognition, emotion, and motivation. Their analysis is informed by in-depth analyses of two broadly defined regions of the world, namely, European-American cultures and East Asian cultures. Although each cultural region is diverse by itself and, therefore, there is likely to be considerable within-regional variations, it remains to be the case that each of the two regions has historically shared substantial amount of pertinent ideas, practices, and social institutions.

Specifically, in European and North American cultures such as the American middleclass culture there is a strong belief in the independence and autonomy of the self. The self is believed to be the center of thought, action, and motivation. It is bounded and separate from other such selves. Social relations are quite important; yet, they are constructed in accordance with the fundamental assumption about the independence of each self. Specifically, they are based on choice of each self to enter such relations. These ideas are widely distributed in European-American cultural contexts and, in fact, they are quite instrumental in organizing daily practices, routine discourses and narratives, and institutions of these contexts.

Given the independent model, the most central aspect of the self is a set of internal attributes. Individuals are therefore highly motivated to find and affirm the positivity of these attributes. This implies that happiness in European-American cultures is likely to hinge critically on the affirmation of positive attributes of the self. Moreover, happiness itself is often construed as one of those internal attributes that are to be pursued and attained via personal striving. In other words, happiness is likely to be constructed as *personal achievement.*

In contrast, in East Asian cultures, there is a contrasting assumption about the connectedness and interdependence of self with others. The self-in-relationship-with-others is believed to be the locus of thought, action, and motivation. The symbolic boundary between the self and other such selves is blurred and constantly negotiated through social interaction. Personal selves are quite important; yet, they are constructed in accordance with the fundamental assumption about the interdependence of the selves involved. For example, in East Asian cultural contexts, strong personal egos appear to emerge through identification with significant others or rebellion against them, both of which involve an immersion into close interpersonal relations. Ideas about the interdependent nature of human being are quite widespread in East Asian cultures. Moreover, these ideas are often underlying the practices, daily routines, discourses and social institutions that, as a whole, define the social realities of these cultural contexts.

Individuals in East Asian cultural contexts are highly motivated to adjust and fit themselves to the pertinent social relations. Commitments to social roles, social obligations, and readiness to respond to social expectations are all manifestations of this socially oriented motivation for realizing an interdependent self (Morling et al. 2002; Weisz et al. 1984). This implies that happiness in East Asian cultures is likely to depend crucially on the realization of positive social relationship of which the self is part. Personal happiness often damages social relationship. For example, emphasizing a success of the self may lead to jealousy and envy by others. The personal form of happiness is therefore often perceived to be tainted and incomplete, and as a consequence, there is no strong desire to pursue personal happiness at the expense of social harmony. Instead, happiness is seen as an inter-subjective state that is grounded in mutual sympathy, compassion, and support. In short, happiness is constructed as *realization of social harmony* (Kitayama and Markus 2000).

The foregoing analysis offers some important implications regarding the nature of happiness in different cultural contexts. Specifically, recent evidence suggests that there are systematic cross-cultural differences in three domains, namely: (1) cultural meanings of happiness, (2) motivations underlying happiness, and (3) correlates of happiness. We now turn to a review of this empirical evidence.

14.2 Empirical Evidence

14.2.1 Cultural Meanings of Happiness

Happiness may be defined as a positive emotional state that is most general and, thus, not restricted to any specific circumstances or events (Kitayama et al. 1995a, 2000). Defined in this broad term, happiness is likely to be universal. Although happiness is experienced as unqualified, this experience itself is embedded in specific socio-cultural contexts and circumstances and, therefore, is likely to be highly contingent on these contexts and circumstances. In accordance with the foregoing analysis on culture and self, we propose that happiness is encompassed in a rich associative network that is largely culture dependent and, thus, cross-culturally variable.

Specifically, in North America happiness may most typically be construed as a state contingent on both personal achievement and positivity of the personal self. Negative features of the self and negative feelings are thus perceived to be a hindrance against positivity and happiness. In contrast, in East Asia happiness is likely to be construed as a state that is contingent on social harmony and, thus, on a balance among different selves in a relationship.

These cultural views of happiness are grounded in historically nurtured ideologies and religious ideas. It is easy, for example, to identify some close affinities between the European-American view of happiness as personal achievement and the Protestant worldview (Kitayama and Markus 1999). According to this worldview, individuals are predestined to be either "select" or "doomed" (Weber 1930). The belief in predestination, in turn, generates a strong desire for affirming the self as worthy, competent, true to the intent of the God and, thus, as "select". Affirmation of personal worthiness ("me" as smart, friendly, kind, etc.) may therefore serve as a quite effective buffer against anxiety of a negative prospect of the self as "doomed" (e.g., "me" as dumb, stupid, and ugly). Along with other ideas such as person as commodity, social relations as market, and personal choice as a God-given right, the Protestant view of personhood has historically encouraged the construal of happiness as personal achievement and as a state that is contingent on the affirmation of personal self.

Likewise, there are some close links between the East Asian view of happiness as realization of social harmony and certain Asian strands of ideas as revealed in Confucianism, Taoism, and Buddhism. All these ideologies and worldviews emphasize a holistic world order where everything is assumed to be connected with everything else. In particular, what is good in personal domains are often assumed to lead to certain social problems (Kitayama and Markus 1999; Suh 2002). There is an explicit recognition, for example, that a personal success may entail a negative consequence by inviting someone's jealousy. Likewise, what is bad personally is often seen as a cause for certain positive social consequences. A personal failure, for example, may be an opportunity for receiving social support and compassion from others. These dialectic views of the world in general and of happiness in particular, are part and parcel of the happiness as that results from social harmony and social balance.

In the recent years, some researchers have empirically investigated the culturally divergent meanings of happiness. These studies suggest that whereas in European-American cultures positivity and negativity are often seen as contradictory, in East Asian cultures they are seen as complementary. For example, Ji et al. (2001) presented Chinese and American participants with graphs representing either a linear or nonlinear trend and asked them to indicate which graph might best represent the change of happiness in the life. Whereas Chinese respondents were likely to choose a nonlinear graph, Americans were likely to choose a linear graph.

A similar point has been made in recent studies that examine cross-culturally different associations between positive and negative emotions. Bagozzi et al. (1999) measured the intensity of pleasant and unpleasant emotions and found that whereas these two types of emotions were negatively correlated in the U.S., they were positively correlated in China and Korea. Hence, Americans experience positive and negative emotions as bipolar opposites, but East Asians appear to experience these emotions in a more simultaneous fashion. Kitayama et al. (2000) found a similar pattern with a different measure. These researchers asked American and Japanese participants to report how frequently they experience some different types of positive and negative emotions. Some emotions were interpersonally engaging (e.g., friendly feelings, ashamed), but some others were interpersonally disengaging (e.g., pride, angry). Still some others were general ones that are much less specific in their antecedents and consequences (e.g., calm, elated, happy). The correlations between the positive and negative emotions are shown in Fig. 14.1. For the most part, they are highly negative in the U.S., but in Japan, most of them

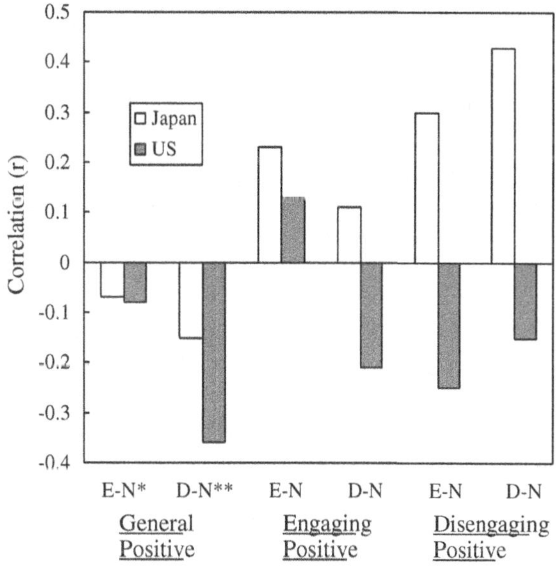

Fig. 14.1 Correlations between positive and negative emotions in Japan and the United States. (Fig. 2 in Kitayama et al. 2000)* Engaging negative,** Disengaging negative

are positive. On the basis of this evidence, Kitayama and colleagues speculate that people in independent cultures (e.g., Americans) may be motivated to maximize pleasant emotions and minimize unpleasant emotions, but people in interdependent cultures (e.g., Japanese) may be motivated to maintain a balance between positivity and negativity. We now turn to a discussion on cultural differences in motivation involved in happiness.

14.2.2 Motivations Underlying Happiness

If the meaning of happiness is cross-culturally divergent, it is likely that motivations implicated in happiness are also likely to vary. Specifically, in cultures where happiness is construed to be a personal achievement, individuals are likely to be highly motivated to affirm positive personal attributes as an integral part of their pursuit of happiness. In contrast, in cultures where happiness is construed to be a realization of social harmony, there will be little or no strong desire for achieving personal happiness insofar as there is an explicit recognition that doing so is likely to hinder the realization of social harmony and thus of a more socially grounded form of happiness (Diener et al. 1995b).

Quite consistent with this analysis, a growing body of literature on self-serving motivations across cultures has demonstrated that Americans are much more likely than Asians to seek and confirm positive internal attributes of the self. The cross-cultural difference in self-serving or self-enhancing motivations has been demonstrated in causal attribution of success and failure (Kitayama et al. 1995b), self-referent judgments (Heine and Lehman 1995; Markus and Kitayama 1991b), judgment about ingroup (Conner-Snibbe et al. 2003), and readiness to accept either positive or negative feedback about the self (Heine et al. 2001; Kitayama et al. 1997). Summarizing this literature, Hiene et al. (1999) note that the tendency toward positivity of the self is constantly reinforced and required to be a respectable cultural member in North America, but probably not in Japan.

Evidence also suggests that Americans are more likely than Asians to actively seek to achieve personal happiness. For example, Kitayama et al. (2000) found that Americans are far more likely than Japanese to reportedly experience positive emotions. This evidence is consistent with evidence from a large-scale international survey that shows that the average levels of subjective well-being are much higher in individualist cultures than in collectivist cultures (Diener et al. 1995). More recently, Oishi (2002) suggests that the cross-cultural difference observed here is unlikely to be due to any difference in actual emotional experience. Instead it seems to be due largely to a motivated tendency of Americans to remember positive emotional experience (see also Diener et al. 2002).

Instead of pursuing personal happiness, Asians may be strongly motivated to seek more communal or intersubjective forms of happiness. In a recent cross-cultural survey (Morling et al. 2003), Japanese pregnant women were more likely than their American counterparts to seek and rely on advice, opinions and judgments of their close others such as their partner, parents and doctors. Moreover, evidence suggests that individuals with Asian cultural heritage are more prone than those with European-American heritage to use expectations by close others in organizing their own behaviors (Iyenger and Lepper 1999). It is likely, then, that Asians are more likely than European-Americans to be concerned with approvals by close others (Kitayama et al. 2004a). It may then be predicted that care and support by close others are likely to be directly implicated in the happiness of many Asians.

14.2.3 Predictors of Happiness

Depending on the cultural meanings of happiness and the corresponding motivations underlying happiness, there should be quite divergent sets of factors that predict happiness in different cultures. Specifically, our analysis suggests that whereas in European-American cultures factors that are related to personal achievement should be the primary predictor of happiness, in East Asian cultures those that are linked to realization of social harmony should serve as much more reliable predictors of happiness.

The factors that are almost always correlated with happiness in North American cultures are personal accomplishment (e.g., Emmons 1986, 1991) and self-esteem (Campbell 1981; Diener and Diner, 1995; Diener et al. 1985). Taylor and Brown (1988) argue that perception of one's positivity, even when it is illusory, can contribute to mental health.

In other cultural contexts, especially in East Asian contexts, however, the significance of self-esteem is questionable. Diener and Diener (1995) investigated 31 countries and found that self- esteem is more strongly correlated with subjective well-being in individualistic (e.g., European-American) cultures than in collectivistic (e.g., East Asian) cultures. We have suggested that in these latter cultures, happiness is grounded in social harmony and connectedness. In these cultures, then, factors that are related to social harmony should more reliably predict happiness (Endo 1995; Kitayama and Markus 2000; Suh et al. 1998). Consistent with this reasoning, Suh et al. (1998) have shown that positive affect enhances the feelings of happiness in North America, but it is other, more social factors (such as adapting to social norms and fulfilling relational obligations), that increase happiness in East Asia. These social factors contribute to social harmony.

More recent studies have simultaneously examined both self-esteem and social harmony in predicting happiness. In one such study, Oishi and Diener (2001) asked European-American and Asian-American participants to list five important goals they hope to accomplish in the next one month. The participants then judged the extent to which each goal was related to independence (i.e., an attainment of one's own fun or enjoyment). One month later, participants evaluated their satisfaction with life during the past one month. They also judged the extent to which each goal had been achieved. As can be seen in Fig. 14.2, for the

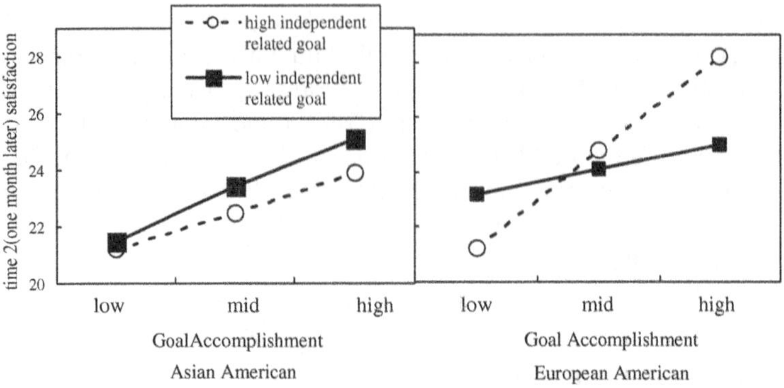

Fig. 14.2 Adjusted monthly satisfaction as a function of goal attainment for Asian Americans and European-Americans with high and low independent goal pursuit. (Modified version of Fig. 1 in Oishi and Diener 2001.)

European-American sample, happiness increased as more independent goals were achieved. In contrast, for the Asian sample, happiness increased instead as a function of the achievement of goals that were rated to be less independent (and therefore probably more interdependent, e.g., bringing happiness to parents).

A similar point has been made by Kitayama et al. (2000). These researchers asked American and Japanese participants to report how frequently they experience interpersonally engaging positive emotions—emotions resulting from social harmony (e.g., friendly feelings), interpersonally disengaging positive emotions—emotions resulting from personal achievement (e.g., pride, self-esteem), and general positive emotions (e.g., happy, calm, elated, relaxed). The correlations among these emotions, shown in Fig. 14.3, indicate that in the U.S., the reported frequency of experiencing general positive emotions (e.g., happy) is more closely correlated with the reported frequency of experiencing disengaging positive emotions (e.g., pride) than with the frequency of experiencing engaging positive

Fig. 14.3 Predicting general positive emotions as a function of engaging emotions (e.g., friendly feelings) and disengaging emotions (e.g., self-esteem) in the US and Japan. (The data reported in Kitayama et al. 2000.)

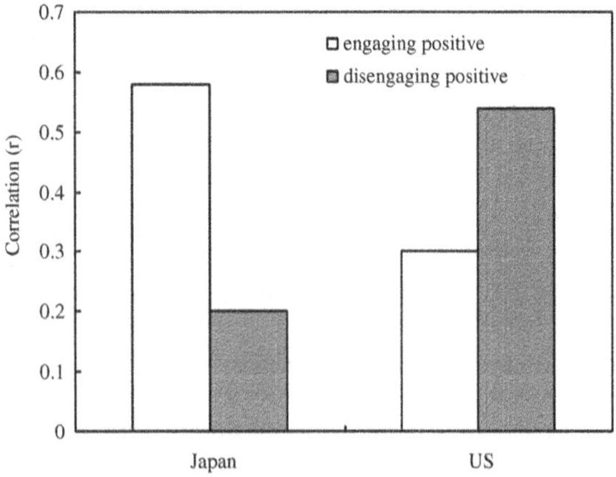

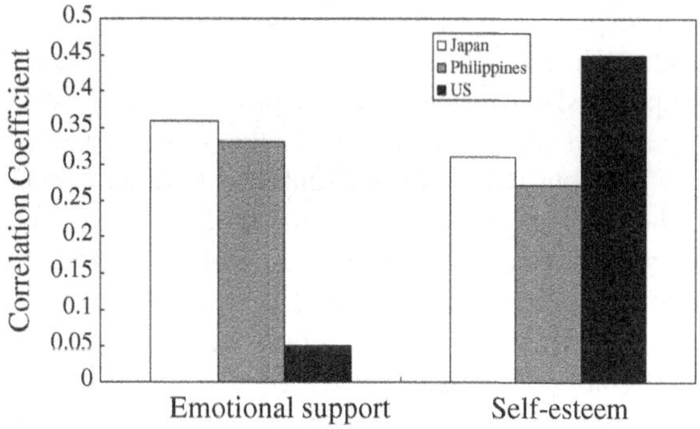

Fig. 14.4 Predictors of happiness in Japan, the Philippines, and the United States. (Modified version of Fig. 1 in Uchida et al. 2001)

emotions (e.g., friendly feelings). In contrast, in Japan, the frequency of experiencing general positive emotions was more strongly correlated with the frequency of experiencing engaging positive emotions than with the frequency of experiencing disengaging positive emotions. This data pattern suggests that whereas in European-American cultures personal achievement is a primary antecedent of happiness, in Asian cultures, social harmony may be more important.

Some other studies have made the same point with trait measures. In one of the earlier studies of this type, Kwan et al. (1997) examined the relative importance of self-esteem and relationship harmony to attain life satisfaction in Hong Kong and the U.S. These researchers found that in the U.S., self-esteem was the only predictor of life satisfaction, but in Hong Kong, relationship harmony was equally important in predicting life satisfaction. More recently, Uchida et al. (2001) examined both self-esteem and perceived emotional support from close others as potential predictors of happiness. These researchers found that in two different Asian cultures (Japan and the Philippines) both self-esteem and perceived emotional support were equally predictive of happiness. As predicted, however, in the U.S. happiness was reliably predicted only by self-esteem (see Fig. 14.4). It is likely that in independent cultures emotional supports such as encouragement, compassion, and sympathy often carry ambivalent meanings: They may signify both the worthiness of the self and the weakness of the self. As a consequence, emotional supports may contribute to happiness only to the extent that they do not threaten self-esteem. Quite consistent with this line of analysis, Uchida et al. (2001) found that in the American sample, the effect of perceived emotional support on happiness was entirely mediated by self-esteem.

14.3 Conclusions

In this chapter, we have shown some substantial cross-cultural variations in happiness. Overall, in European-American cultures happiness tends to be defined and experienced as personal achievement, in East Asian cultures it tends to be defined and experienced as a realization of social harmony. Three lines of research (i.e., cultural meanings of happiness, happiness-related motivations, and predictors of happiness) have converged to provide empirical evidence for this analysis. Yet, there are some significant issues that must be addressed in future work.

To begin with, Norasakkunkit and Kalick (2002) have argued that there is an inherent bias in the concept of well-being that is tacitly embedded in conventionally used measures of emotional distress in favor of independent goals and their social-cognitive constituents (i.e., self-enhancing tendencies). Given this standard, those with interdependent selves (i.e., Asians) may be judged to be less healthy and emotionally more distressed than those with independent selves (European-Americans). Future work in this area may benefit from an effort to develop culture-specific measures of happiness and well-being.

Moreover, it is important to extend the analysis of happiness to mental illness. Although it is likely that factors related to happiness and subjective well-being are also related to other aspects of health (i.e., physical health) and illness in general, this point has yet to be examined in cross-cultural contexts. It is well known that mental illness can take quite divergent forms across cultures (e.g., Al-Issa and Oudji 1998; Kirmayer 1991; Kleinknecht et al. 1997; Kleinman and Good 1985; Marsella et al. 1996). Correspondingly, effective strategies of health-related interventions may also be different. Thus, future work may seek to find the specific forms of interventions that are culturally appropriate and, thus, effective.

In conclusion, empirical work over the last decade has provided initial evidence for the hypothesis that happiness and well-being are significantly grounded in socio-cultural modes of being a person and interacting with others. This by no means denies universal underpinnings of happiness and well-being. However, it does mean that any adequate understanding of seemingly universal factors can never be complete without taking into account culture-dependent ways in which such factors are realized and allowed to shape happiness and well-being.

Acknowledgments Yukiko Uchida, Research Fellow of the Japan Society for the Promotion of Science, was supported by Grant-in-Aid for JSPS Fellows. Also, this research was supported by the 21st Century COE Program (D-2 to Kyoto University), MEXT, Japan and grants-in-aid from the Ministry of Science and Education, Japan.

References

Al-Issa I, Oudji S (1998) Culture and anxiety disorders. In: Kazarian S, Evans D (eds) Cultural clinical psychology: theory, research, and practice. Oxford University Press, Oxford, pp 127–151

Bagozzi RP, Wong N, Yi Y (1999) The role of culture and gender in the relationship between positive and negative affect. Cogn Emot 13:641–672

Benson C (2000) The cultural psychology of self: place, morality and art in human worlds. Routledge, Philadelphia

Bruner J (1990) Acts of meaning. University Press, Cambridge

Bruner J (1996) The culture of education. University Press, Cambridge

Campbell A (1981) The sense of well-being in America. McGraw-Hill, New York

Conner-Snibbe A, Kitayama S, Markus HR, Suzuki T (2003) They saw a game: a Japanese and American field study. J Cross Cult Psychol 34:581–595
Diener E (2000) Subjective well-being: the science of happiness and a proposal for a national index. Am Psychol 55:34–43
Diener E, Diener M (1995) Cross cultural correlates of life satisfaction and self-esteem. J Pers Soc Psychol 68:653–663
Diener E, Suh EM (eds) (2000) Cultural and subjective well-being. The MIT Press, Cambridge
Diener E, Emmons RA, Larsen RJ, Griffin S (1985) The satisfaction with life scale. J Pers Assess 49:71–75
Diener E, Diener M, Diener C (1995a) Factors predicting the subjective well-being of nations. J Pers Soc Psychol 69:851–864
Diener E, Suh EM, Smith H, Shao L (1995b) National differences in reported subjective well-being: why do they occur? Soc Indic Res 34:7–32
Diener E, Lucas RE, Oishi S, Suh EM (2002) Looking up and looking down: weighting good and bad information in life satisfaction judgement. Pers Soc Psychol Bull 28:437–445
Ekman P (1992) An argument for basic emotions. Cogn Emot 6:169–200
Emmons RA (1986) Personal strivings: an approach to personality and subjective well-being. J Pers Soc Psychol 51:1058–1068
Emmons RA (1991) Personal strivings, daily life events, and psychological and physical well-being. J Pers 59:453–472
Endo Y (1995) Argument of the self as an index of mental health. Jpn J Soc Psychol 11:134–144
Heine SJ, Lehman DR (1995) Cultural variation in unrealistic optimism: does the West feel more vulnerable than the East? J Pers Soc Psychol 68:595–607
Heine SJ, Lehman DR, Markus HR, Kitayama S (1999) Is there a universal need for positive self-regard? Psychol Rev 106:766–794
Heine SJ, Kitayama S, Lehman DR (2001) Cultural differences in self-evaluation: Japanese readily accept negative self-relevant information. J Cross Cult Psychol 32:434–443
Iyengar SS, Lepper MR (1999) Rethinking the value of choice: A cultural perspective on intrinsic motivation. J Pers Soc Psychol 76:349–366
Ji L, Nisbett RE, Su Y (2001) Culture, change, and prediction. Psychol Sci 12:450–456
Kirmayer LJ (1991) The place of culture in psychiatric nosology: Taijin kyofusho and DSM-III-R. J Nerv Ment Dis 179:19–28
Kitayama S (2002) Culture and basic psychological processes—toward a system view of culture: comment on Oyserman et al. (2002). Psychol Bull 128:89–96
Kitayama S, Markus HR (1999) Yin and yang of the Japanese self: the cultural psychology of personality coherence. In: Cervone D, Shoda Y (eds) The coherence of personality: social cognitive bases of personality consistency, variability, and organization. Guilford, New York, pp 242–302
Kitayama S, Markus HR (2000) The pursuit of happiness and the realization of sympathy: cultural patterns of self, social relations, and well-being. In: Diener E, Suh EM (eds) Cultural and subjective well-being. The MIT Press, Cambridge, pp 113–161
Kitayama S, Markus HR, Matsumoto H (1995a) Culture, self, and emotion: a cultural perspective on "self-conscious" emotions. In: Tangney JP, Fischer KW (eds) Self-conscious emotions: the psychology of shame, guilt, embarrassment, and pride. Guilford Press, New York, pp 439–464
Kitayama S, Takagi H, Matsumoto H (1995b) Cultural psychology of Japanese self: causal attribution of success and failure. Jpn Psychol Rev 38:247–280
Kitayama S, Markus HR, Matsumoto H, Norasakkunkit V (1997) Individual and collective processes in the construction of the self: self-enhancement in the United States and self-criticism in Japan. J Pers Soc Psychol 72:1245–1267
Kitayama S, Markus HR, Kurokawa M (2000) Culture, emotion, and well-being: good feelings in Japan and the United States. Cogn Emot 14:93–124
Kitayama S, Conner-Snibbe A, Markus HR, Suzuki T (2004) Is there any free choice? Self and dissonance in two cultures, Psychol Sci (in press)

Kitayama S, Mesquita B, Karasawa M (2004) The emotional basis of independent and interdependent selves: socially disengaging and engaging emotions in the US and Japan. University of Michigan, Michigan

Kleinknecht RA, Dale DL, Kleinknecht EE, Hiruma N (1997) Cultural factors in social anxiety: a comparison of social phobia symptoms and Taijin Kyofusho. J Anxiety Disord 11:157–177

Kleinman A, Good B (eds) (1985) Culture and depression: studies in the anthropology and cross-cultural psychiatry of affect and disorder. University of California Press, Los Angeles

Kwan VSY, Bond MH, Singelis TM (1997) Pancultural explanations for life satisfaction: adding relationship harmony to self-esteem. J Pers Soc Psychol 73:1038–1051

Markus HR, Kitayama S (1991a) Culture and the self: implications for cognition, emotion, and motivation. Psychol Rev 98:224–253

Markus HR, Kitayama S (1991b) Cultural variation in the self-concept. In: Goethals GR, Strauss J (eds) Multidisciplinary perspectives on the self. Springer, New York, pp 18–48

Markus HR, Kitayama S (2004) Models of agency: sociocultural diversity in the construction of action. In: Murphy-Berman V, Berman JJ (eds) Nebraska symposium on motivation, vol 49. Cross-cultural differences in perspectives on the self, University of Nebraska Press, Lincoln, pp 1–57

Marsella AJ, Friedman MJ, Gerrity ET, Scurfield RM (eds) (1996) Ethnocultural aspects of post-traumatic stress disorder: issues, research, and clinical applications. American Psychological Association, Washington

Michalos AC (1991) Global report on student well-being, vol 1–4. Springer, New York

Morling B, Kitayama S, Miyamoto Y (2002) Cultural practices emphasize influence in the United States and adjustment in Japan. Pers Soc Psychol Bull 28:311–323

Morling B, Kitayama S, Miyamoto Y (2003) American and Japanese women use different coping strategies during normal pregnancy. Pers Soc Psychol Bull 29:1533–1546

Norasakkunkit V, Kalick SM (2002) Culture, ethnicity, and emotional distress measures: the role of self-construal and self-enhancement. J Cross Cult Psychol 33:56–70

Oishi S (2002) The experiencing and remembering of well-being: a cross-cultural analysis. Pers Soc Psychol Bull 28:1398–1406

Oishi S, Diener E (2001) Goals, culture, and subjective well-being. Pers Soc Psychol Bull 27:1674–1682

Ryan RM, Sheldon KM, Kasser T, Deci EL (1996) All goals are not created equal: an organismic perspective on the nature of goals and their regulation. In: Gollwitzer PM, Bargh JA (eds) The psychology of action: linking cognition and motivation to behavior. The Guilford Press, New York, pp 7–26

Ryff CD, Keyes CLM (1995) The structure of psychological well-being revisited. J Pers Soc Psychol 69:719–727

Shweder RA, Sullivan MA (1993) Cultural psychology: who needs it? Annu Rev Psychol 44:497–523

Suh EM (2002) Culture, identity consistency, and subjective well-being. J Pers Soc Psychol 83:1378–1391

Suh EM, Diener E, Oishi S, Triandis HC (1998) The shifting basis of life satisfaction judgments across cultures: emotions versus norms. J Pers Soc Psychol 74(2):482–493

Taylor SE, Brown JD (1988) Illusion and well-being: A social psychological perspective on mental health. Psychol Bull 103:193–210

Uchida Y, Kitayama S, Mesquita B, Rayes JA (2001) Interpersonal sources of happiness: the relative significance in three cultures.In: Paper presented at 13th annual convention of the American Psychological Society, Toronto, Canada

Veenhoven R (1991) Is happiness relative? Soc Indic Res 24:1–34

Weber M (1930) The protestant ethic and the spirit of capitalism (trans: Parsons T) Routledge, New York

Weisz JR, Rothbaum FM, Blackburn TC (1984) Standing out and standing in: the psychology of control in America and Japan. Am Psychol 39:955–969

Chapter 15
Development as Happiness: The Subjective Perception of Happiness and UNDP's Analysis of Poverty, Wealth and Development

Jörg Schimmel

Abstract This chapter examines to what extent the concept of happiness is complementary to the United Nations Development Program's (UNDP) human development approach in the evaluation of poverty, wealth and development. The deconstruction of UNDP's discourse on and its measurement of these concepts show that its perspective is highly arbitrary. Poverty is exclusively defined as lack and state of ill-being, inferior to wealth regarded as a state of abundance and well-being. Development then becomes a teleological process trying to promote well-being through abundance. Yet, this external perspective of UNDP on well-being is questioned by the subjective perception of the individuals themselves. Happiness studies—which define happiness as the degree to which an individual judges the overall quality of his life-as-a-whole favorably—prove that higher levels of UNDP's development indicators are not necessarily better for subjective well-being. Despite methodological and conceptual problems, happiness studies discover that the individuals' perception of poverty, wealth and development can differ considerably from UNDP's perspective. Increased income, better objective health and higher levels of education do not automatically lead to greater happiness. Furthermore, additional dimensions essential for human happiness are detected by the research, yet not taken into account by UNDP. A country ranking comparison between the two approaches confirms the different visions of well-being. The integration of a happiness indicator in its analysis of poverty, wealth and development is thus indispensable for UNDP in order to correct its analytical and also practical approach to development.

Keywords Happiness • Subjective perception • Well-being • Indicator • Poverty • Human development • United Nations Development Program (UNDP)

J. Schimmel (✉)
United Nations Development Programme, PO Box 101, UN House, Deloitte Tower, Level 14, Douglas Street, Port Moresby, Papua New Guinea
e-mail: jorg.schimmel@undp.org

A. Delle Fave (ed.), *The Exploration of Happiness*, Happiness Studies Book Series, DOI: 10.1007/978-94-007-5702-8_15, © Springer Science+Business Media Dordrecht 2013

"If this development project had never been put into place here, we would be far happier!" [1].

15.1 Introduction

The above quotation shows a low degree of subjective appreciation of a development project, which perfectly fulfills UNDP's (United Nations Development Program) criteria of a successful development implementation. Nevertheless, the vision of well-being applied by the project contradicts the subjective perception of well-being of the targeted population. Despite development activities, people do not feel happier. The individual perception of happiness thus seems an important evaluation tool in the realm of development. This essay examines, to what extent happiness is a complementary device to UNDP's analysis of poverty, wealth and development.

For this purpose, the essay is divided into three main sections. The first section analyses UNDP's perspective on poverty, wealth and development through its discourse on and its measurement of these three concepts. The second section presents and defines the concept of happiness. The third section then applies the concept of happiness to the three dimensions of UNDP's development approach, detects and examines further dimensions important for human happiness, and eventually compares the country rankings of UNDP and happiness studies.

Happiness studies are still in their infancy. Consequently, the idea of measuring happiness often harvests mere smiles. However, although it might be too optimistic to integrate a happiness indicator in the realm of development immediately, a more extensive research on the subject can support this new initiative in the medium and long term, and stimulate thoughts and debates. We have to think the unthinkable and throw ourselves into the adventure in order to achieve progress in this vital field 'human happiness' for the research and the practice in the realm of development.

15.2 UNDP's Perspective on Poverty, Wealth and Development

The document which accounts best for UNDP's perspective on poverty, wealth and development is the annual Human Development Report (HDR), first introduced in 1990. This report represented a temporary peak of the expansion of new development paradigms throughout the 20th century, shifting the focus of development away from the purely monetary focus on the Gross Domestic Product (GDP). The origins of this movement can be traced back as far as 1954, when the "Report on International Definition and Measurement of Standards and Levels of Living" proposed twelve components in order to provide a comprehensive picture

---

[1] This comment was made in 2001 by a man affected by a local development project in the periphery of the city Sucre in Bolivia.

of standards of living and thus of poverty, wealth and development (Noorbakhsh 1998, p. 517). During the 1960s and 1970s, an increase in depletion of resources and environmental degradation brought about the so-called social indicator movement in its search for alternative measures that would provide a more comprehensive understanding of human well-being (Noorbakhsh 1998, p. 517). After the 1980s when structural adjustment programs—despite growing poverty and inequality—brought the economy back onto the centre stage of development, UNDP reacted to by integrating dimensions of human well-being which do not necessarily figure in income-related variables (Sen 1999, p. 14).

The conceptual framework of the HDR is the so-called capability approach. This theoretical backbone of UNDP seeks "to put people back into the centre of development" (UNDP quoted in Hicks 1997, p. 1283) recognizing that human beings are the primary ends as well as principal means of development (Anand and Sen 2000, p. 83). Development should hence be centered on enhancing their achievements, freedoms, and capabilities. "It is the life they lead that is of intrinsic importance, not the commodities or income that they happen to possess." (Anand and Sen 1994, p. 1) The ultimate aim is human well-being. According to the capability approach, this well-being is achieved through a process of expanding the real freedoms that people enjoy (Sen 1999, p. 3). Freedom is intrinsically good and thus an objective for the development process. It is a "constitutive role of development" (Sen 1999, p. 36). At the same time, "development as freedom" (Sen 1999, p. 36) changes the individual from an object to a subject and agent of this process, which can shape its own destiny instead of being primarily a passive recipient of the benefits of cunning development programs (Sen 1999, p. 11). Freedoms hence also have an instrumental role of development (Sen 1999, p. 36).

This approach puts human efforts, skills and talents, i.e. human capital, above physical capital (Anand and Sen 2000, pp. 83/84), and hence human development above economic development. The latter's role in development is not lost, but it has changed. Instead of being the primary end of development, economics is one of the principal means to achieve human well-being and happiness. Human development is thus motivated by the search for freedom, dignity and well-being of individuals in all societies (Fukuda-Parr 2002, p. 4).

This conceptual framework, and thus UNDP's enlarged vision on wealth, poverty and development, merits great recognition and must be considered a major and successful leap in development analysis and politics. Yet, at the same time, it leads to a very particular vision of poverty, wealth and development, as UNDP's discourse on and its measurement of the three concepts illustrate.

15.2.1 Discourse

A discourse always represents a choice of words which intrinsically implies a way of looking at, feeling and understanding the world. It is never neutral but secretly carries an epistemology. A deconstruction of UNDP's discourse on poverty, wealth and development thus detects its *Weltanschauung* concerning these concepts.

UNDP equates poverty with disease, high infant mortality, low life expectancy, malnutrition, hunger, lack of access to water, education, knowledge, public and private resources, housing, clothes, and security (UNDP 2005)—in other words with lack and deficiency. It contemplates exclusively what poor people do *not* have and what they are *not*. Hence, poverty is an anomaly compared to a standard norm seen as natural, i.e. it is denaturalized. In terms of happiness this means that poor people are unhappy.

The natural norm of reference to which poverty is compared emerges out of UNDP's ideally developed individual, which is "affluent, healthy and well educated individual" (Ryten 2000, p. 7). This state of reference is one of abundance, i.e. the state of wealth, a state that allows for individual well-being.

This dichotomy between the victims of poverty and deficiency which suffer from ill-being on the one side, and the wealthy, modern, western, scientific, bureaucratic people enjoying well-being on the other (Grillo and Stirrat 1997, p. 13) follows a clear hierarchy, which judges poverty an inferior state of life than wealth.

Based on this perspective UNDP deducts the concept of development, which it sees as a process from the inferior state of poverty and ill-being towards the superior state of wealth and well-being. Development is thus a teleological process according to which, in terms of well-being, quantity is quality, i.e. *more* is automatically *better*, and maximized indicators necessarily mean optimized well-being.

UNDP does include into the HDR the perception of poverty by the poor and also the phenomenon of the 'new poverty' in developed countries. This enlarges the concepts providing individual definitions from outside UNDP. However, this recognition is still based on the same dichotomy of poverty, deficiency and ill-being on the one side, and wealth, abundance and well-being on the other.

15.2.2 Measurement

Concerning the measurement of poverty, wealth and development, UNDP's main indicator, the Human Development Index (HDI), reflects the same *Weltanschauung*.

This indicator reflects the mathematical average of three human development dimensions (UNDP 2005, p. 352) and is presented on a scale from zero to one, one being the perfect state of human development. One dimension is the decency of the living standard measured through the GDP per capita. A second dimension is health, measured in terms of life expectancy at birth. The third dimension is education, calculated through adult literacy—for two thirds—and the average school enrolment of adults above 25 years—for one third. This composition mirrors UNDP's arbitrary perspective on poverty, wealth and development.

First, its reductionist approximation through a simple average (Ryten 2000, p. 3) suggests that a perfectly developed individual is about 16 years old, affluent, healthy, well educated, has a given life expectancy at birth and an income attributed independently of age, has no sex and no occupation, and lives nowhere and everywhere in a country (Halis 1994, p. 2). This state of development is the norm of reference against which the other individuals are measured. The bigger the discrepancy to this state of development, the poorer the individual is considered. UNDP's perspective of dichotomy becomes evident.

Second, UNDP has chosen minimum and maximum values for each of the three human development dimensions (UNDP 2005, p. 352) which form the mathematical basis. For life expectancy, 25 and 85 years were chosen, for literacy and school enrolment 0 and 100 % respectively, and concerning the income component, 100 and 40,000 US$ form the determination points. If those points change, the HDI changes as well and thus puts countries further away or closer to the development optimum. In 1991, by choosing 71 instead of 75 years of life expectancy, China would have improved her index from 0.72 to 0.78 (Kelley 1991, p. 318).

These values represent thus a norm of reference. The level of poverty is defined in comparison to the highest possible end points. Hence, the HDI is a 'catch-up indicator' which makes operational sense only for those far away from these end points. The state of development of those close to these optimum values is considered as adequate (Veenhoven 2004, p. 15). The higher the numerical level of the HDI, the better it is considered for people's well-being. But the fact that UNDP has situated the norm of reference high increases the likelihood that individuals and countries fall short of the norm and are thus categorized as poor.

The only dimension, where UNDP agrees that *more* is not unlimitedly *better* for individual well-being is the variable of income. UNDP does take into account a diminishing utility of income from 5,120 US$ upwards. For example, if an income rises by 2,000 US$ from 3,120 US$ to 5,120 US$, the IDH rises by 0.1286. If it rises by the same amount but from 5,120 US$ to 7,120 US$, the HDI rises only by 0.0057. An increased income does thus not proportionally contribute to human development.

A third problem that UNDP faces is the fact that it has selected three human development dimensions, and thus excludes others which might also be important for the concept, such as human rights and political participation (Fukuda-Parr 2002, pp. 5–6), inequalities (Kelley 1991, p. 320), gender issues (Bardhan and Stephan 2000, pp. 191–195), the environment (Neumeyer 2001, pp. 104–114) as well as good governance and corruption. However, for UNDP these other dimensions are either not important, or they are supposed to be indirectly represented through the income variable. Yet, by reducing human development to only three dimensions, UNDP largely misses out on on the multidimensionality of poverty and wealth (Rahman et al. 2005, p. 3). It is true that, since 1991, UNDP has increasingly integrated other dimensions in the HDR (UNDP 2005, pp. 221–222), but they have not been included in the HDI.

Despite its successful extension of the development perspective, UNDP remains too selective in its HDI and thus provides an arbitrary image of an ideal state of development and thus of poverty and wealth, ill-being and well-being. Certainly, the HDI as well as any other kind of externally defined indicator on well-being will never be able to avoid their partiality, incompleteness and reflection of the values of its creators. But this means, as long as people are not directly asked for their opinion, UNDP's perspective on ill- and well-being might not necessarily correspond to their subjective perception of these concepts.

This is where happiness studies become important. They can help identify whether people's individually perceived level of well-being correspond to the one identified externally by UNDP. If perceptions diverge, happiness studies represent a complementary device for UNDP's analysis of wealth, poverty and development and consequently its perspective on ill- and well-being. The degree of correspondence between UNDP's perception and subjective perceptions of well-being—from now on called happiness—is examined now (for an overview, refer to Table 15.1 at the end of the essay). First, however, happiness has to be defined more precisely.

15.3 Happiness: The Concept, Its Methodology and Its Problems

The reflection on happiness is as old as humanity itself. Herodotus and Aristotle theorized about *eudemonia* as the best possible and flourishing life (Veenhoven 1984, p. 15), Thomas Aquinas and the Christian discourse in general defined it as "proximity to God" (Diener Suh 1999, p. 434). As different as the understanding of the concept was, happiness was commonly treated as *happ* (luck), i.e. as being determined by a force outside the human being hardly to be influenced (McMahon 2006, p. 7). This changes with Enlightenment which put forward the conviction that the individual is responsible and wise enough to chose their own destiny without the a dependence on a king or God. Happiness became thus a concept attainable for all that could be reached in the 'here' and 'now'. The fact that "we can be happy, we will be happy, we should be happy" (McMahon 2006, p. xii) turned happiness into a value of society and laid the basis for our modern welfare state.

Yet, throughout history confusion exists around the terms happiness, subjective well-being, life satisfaction, and quality of life. This confusion has continued in the scientific debate and consensus has never emerged (Veenhoven in Strack et al. 1991, p. 8). However, whilst there might be differences of meaning, for the purpose of this essay these concepts are used interchangeably. Happiness is then defined as: "degree to which an individual judges the overall quality of his life-as-a-whole favorably" (Veenhoven 1984, p. 22). The degree is measured on a scale from zero to ten, ten being the highest degree attainable.

Happiness can be measured for life-as-a-whole but also for the various domains of life, such as work, social relationships etc. Important is to approach research with the open happiness question in order to avoid any biased predetermination of domains and thus allow for a maximum of subjectivity (Veenhoven in Karma and Karma 2004, p. 298). Furthermore, happiness consists of a "hedonic level" (Veenhoven 1991, p. 2) on the one side, and of a "level of contentment" (Veenhoven 1984, p. 27) on the other. While the former represents the mood of the moment, which is evaluated through unconscious cognitive activity, the latter is happiness in the long term, which is judged by a conscious, voluntary cognitive activity including past, present and future (Layard 2005, p. 74). Happiness is thus a global term which contains people's different evaluations concerning their lives, the events affecting them, their bodies and brains, and their living conditions (Diener 2005, p. 4) However, research has shown that the influence of external factors, such as living conditions, is far more important for individual happiness than internal factors, such as personality (Diener 1984, p. 565).

It is obvious that this complex and rather vague concept of happiness provokes methodological and conceptual problems which have to be taken into account.

Concerning the methodology, the validity of the answers is questionable. People might never think about happiness as such and thus not have an opinion at all. Their answers might also reflect rather desires rather than reality, leading to self-defense or cliché answers. However, research proves that people do think about happiness regularly and that they have a rather definitive idea of what happiness is (Veenhoven in Karma and Karma 2004, p. 298). Some distortion can be observed (Ibid.), especially through a general overrepresentation of happiness and a "sense of relative superiority" (Heday and Wearing 1988, p. 497). But the influence is generally very weak.

As far as the credibility of the results is concerned, people fear that the data might not be stable enough through time since happiness depends on mood swings (Veenhoven 2004, p. 19). Research, however, proves a high stability in case of repetition (Veenhoven 1984, p. 41). Also, people suspect measurement errors (Veenhoven in Karma and Karma 2004, p. 298) and interview biases (Veenhoven 1984, p. 55). This phenomenon does certainly influence the results. Yet, it is a phenomenon common to all social sciences, not happiness studies exclusively.

The biggest problem seems to be the comparability of happiness between individuals and countries. Individuals might have different scales of happiness in mind. A degree of six out of ten might mean different things to different people. Moreover, people can perceive objectively different situation as identical or vice versa (A. Parducci quoted in Rojas 2004, p. 10). However, these doubts are not confirmed by happiness research. The individual experience of happiness seems to be similar for everyone, just like phenomena such as hunger and pain (Veenhoven in Karma and Karma 2004, p. 299).

Concerning comparison between countries, critiques refer to language biases or cultural differences. Americans might generally declare themselves happier than Japanese people, whose society underlines modesty (Frey and Stutzer 2001, pp. 33/34). Some studies in bilingual countries showed no linguistic bias whilst others prove the contrary. Research findings are not yet uniform.

As far as conceptual problems with happiness in general are concerned, critiques blame happiness to be a Western ideology (Bruckner 2000). However, first of all, it is a universal concept. Certainly, its content might vary—happiness in the eyes of a Buddhist is different from happiness perceived by an Islamic fundamentalist and by utilitarian Bentham—but the concept as such is universally valid. Second of all, an ideology assumes the potential to attain a perfect state of happiness. This, however, will never be the case. Unhappiness will always remain prominent; happiness can thus never be absolute. Moreover, a certain degree of unhappiness might be important to appreciate happiness.

It is true however, that happiness can be dangerous, if it is pursued as the only value of society. Dictatorial regimes, for example, can base their legitimacy on the happiness of society.

Lastly, there is a problem with the geographic focus of happiness research which deals almost exclusively with happiness in developed countries. The deficit of research on developing countries implies not only a lack of rich information, but also obstructs a comparative analysis on happiness on the international level.

Happiness studies are not free of problems. It is obvious that individual cognitive processes are highly complex and thus far from being understood. Also, the concept of happiness as such is confronted with heavy critiques. Some doubts cannot be discarded. On the other hand, many critiques are proved wrong by this research. These observations have to be taken into account. They can contribute to a flourishing debate. Unfortunately, critiques have led more or less automatically to the refusal of the concept of happiness as a whole. While this concept is still in its infancy, it merits the benefit of the doubt. The observations to follow on happiness studies and their perspective on poverty, wealth and development illustrate that these studies have a strong case and need to be integrated a lot more in the realm of development.

15.4 Application of 'Happiness' in the Analysis of Poverty, Wealth and Development

In order to illustrate the differences between UNDP's and the happiness studies' perspective on poverty, wealth and development, this chapter first examines the three human development dimensions from both angles and then considers additional dimensions that seem to be important for individual happiness.

15.4.1 Income and Happiness

The income component can be divided into GDP and personal income. As we have seen, for both types UNDP suggests a positive correlation between higher revenue and happiness, though with diminishing utility. Happiness studies, on the contrary, give a far more nuanced account of this relation.

Concerning GDP, they find out that this measure counts disaster positively. For example, natural disasters, criminality and divorce—despite their negative impact on happiness—contribute through fixing measures to an increase in GDP. UNDP's economic hero is thus a terminal cancer patient who is going through a costly divorce, and the happiest event is an earthquake or a hurricane (Cobb et al. 1995, p. 65). Furthermore, GDP does not include goods and services that do not pass through the market (Lane 2000, p. 104), such as work in households or communities (Association Redefining Progress 2005). Yet, this economy of love, compassion, reciprocity and solidarity (F. Brancho in Karma and Karma 2004, p. 434) is highly important for human happiness. GDP makes no distinction between the desirable and the undesirable, or costs and gains in terms of human happiness (Cobb et al. 1995, p. 60). This observation undermines UNDP's conviction that the maximum of income is necessarily the optimum for happiness.

As far as personal income is concerned, happiness studies detect a similar phenomenon. The "Easterlin paradox" (Layard 2005, p. 3) discovers that in the United States and in Western Europe, despite a doubling in personal income since 1945, the level of individual happiness had hardly or not at all increased. Sometimes it had even diminished (Easterlin 1995, p. 38). A study of Switzerland, for example,—a country categorized by UNDP with a high level of human development and with the 5th position concerning PIB per capita—shows a generally positive relation between income and happiness. However, it also reveals that this relation is not linear and sometimes even negative. The richest quintile, for example, is less happy than the quintile before (Leu et al. in Stutzer 2004, pp. 89–109). Psychologists explain this paradox with three theories. First, the theory of aspiration states that a rise in living standards increases personal aspirations in income. Hence, monetary needs and desires can never be fully satisfied (Easterlin 2001, p. 481). Consequently, happiness rises less rapidly, the higher personal income is. Second, the theory of social comparison is based on the observation that the human being is a social animal. Our desires and pleasures thus have their origin in society. We measure them in relation to society; we don't measure them in relation to objects that serve for their gratification (Karl Marx quoted in Frey and Stutzer 2003, p. 11). When this social norm of reference rises and personal income stays the same, the individual is more likely to feel "relatively deprived", even though its personal situation has not changed (Runciman 1966, p. 11). Given the human desire to be relatively superior to others (Heady and Wearing, 1988), this social comparison is generally made upwards (Stutzer 2004, p. 91)—i.e. with those members of society with whom the individual still has to catch up—and hence leads to so-called "frustrated achievers" (Graham 2004, p. 13) with a lower level of happiness. Third, the theory of adaptation reveals that individuals adapt to their income and thus always needs an increase in order to satisfy their needs and desires. This "hedonic treadmill" (Layard 2005, p. 48) renders joy a mere transitory state (Stutzer 2004, p. 91) and lowers individual happiness.

In a happiness study in Mexico—a country very close to UNDP's category of medium human development (UNDP 2005, p. 220)—55 % of the respondents are 'poor' by UNDP definitions. However, only around 5 % declared that they did not have a happy life. The study did reveal a positive correlation between personal income and happiness, yet, this relation was not linear. The rate of increase in happiness diminished with a rising personal income (Rojas 2004, p. 7). The study detects an extremely high percentage of "happy poor" people and a relatively high rate of "unhappy rich" people (Ibid., p. 5). The explanation for the Mexican case might lie in the theory of basic needs. This approach assumes that not everything is relative. Some needs are fundamental to human life, such as subsistence, protection and affection (Nic Marks in Karma and Karma 2004, p. 322). Their satisfaction increases individual happiness. The high rate of happy poor people seems to suggest that these individuals are happy to be able to satisfy their absolute needs. They do not compare themselves to other members of society whose standard of living they aspire to. The relative character of income seems to become more important for the unhappy rich people.

These studies challenge UNDP's perspective of an exclusively positive relation between income and happiness and suggest a relation of a far more complex nature. There are people whose life, according to UNDP, is marked by poverty and ill-being. Yet they declare themselves highly happy. Equally, there are people whose life, according to UNDP, is coined by wealth and well-being. However, they declare themselves highly unhappy (Stutzer 2004, p. 105). This counts for developed as well as for developing countries. While happiness studies confirm UNDP's perspective for the people who are unable to cover their basic needs, they reveal at the same time that people's picture of poverty, wealth and thus development does hence not necessarily correspond to that perspective. An integration of a happiness indicator could thus provide UNDP with valuable information on whether its development analysis and policy contribute to people's well-being.

15.4.2 Health and Happiness

UNDP is convinced that more health increases individual happiness. This is entirely confirmed by happiness studies. However, the latter make a distinction of two levels of analysis unknown to UNDP: the distinction between objective and subjective health. Objective health—the state of health as it is analyzed by an outside expert—is positively correlated with individual happiness. Life-threatening diseases such as cancer, HIV/AIDS, hepatitis and malaria, and diseases obstructing a normal functioning of the human body, such as rheumatism, generally have a negative impact on happiness (Diener and Seligman 2004, p. 13). Yet, this correlation is relatively low, probably because of human adaptation to lots of diseases (Layard 2005, p. 69). The variable that is very highly correlated with happiness is subjective health, i.e. the state of health as it is perceived by the concerned individual itself. Neurotics, for example, remember more respiratory symptoms than they had reported on a daily basis before (Diener et al. 1999, p. 287). This variable thus includes the physical condition and the emotional adaptation which explains why an individual can feel good despite a serious disease, and why it can feel bad despite objectively attested good health. Happiness studies hence offer an additional level of analysis important for human well-being.

A second hypothesis of UNDP is that a rising level of development increases the state of health, since it facilitates the prevention of disease, not least because of financial means. Indeed, a high level of human development does facilitate prevention through education or increased income, which allowed eradicating diseases such as tuberculosis, cholera and typhus in the developed countries. However, these developed countries witness a new form of disease, the so-called "luxury diseases", which appear exclusively, increasingly widespread and more frequently in developed countries. Examples are depression, eating disorders, and heart attacks (Diener and Seligman 2004, pp. 13–16). Hence a higher level of development as seen by UNDP simultaneously provokes this new type of disease among the rich and well-educated.

Moreover, a high level of economic development does not automatically guarantee a good state of health. There is, for example, no demonstrated link between the level of GDP and the mortality rate of a country. The USA witnesses a high economic growth but at the same time a high rate of premature mortality. Japan, Switzerland, France and Germany, on the other hand, have a weaker economic growth but also a lower rate of premature mortality.[2] Similarly, countries like Vietnam, China, Sri Lanka, and Costa Rica are economically poor, but their populations are characterized by a high level of health (Sen 1999, p. 6). Contrary to the assumption of UNDP, healthy populations and populations characterized by a low level of health can thus be found everywhere on the GDP scale.

Third, UNDP exclusively measures life expectancy, but ignores the quality of the years lived. Happiness studies, on the contrary, suggest a measurement of happy life years (Veenhoven in Karma and Karma 2004, p. 304), an approach that adds the quality of years lived to UNDP's quantitative perspective.

Lastly, happiness studies also reveal that happiness has a major influence on health. For example, they show that happy people show extremely little sign of mental disease (Diener and Seligman 2004, p. 16), that patients with an identical level of objective health lived longer when their self-confidence was higher (Layard 2005, p. 23), and that optimists live about eight years longer than pessimists (T. Maruta quoted in Diener and Seligman 2004, p. 14). The relationship between health and happiness is thus bidirectional; a phenomenon not considered by UNDP.

UNDP's position concerning health and well-being is incomplete. Undoubtedly, increased health does raise the level of well-being. But happiness research shows, that contrary to UNDP's assumption more development does not necessarily lead to happiness and money does not buy health. Moreover, they add the quality of years lived as well as the mutual relationship between health and happiness to UNDP's perspective, two crucial factors for human happiness. Happiness studies then represent a complementary tool for UNDP to analyze its perspective and policy of well-being.

15.4.3 Education and Happiness

UNDP's human development approach suggests that a higher level of education automatically leads to higher level of well-being, since it facilitates employment, revenue, creativity, and self-confidence. Happiness studies, however, provide a

[2] Jean-Daniel Rainhorn in his presentation in the margins of the seminar 'Le défi social du développement, mondialisation, croissance, pauvreté et inégalités', Institut Universitaire d'Etudes de Développement, Geneva, 9 February 2006.

more nuanced perspective. They do confirm that education contributes to happiness, especially when people enjoy little or no education. Yet once basic needs are met, the correlation becomes more multifaceted. Especially high levels of education can cause unhappiness. The three relative theories presented in relation to the income component also explain the phenomenon in terms of education. The higher the level of education, the more likely people are to have increased aspirations, social comparisons and adaptation which lower the level of happiness (Michael Argyle in Kahnemann et al. 1999, p. 355). Moreover, if job offers do not match the level of education, frustration can emerge and have detrimental effects on happiness (ILO 2005, p. 321). Beyond the satisfaction of basic needs, happiness research suggests, contrary to UNDP's assumption, that the correlation between education and well-being is not linear and sometimes even negative.

Also, happiness studies, as opposed to UNDP, take into consideration that the causality between education and happiness is bidirectional. Happiness can increase the individual performance in education. Happier people have, for example, better results in school, a greater mental efficiency, higher autonomy and self-confidence (Veenhoven 1984, p. 200).

UNDP is right to consider education to be one of the three main determinants of well-being, especially at low levels of human development. Yet, happiness studies with their more nuanced approach serve as an important device to find out in how far UNDP's vision and the people's subjective perception of well-being correspond.

15.4.4 Other Dimensions Determining Individual Happiness

UNDP not only ignores important findings on the relation between the three human development dimensions and well-being. It also completely disregards other dimensions that seem to determine individual happiness, as studies have found out. These include external factors, i.e. domains and conditions of life external to the individual, and internal factors, i.e. traits of character and personality of the individual itself. The following paragraphs thus illustrate that UNDP's development analysis and policy could and should be completed through the integration of a happiness indicator.

15.4.5 External Factors

15.4.5.1 Social Relations

Human beings are social beings and thus prefer to be in company rather than being all by themselves. Happiness studies show that no or bad social relationships have a strong negative impact on happiness (Campbell 1981, p. 112). Equally, strong and positive social relations provide personal ties, support and feelings of belonging and identity (Diener and Seligman 2004, p. 18). Receiving these elements, but also to giving them to others increases individual happiness (E. Fromm in ibid.). It is hence little surprising, that most individuals that declare themselves happy in the studies on happiness have good social relationships (Diener and Seligman 2004, p. 18). Especially marriage goes hand in hand with happiness (Frey and Stutzer 2003, p. 18). But the causality between social relations and happiness is bidirectional. Studies show that happier people are more sociable (M.R. Cunningham in Diener and Seligman 2004, p. 20). Despite this great importance of this dimension, UNDP does not take it into account. The three human development dimensions might represent an increased capacity to enter into social relations. However, the example shown that a divorce increase GDP illustrates that the relationship is far more complex.

15.4.5.2 Work

The idea of human development is obsessed by the idea of full employment, where people are employed at any price without questioning the quality of those jobs (Bruckner 2000, p. 195). However, the quality of work is crucial for individual happiness. The determinants of happiness with work are intrinsic and extrinsic and include the opportunity to have control over personnel, the application of one's capacities, the existence of objectives, the variety of tasks, the transparency and the sharing of information, the access to a revenue, the physical security, the supportive supervision, the opportunity to interpersonal contact, the social status of the occupation (Peter Warr in Kahneman et al. 1999, pp. 396/397), and the contribution to larger society (Layard 2005, p. 62). Unemployment, on the contrary, fosters higher rates of depression and suicide (A. Kposow in Diener and Seligman 2004, p. 12).

Moreover, the causality between work and happiness is of bidirectional character. Happy employees have a better performance at work, they are more productive, more punctual and more cooperative, and they show less absenteeism (Diener and Seligman 2004, pp. 10–12).

UNDP, however, reduces the correlation between work and well-being to the three dimensions of human development, which indirectly represent the dimension of work, since income, education and health are important preconditions or results of an employment. Yet, happiness studies show that the correlation is more complicated and that this dimension should be considered in the evaluation of well-being.

15.4.5.3 Political and Societal Conditions

The political and societal environment of an individual has great effects on his/her level of happiness. Inequalities, for example, have a considerable detrimental effect on happiness. Given the relative character of the individual living standards which has been shown, it is not surprising that inequalities foster a feeling of deprivation and thus unhappiness. These inequalities can be endogenous to society—such as economic, cultural, ethnic or sexual minorities (Veenhoven 1984, p. 158)—or exogenous, i.e. new living standards formerly unknown are introduced from the outside (Runciman 1966, p. 24). Also, there can be a different tolerance level of inequalities. One study found that this level is considerably higher in the US than in Europe (Alesina et al. 2001, p. 1). It might also be less important in places where basic needs are not satisfied. Despite the importance of inequalities for happiness and the complex nature of the relation, UNDP disregards this dimension.

The same observation can be made concerning political stability. Political troubles, violence, civil disorder and war are negatively related with happiness. Given the physical and psychological hardship, this is little surprising (Veenhoven 1984, p. 167). Yet UNDP does not integrate this dimension in its development indicators. True, one could consider its human development dimensions indirect indicators for political stability. However, born in mind that disaster is counted positively in the GDP these indicators might be misleading.

Another dimension strongly related with happiness is human rights (Diener and Seligman 2004, p. 6). Individuals who live in countries where human rights are recognized declare themselves generally happier than individuals who live in other countries (Veenhoven 1984, p. 160). UNDP does increasingly integrate human rights in its annual human development reports. However, they do not feature in the HDI.

A dimension closely related to human rights is democracy. Due to the greater likelihood of benefits for the population and its active participation in the political process (Frey and Stutzer 2001), this political system is highly correlated with happiness (R. Inglehart and H.-D- Klingeman quoted in Diener and Seligman (2004, p. 6). However, it seems as if it were rather certain criteria a political system had to fulfill in order to guarantee happiness. These criteria include an efficiency of social and political institutions, a high mutual trust and a low level of corruption (John Helliwell quoted in Graham 2004, p. 4). Hence democracy is not necessarily a good system to provide happiness, and other systems are not necessarily bad ones. For example, happiness parachuted after the introduction of democracy in Eastern Europe after the fall of communism (John Helliwell quoted in Diener and Seligman 2004, p. 6).

UNDP does not take into account this dimension; and the example of the different countries with distinct political systems and levels of health renders its three human development dimensions little useful as indirect indicators, too.

15.4.5.4 Security

Individual security is very likely to have a positive correlation with happiness. Studies confirm this hypothesis in the case of socioeconomic security (ILO 2005, p. 576). Yet, another study in 42 countries shows that a social safety net does not necessarily guarantee a higher level of happiness (Ouweneel 2002, pp. 167–192). What might be important to people is, instead of monetary safety, psychological safety which is not provided by safety nets. Likewise, even though for this essay no correspondent studies have been found, given the results on violence and happiness, physical security is highly likely to be positively correlated. However, UNDP disregards this dimension in its well-being analysis.

The list of external factors is far from being exhaustive. Only the most frequently mentioned dimensions have been considered. Contrary to common assumptions, demographic factors, such as age and sex, have no significant influence on happiness (Diener et al. 1999, p. 581). It is then interesting to see, that UNDP takes a rather firm stand on the inclusion of these factors into its analysis of living standards and well-being.

15.4.6 Internal Factors

For a long time, it was commonly assumed that the individual personality and hence the biological determination of traits of character is the most essential determining factor of happiness. However, happiness studies reveal that they only explain a minority of the variances in happiness (Diener 1984, p. 558). Notwithstanding, they are crucial for our analysis, since they decide on how external factors are perceived and assimilated. Traits examined are self-confidence, internality, extraversion and ambition.

Self-confidence is one of the most important traits of character for happiness (Ibid.). It generally lifts individual satisfaction. And the causality is bidirectional. Research shows that confidence parachutes in times of unhappiness (R.M. Laxer in ibid., p. 559).

Another determining trait is internality, i.e. the tendency to attribute events to one self rather than to external causes. Happiness studies illustrate that, contrary to unhappy people, happy people are far more convinced of their capacity to influence their personal destiny (Veenhoven 1984, p. 354). The causality between internality and happiness is also bidirectional. Research demonstrates that the capacity to manage one's life enhances the level of happiness.

Extraversion is another trait of personality highly influential on happiness. It involves the tendency to appreciate things. Its correlation with happiness is mutual. Happiness studies prove that higher happiness also allows for more openness, as the case of social relations illustrated.

Lastly, ambition is an important trait of character. To set and to meet personal objectives increases happiness. The goals to be achieved have to represent a challenge, but should not be unreachable (Layard 2005, p. 73). Moreover, intrinsic goals seem to have a greater influence on happiness than extrinsic goals do. Physical attractiveness, celebrity and wealth are not positively related with happiness, whilst self-acceptance, affiliation, and help for the community are (Ed Diener and Mark Eunkook Suh in Kahneman et al. 1999, p. 445).

UNDP does not take into account these internal factors. It is true that their measurement is extremely difficult, but this difficulty should not lead to the

Table 15.1 Perspectives on well-being dimensions of UNDP and Happiness Studies—a comparison

Category of indicator	Indicator	Aspects of indicator	UNDP	Happiness studies
Human Development Indicators	Income	National income (GDP)	• Positive correlation; counts disaster positively	• Counts disaster negatively; distinguishes between desirable and undesirable outcomes • Accounts for work that does not pass through the market (household, 'economy of love' etc.)
		Personal income	• Positive correlation but diminishing utility	• Includes 'Easterlin paradox': no linear correlation but diminishing utility • Correlation is more complex: once basic needs are met there can be 'happy poor' and 'unhappy rich'
	Health	Causality between health and happiness	• Health increases happiness	• Health increases happiness, yet subjective health is more important than objective health
		Causality between development and health	• Higher levels of development increase levels of health	• There is no automatic causality; development can also lead to 'luxury diseases'
		Life expectancy vs. quality of life	• Focus on life expectancy	• Takes into consideration 'quality of life years'
		Causality between happiness and health	• Bidirectional causality is not considered	• Mutual causality between health and happiness. Happy people are healthier
	Education	Correlation between education and happiness	• Exclusively positive correlation	• Correlation is mostly positive, especially for low levels of education. Afterwards, it is more complex. At higher levels of education, this correlation can be neutral or even negative
		Causality between happiness and education	• Not considered	• Takes into account the bidirectional influence. Happy people can perform better

(contninued)

Table 15.1 (continued)

Category of indicator	Indicator	Aspects of indicator	UNDP	Happiness studies
Factors external to the individual	Social relations	Importance	• Not taken into account	• The quality of social relations has a strong impact on levels of happiness
	Work	Causality between work and happiness	• Employment is expressed through personal income	• Consideration of quality of work (intrinsic and extrinsic values of work). This quality strongly influences happiness
		Mutuality of causality	• Not taken into consideration	• Happiness influences work. Happy people perform better
	Political and societal conditions	Inequality, political stability, human rights and good governance	• Ignores questions of inequality, political stability and good governance, and only slowly integrates questions of human rights	• Takes into account the overall political and societal conditions, and thus considers questions of inequality, political stability, good governance and human rights; all being important determinants of individual happiness
	Security	Socioeconomic and physical	• Disregard of these factors	• Integration of socioeconomic and physical security, an important factor for individual happiness
Factors internal to the individual	Self-confidence, internality, extraversion and ambition	Importance and mutual causality	• Does not account for these factors	• These factors are taken into account and considered important for individual happiness • The bidirectional causality between these factors and individual happiness is taken into account

standpoint that what is hardly measurable should be completely ignored. These factors provide crucial information concerning the subjective evaluation of well-being and UNDP's analysis and policy to achieve the latter and should therefore be incorporated into UNDP's development indicator.

The same conclusion can be drawn for all the dimensions detected by happiness studies as well as the additional information concerning the three human development dimensions. Only the integration of a happiness indicator can render UNDP's perspective on poverty, wealth and development and the respective policy applied a more comprehensive one.

15.4.7 Comparison of Country Rankings: UNDP vs. Happiness Studies

The analysis of all the above dimensions has shown that UNDP's perspective on ill- and well-being does not necessarily correspond to the subjective perception of the standard of living the affected individuals themselves have. This phenomenon is well illustrated through a comparison of the country rankings of UNDP and happiness studies.[3]

Certainly, this comparison implies some methodological problems. While the HDI ranking has continuously been updated since 1990, the happiness results date from a period from 1995 to 2005. Some of the data are thus not a result of research done over the last couple of months. Moreover, the number of studies in each country varies considerably. In Australia there have been fourteen studies carried out, thirteen in Russia, eight in Hungary, six in Sweden, and five in Spain and Slovenia. In various European countries there have been four, three or two studies. The data of 38 countries is based on merely one single study. Furthermore, the HDI comprises 177 countries; 55 with a high, 86 with a medium, and 36 with a low human development. The happiness ranking on the other hand includes only 91 countries, out of which only ten belong to the poorest UNDP category, 36 to the medium and 42 to the highest one. The representation is thus biased towards countries with a higher human development. Yet, despite its problems the happiness ranking serves as a first approximation for our analysis and reveals surprising results.

The happiness average goes from 8.2 for Denmark down to 3.9 for Tanzania. In general terms, the happiness roughly follows the human development ranking. Most countries which UNDP classifies having a high level of human development can be found in the upper third of the happiness ranking as well, while countries

[3] The HDI country ranking of the year 2005 provides the necessary data for the UNDP ranking (UNDP, 2005, pp. 219-222). As far as the happiness ranking is concerned, this essay uses the data accumulated by Ruut Veenhoven published on the World Database of Happiness (Veenhoven, 2006).

with a medium human development are situated in the centre and those with a low human development towards the end of the happiness ranking. However, there are important exceptions.

First, there are countries that have a far better position in the happiness than in the HDI ranking. Colombia, for example, is found in the second position—together with Switzerland—with a happiness average of 8.1. Guatemala acquires the 4th position—together with Austria and Iceland—with a happiness average of 7.8. And Mexico is in the 7th position—together with Australia, Finland and Sweden—all with a happiness average of 7.7. Other countries like Honduras, El Salvador, Venezuela and Brazil all have a position in the twenties. Nigeria also makes a great leap and can be found in position 41. The HDI ranking, however, gives them a place among the countries with a medium or even low human development and thus a moderate or low level of happiness.

Second, there are countries which have a worse position in the happiness than in the HDI. The Baltic states, Hungary and Slovakia, for example, find themselves among the last 30 countries in the happiness ranking, whilst the HDI attests them a high level of human development. Also, Japan—positioned on 9th in the HDI ranking—France and Portugal—which are among the most developed countries according to UNDP—are only found in the middle of the happiness ranking, surrounded by countries such as Uzbekistan, Taiwan, Peru and Iran.

Whilst Latin America achieves positions better than expected Eastern Europe surprises negatively. In Africa, Nigeria is the only big surprise—yet a positive one. These results indicate that poverty as defined by UNDP does not necessarily imply a state of deficiency and ill-being, and that wealth as defined by UNDP does not necessarily represent a situation of abundance and well-being. Two explanations are possible. Either people do not perceive their situation as one of poverty and wealth, or they do, but they take into consideration other dimensions to measure these concepts—dimensions UNDP disregards in its analysis. This redefinition of poverty and wealth then implies changes for the concept of development, which can no longer be seen as a teleological process from deficiency and ill-being to abundance and well-being. Yet, UNDP fails to consider these different perceptions and hence misses out a great deal of valuable information in its analysis of poverty, wealth and development.

UNDP's capability approach takes into consideration the potentials that exist in life, either the individual capacities or its surrounding conditions (Veenhoven in Karma and Karma 2004, p. 289). However, these capacities and conditions do not say anything about the real outcomes in life. The potential to be happy is very different from actually being happy (Gasper 2004 p. 24). In order to evaluate the real consequences of development dimensions on people's well-being, the subjective perception of individuals has to be incorporated in the analysis. UNDP thus has to enlarge its approach from "having", "being" and "doing" (Cobb 2000, p. 13) by the 'feeling' about 'having', 'being' and 'doing'. Therefore, happiness studies are the complementary tool to UNDP's development indicator in order to obtain a more comprehensive picture of ill- and well-being as well as the impacts of its respective policy approach.

15.5 Conclusion

This essay examined whether happiness is a complementary tool for UNDP's analysis of poverty, wealth and development. The deconstruction of UNDP's discourse and measurement revealed a perspective of poverty which centers on the notion of deficiency and ill-being, whereas wealth is considered a superior state of abundance and well-being. Consequently, development becomes a teleological process towards well-being through the provision of profusion. Yet, happiness studies reveal that many people's subjective perception of well-being, or happiness, is different from UNDP's vision.

Happiness, defined as the degree to which an individual judges the overall quality of his life-as-a-whole favorably, is a global term which contains people's different evaluations concerning their lives, the events affecting them, their bodies and brains, and their living conditions. Although methodological and conceptual problems remain acute, the concept discovers crucial information about the dimensions of human development. Contrary to UNDP's assumption that *maximizing* levels of the HDI components always brings *optimum* results for people's well-being, happiness research illustrates that increased national and personal income and a higher level of education do not necessarily lead to greater happiness. Nor do they automatically guarantee better health and thus a higher level of happiness. Correlations prove to be much more complex, especially once basic needs are met. Moreover, happiness studies discover other dimensions essential for human happiness which are largely ignored by UNDP. The comparison between the two country rankings eventually confirms that individuals perceive their state of living differently from UNDP's perspective. Poverty is not exclusively a state of deficiency and ill-being, wealth is not necessarily a situation of abundance and well-being, and development is hence not automatically a teleological process providing greater well-being.

Analogue to UNDP's capability approach, happiness represents an end and thus a constitutive part of development. Simultaneously, the implementation of the development process is likely to depend on the happiness of the people. This renders happiness a mean, i.e. an instrumental part of development. In order to obtain a comprehensive analysis of poverty, wealth and development, and to meaningfully engage in the promotion of people's well-being, UNDP has to integrate the element of 'feeling' about 'having', 'being' and 'doing' as an evaluative tool. In the long term, only the inclusion of a happiness indicator can reflect the whole impact of UNDP's policy and thus change its perspective from a 'development as freedom' to a 'development as happiness'.

References

Alesina A et al (2001) Inequality and happiness: are Europeans different from Americans? Working Paper 8198, National Bureau of Economic Research, Cambridge

Anand S, Sen A (2000) The Income Component of the Human Development Index. J Human Dev 1(1)83–104

Anand S, Sen A (1994) Human development index: methodology and measurement, occasional papers, Human Development Report Office, New York

Association Redefining Progress (2005) What's wrong with the GDP as Measure of Progress. on http://www.rprogress.org/newprograms/sustIndi/gpi/whatswrong.shtml. Retrieved 1 Dec 2005

Bardhan K, Klasen S (2000) On UNDP's revision to the gender-related development index. J Human Dev 1(2)191–195

Bruckner P (2000) L'Euphorie perpétuelle—Essai sur le devoir de bonheur. Grasset et Fascelle, Paris

Campbell A (1981) The sense of well-being in America—Recent patterns and trends. McGraw-Hill, New York

Cobb CW (2000) Measurement tools and the quality of life. Redefining Progress, San Francisco

Cobb CW et al (1995) If the GDP is up, why is America down? The Atlantic Monthly 276(4)59–78

Diener DR (2005) Guidelines for national indicators of subjective well-being and ill-being. University of Illinois, SINET

Diener ED (1984) Subjective well-being. Psychol Bull 95(3)542–575

Diener ED et al (1999) Subjective well-being: three decades of progress. Psychol Bull 125(2)276–302

Diener ED, Seligman MEP (2004) Beyond money—Toward an economy of well-being. Psychol Sci Public Interest 5(1)1–31

Easterlin RA (1995) Will raising the incomes of all increase the happiness of all? J Econ Behav Organ 27:35–48

Easterlin RA (2001) Income and happiness: towards a unified theory. Econ J 111(473)465–84

Frey BS, Stutzer A (2001) Happiness and economics; how the economy and institutions affect well-being. Princeton University Press, Princeton and Oxford

Frey BS, Stutzer A (2003) Testing theories of happiness, working paper series, n 147. Institute for Empirical Research in Economics, University of Zürich

Fukuda-Parr S (2002) Rescuing the human development from the HDI: reflections on a New Agenda. Retrieved on http://www.nu.or.cr/pnud/docs/fukuda-parr2.pdf. 17 Mar 2006

Gasper D (2004) Human well-being: concepts and conceptualizations, discussion document n 2004/06 (United Nations University (UNU) & World Institute for Development Economics Research (WIDER), Helsinki)

Graham C (2004) Globalization, poverty, inequality, and insecurity: some insights from the economics of happiness; UNU/WIDER conference. The impact of globalization on the world's poor, Helsinki, UNU/WIDER, Helsinki, 29/30 Oct 2004

Grillo RD, Stirrat RL (1997) Discourse of development—Anthropological perspectives. Berg, Oxford

Halis A (1994) A means to closing gaps: disaggregated Human Development Index. http://hdr.undp.org/docs/publications/ocational_papers/oc18a.htm. Occasional Paper 18, retrieved 20 Jan 2005

Heady B, Wearing A (1988) The sense of relative superiority—central to well-being. Soc Ind Res 20(5):497–516

Helliwell JF (2003) How's life? Combining individual and national Variables to explain subjective well-being. Econ Model 20(2):331–360

Hicks D (1997) The inequality-adjusted human development index: a constructive proposal. World Dev 25(8):1283–1298

International Labour Organisation (ILO) (2005) Socioeconomic security for a better World, ILO Geneva

Kahneman D et al (1999) Well-being: the foundations of hedonic psychology. Russell Sage Foundation, New York

Karma U, Karma G (2004) Gross national happiness and development. The Centre for Bhutan Studies, Thimphu

Kelley A (1991) The human development index: handle with care. Popul Dev Rev 17(2)

Lane RE (2000) Diminishing returns to income, companionship and happiness. J Happiness Stud 1(1):103–119
Layard R (2005) Happiness—lessons from a new science. Penguin Press, New York
Neumeyer E (2001) The human development index and sustainability: a constructive proposal. Ecol Econ 39(1):101–114
Mcmahon DM (2006) Happiness—a history. Atlantic Monthly Press, New York
Noorbakhsh F (1998) A modified human development index. World Dev 26(3):517–528
Ouweneel P (2002) Social security and well-being of the unemployed in 42 nations. J Happiness Stud 3(2):167–192
Rahman T et al (2005) Measuring the quality of life across countries—A sensitivity analysis of well-being indices, Research Article n 2005/06, UNU/WIDER, Helsinki
Rojas M (2004) Well-being and the complexity of poverty—A subjective well-being approach, Research Article n 2004/29, UNU/WIDER, Helsinki
Runciman WG (1966) Relative deprivation and social justice: a study of attitudes to social inequality in twentieth-century England. University of California Press, Berkeley and Los Angeles
Ryten J (2000) Should there be a HDI? Conference IASO Statistics, development and human rights, Montreux, September 2000, retrieved 15 January 2005 on www.portal-stat.admin.ch/iaos2000/ryten_final_paper.doc
Sen A (1999) Development as freedom. Oxford University Press, Oxford
Strack F et al (1991) Subjective well-being—An interdisciplinary perspective. Pergamon Press, Oxford and New York
Stutzer A (2004) The role of income aspirations in individual happiness. J Econ Behav Organ 54:89–109
UNDP Human Development Report (2005) Oxford University Press, New York
Veenhoven R (2004) Subjective measures of well-being, discussion article n 2004/07, UNU/WIDER, Helsinki
Veenhoven R (1984) Conditions of happiness. Reidel, Dordrecht
Veenhoven R (1991) Is happiness relative? Soc Ind Res 24(1):1–34
Veenhoven R (2006) Average happiness in 91 nations 1995–2005, World Database of Happiness, Rank Report 2006-1, retrieved 4 May 2006 on http://www.worlddatabaseofhappiness.eur.nl

Chapter 16
Should Happiness-Maximization be the Goal of Government?

Grant Duncan

Abstract Recent social surveys of happiness (subjective well-being) have given a new stimulus to utilitarian political theory by providing a statistically reliable measure of the 'happiness' of individuals that can then be correlated with other variables. One general finding is that greater happiness does not correlate strongly with increased wealth, beyond modest levels, and this has led to calls for governments to shift priorities away from economic growth and towards other social values. This chapter notes how the conclusions of this research help to address some of the traditional objections to utilitarianism. The question of how happiness research findings can be used to set happiness-maximization goals for public policy needs careful examination, as the translation from research to policy is not always straightforward. Some empirical and ethical objections to this 'new utilitarianism' are raised. The complicating factors of public expectations of, and trust in, governments pose obstacles to any proposal that happiness research may lead to changes in public policy and hence to 'happier' populations.

Keywords Happiness • Public policy • Government • Utilitarianism

16.1 Introduction

Recent research on happiness and subjective well-being has prompted a re-examination of the traditional utilitarian principle that the maximization of happiness should be adopted by governments as an aim of law and public policy. This is an old idea that reappears in various guises, for example:

> Whatever the form or Constitution of Government may be, it ought to have no other object than the *general* happiness.
>
> Thomas Paine, *The Rights of Man* (1790) (1996, p. 164).
>
> A measure of government … may be said to be conformable to or dictated by the principle of utility, when … the tendency which it has to augment the happiness of the community is greater than any which it has to diminish it.
>
> Jeremy Bentham, *An Introduction to the Principles of Morals and Legislation* (1789) (Warnock 1962, p. 33).

G. Duncan (✉)
School of People, Environment and Planning, Massey University Albany,
Private Bag 102-904, North Shore MSC, Auckland, New Zealand
e-mail: L.G.Duncan@massey.ac.nz

A. Delle Fave (ed.), *The Exploration of Happiness*, Happiness Studies Book Series,
DOI: 10.1007/978-94-007-5702-8_16, © Springer Science+Business Media Dordrecht 2013

The US Declaration of Independence of 1776 specifies 'the pursuit of happiness' as one of the principal inalienable rights of all citizens. The 1942 Beveridge Report in the UK, which laid the groundwork for Britain's welfare state, referred to 'the happiness of the common man' as the basic objective (Beveridge 1942, p. 171). And, according to an influential, though Whiggish, history of New Zealand:

> Social Security is … clearly an investment in the future personnel of industry as well as in the happiness of the citizenry (Sinclair 1991, p. 271).

For present purposes, I am mainly interested in that version of the happiness-maximization principle that has re-emerged from research on happiness in the fields of psychology, sociology and economics over the last three decades. To reiterate the question, then, this article asks whether the maximization of happiness *should* be adopted by governments as an aim of law and public policy. I emphasize the word *should*, moreover, because the theory that I am considering here involves an ethical case for a re-evaluation of social-political aims. Let me illustrate this with a few quotes from the recent happiness literature.

> People can and do experience lasting changes in their well-being as a result of life events. *Appropriate public policies can increase the average level of subjective well-being*, and it is conceivable that individuals, with greater knowledge of the social mechanisms governing their lives, might themselves deliberately choose courses of action that would permanently improve their happiness (Easterlin 2003a, italics added).
> … [P]ublic policy should be about enhancing happiness or the welfare of people, now and in the future (Ng and Ho 2006, p. 1).
> … [T]he greatest happiness principle deserves a more prominent place in policy making (Veenhoven 2004, p. 676).

Veenhoven (2004) gives one of the most carefully considered examples of this case for the application of happiness research to public policy, based on what he calls a 'new utilitarianism'. He points out that a number of social factors over which governments have some authority and control (such as respect for the rule of law and civil rights, economic freedom, and tolerance of minorities) are positively correlated with popular happiness levels. He concludes that the happiness of a society could therefore be raised through the application of appropriate public policies, just as public health promotion requires appropriate policy actions.

Diener and Seligman (2004) put forward a well-researched case in favour of nations adopting systems of well-being indicators, partly to supplement existing economic indicators. They do not argue that such social indicators should serve a prescriptive function in the field of public policy. They see them as serving an evaluative role in assessing the impact or success of national policies, and hence their conclusion is more modest than Veenhoven's. In each case, though, the conclusion is based on retrospective data and on statistical correlations. We do not yet have prospective research that indicates a causal relationship between the implementation of a new policy and an effect on happiness.

The present discussion takes its impetus, then, from philosophical and social-research literature. Apart from the well-known examples of the Kingdom of Bhutan's policy of Gross National Happiness and the reference in the US Declaration of Independence to 'the pursuit of happiness', governments around the world have so far not yet firmly established happiness as an over-arching goal or evaluative criterion of public policy in practical terms. So, the question posed here is a largely hypothetical one about the *possible* political applications of happiness research. It considers some of the pragmatics of public policy, and some of the ethical and empirical questions that have yet to be addressed by any proposal to use happiness research to directly inform policy-making. As such, this chapter does not seek to take a fixed stand one way or the other, but it considers the 'pros and cons', poses some critical questions, and seeks to stimulate future theory and research on this question.

So, what are some of the key conclusions of happiness research that are said to have some relevance for public policy? Diener and Seligman (2004) provide a useful literature review. Well-being surveys across nations have suggested that there are diminishing returns to incomes above US $10,000 per annum. Further, once other health and social factors that also correlate with both affluence and subjective well-being are statistically controlled, "the effect of income on national well-being becomes nonsignificant" (Diener and Seligman 2004, p. 5). In fact, aggregate happiness-survey scores remained static in the USA and Japan, even after decades of strong economic growth; and the self-reported happiness of individuals does not increase into middle-age, even when incomes and wealth do. The communities with the highest subjective well-being or happiness are not, therefore, those who are the wealthiest, but rather those who enjoy good health, effective social and political institutions, high trust and social cohesion, and low corruption. More pertinent to matters of government and policy, Diener and Seligman (2004) review research reports that have found correlations between subjective well-being and countries' respect for human rights and freedoms, democratic institutions and political stability.

Below, I introduce some reasons for interpreting such results with caution. But, at face value, they appear to carry a message for policy-makers whose goals may have been focused narrowly on economic growth as an objective and less concerned about health and social issues and about good governance. But, does it also mean that happiness surveys could become a tool for planning and evaluating public policy, and that happiness itself should be a *goal* of public policy and/or a means of assessing its success? To address this, we need a way of defining public policy, and of understanding its aims and methods and how these are chosen and enacted. We also need to consider the bridge between social research and policy actions, as this may not be as simple and unobstructed as it may at first seem. Does research simply quantify pre-existing social problems and test hypotheses about their causes for policy-makers then to digest the results and take appropriate actions; or is the process of research somehow constructive of social problems and thus actively shaping political concerns? But, before we do that, let us consider how happiness researchers define *happiness* itself.

16.2 How do Researchers Define Happiness?

Statistical data about the happiness of populations come from various surveys. This is usually done in the form of questions about how happy or how satisfied with life the respondent feels. It is a question about *subjective* well-being, but the results tend to be fairly consistent and to correlate well with other measures of well-being factors. One might say that 'happiness' is whatever the survey respondents think it is when asked, but researchers often see a need to define the term. Authors in this field have provided definitions that are quite diverse. Layard defines *happiness* as 'feeling good—enjoying life and wanting the feeling to be maintained' (2005, p. 12); and Myers calls it 'a high ratio of positive to negative feelings' (2004, p. 522). These definitions of happiness are the simplest, based on positive feelings, and are the closest to the traditional Benthamite meaning. Others take a slightly broader view, using the term 'subjective well-being' to encompass both an affective evaluation of oneself at present, as well as a rational evaluation of satisfaction with one's life a whole. Frey and Stutzer point out that surveys can measure such subjective well-being, and that these measures 'serve as proxies for "utility"' (Frey and Stutzer 2002, p. 405).

Happiness, according to some psychologists, needs to be broken down into three strongly correlated, but independent, factors: subjective well-being, life satisfaction, and absence of depression or anxiety. Subjective well-being is the moods or feelings that people have of joy or elation. Life satisfaction refers to qualities or circumstances of life, such as personal wealth, family relationships, community participation, employment, goal achievement etc., that may cause satisfaction or dissatisfaction. And, finally, the absence of depression, anxiety, insecurity, etc., does not in itself constitute happiness or well-being, but is nonetheless an important prerequisite (Argyle 2001).

There is another definition of happiness that deserves attention here, because it has been developed in the context of a discussion that addresses the same question as the present paper: the relevance of happiness to the aims of government. Veenhoven, who advocates a 'new utilitarianism' and argues that happiness can be promoted by public policy, defines happiness as 'the overall enjoyment of your life as a whole' (2004, p. 664). This sounds more like Aristotelian *eudaimonia* than Benthamite utility. In fact, the quote comes from a chapter in a volume on 'positive psychology' which explicitly seeks its historical and philosophical roots in Aristotelian ideas about character and virtue, and hence advocates a eudaimonic approach to 'the good life'—in which happiness (as good feelings or satisfaction with life) would be only one dimension alongside 'authenticity', 'continuous development' and 'the meaningful life' (Jorgensen and Nafstad 2004).[1]

So, while each of the definitions of happiness may be sound enough in its own right, the happiness literature in economics and psychology proposes diverse definitions deriving from well-established, but rival, philosophical positions. Are we talking about subjective feelings of pleasure, as balanced against pain—or are we using the term in reference to a broader moral evaluation of 'a good life'? Clearly, the happiness research field has diverging definitions of its key term, but this may be seen as a healthy diversity of opinion, rather than a fundamental flaw. And both

[1] The eudaimonic approach to happiness research is given more thorough discussion in a recent issue of the *Journal of Happiness Studies* (issue 1, 2008).

the eudaimonism of the Aristotelian tradition and the utilitarianism of Bentham and Mill have one significant thing in common: they both hold up the potential for the realization of happiness/eudaimonia as an ultimate goal, achievable in *this* worldly life. It is neither an abstract ideal, nor something to be hoped for in an after-life. And both traditions have proposed that happiness is relevant to the ethics and goals of the individual and of the state.

The matter would become even more complicated if one were to include non-western concepts of happiness. Bhutan, which has adopted the policy of Gross National Happiness, is officially a Buddhist state with a Buddhist concept of happiness (Mancall 2004). Buddhism advocates a detachment from worldliness as a means to overcome suffering and to achieve enlightenment; and it is not really about individual happiness as an immediate or transient experience. By contrast, western utilitarianism and eudaimonism tend to be more oriented towards achieving life-satisfaction or pleasure in the world as we know it empirically.

16.3 What is Public Policy?

So, while both eudaimonism and utilitarianism see happiness as an ultimate goal for the individual, they both also extend this goal, by aggregation, to the political community as a whole. In his *Politics*, Aristotle argues that the state exists to ensure the survival of its members, but, more than that, it also exists to achieve 'the good life' (*eudaimonia*). In a similar vein, Bentham says that the actions of governments can be evaluated in terms of the aggregate effects they have on people's happiness. Both assume that the goals of the state can be inferred from the goals of its members, by aggregation.

It should be noted at this point that some other prominent thinkers have rejected happiness as an ethical–political goal. Kant did not dismiss the importance of happiness, but he did not see it as a suitable guide to moral reasoning, as it is too self-regarding. He preferred instead a deontological approach as expressed in his categorical imperative. More recently, Amartya Sen (1985) has extensively critiqued happiness and utilitarian ethics in relation to development policy, and he advances a theory of capabilities instead.

Nonetheless, contemporary happiness researchers promote happiness as a political goal based on correlations between social and institutional factors, over which governments have some control or influence, and subjective well-being. The latter, moreover, has been associated with other well-being factors, such as good health and longevity. Although real-world governments do not have 'Ministries of Happiness', it would appear logical to argue that, in as much as public policy can influence people's happiness, governments have (at least) an *interest* in maximizing it—if not a moral *obligation* to do so. By this view, a low level of subjective well-being among some populations is as much a 'problem' for policy-makers as, say, poor public hygiene would be, even if it may require less urgent attention. And thus hypothetically a suitable happiness objective needs to be set, and policy programmes put in place to achieve it. The UK Prime Minister's Strategy Unit, for example, considered a paper on life-satisfaction and happiness research in 2002. This discussion paper concluded that there is 'a case for state intervention to boost life satisfaction due mainly to evidence of direct impacts on life satisfaction of government activities, together with strong evidence of the dependence of individuals' wellbeing on the actions of others' (Donovan and Halpern 2002, p. 4).

Such a case relies upon a rational-instrumental model of public policy. It maintains that scientific evidence of social conditions and problems is objective and that it leads logically to proposals for remedies. The job of the policy analyst is to examine alternative courses of action and to advise political decision-makers on the most economical or cost-effective option. This assumes that implementation of such a remedy is a technical process that has reasonably predictable outcomes, *and* that governments have the authority and the means to carry out the desired programmes. When it comes to something as inoffensive and universally desirable as happiness, moreover, how could anyone rationally object? Social researchers and policy technocrats could rule, provided we know it is making people happier.

Even if one cannot object to happiness *per se*, the instrumental model of public policy that would see happiness research as translatable unproblematically into policy programmes, and hence into social outcomes, is not the only way in which to consider the role of policy. A second model of public policy could be called 'interactionist'. This considers the complex set of institutions and actors that form and perform policy as a system, with subsystems and feedback processes. By this model, policy involves more than just routinely-acting and stable hierarchies, but depends also on the complex and less predictable effects of changeable networks and complex governance structures, some of which occur outside the scope of state authority. For example, Rhodes (1996) talks about 'governance as self-organizing networks' operating across organizations in private enterprise, civil society and central and local government. These networks challenge rational, hierarchical models of government because they 'become autonomous and resist central guidance' (p. 667). Policy objectives from the centre may be modified, renegotiated, or even resisted, on such terrain. Such a model would place a notion like happiness onto complex and contestable territory. So any liberal-democratic polity would then need to consider how the ideal of happiness may be expressed within diverse communities, be they secular or fundamentalist, mainstream or minority-group, etc. Individual and cultural differences in values and policy priorities regarding *how* people achieve happiness or 'a good life' would thus come to be relevant, and contestable, matters in such a policy-making process.

A third approach to public policy could be called the 'constructivist' model. By this model, the political process of 'problem-formation' is itself treated critically as problematic (e.g. Dean and Hindess 1998). Hence, social conditions are not simply objective states waiting passively to be measured by social researchers for the information of policy-makers. Rather, the surveying of communities, especially concerning something as subjective as happiness, actively constructs the awareness of the phenomenon, and hence pre-forms the framework in which it may be treated as a 'problem' that legitimates political attention and governmental actions.

The constructivist approach is then also concerned with the ways in which policy instruments give effect to programmes that normalize certain predictable or calculable patterns of behaviour in the interests of, say, safety, financial prudence, healthy eating, or indeed happiness and well-being. Such a perspective takes a critical view of the power relations and strategies that enact programmes of problem-formation and normalization, treating them as interested and contingent, rather than as neutral and necessary. By this approach, then, one may ask how happiness research, once released into the domain of political actions, is actively *re*constructing our understanding of our own well-being as a 'problem' that requires collective efforts and powers to address it; and also how the resultant debates and practices may serve to redirect values and behaviours into normative patterns. For example, a presumed governmental duty to maximize happiness could become implicitly an individual duty to be happy—and hence this may imply a moral failure in those who fall short of that, due to not following socially prescribed norms, and hence elicit a range of new constraints and imperatives around the lives of citizens who are construed as 'autonomous', but whose 'well-being' is taken to be a collective concern.

My impression is that happiness researchers—like many other researchers in social sciences and public health—tend to assume the rational-instrumental model of public policy. The above discussion of alternative models does *not* invalidate the instrumental model in practice, though, and I am not privileging any one of them. After all, one would still expect well-formulated policies to have some rational grounding in evidence, to have clear instrumental goals with authoritative backing, and to be performed by regulated systems that seek to achieve those goals. But the alternative models do call us to exercise, at the very least, some caution and modesty about understanding the complexity and subtlety of policy processes and their origins and outcomes. They help us to understand how sometimes well-intentioned political programmes can come to grief through public misunderstanding and opposition, or how some critical reflexivity may be required in order to fully appreciate the complex and *political* nature of apparently technical processes of public policy.

To illustrate the complexity of the relationship between research findings and their application to policy, consider the case of obesity as a social problem. Obesity is a major concern for all affluent nations, it has well-known health risks, and it has worrying cost implications for governments and health-care systems. It would appear to be a simple matter to translate the mass of scientific evidence into effective public policy. After all, unfettered food production and consumption in affluent societies is only resulting in higher rates of obesity; so governments should take action where markets have failed. All they have to do, it would seem, is to encourage people to change their diets and to get more exercise. But the reality is much more complex than that. Policy-makers are confronted with competing theories, complex and cross-cutting issues, huge vested interests, ideological disagreements, a multitude of possible interventions, and frequent resistance to perceived government 'interference'. Despite the growing sophistication of publicly available knowledge about obesity and its prevention, the rates of obesity seem not to decline (Lang and Rayner 2007).

The skeptical note that this introduces is *not* meant to imply that either obesity-reduction or happiness cannot or should not be a goal of public policy. It is only to suggest that the translation from social research into effective political action is often fraught with complexity and frustration. The next sections of this chapter take up the theme mainly from the point of view of utilitarian prescriptions for governments, rather than the Aristotelian perspective—partly to simplify and to shorten the discussion, but also to recognize that the utilitarian approach appears to be the more common in the happiness research literature, especially among economists. The points arising from this discussion will show that the case for happiness as a goal of good government does run into complications, in the light of ethical and empirical issues.

The ensuing discussion will largely assume that public policy takes place in the environment of a developed nation with a good standard of governance, although the situation of developing or less stable countries will be taken into account when necessary.

16.4 Traditional Objections to Utilitarianism

The findings of happiness research represent an interesting development in utilitarian thought. Now, utilitarianism has become a diverse set of doctrines, and has had to adapt to numerous problems. One of the basic problems was that utility, being subjective and having no basis for interpersonal comparison, could not be measured. So, the Benthamite principle of utility (based on 'the greatest happiness') was, for the purposes of economics, stripped of its subjectivism by Samuelson's principle of 'revealed preference'. This meant that preferences are not regarded in subjective terms, but defined purely by the behavioral choices that consumers make in a market. This led some policy-makers to the idea that measures of aggregate economic output or income could be used as proxies for the welfare of the people, as if greater consumption implicitly means greater happiness. (That is, if we get more of what we prefer, we must be better off.) It appears that this simple equation is no longer taken literally. United Nations guidelines on national accounts, for example, point out that GDP is an *economic* indicator, should *not* be used to stand for 'well-being', and is *not* supposed to represent directly the 'utility' that people may (or may not) derive from the consumption of goods (United Nations Statistics Division 2007). So, let us assume that utilitarianism, in the field of public policy, is not necessarily about the reduction of public values to economic statistics—and hence that happiness research may now have something useful to add to political deliberation and policy decision-making.

Furthermore, while Bentham had a theory about calculating and maximizing happiness, but lacked any interpersonally comparable data, contemporary happiness researchers might claim that social surveys now supply data that is reasonably reliable and valid, thus filling that gap. Veenhoven (2004), for example, argues that happiness surveys are valid and reliable measures, and that the construct of happiness that the surveys are using is interpersonally and cross-culturally comparable.

Hence, this research literature may be seen as giving new stimulus to utilitarianism. Although some, especially in the American 'positive psychology' movement, as pointed out above, appear to take a more eudaimonistic approach to happiness, it is assumed here that contemporary happiness research is predominantly utilitarian in its philosophical foundations. From a political point of view, it leads us to the conclusion that the results of happiness research, based on social surveys and multi-variate analyses, provide evidence of the personal, social and economic conditions that are most likely to maximize happiness. This seems to result in a form of rule-utilitarianism which says that, if governments adopt certain policies and institutional practices, then people will be happier.

The precepts and prescriptions of contemporary happiness research have succeeded in overcoming some of the traditional objections to the political applications of utilitarianism. Relevant authors argue that happiness, as a mental state, is now measurable and can be enhanced through appropriate actions (Layard 2005; Veenhoven 2004), and so happiness surveys, results from which are now quite widespread and available globally, provide the ability to observe and aggregate—and hence potentially to predict and even to enhance—people's happiness. Below, I place in italics some common objections to utilitarianism, and immediately following is the kind of response that happiness researchers can plausibly give in reply.

Objection 1: *So long as the person is 'happy'—even if it requires the administration of opiates—it does not matter if she is illiterate and malnourished.*[2]

Happiness surveys find that greater happiness is correlated with good health, longevity and higher levels of educational achievement, and so it supports the pursuit of a wider range of well-being and development factors (see for example Easterlin 2003b), and the spectre of a starving, yet 'happy', person is nothing but a 'straw man' in this argument. Further, it is sensible to suppose that policies with a happiness goal may be quite different in a country where illiteracy and malnourishment are widespread compared with a country where unmet needs are not as 'basic' and which is instead concerned more with social inclusion in the context of material prosperity. It is thus unfair to attribute to happiness research literature a narrow subjectivism, devoid of interest in objective and variable social conditions.

Objection 2: *'The greatest happiness' of the majority may be sought by means that produce misery for a minority, or that at least involve some trade-off between people, in a way that violates our understandings of human rights or moral principles.*[3]

---

[2] 'If a starving wreck, ravished by famine, buffeted by disease, is made happy through some mental conditioning (say, via the "opium" of religion), the person will be seen as doing well on this mental-state perspective, but that would be quite scandalous' (Sen 1985, p. 188).

[3] A typical hypothetical example used here would be that of a surgeon who has five patients whose lives depend on organ transplants. Should he dissect, and hence kill, one person with healthy organs to save five others? To do so would appear to maximize utility, but is also fundamentally wrong. A real-world example comes from the Kingdom of Bhutan, which espouses a policy of Gross National Happiness, but in 1991 rescinded citizenship from, and then expelled, its Nepalese-Hindi minority—about 100,000 people—who continue to languish in refugee camps. At the time of writing, a group of these refugees was resettling in my own community. Can the forced expulsion of an unwanted minority be justified by the happiness of the majority?

Happiness research findings may suggest that the greatest gains in aggregate happiness can be made by attending to the well-being of society's worst-off, especially those who are poor (by progressive taxation and redistribution, and by employment security) and those with mental illness (by improving mental health services) (Layard 2005). Furthermore, democratic societies that respect universal human rights tend to have happier people (Diener and Seligman 2004).[4]

Objection 3: *'Happiness' as an ultimate goal lacks adequate normative content, so a person may justify, say, gambling, taking drugs or spending his savings on the grounds that it makes him as happy as, or happier than, he would be if saving for retirement and adopting a healthy lifestyle.*[5]

Happiness research (for example Easterlin 2003b) does inquire into which happiness-altering circumstances or behaviours avoid the effects of 'adaptation' (a short-term boost in happiness, after which there is no long-term benefit), and hence can reach conclusions that reflect upon more 'sustainable' gains in well-being.

But, while the conclusions about social and political values that may be derived from happiness research can possibly withstand some of the standard objections to utilitarianism, there are other obstacles in the way of drawing the conclusion that these research results (regardless of how rigorous they may be) *should* be applied to public policy. To make this case, we can explore some logical, philosophical problems, as well as some potential empirical grounds that may lead us to ask whether public policy can achieve any further gains in happiness (as reflected in surveys).

The proposition that happiness should become an aim of public policy relies on two main types of assumption: an ethical assumption about political obligations, and an empirical assumption about effectiveness. The ethical assumption is basically that, because we have statistical analyses that show the conditions under which people are most likely to say that they are happy, then we *ought* to use collective political means to maximize those conditions. The empirical assumption is that, by having governments make the policy reforms that appear to be needed, happiness-survey responses will improve. I will examine each in turn.

---

[4] This is perhaps being too generous to Diener and Seligman, however, as their review article does contain the assertion that '... market democracies have much more well-being than totalitarian dictatorships, so military expenditures that protect and extend democracy will increase global well-being' (2004, p. 24). Published not long after the invasion of Iraq, this statement seems to be guilty of the kind of moral problem often associated with utilitarianism.

[5] This is a version of one of oldest objections to utilitarianism. It may be put somewhat like this: Suppose playing tic-tac-toe gives me more pleasure than listening to Bach; then we would have to suppose that the former is of higher moral worth, in my case. There is something inherently wrong with this, and Mill struggled to get around the problem by arguing that, in the estimation of anyone with sufficient experience of both forms of pleasure, Bach would be the clear favourite. So, similarly, we might argue that anyone with sufficient experience and knowledge of both will see that saving one's money for retirement is morally superior, because it will bring greater *lasting* happiness, to spending one's money in a casino.

16.5 Some Ethical Issues

The ethical claims for happiness as a political goal are often premised on the notion that happiness is a universally understood and desired goal. For Richard Rorty (1999), for example, the goal of giving all people 'an equal chance of happiness' is of prime importance and has an a priori status for which there are no rational, empirical or supernatural grounds. It is simply 'a goal worth dying for', about which there can be no further argument. While it may be true that all languages contain words like the basic idea of happiness as 'good feelings' (Wierzbicka 1999), however, the supposedly 'self-evident' idea that happiness is something all humans universally want may only be self-evident in the sense of being tautological. Happiness is defined as a good or desirable state and hence, purely by definition, it is good, or all desire it. Hence, the statement 'happiness is a universal good' is quite circular, and no more informative than saying 'pain always hurts'.

We may be able to get a little further, though, by stating the conditions which appear to lead to a higher frequency of reports of high levels of happiness—just as it helps to know what is most likely to cause pain, so that we can avoid such things. Now, a common problem with any simplistic version of utilitarianism is the desire to leap from the possession of such facts to the claim that we *ought* to do something. So, while it may be perfectly 'natural'—an observable fact of human behaviour—that we take steps to make our lives happier and to avoid pain, it should not automatically be assumed that this can be used as a fundamental principle of ethics. Certainly, those happiness researchers who use their empirical findings as premises for an ethical and political case may be guilty of overlooking the extra logical steps needed. They generally do not stop to argue why the achievement of higher aggregate scores on happiness surveys is *good* (given that it would be circular simply to say that this result would be 'good' because it would signify that people are happier). The *fact* that we want to be happy does not ineluctably lead to the conclusion that happiness-maximization should be our *ethical* guide. Indeed, there are respectable branches of moral philosophy that argue that it should *not* be, and instead principles such as freedom, human rights, duties, virtue, capabilities or fairness may be more relevant.

I will not try to settle this particular philosophical debate, but simply present it as a problem worth considering. The grounds for happiness get marshier, however, when we examine another common assumption in the happiness research literature. This is the 'leap' involved in proceeding from matters based upon personal subjective feelings to matters of collective political decision-making. Happiness is subjective, and refers to feelings of pleasure and satisfaction with life that can only be directly experienced by a person privately. Hence, we have to be cautious about the scope of reference appropriate to the word *happiness*. I can comment as the expert on my own happiness, and can share empathetically in the happiness expressed by someone else who is close to me. So, it may even be meaningful to assert 'we are happy', if the 'we' is inclusive of people close enough to share each other's feelings. But does the statistical aggregation of many anonymous individuals' estimation of their own private feelings of happiness amount to something that is simply the sum of its parts? Or, is the well-being of the whole something *more* than the net-sum 'well-beings' of its members?

It is clearly feasible to ask individuals to rate their own happiness numerically, and we can aggregate and analyze those responses statistically. But, a large collection of people is not the subject of happiness. Happiness, as an experience, or as something expressed verbally or non-verbally, does not apply to more than one person at a time—or, at best, to no more than a close group of persons. Any expression of personal happiness, moreover, is mediated by factors unique to each context, such as a survey respondent's interpretation of the questioner's motives for asking about happiness, or willingness to disclose feelings to strangers. Aggregated scores from national surveys of happiness, therefore, may not be the best way to estimate the well-being of Belgian or Japanese *society*—because whole societies are not the grounds upon which the feeling of happiness has content or practical meaning.[6]

Coming back to the ethical issues, then, a similar problem applies in moving from matters of individual choice to matters of social or political choice. Even if I accept that happiness can form a guide to my own ethical reasoning and decision-making, it is quite another matter to generalize this to a category to which happiness may not properly apply (that is, a whole society). As John Rawls put it, '[utilitarianism] improperly extends the principle of choice for one person to choices facing society' (Rawls 1999, p. 122), and the same critique may be applicable to happiness survey findings if applied to collective political decision-making. Even if we assumed that happiness is the ultimate personal goal, happiness does not automatically become the ultimate *political* goal.

Communities do not feel happiness, only individuals feel it. So, while it may behove one person to act in a certain way to see to his or her own happiness, the 'happiness' of a whole collective or community of persons may be empty of content or reference, and there may be no obvious pathway to improving happiness at that level of action. Two different people may find satisfaction in customs or policies that are diametrically opposed to one another. (Think about the legality

[6] J.S. Mill commits all of the fallacies described above. He argues that, because people desire happiness, happiness is desirable. Since all this says is, 'happiness is desirable because people desire it', the so-called 'proof' is tautological. Further, the only reason he can give as to why people desire the 'general happiness' is that people desire their own happiness. Proceeding thus from a tautology, which he assumes to be a 'fact', he surmises that 'happiness is a good'; and because it is a good to each individual person, it must therefore be 'a good to the aggregate of all persons' (Mill, in Warnock 1962, pp. 288–299). He does not stop to ask whether 'happiness' has any meaning beyond the subjective experience of one person at a time. However, he then proceeds to argue that ultimately we desire *only* happiness, because all other desirable things are desired only as a means to greater happiness. But the very premises of his case have to be dismissed. Furthermore, happiness suits his purposes as a super-ordinate goal partly because it is free of content and can thus be linked to any other desirable goals.

of prostitution in one community versus the ‘freedom’ to have child brides in another.) So aggregations of happiness scores may elide underlying social and political conflicts, and hence happiness surveys may *not* always be useful in guiding real-world political decisions about how the law should treat various behaviours.

There is a further logical argument that advocates of happiness-maximization need to make which bridges this gap between the individual level, at which happiness (as an experience and as an ethical precept) may make sense, and the collective level at which public policy actions occur, the level of whole communities and populations. The case would need to be made that the goals of a nation can be viewed simply as the net-sum of the happiness-maximization goals of the millions of individuals who inhabit it. In other words, the whole is simply the sum of its parts, and the ethics of state action are to be determined by the aggregated desires of individuals.

Even if we were persuaded that happiness surveys *are* relevant information for public policy (which they may yet be), they would not overcome the basic ethical–political problems of the policy-making process. No matter how much information is produced to show under what social conditions people report greater happiness, these conclusions, on their own, can have no morally compelling basis for the actions of governments. Indeed, some would argue that happiness, while of paramount importance, is rightly the concern of the individual (including loved ones), but *not* of government. Happiness is a private value, not a public one; and many of the key factors associated with happiness (such as social connectedness and health) may rely more on private choices than on public policy. The neo-liberal suspicion of Big Government, or Nanny State, is likely to be scornful of any well-intentioned ‘therapeutic’ effort to lend the powers of the state to the ‘problem’ of helping us to be happier (Furedi 2006). The obligations of government, it is often argued, are merely to preserve the liberties of the individual. (This is a libertarian standpoint and I will not presently defend it, however.) Further, though, there are other principles for social decision-making, such as Rawls's justice as fairness, or Sen's theory of capabilities, against which happiness-maximization has to justify itself as an equal, if not superior, guide. So, even if we can claim that people in well-governed societies report higher levels of happiness, we have not yet established that happiness is the *aim* of good government.

In fact, happiness has been used by political ideologies ranging from utopian socialist to social-democratic to libertarian, each with its own programme for political, social and economic reforms, and with policy objectives that conflict with one another. Claiming that happiness is *the* goal of good government and that we have scientific evidence about what makes people happier, therefore, does not actually help us to solve the problem of divergent social values and policy objectives. Happiness research can be used persuasively and ideologically for diametrically opposed political aims and does not provide us with a set of recommendations that over-ride political antagonisms and public debate. One may claim that happiness is the goal of good government, as Tom Paine did, but that leaves us back at square one when it comes to arguing about how best to maximize happiness in terms of many practical policy choices. In short, evidence about happiness does *not* trump political opinion-formation and public debates about core social values (Duncan 2007). But it may at least *inform* our public debates with empirical data, as Diener and Seligman (2004) suggest.

16.6 Some Empirical Questions

Having considered some ethical questions so far, what then of the empirical issues that bear upon the idea that governments should act to maximize happiness?

The 'Easterlin paradox' is based on the empirical finding that growing markets have not been associated with growth in aggregate happiness-survey results. This normally is explained by 'rising expectations', and leads to calls for better public policy to restore the pursuit of happiness (Easterlin 1974, 2001). The effects of the acquisition of new material goods or enhanced income tend to be 'self-limiting', and do not lead to sustained gains in subjective well-being. Good health and social connectedness, on the other hand, appear to contribute more sustainably to people's happiness than the pursuit of wealth and material goods (Easterlin 2003b), so governments should do more about the former things, for the sake of our happiness.

While this leads happiness researchers to claim that government should not focus too heavily on economic growth, they have not asked about the potential 'unhappiness' that might result from letting economies stagnate. Happiness research also tells us that high unemployment and job insecurity cause lower levels of happiness (Frey and Stutzer 2002), so the consequences of *not* pursuing economic growth may also be undesirable, if we accept the findings of the research.

Further, there may also be a 'rising expectations' effect around public services and policies—such that 'better' or 'more' public services would also lead to static happiness-survey findings, or even paradoxically to greater *dis*content. Indeed, it must not be forgotten that, as developed countries got wealthier, their public and regulatory services also improved—with massive benefits for health, education and public safety. In most advanced industrial nations, the post-War decades saw rising incomes as well as rising social well-being, in part brought about by improved public policy and technical improvements in public services, such as public health systems—paid for by growing economic output. This resulted in measurable well-being improvements in longevity, infant mortality, educational participation and achievement, public hygiene and safety regulations, etc. And yet, happiness surveys remained static over that period in many countries, including the USA, for which we have data going back to 1946 (Veenhoven 2007). In other words, while Easterlin warned us that rising wealth did not correlate with rising happiness, one must note that rising social well-being and expanding public services (over the same decades) also did not correlate with rising happiness. Perhaps the problem is that, as public services in health, education, etc., improved, public expectations of what governments can and should deliver also rose accordingly, leading people to feel no more satisfied or happy than they did before. And so the citizen fails to see him- or herself as a participant in genuine social progress.

Richard Sennett noted this effect from his experience working with the New Labour government in the UK. While he described that government as genuinely progressive, he also observed that it had a tendency to take a short-term 'consumerist' approach to policy—ever striving to produce new policies for the consumer-citizen and 'abandoning them as though they have no value once they exist'. The beneficiaries of the policies failed to credit the politicians with the achievement of progress; the politicians blamed the public for being 'ungrateful'; and the Opposition accused the Government of being 'out of touch' (Sennett 2006, p. 176). The danger may lie in regarding politics and public policy as if we were consumers of 'products' or 'brands'. Viewing the democratic policy-making process in terms of whether a specific programme of action may 'make me happier' is only going to make that consumerist mentality stronger.

There are some—but only a few—developed countries whose surveys have shown long-term trends towards higher levels of happiness (if we can take the survey results literally for the moment). Notable for this are Denmark and Italy. Meanwhile, Belgium had gradually declining happiness scores, and Great Britain's were static (Veenhoven 2007). But, it is not yet clear what the governments of Denmark and Italy may have been doing, and the governments of Belgium and Great Britain *not* doing, to have contributed to these trends. In the case of Belgium, internal disunity caused by differences between its constituent communities could well be a factor, and it is conceivable that 'better policy' could reduce that. National disunity also exists between northern and southern Italy (not to mention corruption and political instability in Rome) and yet happiness ratings seem to be on the rise there. Moreover, the Thatcher revolution made Britons neither more nor less happy. In light of these paradoxes, it may be more parsimonious to hypothesise that public policies have little at all to do with the trends in national survey results. It may be the case that better public policy does *not* result in greater happiness—at least in countries that already enjoy high levels of social well being—as each improvement in the public services or in the social environment is met with rising public expectations, leaving people's sense of satisfaction or well-being more or less static.

The best evidence supporting the notion that governance and public policy have an effect on happiness comes from the negative cases, such as Russia, where political turmoil, economic failure and corruption since the collapse of communism appear to be correlated with low and declining surveyed happiness levels (Saris and Andreenkova 2001). In general, moreover, there are lower happiness results in those developing countries that suffer from economic hardship and political instability or human rights violations compared with developing countries that are the most prosperous and that are democratic and stable. One would expect the individual happiness of Zimbabweans to rise after political and economic stability is restored there. But one does not need happiness surveys to justify democratic elections in that country, nor in any other. So, the most one can say is that the failure effectively to govern a country may cause *un*happiness. But from this one cannot claim either that better public policies in already well-governed, affluent countries will lead to greater happiness, or that 'the greater happiness' is a necessary or sufficient justification for good governance.

The case in favour of making happiness an aim of government needs also to take account of empirical trends in public attitudes towards government and political engagement in democracies. Surveys of trust in government consistently declined over recent decades in developed nations, though there is some uncertainty about how such public perceptions are related to the actual performance of government agencies (Van de Walle and Bouckaert 2003), and these results bear no correlation with well-being indicators (Killerby 2005). Furthermore, a common trend in western democracies is towards lower participation rates in elections, lower political-party membership rates, and less voter loyalty (or more voter volatility) (Mair 2006). The affluent democracies of the west are showing less trust in and commitment to political institutions and processes. This may be an unfortunate trend, but it is empirically grounded, and it lends no support to the idea that publics in the west will put their trust into governments and public officials in matters of maximizing the happiness of all citizens, even though there is still a reasonable expectation that relevant social and health services *ought* to be provided by government.

So, when thinking about the empirical effectiveness of any public programme aiming to maximize happiness, we need to ask whether governments are in a position to use their legitimate authority to this effect and to gain public consensus. Further, though, we would need to be assured that governmental actions *can* positively influence happiness, as measured by social surveys, and the evidence in favour of this proposition has yet to be gathered. We do have evidence that some of the institutional and social or economic factors over which governments do have some influence correlate with measured happiness; but this does not yet prove that reforms to public policy, beyond what has already been achieved in developed nations, will necessarily raise happiness levels. It may be that the relationship between happiness and public perception of good government is as paradoxical as that between economic growth and happiness. While happiness research may supply us with many useful results, one should *not* leap to the conclusion, as does Layard (2005), that there is now a 'science' of happiness that is capable of showing us how to reform our personal and *political* choices. The application of such findings to political aims and to public policy needs to take account of some of the complexities of the relationship between what governments do, in terms of public services, and how people feel about, or derive satisfaction from, their lives.

16.7 Conclusion

Happiness research, based principally on social surveys of subjective well-being, has given a new impetus to utilitarian prescriptions for good government. One of its most significant findings has been that, beyond poverty, the relationship between wealth and happiness is, at best, weak—and further that aggregate self-reported happiness does not increase, in developed countries, as economies grow and as people get wealthier. Instead, a range of other variables correlate with changes in subjective well-being, including physical and mental health and social belonging. These findings have led to calls for happiness to be adopted as an aim (if not *the* aim) of government, and hence for public policy to be guided by happiness research.

It may, however, be wrong to conclude that happiness research findings can be translated directly into authoritative actions by governments, in the interests of the well-being of all members of society, other than to provide feedback on the social programmes that governments already deliver. Future debate about the politics of happiness would need to take into account the complexity of policy networks and processes, and the diversity of communities and their values, and to treat reflexively the questions of problematization and normalization that may underlie the apparently benign and innocuous prescription that happiness be the goal of good government.

While happiness research does overcome some of the traditional objections to utilitarian political theory, the case for its direct application to public policy is challenged when closely examined on ethical and empirical grounds. The utilitarian case for making happiness a guiding collective value is not as 'self-evident' as it may at first seem; and countervailing trends in rising public expectations of, and reducing trust in, governments and public services may be adding complexity to the scene in which any programme for maximizing happiness would have to take part.

Happiness research appears to support what Aristotle said: that you don't have to be rich to be happy and to live a satisfying life—though poverty is a major drawback. Growing economic productivity and personal material wealth in developed countries appear not to result in higher scores on happiness surveys. But, if this means that the growth of economies in the developed world has not caused much progress towards a post-Enlightenment objective of happiness-maximization, would governmental action succeed instead? I have raised some doubts about that, but conclusive evidence has yet to be produced. Public policy does not lend itself to controlled trials, but future evaluative research on the impact of policy reforms on happiness-survey results may assist us. Perhaps such prospective research on governmental effectiveness needs to be performed. In the meantime, I conclude that happiness-maximization, as a social goal, is not an obligation of government.

Acknowledgments I am grateful to Nikil Mukerji for comments on an early draft, and to Professor Ruut Veenhoven for supplying data.

References

Argyle M (2001) The psychology of happiness, 2nd edn. Routledge, Hove

Beveridge W (1942) Social insurance and allied services. His Majesty's Stationery Office, London

Dean M, Hindess B (eds) (1998) Governing Australia: studies in contemporary rationalities of government. Cambridge University Press, Cambridge

Donovan N, Halpern D (2002) Life-satisfaction: the state of knowledge and the implications for governments. Strategy Unit, London

Duncan G (2007) After happiness. J Political Ideologies 12(1):85–108

Diener E, Seligman MEP (2004) Beyond money: toward an economy of well-being. Psychological Sci Publ Interest 5(1):1–31
Easterlin RA (1974) Does economic growth improve the human lot? Some empirical evidence. In: David IPA, Reder MW (eds) Nations and households in economic growth: essays in honor of Moses Abramovitz. Academic Press, New York, pp 89–125
Easterlin RA (2001) Income and happiness: towards a unified theory. Econ J 111(473):465–484
Easterlin RA (2003a) Towards a better theory of happiness. Conference abstract, The paradoxes of happiness in economics, University of Milano-Bicocca, pp 21–23
Easterlin RA (2003b) Explaining happiness. Proc Natl Acad Sci USA 100(19):11176–11183
Frey BS, Stutzer A (2002) What can economists learn from happiness research? J Econ Literature 40(2):402–435
Furedi F (2006) Why the 'politics of happiness' makes me mad. Spiked-Online, 23 May 2006. Available at http://www.spiked-online.com/index.php?/site/article/311/ accessed 30 January 2007
Jorgensen IS, Nafstad HE (2004) Positive psychology: historical, philosophical and epistemological perspectives. In: Linley PA, Joseph S (eds) Positive psychology in practice. Wiley, Hoboken, pp 15–34
Killerby P (2005) 'Trust me, I'm from the government': the complex relationship between trust in government and quality of governance. Social Policy J New Zealand 25:1–15
Lang T, Rayner G (2007) Overcoming policy cacophony on obesity: an ecological public health framework for policymakers. Obes Rev 8(suppl. 1):165–181
Layard R (2005) Happiness: lessons from a new science. Penguin, New York
Mair P (2006) Ruling the void? The hollowing of western democracy. New Left Rev 42:25–51
Mancall M (2004) Gross national happiness and development: an essay. In: Ura K, Galay K (eds) Gross national happiness and development. Centre for Bhutan Studies, Thimpu, pp 1–54
Myers DG (2004) Psychology. Worth, New York
Ng Y-K, Ho LS (2006) Introduction: happiness as the only ultimate objective of public policy. In: Ng Y-K, Ho LS (eds) Happiness and public policy: theory, case studies and implications. Palgrave Macmillan, Houndmills, pp 1–16
Paine T (1996) Rights of man. Wordsworth, Ware
Rawls J (1999) A theory of justice revised. Belknap, Cambridge
Rhodes RAW (1996) The new governance: governing without government. Political Studies, XLIV, pp 652–667
Rorty R (1999) Philosophy and social hope. Penguin, London
Saris WE, Andreenkova A (2001) Following changes in living conditions and happiness in post communist Russia: the Russet Panel. J Happiness Stud 2(2):95–109
Sen A (1985) Well-being, agency and freedom: the Dewey lectures 1984. J Philos 82(4):169–221
Sennett R (2006) The culture of the new capitalism. Yale University Press, New Haven
Sinclair K (1991) A history of New Zealand. 4th edn. Penguin, Auckland
United Nations Statistics Division (2007) 1993 system of national accounts, introduction: the aggregates of the system as indicators of economic activity and welfare. http://unstats.un.org/unsd/sna1993/tocLev8.asp?L1=1&L2=10. Accessed 7 Sept 2007
Van de Walle S, Bouckaert G (2003) Public service performance and trust in government: the problem of causality. Int J Public Administration 26(8&9):891–913
Veenhoven R (2004) Happiness as a public policy aim: the greatest happiness principle. In: Linley PA, Joseph S (eds) Positive psychology in practice. Wiley, Hoboken, pp 658–678
Veenhoven R (2007) Trend average happiness in nations 1946–2006: how much people like the life they live. World database of happiness, Trend report 2007–1
http://www.worlddatabaseofhappiness.eur.nl/hap_nat/nat_fp.htm
Warnock M (ed) (1962) Utilitarianism. Collins, Glasgow
Wierzbicka A (1999) Emotions across languages and cultures: diversity and universals. Cambridge University Press, Cambridge

Chapter 17
Greater Happiness for a Greater Number: Some Non-controversial Options for Governments

Jan Ott

Abstract There are dramatic differences in average happiness across nations ranging from 3.24 in Togo to 8.00 in Denmark on a 0–10 points scale. These differences are an indication that collective conditions in nations are important for happiness. Can governments play a role in the creation of such conditions? This question is addressed in an analysis of average happiness in 131 nations in 2006. The following sub-questions are considered. (1) Is there a positive correlation between average happiness in nations and the quality or the size of governments? (2) Can we explain a positive correlation in terms of causality? (3) Can we specify causality by discerning direct and indirect effects? (4) What about governments and inequality in happiness? (5) What can governments do to increase happiness intentionally? The conclusion is that the technical quality of governments is an important cause for average happiness in nations, and this causality can be specified to some extent. Good governments also reduce inequality of happiness in nations eventually. The implication is that governments can increase average happiness, and in due time reduce inequality in happiness, and that they have some non-controversial options to do so on purpose.

Keywords Happiness • Utilitarianism • Good governance • Democratic quality • Technical quality • Size of governments

17.1 Introduction

Utilitarians believe that governments should have the ambition to create the greatest happiness for the greatest number by legislation, jurisdiction and administration. This point of view raises two different questions: can governments increase happiness, and should they do so if they can. I try to answer the first empirical

J. Ott (✉)
Erasmus University Rotterdam, Rotterdam, The Netherlands
e-mail: jan.ott@planet.nl

A. Delle Fave (ed.), *The Exploration of Happiness*, Happiness Studies Book Series,
DOI: 10.1007/978-94-007-5702-8_17,

question, but the answers are relevant for discussions about the second ethical one. In the discussion, at the end of the last section, I make some personal remarks about a possible relationship between the two.

Many people are sceptical or even suspicious about governments, because they associate governments with bureaucracy, high taxes and inefficiency. Some of them can vividly report about government agencies making funny 'Kafkaesque' decisions, without adequate options to correct them.[1] Since the break-down of communism there is more faith in free-markets as a source of well-being. The financial crises in 2008 made people more aware of the need to control and supervise markets, but did not boost their love for governments. Many people are unwilling to accept a strong or big government, always watching and acting as a 'big brother', because they are afraid they will lose their personal autonomy and freedom. But what can we conclude about the relationship between government and happiness, if we analyze the available data? In this contribution I will assess the potential importance of governments for happiness, but not by evaluating the impact of specific policies. I will do so by an evaluation of the relations between the quality and the size of governments and happiness. I discussed some aspects of these relations earlier (Ott 2010a).

17.1.1 Research Questions

1. How are the correlations between the quality and the size of governments and average happiness?
2. Are these correlations consequences of causality?
3. Can we specify a possible causal impact in terms of direct and indirect effects?
4. What about governments and inequality in happiness?
5. What can governments do to increase happiness intentionally?

17.1.2 Plan of this Chapter

I will discuss the concept of happiness first in Sect. 17.2, including its measurement and available data. The qualities and the size of government are discussed in Sects. 17.3 and 17.4. The answers to the research questions are presented in Sects. 17.5, 17.6, 17.7, 17.8 and 17.9, respectively. The conclusions are summarized and discussed in Sect. 17.10.

---

[1] One typical Dutch example: a civil servant is fired, even though everybody agrees he is an excellent worker. He wants to continue his work and there is a serious shortage of staff. He is fired because of his age. This is prohibited by law, but it was impossible nevertheless to redress this decision, made by the Dutch Ministry of Justice!

17.2 Happiness in Nations

17.2.1 Concept

Following Veenhoven (1984) I define happiness as 'the degree to which an individual judges the overall quality of his or her life-as-a-whole favourably'; in other words 'how much one likes the life one lives'. This is close to what Jeremy Bentham had in mind when he defined happiness as 'the sum of pleasures and pains' (Bentham 1780).[2] Happiness, life- satisfaction, personal utility, and subjective well-being are treated here as identical concepts, all referring to the subjective appreciation or enjoyment of life.

17.2.2 Measurement

Since happiness is defined as something that an individual has in mind, it can be measured using questions. Many different questions are used; for an overview see the item bank in the World Database of Happiness (Veenhoven 2009a). The present analysis draws on responses to a survey question, developed by Cantril (1965), which reads as follows:

Suppose we say that the top of the ladder represents the best possible life for you and the bottom of the ladder represents the worst possible life for you. Where on this ladder do you feel you personally stand at the present time? Please use this card to help you with your answer.

0 1 2 3 4 5 6 7 8 9 10
Bottom of the ladder *Top of the ladder*

The formulation *'best and worst possible life'* invites respondents to take into account all relevant domains of their life, like social relations, work, housing, leisure and so on. This question invites a comparative appraisal of life and measures the cognitive dimension of happiness in the first place. As such it is classified as an indicator of 'contentment' in the Item Bank of the World Database of Happiness.

17.2.3 Data-Source

The question developed by Cantril has figured in many national surveys and has been used since 2006 in the Gallup World Polls. The samples used in these international studies, with usually around 1,000 respondents per nation but more for nations like India and China, are representative for the general population aged

[2] In Bentham's view such pleasures and pains are more than just simple positive or negative emotions. In chapter three of 'The principles of Morals and Legislation', 'of the four Sanctions or Sources of Pain and Pleasure', he discerns four origins of pleasures and pain: the physical, the political, the moral, and the religious. This is an indication that such emotions can derive from complex cognitive states of mind.

15 and older. All findings gathered with this question, the Gallup-data included, are brought together in the collection 'Happiness in Nations' under item type 31 (Veenhoven 2009b). This analysis draws on that source and uses the available data for the year 2006 for 131 nations. I use the mean as an indicator for level of happiness (average) and the standard deviation (sd) as an indicator for inequality of happiness, since this is an appropriate measure for this concept (Kalmijn and Veenhoven 2005). A low standard deviation indicates low inequality; a high standard deviation indicates high inequality.

In recent years the supply of data has been growing steadily. Around 2,000 data about happiness was available for 78 nations, in particular for relatively rich and developed nations. For the year 2006 there are data for 131 nations, not just rich nations but also relatively poor and less developed nations. Such changes, in the composition of the samples of nations to be analyzed, have consequences for the outcomes. One example is discussed in Sect. 17.8. There are 195 nations, so more data about happiness in more nations will be available in the future.

17.2.4 Reliability and Validity of Self-Reported Happiness

The reliability and validity of self-reported happiness deserves some additional attention. The reliability of the individual answers on happiness-questions is limited. There is some instability in the answers and the answers are not invulnerable to contextual factors, like the sequence of the questions in the survey, the interviewer and the weather. Much of these 'random-errors' usually offset each other in the average happiness in nations.

The above-mentioned question on life-satisfaction has evident face validity; the question clearly addresses happiness as defined. Previous research has also shown high internal validity as expressed in consistency in responses to this question, when asked in different ways, such as in written questionnaires, face-to face interviews or interrogation by professional psychologists (Wessman and Ricks 1966; Oswald and Wu 2010). External validity appears in logical correlations with various factors that are likely to be related to happiness.

17.2.5 Complications

To answer happiness-questions people have to balance the good and bad things of their life. A positive answer does not exclude serious problems, and a negative answer does not exclude positive emotions about specific issues. This is not a problem in terms of reliability or validity, but the implication is that self-reported happiness is not always a comprehensive indicator for an individual or collective state of mind. Another complication is that people may be positive or negative about their lives without much justification in actual conditions. Individually or collectively they can be happy in bad conditions, because they expect a better life, or because their conditions are better than what they expected. They can also be unhappy in good conditions because they expect misery, or because their conditions are worse than expected. This is again not a problem in terms of reliability or validity, but the implication is that the relation between happiness and actual 'objective' conditions can be somewhat loose in specific situations.

17.3 Quality of Governments in Nations

17.3.1 Concept

I follow Helliwell and Huang (2008) and use the terms governance and government as equivalents. This is acceptable since both terms are very broad, including administration by governments and their legislation and jurisdiction.

The World Bank defines governance as follows: "governance consists of the traditions and institutions by which authority in a country is exercised. This includes the process by which governments are selected, monitored and replaced; the capacity of the government to effectively formulate and implement sound policies; and the respect of citizens and the state for the institutions that govern economic and social interactions among them" (Kaufmann et al. 2008; World Bank June, p. 7). The following aspects of good governance are discerned (ibid, pp. 7–8).

Voice and Accountability: the extent to which a country's citizens are able to participate in selecting their government, as well as freedom of expression, freedom of association, and a free media.

Political Stability and Absence of Violence: perceptions of the likelihood that the government will be destabilized or overthrown by unconstitutional or violent means, including domestic violence and terrorism.

Government Effectiveness: the quality of public services, the quality of the civil service and the degree of its independence from political pressures, the quality of policy formulation and implementation, and the credibility of the government's commitment to such policies.

Regulatory Quality: the ability of the government to formulate and implement sound policies and regulations that permits and promotes private sector development.

Rule of Law: the extent to which agents have confidence in and abide by the rules of society, and in particular the quality of contract enforcement, the police, and the courts, as well as the likelihood of crime and violence.

Control of Corruption: the extent to which public power is exercised for private gain, including both petty and grand forms of corruption, as well as 'capture' of the state by elites and private interests.

The six aspects of governance are all highly correlated, but the correlations between the first two, and between the first two and the last four, are somewhat lower (see Table 17.1). There is also a conceptual difference: the first two have to do with the political situation and the remaining four have to do with the

Table 17.1 Correlations between government indicators around 138 nations, data-source: World Bank 2006

	Voice + Acc.	Political stability	Goverment effective	Regulatory quality	Rule of law
Voice + accountability	X				
Political stability	0.69	X			
Government effectiveness	0.81	0.77	X		
Regulatory quality	0.85	0.75	0.95	X	
Rule of law	0.80	0.78	0.97	0.94	X
Control of corruption	0.79	0.77	0.96	0.91	0.98

All correlations in this table and in the next tables are based on a pair-wise comparison of variables. The correlations are comparable because they are still related to practically the same sets of nations. I do not report the significance. Significance is the chance that the correlation observed in the sample does not correspond with the correlation in the population from which the sample was drawn. My set of nations is not a random sample of all nations; nations were included if the required data was available

institutional quality and effectiveness. I follow Helliwell and Huang (2008) who discern these types of quality and call them GovDem (average of the first two) and GovDo (average of the last four). I will call them democratic and technical quality. The correlations between the four components of the technical quality are always very high (>0.90 for 2006), which is an indication that we are dealing with one consistent concept. The correlation between the two components of democratic quality is relatively low (0.69 in 2006). In general political stability goes together with a good score for voice and accountability, but stability can also be the outcome of repression without much voice and accountability. Democratic quality as a concept is therefore less homogeneous than technical quality. It is an alternative to use ‘voice and accountability’ as a single indicator for democratic quality, but this approach does not produce substantially different results.

17.3.2 Measurement

To assess the above mentioned aspects of quality of governments the World Bank collects data from independent sources produced by different organizations. These data sources consist of surveys of firms and individuals, the assessments of commercial risk rating agencies, non-governmental organizations, and a number of multilateral aid agencies and other public sector organizations.[3] For 2006 data were used from 33 different sources from 30 different organizations.[4]

[3] For a discussion see 'Governance Indicators: Where Are We, Where Should We Be Going?' by Daniel Kaufmann and Aart Kraay (Kaufmann et al. 2008).

[4] The World Bank transforms this information into scores for each of the six sub-indicators with a mean of 0 and a standard deviation of 1 in the original sample of 212 nations and regions (standardized z-scores, approximately between −2.5 and +2.5; indicating relative positions in a specific year, in my sample in 2006).

17.3.3 Data-Source

All these data, background information included, is available at the site of the World Bank; Governance Matters VII: Aggregate and Individual Governance Indicators for 1996–2007; as published in 'World Bank Policy Research Working Paper 4654, June 2008′ (Kaufmann et al. 2008; World Bank).

17.4 Size of Governments in Nations

17.4.1 Concept

The phrase 'size of government' suggests quantitative exactness, but this is misleading. It would be more realistic, but somewhat long winded, to use the more qualitative phrase 'the relative importance of the level of government activities in society'. This is usually what it is all about, and this is what I mean if I use the term 'size of governments'. This size of governments is about the level of all government activities taken together, and not just the level of specific activities, like military activities, social security, police, public health services, and so on. The popularity of this subject, whatever the phrase, is understandable. In every society we can make a distinction between horizontal and vertical relations between people or organizations (parties/agents). Horizontal relations are based on equality and free will, while vertical relations are based on hierarchy, power and authority. The typical juridical arrangement for horizontal relations is a contract based on consensus. For vertical relations it is an order, a legal decree, or a decision; in democratic nations eventually based on legislation, but not on consensus. The size of governments determines the relative importance of vertical relations in societies.

The distinction between horizontal and vertical relations is important because it runs parallel with the distinction between individual and collective responsibility. People have a clear and full individual responsibility in horizontal relations, but in vertical relations their responsibility is rather limited. The nature of this distinction also explains many negative feelings about governments: it is very difficult to defend yourself against misbehavior by governments; the juridical steps do so are usually complicated, expensive, long-winded, and very unpleasant. This background, plus the consequences in terms of regulation and taxation, explains the importance of the size of governments as a political issue.

17.4.2 Measurement

I will use Government Consumption as a percentage of total national consumption as an indicator for size. Government Expenditures, as a percentage of GDP, is a more comprehensive indicator for the financial importance of governments, but Government Consumption is more informative for the level of actual activities.

Table 17.2 Zero-order and partial correlations between qualities and size of governments and happiness in nations (around 125 nations)

Government characteristics	Zero-order	Control technical quality	Control democratic quality	Control size of government	Control wealth
Technical quality	+0.75	X	+0.58	+0.68	+0.14
Democratic quality	+0.61	−0.17	X	+0.50	+0.04
Size of government	+0.46	+0.10	+0.30	X	+0.03

Data-source States of nations (Veenhoven 2009c)

17.4.3 Data-Source

Data about Government Consumption are obtained from the Fraser Institute (Gwartney and Lawson 2006).

17.5 Correlation Between Quality and Size of Governments and Average Happiness

17.5.1 Quality

In previous research (Ott 2010a) with 127 nations I found high correlations between happiness, and democratic and technical quality, but higher for technical quality. Both correlations are independent of culture. The correlation between technical quality and happiness does not depend on wealth either, but the correlation between democratic quality and happiness is limited to relatively rich nations. I get the same results in my sample of 131 nations. Average happiness appears to be more connected with the technical quality than with democratic quality; the zero-sum correlations[5] are +0.75 and +0.61, respectively. The technical quality is apparently the most dominant quality, with higher and more autonomous correlations (see Table 17.2). For this reason I will concentrate on the relation between technical quality and happiness.

The relation between technical quality and average happiness is visible in Fig. 17.1. The relationship is clearly positive and quite strong. The relationship is apparently linear; there is no clear pattern of diminishing or increasing returns. Consequently a quadratic function does not fit the data substantially better than a linear one.[6]

[5] A zero-order correlation is the correlation between two variables 'as such', without taking into account the effect of any other variable(s). A partial correlation measures the correlation between two variables with the effects of one (or more) variable(s), interaction effects included, controlled or removed.

[6] A linear function explains 56 % of the variance (R squared) in average happiness, a quadratic function 57 %.

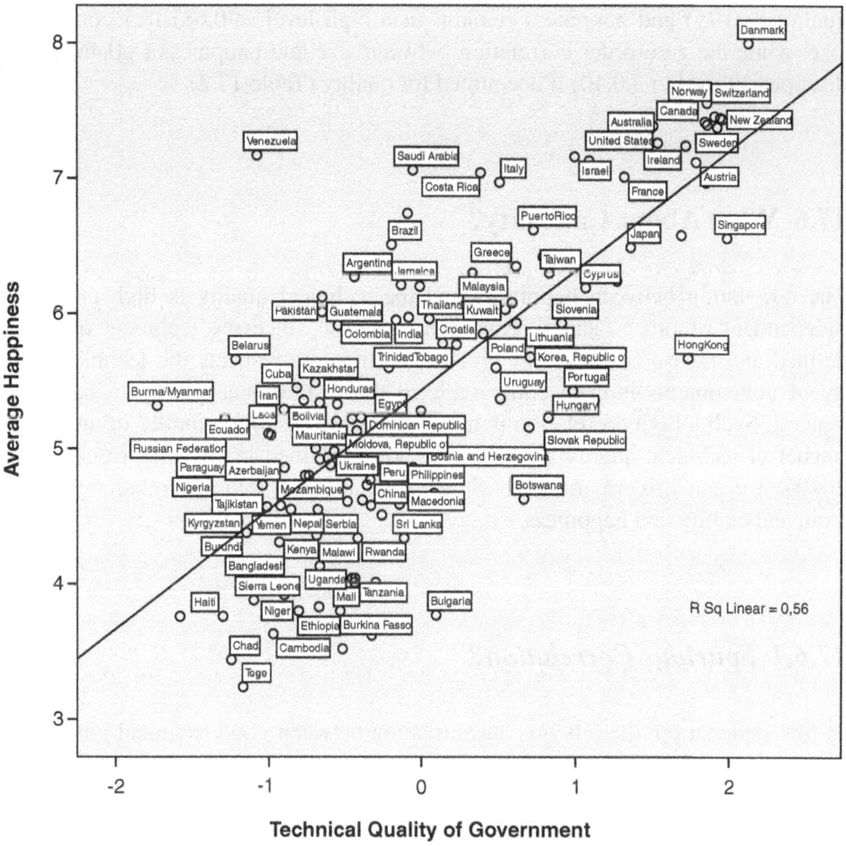

Fig. 17.1 Technical quality of governments and average happiness in nations in 2006

In the right top section of Fig. 17.1 the correlation is higher than in the bottom left section, i.e. scores are closer to the fit-line. Nations seem to need some minimal level of technical competence when it comes to governance, before their quality can develop a substantial correlation with happiness. An additional explanation for the low correlations at the left sides is 'natural resources'. Some governments can collect and distribute a lot of money by the exploitation of natural resources. Even if their qualities are at a low level, they can still contribute to average happiness.

17.5.2 Size

As concluded in my previous research the relation between the quality of governments and happiness is independent of their size, while the relation between size and happiness depends fully on the quality. The zero-order correlation between quality (+0.75) and happiness remains at a high level (+0.68) if accounted for size, while the zero-order correlation between size and happiness (+0.46) almost disappears (goes to +0.10) if accounted for quality (Table 17.2).

17.6 What About Causality?

The correlation between happiness and the technical quality is high and rather independent of other factors. This is no surprise since the technical quality is defined and measured in a very broad way. In some respects the technical quality of governments is even comparable to the institutional quality in nations in general. Such a high correlation is however not necessarily a matter of any causal impact of technical quality on happiness. As explained in previous research (Ott 2010a) we can discern three possible explanations for the correlation between technical quality and happiness.

17.6.1 Spurious Correlation?

In this explanation, there is no causal relation between good technical governance and happiness, but both variables are dependent on a third variable. Wealth could be such a variable since it is likely to affect both happiness and the quality of government. Yet this cannot be the whole story since the correlations between technical quality and happiness does not completely disappear if the effect of wealth is accounted for first (Table 17.2). In addition to that good technical governance is important for wealth and wealth contributes to happiness. In other words: technical quality can have a causal impact on happiness in several ways, directly, and indirectly with intervening factors in between. Wealth is obviously a key-candidate to play such an intervening role (see next section).

17.6.2 Causality: Impact of Happiness on Government Quality?

In this explanation happiness affects quality of government rather than vice versa. Various effects can be involved: e.g. happy citizens being more apt to vote for investment in the public good, more willing to participate in government, and less apt to obstructive behavior. Such explanations fit the literature on benefits of happiness (Lyubomirsky et al. 2005; Guven 2009). Still, this is unlikely to be the whole story, for instance because government qualities have roots in historical developments, which were not always particularly happy.[7]

17.6.3 Causality: Impact of Government Quality on Happiness?

The last explanation is that better government makes happier citizens and this explanation appeals most to common sense. There must be some truth in this explanation, since alternative explanations are insufficient to explain the correlation completely.

17.7 Specification of Causality: Direct and Indirect Effects

The causal impact of technical quality on happiness can be explained in two ways. There can be a direct or an indirect impact. This distinction is similar to the distinction between 'procedural utility' and 'output utility', as developed by Frey and Stutzer (2005). Referring to Deci and Ryan (2000) they define procedural utility as "… the well-being gained from living and acting under institutionalized processes that also contribute to a positive sense of self and address the innate needs for autonomy, relatedness, and competence". The perceived fairness of procedures, and opportunities to participate, are important conditions for procedural utility. It obviously makes a difference if people can participate and are treated professionally, respectfully and carefully, and without too much bureaucracy and delay. Frey and Stutzer have shown that democratic quality has a direct impact on happiness, even if people dislike the outcomes of democratic procedures. We may assume however that technical quality, as determined by effectiveness, regulatory quality, rule of law and control of corruption, are also important in direct contacts. In the context of rule of law adequate procedures are obviously indispensable to correct misbehavior by government agencies.

[7] Data about the quality of governments are considered as 'external' and are not explained. We may speculate however that the principle of the separation of three independent powers for legislation, administration and jurisdiction; provide for an explanation. This principle of the 'Trias Politica' was introduced by Montesquieu in 1748 before the American and French revolution. Since then this principle has had a positive impact on nation building and institutionalization in western nations. It has contributed directly to regulatory quality and rule of law, and, more indirectly, to political stability and control of corruption. In most other nations in the world the struggle against repression by some social class, or a colonial power, has been an alternative driver for nation building and institutionalization. In many nations this has eventually led to the formation of one political party with a very dominant position. In such nations the separation of powers is obviously problematic. Many nations are still in such situations, or in their aftermath.

Table 17.3 Correlations between social-economic conditions and happiness in the second column, and between these conditions and technical quality of governments in the third column

Conditions	Correlations with average happiness	Correlations with technical quality	Partial correlation technical quality average happiness
Wealth	+0.80	+0.89	+0.14
Gender equality	+0.79	+0.75	+0.39
Safety and health	+0.75	+0.70	+0.47
Gross school enrollment-ratio	+0.73	+0.70	+0.49
Economic freedom	+0.62	+0.79	+0.53
Unemployment	−0.40	−0.26	+0.73
Income-inequality (gini)	−0.29	−0.41	+0.72

In the last column the partial correlations between technical quality and happiness, after controlling for these conditions. Variables and data-sources described in the Appendix. Around 110 nations

The indirect impact of quality, and of technical quality in particular, is probably also substantial. If governments are at an optimal quality-level they will be more effective in the realization of conditions that contribute to happiness. Such conditions can operate as intermediate or intervening factors between government and happiness. Some conditions are frequently put forward as important factors for average happiness.

In the second column of Table 17.3 the zero-order correlations are presented between average happiness and seven living conditions; and in the third column the zero-order correlations between technical quality and these conditions. These correlations are high for the first five conditions. In the last column the partial correlations are presented between technical quality and average happiness after controlling for these conditions. This is the usual test to assess the importance of intervening factors. The zero-order correlation of +0.75, between technical quality and average happiness, goes down to +0.14; +0.39; +0.47; +0.49, and +0.53 if controlled for wealth, gender equality, safety and health, gross school-enrollment, and economic freedom. The implication is that wealth in particular is an important intervening variable between technical quality and average happiness, and the other four at a somewhat lower level. Unemployment and income-inequality are not very important as intervening variables, because the original correlation of 0.75 is not really reduced if controlled for these variables. This might be due to complications in the measurement of unemployment and income-inequality (see Appendix).

Combinations of the first five conditions can explain the differences in average happiness quite well. The explained variance in happiness goes up to 75 %, if all these conditions are used as independent variables in a linear regression to explain average happiness in nations. The importance of individual conditions 'in general' is however difficult to assess, because of their intensive interaction, resulting in high mutual correlations (statistical multicollinearity).[8]

[8] As a consequence (of this multicollinearity) it is not fruitful to apply more sophisticated statistical tests like path-analysis.

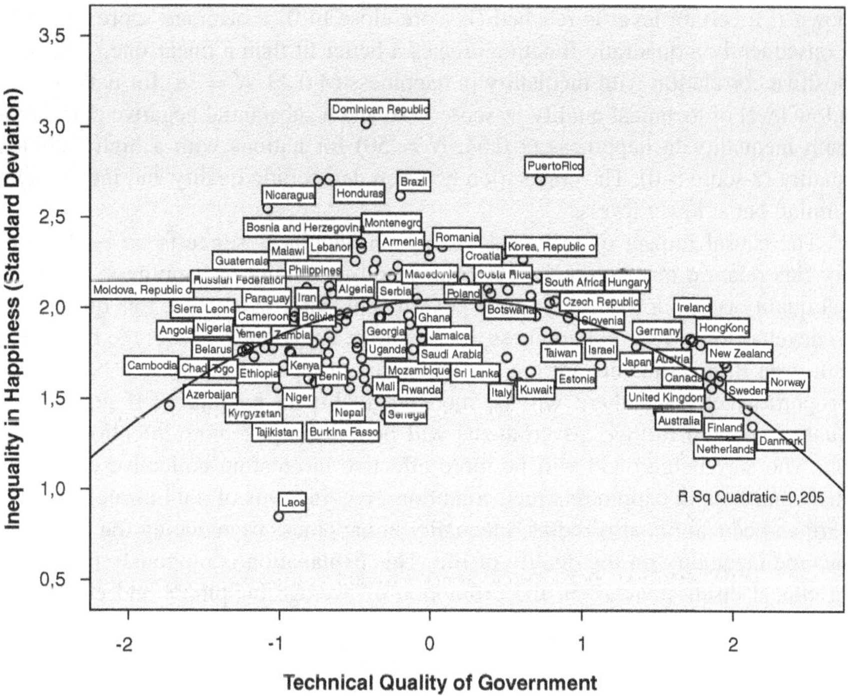

Fig. 17.2 Technical quality of governments and inequality in happiness in 2006

17.8 Good Governance and Inequality in Happiness in Nations

Increasing average happiness is a logical way to promote happiness for the greatest number, since there are no evident reasons to prioritize the happiness of specific groups. One traditional dilemma however is the relative importance of average happiness and inequality in happiness. In this section I will discuss the correlation between the technical quality of governments and inequality in happiness.

17.8.1 Less Inequality with Technical Good Governance?

In Fig. 17.2 we see the relationship between technical good governance and inequality in happiness as expressed in the standard deviation. There is a low negative correlation (-0.18, $N = 128$), suggesting that a higher technical quality goes together with less inequality. But this correlation is misleading because the relation is not linear. Inequality goes up first with higher technical quality and goes down if a certain level is reached (z-score close to 0, = average score in 2006). Consequently a quadratic function creates a better fit than a linear one.[9] We see a positive correlation with inequality in happiness (+0.29, $N = 78$) for nations with a low level of technical quality (z-score < 0) and a substantial negative correlation with inequality in happiness (−0.64, $N = 50$) for nations with a high technical quality (z-score > 0). The correlation between democratic quality and inequality is similar, but at lower levels.

The causal impact of technical quality on happiness suggests an explanation for this relation between technical quality and inequality in happiness. If technical quality is at a low level, and the government starts to improve this quality and to develop some grip on happiness, there will be an increase in average happiness. But even if governments are not corrupt, some groups in society will benefit disproportionately, and there will be more inequality in happiness. If government quality goes up further, governments will be able to pay more attention to people who stay behind and will be more effective in creating collective conditions that contribute to happiness. Such conditions, e.g. in terms of public safety, healthcare and education, also reduce inequality in happiness by reducing the impact of income-inequality on the quality of life. This explanation is obviously interesting in ethical discussions about the promotion of average happiness and equality in happiness.

If we compare Figs. 17.1 and 17.2 we see that the conclusion of Ott in earlier research (2005), that there is in general a positive relation between average happiness and equality in happiness, is not replicated. This is clearly a consequence of a difference in the composition of the samples of nations that were analyzed. The sample Ott used for the years around 2,000 consisted of 78 nations with relatively high levels of government qualities. The sample now used consists of 131 nations, including nations with relatively low levels of government qualities. In other words: the left side in Fig. 17.2 is 'quite new'.

17.8.2 Size of Government and Inequality?

We concluded in Sect. 17.5 that the relation between size of governments and average happiness depends on the qualities of governments, and in particular on technical quality. The same is true for the relation between the size of governments and inequality in happiness. This is very visible in Table 17.4: in the sample of nations with a low technical quality the correlation between size and inequality is very low but positive: bigger governments go together with more inequality. In the sample of nations with a high technical quality the correlations is substantially negative: bigger governments go together with less inequality.

---

[9] A linear function explains 3 % of the variance (*R* squared) in the inequality of happiness, a quadratic function 21 %.

Table 17.4 Correlations between size of government and inequality in happiness (standard deviation) for all nations, nations with a low government quality and nations with a high technical government quality *(number of nations in italics)*

All nations	Technical quality < 0	Technical quality > 0
−0.23	+0.02	−0.46
116	*69*	*47*

Data-source States of Nations (Veenhoven 2009c)

17.9 What Governments can do to Increase Average Happiness: Some Non-controversial Options

The fact that the technical quality of governments has a substantial impact on happiness is important. The implication is that governments can increase happiness by improving their technical quality. This can be achieved by improving government effectiveness, regulatory quality, rule of law, and control of corruption. There are many options[10] and the World Bank and other international organizations, like the UN, the IMF and the OECD, provide practical guidelines and support. Governments can select the best options after an inventory of their specific weaknesses and opportunities. This conclusion is interesting because the improvement of technical quality is usually not a controversial issue; most people will agree that improving the technical quality is perfectly all right, even if they have different political priorities otherwise. Improving the democratic quality or changing the size of governments will be more problematic and controversial, because such alternatives are more likely to have consequences for the distribution of power.

One additional non-controversial way to increase happiness is by carefully discerning three methods to assess happiness or subjective well-being.

[10] Three more specific but interesting 'down-to-earth' options to improve the technical quality are:

a. the registration of property rights, in particular for real estate, i.e. have a land registry. As has been demonstrated by De Soto (2000) this is an important condition for economic development
b. to register people, i.e. set up registrar's offices, as a necessary condition to organise adequate public education and health services.
c. to develop and implement general principles of good governance, to achieve decent and respectful relations between government institutions and citizens. This is really important because people can get very angry and upset by unfair government-decisions. Well-known examples of such principles are: carefulness and accuracy of decisions, respecting all interests, accounting for decisions, fair-play and equality (equal situations are treated equally), respect for reasonable expectations, no 'détournement de pouvoir' (powers have to be used in accordance with their legal background), proportionality (no disproportional consequences for citizens, relative to public interests).

1. Governments can analyze the behavior and the decisions of citizens, to find out what they want. In other words: they can observe their 'revealed preferences'. This is common practice in economics and leads to a high priority for economic growth. Unfortunately revealed preferences depend on the actual supply of goods and services, the knowledge and disposable budgets of consumers, the honesty of producers, and the transparency of markets in general.
2. Governments can analyze the 'stated preferences' of people, as they express them explicitly in inquiries, referenda, polls and elections. The weakness of stated preferences is that they also depend on the knowledge and imagination of respondents, and that they are not binding. People can say whatever they like without personal consequences.
3. Governments can analyze the conditions that make people happy, by comparing the conditions of people at different levels of happiness. People can adequately report about their own happiness, and this self-reported happiness is not directly dependent on their imagination, or on their knowledge of available products and services. A practical problem is the fact that happiness depends on many conditions, which makes it difficult to assess the importance of specific conditions. Happiness research requires a lot of data to reach meaningful conclusions, but the collection of this data is relatively easy and cheap.

Most governments and political parties only use the first and second approach and neglect the third. Their assessments of happiness or subjective well-being are therefore unbalanced, and the measurement and analysis of self-reported happiness can help to overcome this problem (Ott 2010b). In addition to maximizing their technical quality, governments should therefore facilitate such efforts by stimulating the collection and analysis of happiness data. This would improve the assessments of subjective well-being, and such improved assessments would be valuable input for political debates and democratic decision-making.

17.10 Conclusions and Discussion

17.10.1 Correlations

The technical quality of governments is assessed by the average score of four government indicators, as measured by the World Bank: government effectiveness, regulatory quality, rule of law and control of corruption. It is a broad concept but the correlations between the four components are high. The democratic quality is assessed by the average score of two government indicators: voice and accountability and political stability. The correlation between these components is somewhat lower. Both qualities are in a positive way correlated with average happiness in nations, but the correlation between the technical quality and average happiness is the highest and the most independent. The qualities, and in particular the technical quality, are also important for inequality in happiness but in a different fashion. In a sample of nations with a low level of technical quality there is a positive correlation with inequality: more quality implies more inequality. Above a certain level, in 2006 a level close to the average, the correlation becomes substantially negative: more quality implies less inequality.

17.10.2 Causality

The correlations between technical quality and happiness are, at least to some extent, a consequence of causality. We can discern a direct and an indirect causality. The quality 'as such' is probably appreciated by citizens and creates 'procedural utility'. Quality also creates 'output utility', because better qualified governments are more effective in creating conditions that contribute to happiness. Such conditions can be perceived as intermediate or intervening factors between government qualities and happiness. The actual importance of such intermediate factors will be different in nations, and even in one nation it is difficult to assess the importance of individual conditions, because of their intensive interaction. Gender equality, wealth, economic freedom, education, and safety and health are examples of 'positive' intermediates.

17.10.3 Causality and Inequality

If technical quality is at a low level, and the government starts to improve this quality and to develop some grip on happiness, there will be an increase in average happiness. But even if governments are not corrupt, some groups in society will benefit disproportionately, and there will be more inequality in happiness. If government quality goes up further, governments will be able to pay more attention to people who stay behind and will be more effective in creating favourable collective conditions. Collective conditions, e.g. in terms of public safety, healthcare and education, contribute to equality in happiness, also by reducing the impact of income-inequality on the quality of life.

17.10.4 Some Non-controversial Options to Increase Happiness

Governments can increase happiness by improving their technical quality. They can do this by improving government effectiveness, regulatory quality, rule of law, and control of corruption. There are many options, and governments can select the best options after an inventory of their specific weaknesses and opportunities. This conclusion is interesting because the improvement of technical quality is usually not a controversial issue; most people will agree that improving the technical quality is perfectly all right, even if they have different political priorities otherwise. In addition to that governments can facilitate the collection and analysis of self-reported happiness data, to make the assessments of happiness, life satisfaction, utility, or subjective well-being, less dependent on revealed and stated preferences. Such improved assessments are valuable input for political debates and democratic decision-making.

17.10.5 Discussion: Should Governments Increase Happiness?

The conclusion that governments can increase happiness leads us to the next question: should governments increase happiness intentionally? In my view this is very acceptable in some respects. Happiness is measurable and widely appreciated in different cultures as a social value (Veenhoven 1984; Oswald and Wu 2010). Even if people focus not on happiness, but on other goals, they can still appreciate happiness as a positive 'by-product'. Happiness has also some appreciated consequences. It has a positive impact on health (Veenhoven 2008) and happy people are more willing to participate in government and are less apt to obstructive behavior (Guven 2009). And in research no serious structural tensions have been found between happiness and alternative values, like personal autonomy, justice, solidarity and freedom (Duncan 2010; Layard 2005, Diener and Seligman 2004). In my view governments should nevertheless primarily respect the personal autonomy of citizens, and as a consequence they should work within the context of democracy. I do not believe that governments should ever apply some general ideology as a substitute for democracy, or as an excuse for paternalism. The implication is that governments can always promote happiness directly by maintaining law and order and creating 'procedural utility', but, apart from that, they can only promote happiness intentionally, if they are entitled to do so by legitimate democratic decisions. In most nations it will be rather easy however, to achieve consensus about the non-controversial options just mentioned: improving the technical quality of the government and facilitating the collection and analysis of happiness data.

Appendix: Additional Information About Variables Related to Social-Economic Living Conditions

1. Wealth. Purchasing power parity per capita (in 2007-international dollars) (HDI 2006; UNDHP, HDR 2008).
2. Gender Equality as measured by the Gender Development Index (GDI 2007; UNDHP, HDR 2009).

3. The expected life-time at birth is used here as an indicator for objective safety and health, because there is no adequate alternative information available (HDI 2006; UNDHP, HDR 2008).
4. Gross School-Enrolment Ratio: % of population in primary, secondary and tertiary education (HDI 2006; UNDHP, HDR 2008).
5. Economic freedom. The freedom to make economic decisions; average score of five aspects of economic freedom as measured by the Fraser Institute: size of governments, legal structure and security of property rights, access to sound money, freedom to trade internationally, regulation of credit, labor and business (Economic Freedom of the World, Fraser Institute 2006).
6. Unemployment (% unemployed of labor force (CIA, The World Fact Book 2009, most data collected in the years 2002–2009)).
7. Income-equality. The Gini-index of the family-income distribution (CIA, The World Fact Book, 2009, most data collected in the years 2002–2009).

The measurement of the last two variables, unemployment and income-inequality, is complicated. In many nations there are extensive informal sectors, and it is difficult to collect economic-data for such sectors. On top of that there are substantial differences in the definitions of unemployment and income.

References

Bentham J (1780) The principles of morals and legislation. Republished in 1988 by Prometheus Books, New York

Cantril H (1965) The pattern of human concerns. New York

De Soto H (2000) The mystery of capital; why capitalism triumphs in the west and fails everywhere else. Bantam Press, London

Deci EL, Ryan RM (2000) The 'what' and 'why' of goal pursuits: Human needs and the self-determination of behavior. Psychol Inq 11(4):227–268

Diener E, Seligman MEP (2004) Beyond Money: toward an economy of well-being. Psychological Sci Publ Interest 5(1):1–31

Duncan D (2010) Should happiness maximization be the goal of government? J Happiness Studies 11(2)

Frey BS, Stutzer A (2005) Beyond outcomes: measuring procedural utility. Economic Papers, Oxford

Guven C (2009) Are happier people better citizens? Economics series SWP 2009/04, Deakin University Australia

Gwartney JD, Lawson RA (2006) Economic freedom of the world. Annual report, Fraser Institute, Vancouver, Canada. Data available at: www.freetheworld.com/206/2006dataset.xls

Helliwell J, Huang H (2008) How's your government? International evidence linking good government and well-being. Br J Political Sci vol 38. Cambridge University Press, pp 595–619

Kalmijn WM, Veenhoven R (2005) Measuring inequality in happiness in nations. In search for proper statistics. J Happiness Studies 6(4)

Kaufmann D, Kraay A, Mastruzzi M (2008) Governance matters VII: aggregate and individual governance indicators, 1996–2007. World Bank policy research working paper No. 4654, World Bank 2008. Data available at: www.govindicators.org

Layard R (2005) Happiness: lessons from a new science. Penguin, New York

Lyubomirsky S, Diener E, King L (2005) The benefits of frequent positive affect: does happiness lead to success? Psychol Bull 131:803–855

Oswald AJ, Wu S (2010) Objective confirmation of subjective measures of human well-being: evidence from the USA. Science 327

Ott JC (2005) Level and equality of happiness in nations: does greater happiness of a greater number imply greater inequality in happiness? J Happiness Stud 6(4)

Ott JC (2010a) Good governance and happiness in nations, technical quality precedes democracy and quality beats size. J Happiness Stud 11(3)

Ott JC (2010b) Happiness, economics and public policy, a critique review article on 'happiness, economics and public policy' by Helen Johns and Paul Ormerod. J Happiness Stud 11(1)

Veenhoven R (1984) Conditions of happiness. Kluwer, Dordrecht

Veenhoven R (2008) Healthy happiness: effects of happiness on physical health and the consequences for preventive healthcare. J Happiness Stud 9(3)

Veenhoven R (2009a) Measures of happiness (Item bank). World database of happiness, Erasmus University Rotterdam. Assessed Oct 2009 from http://www.worlddatabaseofhappiness.eur.nl/hap_quer/hqi.htm

Veenhoven R (2009b) Happiness in nations. World database of happiness, Erasmus University Rotterdam. Assessed Oct 2009 from http://www.worlddatabaseofhappiness.eur.nl/nat_hap/nat_fp.php

Veenhoven R (2009c) States of nations; Dataset for the cross national analysis of happiness world database of happiness, Erasmus University Rotterdam. http://worlddatabaseofhappiness.eur.nl/ statnat/statnat_fp.htm

Wessman AE, Ricks DF (1966) Winn, a case study of a happy man. J Humanistic Psychology 6(1):2–16

The manufacturer's authorised representative in the EU is Springer Nature Customer Service Centre GmbH, Europaplatz 3, 69115 Heidelberg, Germany. If you have any concerns regarding our products, please contact ProductSafety@springernature.com

Printed and bound by CPI Group (UK) Ltd, Croydon, CR0 4YY
30/09/2026
02225436-0008